WRITING GHANA, IMAGINING AFRICA

NATION AND AFRICAN MODERNITY

ROCHESTER STUDIES in
AFRICAN HISTORY and the DIASPORA

Toyin Falola, Senior Editor
The Frances Higginbotham Nalle Centennial Professor in History
University of Texas at Austin

(ISSN: 1092-5228)

*Power Relations in Nigeria: Ilorin
Slaves and Their Successors*
Ann O'Hear

Dilemmas of Democracy in Nigeria
Edited by Paul Beckett and
Crawford Young

*Science and Power in
Colonial Mauritius*
William Kelleher Storey

*Namibia's Post-Apartheid Regional
Institutions: The Founding Year*
Joshua Bernard Forrest

*A Saro Community in the Niger Delta,
1912–1984: The Potts-Johnsons of
Port Harcourt and Their Heirs*
Mac Dixon-Fyle

*Contested Power in Angola:
1840s to the Present*
Linda Heywood

*Nigerian Chiefs: Traditional Power in
Modern Politics, 1890s–1990s*
Olufemi Vaughan

*West Indians in West Africa, 1808–
1880: The African Diaspora in Reverse*
Nemata Blyden

*The United States and Decolonization
in West Africa, 1950–1960*
Ebere Nwaubani

Health, State, and Society in Kenya
George Oduor Ndege

Black Business and Economic Power
Edited by Alusine Jalloh
and Toyin Falola

Voices of the Poor in Africa
Elizabeth Isichei

*Colonial Rule and Crisis in Equatorial
Africa: Southern Gabon ca. 1850–1940*
Christopher J. Gray

*The Politics of Frenchness in Colonial
Algeria, 1930–1954*
Jonathan K. Gosnell

*Sources and Methods in African
History: Spoken, Written, Unearthed*
Edited by Toyin Falola and
Christian Jennings

*Blood Memory: The Legacy of War, Ethnicity,
and Slavery in Early South Sudan*
Stephanie Beswick

*Writing Ghana, Imagining Africa:
Nation and African Modernity*
Kwaku Larbi Korang

WRITING GHANA, IMAGINING AFRICA

NATION AND AFRICAN MODERNITY

Kwaku Larbi Korang

UNIVERSITY OF ROCHESTER PRESS

First published 2003
by the University of Rochester Press

The University of Rochester Press
668 Mt. Hope Avenue, Rochester, NY 14620, USA
and at Boydell & Brewer, Ltd.
P.O. Box 9, Woodbridge, Suffolk 1P12 3DF, UK
www.urpress.com

ISBN 1–58046–146–8

Library of Congress Cataloging-in-Publication Data
Korang, Kwaku, Larbi, 1959–
    Writing Ghana, Imagining Africa: Nation and African Modernity / Kwaku Larbi Korang.
        p. cm. — (African history and the diaspora, ISSN 1092-5228 ; 16)
    Includes bibliographic references and index.
    ISBN 1-58046-146-8 (alk. paper)
        1. Nationalism—Ghana—History.   2. Ghana—Politics and government—
    To 1957.   3. Ghana—Historiography.   4. Ghana—Intellectual life.
    5. Pan-Africanism.   6. Nationalism—Africa—History.   I. Title.   II. Series:
    Rochester studies in African history and the diaspora v. 16.
    DT511.K66 2004
    966.705—dc22
                                                                                2003016339

British Library Cataloguing-in-Publication Data
A catalogue record for this book is available from the British Library

Designed and typeset by Straight Creek Bookmakers
Printed in the United States of America   •
This publication is printed on acid-free paper

The stone that the builders rejected has become the cornerstone.
—Psalm 118:22

CONTENTS

ACKNOWLEDGMENTS

Writing this book has been a journey for me into little-charted waters. I am especially grateful to Stephen Slemon for boosting my morale through his unshakeable conviction that I had it in me to see my intellectual mission through. At a critical stage, he was unstinting in his assistance as a "pathfinder," and has thus greatly helped in making this document the rewarding accomplishment that I feel it is.

I owe a debt of gratitude to a number of people who read and commented on the manuscript in various incarnations, and at various stages of completion. I have profited from their challenging queries, comments, and suggestions. I am greatly indebted in this regard to Ato Quayson, Biodun Jeyifo, and Ania Loomba. Suvir Kaul forced me to bring my abstractions down to earth by insisting that I should always historicize. Joseph Valente's and William J. Maxwell's critique of my original introduction resulted in what I hope is a stronger version.

My "research assistants" Kwadwo Osei-Nyame and Akosua Asabea Boakye-Korang freely gave of their time (and money, in the case of Kwadwo), and combed the archives in London (Colingdale) and Cape Coast, respectively, to find me the material I needed for portions of this book. From Accra, Nana Akua Boakye-Korang sent me photocopies of rare materials. I cannot thank my friend and my nieces enough for their invaluable contributions to this book.

My most ardent supporters, through thick and thin, have been and remain Zohreh Sullivan, Adlai Murdoch, Robert Dale Parker, and Philip Graham. I am lucky to have (had) on my side these wonderful human beings and to have received their encouragement. The list of my supporters and encouragers would of course be incomplete without mention of: Dennis Baron, Alma Gottlieb, Alice Deck, Janet Lyon, Michael Bérubé, Judy Murdoch, Yvette Smith, Shereen Mills, Stephanie Foote, Leon Chai, Joshua Esty, Julia Saville, Jean Allman, Nadine Dolby, Stephen David, Rebecca Starr, Michael Rothberg, Jamie McGowan, and Rene Wahlfeldt. Cary Nelson has been a pillar to lean on in a time of trouble: I can't thank him enough. Jim Hurt and Lori Humphrey-Newcomb were sources of inspiration and assistance when it came time for me to write a book proposal. It is unfair to be selective this way when all I have known and come to expect is the unconditional love of my colleagues in the English Department, University of Illinois at Urbana-Champaign. My heartfelt gratitude goes to the entire faculty of the Department for providing a wonderfully supportive environment for me. I am grateful also for the moral and spiritual support I received from afar—from Patience Sowa (Kansas City), Isaac Quist (Cardiff), and from my sister, Mrs. Henrietta Abban (Accra).

Let me mention in gratitude and appreciation Toyin Falola and Paul Zeleza for working extraordinarily hard to get my sizeable manuscript approved for publication by the University of Rochester Press. I appreciate, too, the contributions of Tim Madigan, the Editorial Director at Rochester, as I do those of my copyeditor, Louise Goldberg. I cannot end without thanking also the anonymous librarian(s) at the University of Nottingham who helped me to track down information on copyright holders for books long out of print.

This book is dedicated to my wife Gifty Ako-Adounvo, and to my sons Kwame Larbi-Korang and Victor Kwabena Larbi-Korang. Thank you for being my source of ultimate succor through difficult times; and for continuing to be a beacon of a hopeful future.

The fourth section of chapter 7 originally appeared as the third section of "Crisis and Accounting: Towards a Spatial History of the African Nation," chapter 11 in *Sacred Spaces and Public Quarrels: African Cultural and Economic Landscapes,* edited by E. Kalipeni and P. T. Zeleza. I am grateful to the publisher, Africa World Press, for permission to reprint.

"Mutilated Congo," by Bankole Awoonor-Renner, is reprinted by permission of Central Books Ltd., London.

The extract from "Gold Coast Customs," by Edith Sitwell, is reprinted by permission of the author and the publisher, Macmillan.

I have not been able find any information on who the executors are of the estate of Dorothy Kurankyi-Taylor, in whose name, her publishers Stockwell have assured me, copyright for the poem "The Sensible Attitude" and the volume *Reflected Thoughts* in which it appears would have been lodged.

Kwaku Larbi Korang
Urbana, Illinois
July 2003

INTRODUCTION

HERE, THERE, AND EVERYWHERE

MODERNITY IN QUESTION

> The basic characteristic of the modern nation and everything con-
> nected with it is its modernity.
> > —E. J. Hobsbawm, *Nations and Nationalism since 1780*

> The continent and people of Africa today are a part of the modern
> world.
> > —C. L. R. James, *Nkrumah and the Ghana Revolution*

A Contested Universal: Debating Nation and Modernity

In his *Imagined Communities*,[1] Benedict Anderson, the Marxist cultural
critic, proposes as a truism that "In the modern world everyone will, can,
should 'have' a nation as he or she 'has' a gender." Commanding everywhere "profound emotional legitimacy" (14), "nation-ness," according to
Anderson, is "the most universally legitimate value of political life in our
time" (12). Anderson's historico-cultural account and assessment of this
condition of global convergence—how and why everyone here, there, and
everywhere has come to subscribe to the nation-form as *the* norm of (self)-
identification—registers as a humanist-universalist approbation of this development of modern history without being sentimental. The global

1

diffusion and institution of nation-ness, "a complex composite of French and American [revolutionary] elements" (78 n. 34), reads as a great story of human differences universally equalized. Anderson's contribution, in one critic's approving evaluation of *Imagined Communities*, stands out as "a reminder that, at its best, imagined nationhood in all its crudity has been the entry ticket for the wretched of the earth into world history."[2]

On the other hand, in his *Nationalist Thought and the Colonial World*,[3] Partha Chatterjee, who, like Anderson, is looking at the nation-form in the unfolding of a universal history, aims to assess *the legitimacy* of the conjoint nationalist basis upon which modernity here, there, and everywhere has been established. Chatterjee focuses his critical eyes firmly on the colonial encounters between the West and "the Rest," and what he sees in these encounters is a dominant West shaping unequal structural and cultural relations between itself and others, and profiting from this inequality. It is the "dominance of the West in the world, [that has] made nationality the canon," as Liah Greenfeld has pointed out.[4] Given this circumstance, the question uppermost for Chatterjee is how, and for whom *really*, the universal history of nationalism—the story retold by Anderson as modernity's triumphant global march—is launched. In Chatterjee's skeptical assessment, what is revealed at work in a post-encounter modernity is a self-interested and manipulative Western logic. This is a colonial logic that has canalized the desire of non-Westerners for independent community into a norm of representation and a form of cognition whose patents are owned by the West.

Chatterjee's *Nationalist Thought* is a densely argued work which generalizes the example of Indian nationalism for the Third World. Its author highlights the interplay of Western power/knowledge and anticolonial desire in a sociological account, offering a combined *marxisant*/Foucauldian critique of nationalist politics within colonial society. His account and critique, set up to question the "authenticity" of the existing postcolonial nation-state by casting a retrospective look at its foundations, engages genealogical questions having to do with the formation of knowledgeable subjects of nationalism and the ontological status of their agency in the colonial Third World. Chatterjee's is a preeminent example of what we might call the "Trojan-horse" interpretation of Third World nationalism—a mode of interpretation in which what *appeared to be* a self-renewing possibility in a given (i.e., nationalism) has turned out more or less to be a self-confining liability.

It emerges in Chatterjee's work that the nation-form, as given to Third World nationalist intellectuals, is part of the apparatus of Enlightenment thought. The historically imperializing and colonizing West has imposed this rationalist apparatus to create a cognitive hegemony over the historically imperialized and colonized non-West. Since these Third World nationalist intellectuals can activate their nationalist agency only in terms of the categories of knowledge given to them, categories not of their own direct making, their nationalist agency is fated to come, as it were, colonially preinscribed. Third World nationalist thought is trapped within the epistemic protocols of Enlightenment Reason. Hence Chatterjee asks rhetorically, "Can [non-Western] nationalist thought produce a [rationalistic] discourse of order while daring to negate the very foundations of [the Western] system of knowledge that has conquered the world?" And his answer is in the negative: non-Western nationalism, "[a] different discourse, [is] yet one that is dominated by another" (42). As such, the vaunted autonomy of nationalist knowledge and practice must remain under postcolonial suspicion.

Chatterjee's suspect nation-form is part of the Enlightenment armature of Western imperial-colonialism, seductive because it dissimulates as a form of liberation from this imperial-colonialism. The reality is that the West hankers after universal dominion. To fulfill its will-to-universal-dominion, the West has imposed—by means of what Chatterjee, referencing Hegel, calls "the Cunning of Reason"—shadow expressions of this hankering, in the form of colonial intellectuals' desire for modern national community. Thus Chatterjee observes:

> Reason is . . . far more cunning than the liberal conscience will care to acknowledge. It sets "the passions to work in its service"; it keeps Itself "in the background, untouched, unharmed," while it "sends forth the particular interests of passion to fight and wear themselves out in its stead." No, the universality—the sovereign, tyrannical universality of Reason—remains unscathed. (168)

No *true* universal narrative has emerged from the global diffusion of the nation-form, as proposed by Anderson; it is only the West masquerading as universal (Reason) and playing the non-West false in this disguise. In Chatterjee's estimation, the Reason of the imperializing, globalizing, and capitalizing West needs the non-West: "Enlightenment itself, to assert its sovereignty as the universal ideal, needs its Other; if it could ever actualize itself in the real world as the truly universal, it would in fact destroy itself" (17). Based on this reading, colonial intellectuals expending their passions in seeking nationhood for their colonized countries have done so merely as Enlightenment's foot soldiers in non-Western territories. They have been warranted only the illusion of universal equivalence, for the nation they have been duped by Enlightenment cunning to will into being can be ever only a universal-in-subordination.

Chatterjee asks, "How far can [non-Western nationalism] succeed in maintaining its difference from a [Western] discourse that seeks to dominate it?" (42), and the import of the work he subtitles "a derivative discourse" suggests that the Third World nationalist apple does not—indeed, cannot—fall far from the rationalist Enlightenment tree. Non-Western nationalisms may have cast themselves in a struggle to affirm and take back Difference, but that struggle is itself preprogrammed to reconfirm the dominion of the Same, the West.

In that sense, recounting the history of modernity as it is instituted in the diffusion of the nation-form, *Nationalist Thought* replicates, albeit in a way more sophisticated than most, a dominant inscription of modernity in knowledge as a one-size-fits-all category. In this dominant inscription, being Western is being modern, and being modern is nothing but being (assimilated as) Western. Modernity, in this mono-contextual resolution, is a priori and nonnegotiably Western: for non-Western societies to be modern, therefore, is for them to be Western(ized). Sociological and cultural modernity in the non-West cast in a narrative of absorption and assimilation, is thus no more and no less than a confirmation of the preeminence of Western power, no more and no less than a reiteration of the West's absolute global hegemony.

On this score we find Ernest Gellner, with none of the equivocation and subtlety that characterize Chatterjee's argument, claiming the general diffusion of nationalism in the non-West as a more or less triumphal expression of the assimilative power of the West-as-modernity. Gellner writes:

> Nationalism is, essentially, the general imposition of a high culture [read Western/modern] on society, where previously low cultures had taken up the lives of the majority, and in some cases of the totality, of the population. It means that generalized diffusion of a school-mediated, academy-supervised idiom, codified for the requirements of reasonably precise bureaucratic and technological communication. It is the establishment of an anonymous, impersonal society, with mutually substitutable atomized individuals, held together above all by a shared culture of this kind, in place of a previous complex structure of local groups, sustained by folk cultures reproduced locally and idiosyncratically by the micro-groups themselves.[5]

"This is what *really* happens,"[6] Gellner concludes, and the emphatic "really" reveals the irreducible thesis of the modern-as-nothing-other-than-

Western, the modern in the non-West as nonnegotiable "imposition," uncompromisingly argued.

This all-or-nothing position has been contested in intellectual debate for some time now, with rereadings of the modern emerging that offer intercontextual illumination and comparative understandings of global cultural geographies and identities.[7] These alternative readings account for a modernity at large in relational terms. Such readings make "modern" a term of exchange between the West and the non-West—between dominant and dominated it is true, but nevertheless, in the spirit of Bakhtinian dialogism, they leave room for the negotiability of the modern in the contexts of the latter. In light of modernity's relativity and negotiability, then, non-Western modernities, at once similar to *and* different from the Western, appear in knowledge. These para-modernities are analyzable as self-activated sociocultural renewals by non-Westerners shaped by the cross-cultural interactions and exchanges attendant on their colonial encounters with the West.

This sort of reading of modernity stands out in Anderson's account, in *Imagined Communities,* of the diffusion and global normativity of the nation-form as a distinguishing feature of the post-encounter world. According to Anderson, the nation-form was spontaneously distilled from "a complex 'crossing' of discrete historical forces" in eighteenth-century Europe. It was nevertheless "capable of being transplanted, with various degrees of self-consciousness, to a great variety of social terrains, to merge and be merged with a correspondingly wide variety of political and ideological constellations" (14). Readings such as Anderson's have produced the modern in an interculturally nuanced post-encounter knowledge, wherein it emerges as a comparative datum, (shaped) between the West and the Rest rather than lying wholly and dominantly within, and explainable exclusively in terms of the former.

The What, the How, and the Why of This Book

Writing Ghana, Imagining Africa: Nation and African Modernity is affiliated with the rereadings that take an intercontextual, inclusively intercultural, and comparative approach to the modern. The book sets out to change the dominant ideas about Africa's relations with modernity and the global history of nationalism by reconstructing African nationalist theory, culturalist thought, and intellectual agency in a modern genealogy. The book does so by recovering and reinterpreting the largely neglected writings of preindependence, nationalist writer-intellectuals of Ghana. (This West African country, until it gained its national independence from British colonial rule in 1957, was known as the Gold Coast.[8]) These thinkers and activists operated under the imperial-colonial order of the nineteenth and twentieth centuries; and they were conscious of themselves as part of an intraregional framework of (anglophone) West African intellectual exchanges.[9] Preeminent among them were Rev. C. C. Reindorf (1834–1917), John Mensah Sarbah (1864–1910), J. E. Casely Hayford (1866–1930), Rev. S. R. B. Attoh Ahuma (1864–1921), Kobina Sekyi (1892–1956), J. B. Danquah (1895–1965), and Kwame Nkrumah (1909–72). The list would be a headless one if we were to leave out E. W. Blyden (1832–1912), the American returnee to Africa and the Liberian doyen of African nationalism, whose pioneer example and seminal thought influenced many of these figures. Nor would the story of West African nationalism be complete without mention of the Sierra Leonean Creole James Africanus Beale Horton (1835–83) who, in outstanding fashion, helped give intellectual shape to the protonationalism that emerged in the Gold Coast in the late 1860s. Brief introductory interpretations of the thought of these two pioneers, Blyden and Horton, appear below.

Crucially, too, these nationalist intellectuals were self-conscious about their being formative contributors to, or heirs drawing on and conscientiously replenishing, an interregional formation of continental and transatlantic Pan-African activist thought and endeavor. Indeed, in Imanuel Geiss's assessment, the Gold Coast was "the most important centre for the development of Pan-Africanism on African soil" (*Pan-African Movement,* 147). And in keeping with the normative parameters organizing the conversations and solidarities, the internal contestations and self-interrogations, of this wider interregional formation, these preindependence thinker-activists necessarily had to engage, at their Gold Coast/West African location, the concept—its thrust now nativist, now racialist—of the "African nation."

This work of Ghanaian and West African retrospection investigates the interconnections between the concepts of "Africa," "modernity" and "nation." It resolves "Africa" as a structure of nationalist self-framing and knowing that has emerged in the interplay between "modernity" and "nation" as these two concepts have been engaged by Ghanaian/West African activist intellection—intellection that in its widest self-understanding is Pan-African. On this basis, this book proposes "African modernity"—mediated by what Blyden first advanced as "African nationality"—as the object both of colonial/preindependence intellection and of (retrospective) postcolonial/postindependence analysis. In doing so, this book cannot but take cognizance of the ongoing debates within and across disciplines and critical formations—postcolonial studies, cultural studies, Third World studies, African and Africana studies, comparative anthropological and sociological studies of modernity—that are restructuring, problematizing, and enriching our understandings of cultural (self)-conceptions and categories. Drawing on insights from these varied critical formations, the distinctiveness of this book lies in its interdisciplinary approach to nation and modernity as African concerns and in its "spatializing" of these concerns so that themes of a wider global relevance emerge out of the book's specific African focus.

To account for the objects of its investigation, *Writing Ghana, Imagining Africa* takes as ideal in approach the "analytic pluralism" recommended by Edward Said, following Gramsci, in *The World, the Text and the Critic*.[10] For Said, as for this book, analytic pluralism is a matter of methodologically acknowledging that only in its interdisciplinary cross-hatching is any cultural object's complicated historical coming to be and mean in the world, as well as its current mode of being and meaning in the world, to be adequately grasped.

As it takes the interdisciplinary and pluralist path in method, *Writing Ghana, Imagining Africa* finds itself, in the substance of its analysis, going part of the way with Anderson. Anderson accomplishes in *Imagined Communities* the interfusion of a global comparative anthropology with local social, cultural, and intellectual histories. And by this multileveled explanatory approach he brings to a resolution how and why the nation-form emerges and validates itself as the intercultural norm of identification within the modern order.

Anderson opens *Imagined Communities* by questioning "in an anthropological spirit" certain overly rationalist and reductively ideological readings that cast the nation-form as a representational and constitutional "anomaly" of and within the modern order. Nationalism is seen as a false ideological consciousness, the reflex of "a pathology of modern developmental history" (14), as Anderson quotes Tom Nairn's *The Breakup of Britain*. It may be true in Gellner's skeptical observation, also quoted by Anderson, that "Nationalism is not the awakening of nations to self-consciousness: it invents nations where they do not exist" (*Imagined Communities*, 15). However, if Gellner's critical agenda is one of ideological delegitimation of the nationalist form of imagining community, in Anderson's estimation he is to be chided for being "so anxious to show that nationalism masquerades under false pretences that he assimilates invention to 'fabrication' and 'falsity'" (15). In Anderson's globalized (comparative) anthropological read-ing, *no* "'true' communities exist which can be advantageously juxtaposed to nations." On the contrary, communities of all types, past and present, distant and near, here and there, "are to be distinguished, not by their falsity/genuineness but by the style in which they are imagined" (15). Gellner's mode of posing the question, Does nationalist form fall inside or outside true community?—a question that presumes to weigh deviant against true norm—is therefore illegitimate. In contrast, Anderson suggests that a legitimate procedure for analyzing and accounting for the nation-form must be one that locates it within a "timeless" and "globally" enfolding structure of collective representation—Community—wherein this nation-form ap-pears as a legitimate variant of an enduring human norm. Comparative anthropological wisdom, for Anderson, begins by inserting the nation-form into a number of queries about community as it was imagined *then* and as it is imagined *now* (that is, a comparative history of collective self-represen-tation) and community as it is (now) imagined *here* and *there,* and *every-where* (that is, a comparative geography of collective self-representation). The critic is to be seen in this light asking: in what form is the language of modern self-representation cast? And how, if this form is unique, does it particularize its subscribers historically in a comparative similarity across the globe as *nothing but* modern?

Anderson, looking at the "large cultural systems" of Eurasia before the nineteenth century—"the religious community" and "the dynastic realm" (19, 20)—locates within them premodern conceptions in which commu-nity, mediated through a hieratic language or through the proxy divinity of an earthly monarch, is identical with divinity or being. The dominant lan-guage of community emerges in what we might call a closed metaphor, a singularity, insofar as "There [was] no idea [then] of a world so separated from language that all languages are equidistant (and thus interchangeable) signs for it" (21). Instead, in what amounted to a foreclosure of differential thinking, "ontological reality [was] apprehensible only through a single, privileged system of re-presentation: the truth-language of Church Latin, Qur'anic Arabic, or Examination Chinese" (21–22). There was the One "over-language" which canceled out all differences, cultural and linguistic, and into whose suprarepresentative self all were absorbed in communal representation; the claims of particular community could not withstand the superior claims of universal community. Premodern understanding was additionally nonrelativistic in holding that "the ruler, like the sacred script, was a node of access to being and inherent in it" (40). And this indifferent conception of the way things were, are, and will always be extended to its apprehension of time since for it "cosmology and history were indistinguishable" (40).

Anderson points out that "the fall of Latin exemplified a larger process in which the sacred communities integrated by old sacred languages were gradually fragmented, pluralized, and territorialized" (25). It was now possible as a consequence to imagine community secularly and historically "in a competitive, *comparative field*" (24; emphasis in original). And what this relativizing conception meant was that the assimilative "supra"—that which is over and above and which indifferently integrates—had given way to the similar-making "inter"—that which falls between and integrates differences—in the *modern* conception of community in representation, the nation-form. Whereas previously the One exhausted all in a closed metaphor, the modern era dawns with metaphor being blasted open by invading metonymy, registered in Anderson's perception of the paradox of the "formal universality of nationality as a socio-cultural concept . . . vs. the irremediable particularity of its concrete manifestations" (14). The nationalist organization of modern self-representation is notionally informed by the universal or general comparability of differences and by the interchangeability—hence the (humanistic) equivalence in status—of particulars. With the waning of the ecumenical globality of the imagined religious community, what offers itself as a norm in global relations is "Internationality . . . a style of thought that generates a plurality of nations."[11] An "inter-language" of the nation-form succeeds the earlier "over-language," and it is generative of plurality of being (metonymy) in competitive similarity or equivalence of status (metaphor). It is on this basis that it has become for Anderson a truism of the modern that "everyone can, should, will 'have' a nation."[12] The nation-form today is a global given; in it communities here and there—communities otherwise different in many particulars from each other—are commonly articulated in a structure of universal representation.

On the basis of Anderson's more or less affirmative generalization of modernity in the ubiquitous form of nationalist self-representation, *Writing Ghana, Imagining Africa* proposes several intellectual objectives and key investigative questions. One of these objectives is to bring African nationalist example into view as a comparative datum to show how the *here* of Africa relates to and is interlinked with a *there* elsewhere, in accordance with a template of representation that offers itself in a global commonality. This book's contribution to intellectual understandings of the nation-form in this mode is thus a matter of *expanding* Anderson's disclosure of modern self-representation in a cross-cultural geography. (Anderson's seventh chapter in *Imagined Communities,* devoted to Third World appropriations of the nation-form as "The Last Wave" in his story of the cross-cultural fertilizing and hatching of the modern, draws heavily on southeast Asian examples and has very little to say directly about Africa.) And this is by way of making Africa a center of significance, from where the following general questions can be validly posed and illumined: How and why have contemporary communities, having inscribed their identities as *modern,* or desiring to do so, come jointly to share and exploit the "inter-language" of the nation-form? How and why have they commonly come to subscribe to a universally normative "syntax" of self-representation? This book's aim is thus to connect social, cultural, and intellectual histories in an African locality to broader global patterns.

It cannot be gainsaid that this project of connecting Africa "here" with a global "out there," and hence naming Africa as a human presence and participant in the unfolding drama of the modern, is a vital one. Africa, represented as the absent relation of the modern,[13] and stereotyped as modernity's incommensurable Other,[14] has consistently been bled by those terms of its historicity and humanity. In short, the continent of Africa has been a part of the world missing from, or misrepresented in, the contemporary and not-so-contemporary conceptualizations of and debates about the making of the modern world's cultural and political order. Yet, looking at the lively nationalism permeating the continent in the 1950s, the great Pan-Africanist C. L. R. James could not help but conclude that "The continent and the people of Africa today are a part of the modern world."[15] This book asks in the spirit of James's affirmative reading: How can the comparative retrieving of African nationalist endeavor for an expansive knowledge of the making of the modern also be a recuperation for Africa of the modernity otherwise withheld from or denied it? In effect, how can the comparative method, brought to bear on the question of African self-appropriation in modern representation—as normatively given in the nation-form—contribute to a modernist[16] knowledge of Africa and an Africanist knowledge of the modern? By focusing on Africa, what sociohistorical, cultural, and philosophical perceptions, hitherto overlooked, and what special analytic insights can this book bring to the multiperspectival and multidisciplinary debates about the constitution of the modern order, and about its possibilities, contradictions, and problems? And how do these African perceptions and insights augment and/or change the conduct of these debates? These are some of the major questions that inform this book.

Fractured Formations: African Modernity in a Constitutive Double Consciousness

Intervening in the debates over the nation-form, Anderson, as we have seen, rescues the category from the critical school that will pathologize it, and he normalizes it as a global given. The nation-form as a model of imagining community may have come late to the colonial world. Yet once it had been instrumentally appropriated by a vanguard native intelligentsia, this intelligentsia defined in its possession of "bilingual literacy, or rather [European] literacy and bilingualism" (*Imagined Communities*, 107), it could serve the same self-validating and equalizing function as it did in the West. However, Anderson, producing and inserting the nation-form as a norm in a universal and universalizing narrative, fails to pose adequately the question: how is its universality—or canonicity, as Greenfeld will have it—given? If in the nation-form "eighteenth-century England presented the world with a new 'canon' consisting at once of nation-state, and industrialising social economy and parliamentary government," as Hastings has it (*Construction of Nationhood*, 28), is this donation a free given? Or is it a hegemonic given, imbricated in a Western logic of domination? And for those interrogating the Andersonian perspective this way—critics from, or identified with, the "postcolonial" and/or Third worlds—it is a matter of how that perspective overlooks Western power and interest playing in the very logic of accessibility of the nation-form and its Enlightenment accessories. Thus we find the Indian-born postcolonial critic Gayatri Spivak interrogating in this vein:

> The master words implicated in Indian decolonization offered four great legitimizing codes consolidated by the national bourgeoisie by way of the culture of imperialism: nationalism, internationalism, secularism, culturalism. If the privileged subject operated by these codes masquerades as the subject of an alternative history, we must meditate on how they (we) are written, rather than read their masque as historical exposition.[17]

Calling for the exposure of the Third World nationalist masque, the demand Spivak imposes on postcolonial critical practice is one of a rigorous Foucault-style genealogical critique, that very mode of critique conducted by Chatterjee in *Nationalist Thought*. Other interventions, grounded in a transnationalist perspective on modern culture, have emerged which probe and call into question the ethical status of the nation-form as modernist self-representation and knowledge. Two of these, with a direct Africanist relevance, are Kwame Anthony Appiah's *In My Father's House: Africa in the Philosophy of Culture* and Paul Gilroy's *The Black Atlantic: Modernity and Double Consciousness*. Their claims are examined in the Postscript to this book.

If everyone can have the nation in the modern world, as Anderson avers, clearly this story of modernist entitlement and achievement does not accommodate itself everywhere to a simple retelling. On the contrary, the story of the modern is fraught with contradiction in the context of the non-Western Third World. Hence, we find the Trojan-horse account Chatterjee gives in *Nationalist Thought* reiterated in Basil Davidson's genealogical account of the nation-form and diagnostic of nationalist subjectivity on African soil given in his *The Black Man's Burden*. This is a book which addresses, as its subtitle has it, "Africa and the curse of the nation state,"[18] a curse conducted into the continent, in Davidson's reading, by the African variant of Anderson's literate, bilingual intelligentsia produced by the colonial encounters. This African intelligentsia belonged to a "middle class,"[19] whose members, their subjectivities collectively molded in the Enlightenment forge of colonial culture, as Davidson argues, related to Africa in the split and alienated mode of "native foreigners."

Writing Ghana, Imagining Africa's response to the insight of the accursed gift of modern subjectivity and agency furnished by the postcolonialist, Third Worldist, and transnationalist critiques is to work this insight into a complex retrieval of the sociocultural and intellectual genealogies of the nationalists it reviews in contradiction and paradox. And the book does so at a conceptual and analytic crossroads, recurrently referred to in a military metaphor as a "frontline." The preindependence Ghanaian, West African, and Pan-African intellectuals whose nationalist thought is reviewed here, the book argues, comprise a group that had arrived at historical and existential understanding of itself as straddling the frontline of the European-African colonial encounters. Blyden, the earliest most articulate African nationalist intellectual, employing the metaphor of being under siege, characterized the place occupied by his middle-class kind in this way: "The *fringe* of European civilization is violence."[20] And in this civilizational siege laid by Europe against Africa, Blyden saw the middle class as standing in the first line of assault, at the receiving end of the violence of psychocultural and cognitive alienation. Yet if European civilization was the adversary to be engaged at the frontline, this was a place of paradoxical engagement, for this adversary turns out to be what Ashis Nandy, the Indian cultural critic, has called "the intimate enemy."[21] The frontline was not in place "out there," dividing Self purely from Other; it happened to be "in here," too, internalized in the psychocultural constitution of those who straddled it. The "enemy" was as much the Other as it was (in) the Self; and it was paradoxically as much a "friend" as it was a "foe."

The desire by the frontline intellectuals for modernist self-identification in the nation-form, therefore, is only possible within this constitutive and untranscendable contradiction. Their very self-conception as nationalist is "gifted" them in (spite of) the violence of the colonial alienation imposed on them by European domination. Imagining African modernity in the nation-form, these writer-intellectuals disclose a paradox at the level of concept. They are to be seen simultaneously affirming—saying an intimate "yes" to—an alien dominant even as they mobilize its categories to say "no" in revolt against it. Their nationalist agency does not come in the form of being able to choose from among pure alternatives native and modern, African and Western. On the contrary these intellectuals straddling a post-encounter frontline are inescapably "Afro-Western," and they are so in a relationship which finds no happy medium, since the foreign element in their makeup dominates the native one. *Writing Ghana, Imagining Africa* models these nationalist intellectuals as representing *in themselves* the place where "Africa" and "modernity," native and alien, intersect as an ontological predicament. And this is the predicament of being the agency by, and subjectivity through, which Enlightenment (indirectly) fastens its grip on native realities. Nationalist intellectuals in this mode, that is, represent "what one may ungenerously call a comprador intelligentsia,"[22] caught in a predicament that is captured in this book as Faustian.[23]

That said, however, this book is additionally compelled to ask whether the Trojan-horse interpretation must have the last word. This is the one which has it that to have consented in the non-West to modernist self-identification in the nation-form is to have been conquered, overmastered, and pacified in another Western colonial form. If the likes of Chatterjee and Spivak draw on poststructuralism, in the form of Foucauldian genealogical critique, etc., to advance this viewpoint, another Indian-born critic, Asha Varadharajan, has noted "the failure of poststructuralism to appeal to the dispossessed." This failure, she points out further,

> inheres in poststructuralism's desire to deconstruct the very notion of the political; to destroy the very possibility of a conjunction between interest, insight and agency; to collapse . . . the distinction between consensus and conquest; or to interrupt the very relation between epistemology and ethics except insofar as knowledge serves to bolster (an often undifferentiated) power.[24]

We must question the perspective identified with Chatterjee also about whether Third World nationalism's imbrication in a Westernizing universal narrative, in which its politics emerges paradoxically canceled out as a politics of the impossible, is *all* there is and can be to this nationalism. Paul Zeleza provides some Africanist food for thought in this regard. "Compared to their Indian counterparts," he writes,

> "cosmopolitan" African intellectuals tend to be less dismissive of nationalism because of Africa's special position as the ultimate negative other of Europe, borne out [by the experience of] the Atlantic Slave Trade, which demands constant discursive redress. Also, African nationalisms were articulated at national, regional, and international levels through Pan-Africanism and Pan-Arabism, and often involved protracted armed liberation struggles, which mean that the nationalist imaginary was not chained to the performance of one particular territory or the interests of the elites, so that hope could always be transferred from one failed country to another, or into the possibilities of the masses being mobilized again as they had been during the liberation struggles. Indeed, the very failures of decolonization, which have been recorded with such a deep sense of anger and betrayal by African writers, were blamed less on the nationalist agenda itself than on the unwillingness or inability of the political class to implement it, abetted by international conditions and inequities.[25]

Zeleza is in danger of homogenizing "cosmopolitan" Indian intellectuals and their African counterparts into pure postmodernist and nationalist stereotypes, respectively, but generally it is a point well made.

Neither the self-inflicted defeatist reading of the nation nor its self-congratulating triumphalist counterpart will do, it seems. Hence *Writing Ghana, Imagining Africa* insists that, analytically, there must be a way of sidestepping the all-or-nothing propositions implied in both positions. It puts Anderson's view of the nation-form as (mostly) modernist possibility and Chatterjee's and Davidson's view of the same as (mostly) liability be-side—not against—each other, in a mode of reading that encompasses a both/and dialectic. It sees thus in the nation-form an African and non-Western politics of representation and action wherein the impossible does not exclude the possible, wherein the signpost facing nationalist agency does not eternally read "No Exit"[26] but reads, instead, "the way out has to be the difficult way *through*." This book seeks to arrive in that at a reading of African—and through that a reconstructed view of non-Western/Third World—modernist and nationalist intellectual agency in terms of a philosophical and cultural *navigation* of terrain already inscribed, in terms of a difficult *negotiation* of political and ideological givens.

In light of the foregoing, this book is arguing, the preindependence intellectuals who engaged with the concept of the African nation under the colonial order, and as something to come after it, were confronting African modernity in a dual interdependent aspect as a *problem* and a *problematic*. In the problem mode, modernity in Africa, that is, appeared to them in the aspect of a limitation, a predicament, a conundrum. But inside limitation and predicament they were also historical actors engaging modernity as a problematic, seeing the modern as such as offering, in Chatterjee's words, "historical possibilities," and warranting them "the practical forms of . . . realiz[ing]" these possibilities (*Nationalist Thought*, 38).

In the nation and its accessory forms of imagining modern community, then, we find these writer-intellectuals negotiating and navigating modernity in a movement away from African predicament towards African potential. Below I identify two broad tendencies, which I designate as "Orphean" and "Promethean," emergent in this African nationalist navigation. This is an exercise that must necessarily take us back in time to the two West African originals Blyden and Horton, for it is in their thought and activist posture that these two tendencies begin to crystallize.

"Africa" in Modernist Navigation: Two Archetypes

Appiah has observed of the African intelligentsia that they are to be known "through the Africa they offer . . . through an Africa they have invented for the world, for each other, and for Africa" (*In My Father's House*, 149). Blyden pioneered this threefold project—"worlding" Africa, "selving" a middle class in an African image, and going native with, or "nativizing," Africa—laying them out in a comprehensive philosophizing that would set the tone and agenda for much that will follow in African nationalist thought. Blyden's work features, too, a critique of Western modernity, a critique angled in particular towards what he conceived as its not-to-be-underestimated potential to rob "Africa" of what he called "African Personality." Those standing in the first line of attack by an "insurgent [Western] civilization" were the educated Africans of the middle-class frontline. Blyden's analyses of, and warnings about, the dangers inherent in the formation of the "intelligent Negro" according to alien pedagogical precepts projected a post-encounter African intelligentsia in a Faustian image. In his diagnosis, like Faust, the African middle class stood in danger of losing its African soul-essence in exchange for gaining the world meretriciously proffered to it by European civilization.

For the pioneer nationalist, however, the solution was not for Africa to turn away from an alienating but paradoxically desirable modernity—an impossible proposition since the historical clock could not be turned back in a mode of completely reversing the psychocultural and material effects on Africa of encounter. Rather, we see Blyden preoccupied with the difficult philosophical question of how the Faustian element in an alien modern might be lived down—the modern, then, as it might be reformulated in a self-serving "African" image. And, in his series of exhortations to educated West Africans—the most empowered by the modernizing, Westernizing changes wrought on Africa by encounter but also, as a consequence, the most in danger of alienation, as he saw it—the solution Blyden proposes is, as it were, an Orphean one. If the modern as a problem is the starting point for the pioneer, then the solution was a return by Africans everywhere, in a mode of racial self-retrieval—or *sankofa,* in its Akan-language popularization in the Gold Coast/Ghana—to the sources of their authentic selfhood. And he locates this selfhood in the nativity that their education and Western acculturation have taught Africans to either forget or reject. It is the modern, therefore, that Blyden required to be made answerable to the priority of a native essence (which he racializes as "Negro"). He stands at the head as the founder, then, of what one might call a tradition of Orphean nationalism. This was a conservative nationalism of culture—or nativism—and, in its more or less "pure" form, it will dominate preindependence Ghanaian—and, for that matter, West African—intellection and anticolonial strategy until roughly World War II.

The other pioneer nationalist contributions came from Blyden's contemporary, Horton, who was among the first Africans to be trained as a doctor—he studied medicine at Edinburgh University in the 1850s—and who spent most of his working years in various parts of the Gold Coast serving British protocolonialism. His projections concerning West Africa's future, nonetheless, were cast in anything but a colonialist rhetoric. Horton's meditations and prognostications took as their theme independent nation-state formation as a practical West African necessity, and they came accompanied by a rationally worked out program for achieving this end. Horton was a major influence in the late 1860s on the modern political self-conception of the short-lived protonationalism of the Fanti Confederation on the Gold Coast's western littoral. He was also in the nineteenth century the first and a most articulate ideologue of modern etatism—or the ideology of state—in African political nationalism.

Horton, in this wise, may be seen standing at the head of an ideological tradition, relatively muted under colonial rule, but rekindled in post

World War II African anticolonialism and embodied centrally by Kwame Nkrumah's nationalist ideopraxis.[27] The goal Horton desired was an ultimately self-sustaining black (or African) power. And this concern is to be understood in terms of the African American Martin Delany's observation about modern relations, made in 1859 to Egba chiefs in Yorubaland, in today's Nigeria, that "The claims of no people are respected until they are presented in national capacity."[28] For a West Africa severally fragmented into ethnic groups—often in conflict with each other—to attain this national capacity, it was a matter for Horton of enlightened Africans seizing on behalf of Africa the instruments of nationalist self-definition, including the institution of the modern state, from European civilization.

Horton's reading of the intelligent Negro at the frontline, then, is different from Blyden's, for the former saw the rationalist instruments of the (West) African's educational acquisition as a boon, available to be put to the work of institutionally reconstructing—or "regenerating," the nineteenth century's word—the region's societies. Unlike Blyden, for whom the modern as African alienation was a moral and existential problem, Horton welcomed this alienation insofar as its rationalist fruits, redirected into the building of national capacity, portended an exponential rise in African power. And the acquisition of modern power, qua the nation-state, was necessary to confer, as in Delany's terms, worldly recognition on the subjects of his 1868 study *West African Countries and Peoples*. In Horton's thought, therefore, alienation appears in a pragmatic calculus: there was no point reinventing an African wheel when the wheel was already in existence, and, on account of its universal applicability, could be—indeed, was waiting to be—appropriated from Europe to serve African purposes. Where it is a Faustian problem requiring an Orphean or *sankofa* solution for Blyden, the modern as an African nationalist theme for Horton arises as a Promethean problematic. It is a project for the frontline intellectual to enact a seizure of universalizing means already to hand for empowering reconstruction in Africa.

The popular soil of West Africa in the latter nineteenth century, however, was unpropitious for the seeding of Horton's ideas of homogenous political community and national sovereignty—ideas whose practical end he saw as "rais[ing] the African to a [self-determining] people."[29] There simply at this time was no social and political base transcending West Africa's fragmented ethnicities, no widespread popular roots to which coastal intellectuals of Horton's ilk were organically connected, that could provide a platform to launch a mass nationalist movement.

Something close to a "mass movement," though, one which presented the intelligentsia with an opportunity to forge an organic linkage with the "popular," did spontaneously emerge out of the crisis in European-African relations on the Gold Coast in the 1860s. This was a crisis born in part of the threatened withdrawal of Britain from West Africa, a move which entailed a relinquishing of the commitment by the Crown to protect groups like the Fanti on the Gold Coast littoral, leaving the latter to almost certain conquest by imperial Asante. It is this crisis that led to the formation on the western Gold Coast, in 1867, of the Fanti Confederation, uniting the intelligentsia and so-called natural rulers of the severally divided Fanti people in a common cause to protect and defend their newly forged confederate sovereignty. The Confederation will spawn its imitator, the Accra Native Confederation, on the east, with both developments enthusiastically endorsed and programmatically supported by the Creole Sierra Leonean doctor. (His 1870 *Letters on the Political Condition of the Gold Coast* is a lengthy and passionate statement of this support.)

Gold Coast protonationalism must have provided Horton in the late 1860s and early 1870s a glimmer of hope of things to come in West Africa. However, at this time the British did a volte-face, reversing their policy of disengaging from West Africa. The crushing of the Confederation movement by the British marked the Gold Coast beginnings of the aggressive New Imperialism which burgeoned, as the nineteenth century drew to a close, into the expansionist colonial Scramble for Africa. Horton's hopes for African sovereign self-determination in the Gold Coast would have been decisively snuffed out when in 1874 the country was formally placed under British Crown Colony rule.

The popular soil will continue to remain unpropitious for the growth of Horton's brand of nationalism for the next sixty years or so with the Gold Coast and West Africa under the colonial yoke. However, by the 1940s, the objective conditions of social change, and the economic, social, and psychological contradictions for the native contained therein, as well as the geographic and political-economic homogenization of colonial territory, had conspired to more or less create in the colonial formation a popular, transethnic convergence of interest. The wide, ethnicity-transcending social base needed for Horton's Prometheanism to be successfully activated in mass nationalist practice had become available. It is this development that Nkrumah, successfully projecting himself as an organic intellectual of the people, would come to exploit, engineering the mass nationalism that brought the Gold Coast to the independence—in 1957—that Horton had vainly dreamed of a century or so earlier. If Nkrumahist nationalism was Hortonian in being Promethean, it supersedes the Blyden-inspired Orphean variety that was long the Gold Coast and West African staple.

The two influential figures in Gold Coast and West African nationalism—Blyden the Orphean and Horton the proto-Promethean—provide two broad interpretive motifs by which this study negotiates its historical and philosòphical-ideological understandings of the domain of thought and practice that is circumscribed by "preindependence." It will be obvious in what follows that this study has disproportionately more to say about the Orphean/*sankofa* variety of nationalism and its Gold Coast and West African negotiations of African modernity, both as a problem and a problematic. And this is so since the preoccupations of this variant of nationalism, falling between the exceptions of Horton, preceding the formal colonial era, and Nkrumah, in the postwar era, dominate much of the period here designated preindependence, accounting for the thought of virtually all the other mainstream nationalist figures mentioned above. That said, however, it will be an error to partition Gold Coast nationalist orientations so neatly. For instance, one does see something of a Horton in the nationalist posture of Attoh Ahuma in the late-nineteenth- and early-twentieth-century colonial Gold Coast. And Nkrumah does not abandon *sankofa* entirely in his ideopraxis, either: Blyden's philosophical ghost hovers over the conception of his classic 1964 work of social philosophy, *Consciencism: Philosophy and Ideology for Decolonization.*

Orphean and Promethean alike, Gold Coaster, West African, and/or Pan-African, the nationalist writer-intellectuals reviewed in this book straddled the frontline of the variegated, but everywhere unequal, European-African colonial encounter.[30] And they were confronted there by the problem—into which the imagining of nation, as a problematic, will come to be folded—of African modernity. The sum of their navigations and negotiations of problem and problematic has been a projection of a modernity that would be African, an African modernity centered in the modernist given of nationality.

The Time and Space of African Intellectual History

Writing Ghana, Imagining Africa is affiliated with the comparatively few recent works of intellectual history in the Africanist domain that seek to alter the ways in which African intellection as historical "event" has been periodized and its modernity (implicitly) theorized in this periodization. This book covers the thought of "preindependence"—as opposed to "postindependence"—intellectuals, Ghanaian, West African, and Pan-African. And it contrives to work "preindependence" back to the mid- to late nineteenth century and the early twentieth. This is a period that has been consigned by and large in the historiography of African cultural thought to exist in the unclarity of a *pre*history to succeeding thought. Early national-ist thought, this book argues however, is not an unselfconscious and colo-nized "before" to a self-conscious and decolonized "after," the latter mark-ing a "break" that is presumed to begin with the approach of the mid-twentieth century. This is what Fanon's mistaken typology of stages of growth in national consciousness in colonized countries, as outlined in *The Wretched of the Earth,* has popularized.[31]

Then, again, the sheer volume of writings about the philosophical and aesthetic movement founded by francophone colonial black intellec-tuals in Paris, Negritude, relative to the paucity of work on what came before it has conduced to the impression that the "true" history of philo-sophically engaged African intellection begins in the 1930s. What this periodization unjustifiably warrants is a demotion of everything that came before Negritude to the status of pre-, proto-, or nascent Negritude: that is, so many faltering, unsystematic steps towards the brilliant illumination that Negritude will become.

Nor, if one is prepared to engage nonprejudicially with the preindependence era, can one countenance the elevation of the spectacular flowering of a culture of letters in the newly decolonized Africa of the 1960s into a mythical Origin, the great postcolonial dawn when Africa awakened into modern literary self-consciousness. That myth is neatly encapsulated in the title of Chinua Achebe's reflections on an African literary culture published in 1975. The Nigerian author informs us that, in the postindependence era, it is *Morning Yet on Creation Day.* Implied in that is a mapping of the institution of a culture of African letters in terms of a prehistoric dusk preceding this great dawn, a dusk (perhaps) forgettable for disclosing only sporadic and accidental creative flashes lighting up the con-tinental literary firmament.

All of these ways of periodizing African intellection imply a theory of history in which succession is supersession, where to be forward in time is to have a consciousness and awareness superior to those behind in time. We might see Philip Zachernuk's recent book on the southern Nigerian intelligentsia, *Colonial Subjects: An African Intelligentsia and Atlantic Ideas,* with its richly detailed account of Nigerian intellection of a century or so, as an important intervention announcing this mode of periodizing as outworn.[32] The histo-rian, indeed, does well to bring the "dark ages" of the nineteenth and early twentieth centuries to light in the fullness of those eras' thought. They are to be deemed in themselves fully historical, not some other era's prehistory.

Zachernuk's own historiographic practice, influenced by recent developments in postcolonial theory, insists on "restoring heterogeneity" to his southern Nigerian colonial subjects and to the terrain over which they think and act. And, in that, it produces a history punctuated by epochal breaks, the historiographic assumption being that in each break the previous epoch is left behind. ("I ask," he notes in this vein, "what *Africa* meant to different people at different times rather than assume some essential or enduring meaning for the term" [*Colonial Subjects,* 9, emphasis in the original].) Writing this Africanist history of contingency, Zachernuk would have us believe that Nigerian, and for that matter African, intellectual history is succession without iteration. And what this way of proceeding involves is the historian looking so hard at the trees that he fails to see the forest—namely, what is *enduring* in the question of "Africa" *in spite of* its being posed differently at different times.

Writing Ghana, Imagining Africa covers roughly the same hundred-year period as *Colonial Subjects.* It proceeds with Zachernuk's care in acknowledging contingencies of time and differences in situation of the intellectuals it looks at. However, this book establishes radically that African intellectual history is ultimately intelligible only within the unbroken continuum of *one* post-encounter epoch, the continuity of this epoch identified in a native intelligentsia's successively straddling and navigating a frontline within it. The theory of periodization that informs its historiography, therefore, is that insofar as there is historical succession this succession has moved the frontline forward but this forward movement has not caused it to be transcended. Thus the chronologies and the writer-intellectuals this book looks at—from the mid- and late nineteenth century to the recent past, the period labeled "preindependence"—are all *contemporary.* These writer-intellectuals commonly address problems within—and this crucial perception is missing from Zachernuk's account—the contemporaneity of a post-encounter frontline, a contemporaneity, we might add, that they share with their postindependence counterparts. Dealing with a *recurrent* problem of African modernity at the frontline, earlier and later African thought are continuous and interilluminating; and, indeed, for the same reason, "preindependence" and "postindependence" are *logically* interchangeable (even if *ideological* responses to the problem of African modernity are historically mutable).

Finally, does the fact that encounter took place here, there, and everywhere mean that the paradoxically given post-encounter frontline that this book sees in African location is globally "spatializable"? Can we out of, and by way of, Africa read the intellectual histories of different sites of colonial encounter—say, Ireland and India; Mediterranean Gibraltar/Cyprus and the South Sea islands; Palestine and Papua New Guinea—in a mode of comparative *similarity*? The answer has to be a "yes." What do we see of the nationalist writer-intellectuals represented in *Writing Ghana, Imagining Africa* but their recurrent engagements self-consciously at the frontline with the question of domesticating the alien and alienating to invent the modern in an African image? If in that their writings disclose a deeply interesting navigation of a post-encounter problem of immense sociocultural and philosophical difficulty, this problem is not the exclusive property of these preindependence African intellectuals. They share them, indeed, with others globally, products of encounter, too, who also happen to straddle a post-encounter frontline and are self-conscious about being so doubly positioned. Thus we find the Irish modernist writer, James Joyce, making his character Stephen Dedalus silently declare his double positioning to his English interlocutor, "so familiar and [yet] so foreign," in *A Portrait of the Artist as a Young Man*:

> The language in which we are speaking is his before it is mine. How different are the words *home, Christ, ale, master,* on his lips and mine! I cannot speak or write these words without unrest of spirit. His language so familiar and so foreign, will always be for me an acquired speech. I have not made or accepted its words. My voice holds them at bay. My soul frets in the shadow of his language.[33]

That moment of truth where the (ex)-colonial subject self-consciously confronts his division from and hostility to the (ex)-colonizing other, and must also acknowledge his at once enabling *and* disabling incorporation into the language and intellectual protocols of this other, is as (recurrently) African as it is Irish. Irish modernism, as is its African counterpart, is a matter of making a virtue out of necessity, of wrenching possibility from the liabilities of colonial encounter. For these reasons, *Writing Ghana, Imagining Africa*, while partial to preindependence Ghanaian and West African example, is alive to the fact that it tells part of a story and is an exemplum of a wider post-encounter navigation of the problem of constituting a postcolonial and/or non-Western modernity. And this as it transpires in a particular ontological position—that doubly disposed frontline as it has historically been given by the (variegated) colonial encounter.

What follows in the next chapter, then, begins by tapping into a self-reflexive insight about the frontline by a post-encounter intellectual of South Asian origin positioned thereon, the aforementioned Gayatri Spivak. With

Spivak's leader setting the investigative focus and tone, the chapter begins the work of reconstructing the post-encounter frontline, its fractured legacy of subjectivity and cognition, from within the more or less globally representative African setting of a Gold Coast/Ghana of West African location. Interwoven in the discussion are pertinent sociohistorical and sociocultural observations that should give the reader an idea about the subjective and objective formation, the structure, and the nature of the field of thought and action circumscribed by the designation "preindependence Ghana." Chapter 1 broadly lays out the contexts of the themes recurrently addressed in this book. Who writes the nation as part of a project of African Reconstruction construed as African modernity? From which sociocultural stratum or location does the nationalist writer-intellectual's endeavor emanate? How is this location to be understood in its objective historical construction and in its formation, as a psychocultural question, of the subjectivity of the writer-intellectual? What existential, historical, and cultural circumstances pressing down on the writer-intellectual's location imposes the necessity of the African nation and its modeling in representation? In these same terms, then, towards what does and must the African nation in the writing or representation gesture?

In *The Wretched of the Earth,* Fanon argues that the contradictions built into the relations between colonizing Europeans and colonized Africans mandate for the latter specific forms of ideological representation that answer back to the colonizer. "[F]or the colonist," writes Fanon, "the Negro was neither an Angolan nor a Nigerian" but "simply . . . 'the Negro,'" an abstraction that lent itself to indifferent denigration. For this reason, Fanon polemicizes, "The native intellectual who decides to give battle to colonial lies fights on the field of the whole continent" (*Wretched,* 211). Crucially, according to Fanon, while the ideological horizons, colonial and anticolonial, may be divided, in their logics of representation colonizer and colonized fall under a common (imperial) sky. Thus Fanon: "The efforts of the native to rehabilitate himself and to escape from the claws of colonialism are logically inscribed from the same point of view as that of colonialism" (212).

The first half of chapter 2 is an extended review of these Fanonian propositions, which are by and large true of the preindependence native and Pan-African intellectuals represented in this study. The second half of the chapter goes into an extended discussion of Blyden's work. I present the thought of the doyen of African nationalism in the light of the circulation of ideas in the latter half of the nineteenth century. These are the ideas underpinning humanitarianism (Buxton), liberal humanism (Mazzini),

romantic racism (Herder), internationalist nationalism (Mazzini), and imperialist historicism (Hegel). We see how Blyden challenges, adopts, and
uniquely modifies these discourses in his pioneer nationalist efforts at giving Africa a worldly presence.

Blyden, who begins the project of African worlding, bequeaths it
through his influential writings to his West African followers. Chapter 3,
"'Worlding' Nativity," looks partly at how the Blydean agenda emerges in
its application to the special historical challenges of self-affirmation and
reconstruction confronting Gold Coast nationalist intellectuals under the
colonial order. The first section of the chapter offers an interpretation of
the historiographic endeavor of Rev. C. C. Reindorf, the Basel Mission
pastor whose pioneer *History of Gold Coast and Asante* was belatedly published in 1895. Reindorf, in a context where contemporary colonial pressures had objectively thrown the Gold Coast's multiple ethnic groups together, deals with this "thrown-togetherness" as a post-ethnic question of
inventing for the colonial territory a confederate *and* corporate identity as
native.

The activity of the Accra-based Reindorf stands as the lone outstanding one in this mode of negotiation to emerge out of the eastern Gold
Coast in the late nineteenth century. From this period into the early twentieth century, Cape Coast on the west takes the prize in being the scene of
a spectacular efflorescence of nationalist writing and activism. This cosmopolitan littoral town has rightly been called "the cradle of Gold Coast nationalism,"[34] and "the 'Mecca' of Ghana's . . . nationalist political
endeavours."[35] At the head of the Cape Coast endeavors stands the outstanding lawyer, legislator, and cultural-political activist, John Mensah
Sarbah, a founding member in 1897 of the Gold Coast Aborigines' Rights
Protection Society (A.R.P.S.), which was "essentially [a nationalist] alliance
of coastal chiefs (especially Fanti) and the Cape Coast intelligentsia" (*Towards Nationhood,* xx). The project of affectively mobilizing Gold Coast
thrown-togetherness begun by Reindorf, to the extent that British policy
was seen through A.R.P.S. lenses as vitiating it to Britain's colonial advantage, is a large part of the raison d'être of this organization.

Sarbah's writings from the late 1890s and early 1900s, like the cote-
rminous ones of his fellow Cape Coasters Attoh Ahuma and Casely Hayford,
continue the nativist project laid down as a nationalist necessity by Reindorf.
The second section of chapter 3 looks specifically at Sarbah's work and how
it discloses an imperative on the middle-class intellectual to either *translate*
the native discovered and reconstituted by him out of the ethnic or, with
this nativity under the iron grip of colonialism's Darwinist logic, leave it to

perish. What we see in Sarbah's example is that colonial circumstances leave the intellectual bent on worlding his nativity with no choice but to, as it were, use the master's tools to reconstruct his own house. Sarbah's specific Gold Coast work provides occasion to illustrate a general frontline imperative: that of the native intellectual who is compelled to make a virtue out of necessity—an imperative which is not without its philosophical and practical pratfalls.

The third section of chapter 3 reads a specific problem of middle-class (self)-consciousness as it registers in the social-critical writings of Attoh Ahuma and Kobina Sekyi. Sekyi, whose literary career takes off in the teens of the twentieth century, is easily the intellectual leader of the generation of the Cape Coast school born in the 1890s. (Sarbah, Casely Hayford, and Attoh Ahuma were born in the 1860s.) An ardent Blydean, Sekyi will emerge as the most consistent *sankofa* ideologue within the ranks of the A.R.P.S. And already in 1914, this shows in his dramatic comedy *The Blinkards,* a withering satire on what Sekyi, referencing the bicultural makeup of the Euro-African subgroup to which he belonged, labeled "Anglo-Fanti." This was a group that colonial education, Western acculturation, and Christianity, in its Europeanized form, had, in Sekyi's understanding, deprived of an authentic self-consciousness and therein rendered existentially bereft of a world. Anglo-Fanti deprivation of a world of its own authentic grounding is the theme of Sekyi's fictionalized autobiography *The Anglo-Fanti* (1919), which goes inside the hero to examine the effects of a psychic bastardy which comes at the price of madness and death.

Sekyi's writings demonstrate centrally that the Socratic injunction of "man, know thyself" that had arisen in Blyden's work in the late nineteenth century had an ongoing urgency in the early twentieth. This know thyself is the premise driving Attoh Ahuma's *The Gold Coast Nation and National Consciousness* (1911), whose fundamental theme, addressed to the Gold Coast and by extension West African middle class is: "if we are a Nation, are we self-conscious?" For these early social critics and reformers, an Orphean recovery of a consciousness of a self otherwise lost in alienation is a foundational requisite for the middle-class project of the nation, folded into the frontline problematic of African modernity.

Chapter 4 looks at the negotiations and compromises required of, as well as the paradoxes and pratfalls haunting, Gold Coast nationalism as it embarks, under the British colonial order and through its middle-class spokesmen, "On the Road to Ghana." The first half of the chapter centers on the nationalist polemics of Attoh Ahuma in *Gold Coast Nation.* There are arguments out there, Attoh Ahuma leads his reader to see, which have perverted the application of the law of nature to unjustly buttress claims that the Gold Coast is deserving of colonial rule. The British nation, in exercising imperial overrule, confirms the universal in itself whereas the Gold Coast lacks the means of such self-confirmation and is hence undeserving of recognition as a nation. Yet for the Gold Coast nationalist his country also deserves the status of a "Nation" by virtue of the universal right conferred by natural law. The Gold Coast nation claimed in the churchman's argument appears not in a pure opposition to Empire; the former, in fact, needs the latter in order to recognize the universal in itself. The British Empire's Gold Coast presence paradoxically provides the universalist mirror in which Attoh Ahuma's Gold Coast sees the modernist visage of her national selfhood.

Attoh Ahuma contends that the Gold Coast nation has its requisite national past but he does not himself provide an image of this past. The second part of chapter 4 looks at the nationalist effort to image the Gold Coast's past in the historiographic efforts involving personnel, European and native, in the country. The English Methodist missionary and educator Rev. W. T. Balmer, between 1907 and 1911, begins the definitive elaboration of the thesis genealogically connecting the Gold Coast's ethnic Akan majority and imperial Ghana of the medieval western Sudan. (His lectures were published in 1925 as *A History of the Akan Peoples of the Gold Coast*.) From the late 1920s on, the business of inventing the Gold Coast as "Ghana," via the ethnohistory of the Akan, becomes the province of J. B. Danquah, the most prominent middle-class nationalist between 1930 and 1947. Danquah's effort is joined and augmented in the mid-1940s by the white expatriate woman Eva L. R. Meyerowitz.

Looking at the collaboration between black and white in the invention of Ghana, the chapter contends that the mythological road to Ghana is by no means smooth in its unfolding. Balmer's and Meyerowitz's rehabilitation of the Gold Coast in a past, both efforts abetted by an interested colonial administration, are political; they serve the ends of Empire. Danquah's anticolonial figurations of Ghana, then, as is his intellectual agency, are manipulated and canalized into a colonialist agenda. There is, in effect, a *genealogical* paradox in the mythological birthing of this national idea. And this may be rendered in terms of the operation, in Gold Coast middle-class agency, of colonialist constraint in modernist bestowal, a condition which extends beyond the Gold Coast and thus requires to be indexed to the African frontline at large—and beyond.

Chapter 5, "Faust in Africa," is an elaboration of the genealogical paradox identified in the previous chapter. At the center of the chapter are two middle-class figures John Ocansey and George Ekem Ferguson. Ocansey authored *African Trading* in 1881, a travel narrative which is a revealing self-presentation of a Christianized "black Englishman." Out of the mercantile story of this product of the three Cs of the Anglo-African civilizing mission—Christianity, Commerce, and Civilization—the chapter reads the materialist underpinnings of the psychocultural dynamics which produce the colonial subject.

Ferguson was one of the more remarkable middle-class personages to emerge in the last quarter of the nineteenth century. His work as a native cartographer and political agent at the service of British colonial expansionism helped in no small way to lay the territorial foundations of modern Ghana. The ends of Ferguson's activities were to rope the territories and peoples of the Gold Coast hinterland into an enlarged colonial political economy. His expeditionary accounts reveal, like Ocansey's travel narrative, middle-class consciousness in the ancillary mode which the Kenyan writer Ngugi wa Thiong'o has captured as the peculiar ontology of a frontline African "messenger class." Analyzing the literary self-presentations of these two, the chapter draws out of their subjective formation and objective field of operation the thesis of a colonialist premise in the modern and a modernist promise in the colonial. They are African emblems, then, of a paradoxical and difficult-to-read doubling, that Faustian condition which comes with straddling the frontline. In the matter of this Faustian condition, the chapter underlines the existential continuity between preindependence then and postindependence now by showing how the compradorial makeup of the middle class continues to figure as a problem in the postindependence writings of Achebe, Ngugi, and the Senegalese writer Cheik Hamidou Kane.

Chapter 6, "Black Orpheus, Or the (Modernist) Return of the Native," presents Casely Hayford's Orphean classic of 1911, *Ethiopia Unbound*. His quasi-fictional autobiography shows the middle-class intellectual negotiating a "third space" of "Ethiopian" (or, interchangeably, "African") nationality to emerge between the native and the modern. We also find the author bringing a critical "Ethiopian" perspective to a sustained reformist critique of European imperialism. Additionally, Hayford casts his quasi autobiography as an Ethiopianist manifesto. As such he offers it as an agenda for the nascent Pan-Africanism of the early twentieth century linking a Western-educated racial vanguard of the black Atlantic in a search for a common platform to prosecute a politics of race. In accordance with Blyden's teachings, Hayford, as he addresses the generality of a black Atlantic public, advocates a rediscovery of the native Ethiopian soul-essence by Africa and her diaspora as the sole basis by which the black race will re-empower itself. For that reason, Hayford argues, the leadership of the Pan-African movement has naturally to be African since it is Africa's intellectuals who are closest to this essence.

That the native African intellectual embodies this essence, or is ratified by it to act on its behalf, is the subject of *Ethiopia Unbound* as the quasi autobiography resolves into allegory. We see the hero, Kwamankra, on a journey back to the abode of the Akan-Fanti gods where he is reconfirmed in a nationalist and racialist mandate to be a public intellectual, the medium through which the Ethiopian soul will find a this-worldly incarnation in the Ethiopian nation.

The final chapter looks at *Ghana: The Autobiography of Kwame Nkrumah*. Its title, which collapses the biography of nation (Ghana's) into autobiography (Nkrumah's), shows that this work continues the claims made, and the prerogatives established, in the middle-class national allegory. The continuity in allegorical self-conception between Hayford and Nkrumah notwithstanding, looking at Nkrumah's pragmatic secular idealism in relation to the conservative metaphysical idealism of Hayford enables us to see the middle-class national allegory in a radically revisionist framework. Nkrumah's motivations are Promethean where Hayford's were Orphean, and that difference may be measured in terms of personality, ideological environment, and historical opportunity. Where Hayford was greatly influenced by Blyden's idealism, Nkrumah's ideological heritage was a left Pan-Africanism which, as the 1930s drew to a close, was beginning to articulate, beyond a reformist anticolonialism, an anti-imperialist politics that rejected Empire altogether. Nkrumah's Pan-African associates were such West Indian Private Private as George Padmore, Ras Makonnen, and C. L. R. James. (James's The *Black Jacobins* [1939])—depicting a heroic Toussaint stealing the fire of Enlightenment, as embodied in 1789, from the imperial-colonial French "god" and gifting it to his people—is a classic statement of left Pan-Africanist Promethean ideology.) Nkrumah could also count on a local West African tradition of anti-imperialism involving Sierra Leone's I. T. A. Wallace Johnson and Nigeria's Nnamdi Azikiwe, who were both active in the Gold Coast of the 1930s. What is more, mass discontent with colonial economic policy in the 1930s and beyond had for the first time created a fertile soil for the growth of a mass politics in the country. This signal development was unavailable for Hayford, whose populism therefore was fated to be merely symbolic, unconnected organically with the masses. The first party with a "national" semblance in the Gold Coast, the United Gold Coast Convention (U.G.C.C.), the party of J. B.

Danquah and others, is an outgrowth of this widening of the social base of the political. However, as Nkrumah came to understand it, the U.G.C.C.'s gradualist liberal-constitutionalist approach to the question of independence was not going to awaken and radicalize the people any time soon. When Nkrumah breaks away from the U.G.C.C., therefore, a middle-class nationalism redefined as to tactics and goals is the basis of his successful politicking. As this politicking, mediated through his Convention People's Party (C.P.P.), marks the beginning of the end of direct colonial rule in Africa, national allegory in *Ghana* affirms a middle-class sense of culmination, of modernist arrival in substantive nation-statehood.

But has the sense of arrival been sustained a generation into Independence? The last section of the chapter, pursuing an answer to this question, reflects on the nationalist heritage reflected in the writing of "Ghana" and the imagining of "Africa" therein. Thus, if this study properly ends with decolonization in the late 1950s and the 1960s, this reflection means looking beyond the moment of the crowning achievement of middle-class nationalism to see what has become of the promise of this class. In our time, what Nkrumah and Fanon once hopefully called the "African Revolution" emerges largely as a spectacle of compromise. The last section of chapter 7 speculates on the wherefore of this failure of the African modernist enterprise. Finally it draws, too, on a revolutionary strand of African nationalist thinking—Amilcar Cabral's—to explore, if only in a tentative fashion, the terms in which Africa's nationalist compact with the modern might be rethought and renegotiated.

1

(IM)POSSIBLE NECESSITIES

READING AN AFRICAN FORMATION IN CONTRADICTION

> One who causes you injury also teaches you wisdom.
>
> —Yoruba proverb

> For the African intellectual . . . the problem is whether—and, if so, how—our cultures are to *become* modern.
>
> —Kwame Anthony Appiah, *In My Father's House*

Gayatri Spivak, in one of her essays, characteristically puts under the microscope "postcolonial persons" like herself, "from formerly colonized countries," for whom access to the "so-called culture of imperialism" has been enabling. Enabling, insofar as it warrants them the good fortune of being "able to communicate to each other (and to metropolitans), to exchange, to establish sociality." Nonetheless, when Spivak goes on to ponder whether, under these fortunate circumstances, "we [shall] assign to that [imperialist] culture a measure of 'moral luck,'" she has no doubt that "the answer is 'no.'" Yet, for all that, the critic admits that this is an *"impossible* no," on account of the fact that it appears contradictorily within "a structure that one critiques and yet inhabits intimately."[1] Spivak implies, therefore, that to inhabit the culture of imperialism—and this culture gives us the structure of our international modernity—as a "formerly colonized," or "postcolonial" person is to be pulled in contrary directions at once. It is to find oneself inside a structure, not of one's (direct) making, that does not afford one the luxury of a standpoint purely outside itself—a structure, that is, that affords no Archimedean standpoint in consciousness and identity. And it is to inhabit this structure under circumstances which impose upon one to simultaneously say to it a reluctant "yes," in desire and intimacy, and a compromised "no," in resistance. It is to know, further, that while saying "no" does not and will not put one outside this structure, a failure to say the same amounts to a shirking of an existential obligation, an ethical charge, and the historic necessity to imagine, in the impossible-to-inhabit outside of the structure, the possibility of the unimaginable.

The problem of a modernity that is imaginably and unimaginably African—a conceptually impossible proposition—should emerge in outline here. For in the frontline nationalist thought under consideration in this study, "Africa" and "African nationality" come inscribed on the "no" of Spivak's impossible refusal.

In a self-analysis of one aware of herself straddling the post-encounter frontline, Spivak therefore gives us the contradictory, split, and complicated outline of a generally post-encounter condition that inhabits both colonial and ex-colonial subjects. We may connect her contradictory exegesis of this condition to the proverbial wisdom of Ghana's ethnic Akan as set out in a conundrum outlining the quandary of desiring ("yes") that which one must fear ("no"). Thus the Akan: *santrofi anomaa, wofa a, woafa mmusu; wogyaw a, woagyaw ade pa.* And this translates: the nature of the *santrofi* bird is such that to carry it home from the wilds is to impose a curse on oneself. And yet a failure to claim and presumably domesticate this creature is an unwise denial of oneself a great fortune. How, then, to live down the necessary curse bound up with equally necessary good fortune?

Africa between Purity and Parity

Mainly analyzing examples of the nationalist thought of preindependence Gold Coast/Ghana, this study is a historically informed attempt to chart an African colonial genealogy of this generally post-encounter contradiction. It is a study that also reconstructs, by way of the nationalist thinkers and ideologues, a navigational map of the different modes in which this contradiction—that is, Africa's contamination and compromise by the very structure it emerges in a refusal to inhabit—has been dealt with. On the one hand, we find in these thinkers' navigation, an Africa that is, that indeed

must be, defined towards a pole of *difference,* a pole of self-centered autonomy and self-consistent authenticity. On the other hand, this difference that yields Africa in autonomy and authenticity must be defined towards a pole of *similarity.* Looking at an Africa done down by and under
the imperial order as subhuman and inferior, historical and ethical necessities arise for these nationalist thinker-ideologues to articulate Africa in a
"worldly" parity with those who dominate the continent. A demand for
"purity"—a demand to inhabit an "outside"—impossibly sits cheek by jowl
beside a demand for parity—a demand to inhabit an "inside" on equal
terms—in the same Africa.

This difficult double order of reclamation is a problem negotiated
with great acuity, and not without its shortcomings, in the seminal nationalist thought of Blyden. An extended review of Blyden's meditations on
African nationality in these terms appears in the next chapter. If Blyden
takes pride of place "naturally" in an introduction to a study of Ghanaian
nationalist thought, it is because the West African returnee of American
origin was the first comprehensively to lay out, in a self-critical social, cultural, and moral philosophy, what he called "the African problem." He
both illuminates and begins the navigation of the problem of African modernity. Hence what transpires after Blyden in the Gold Coast and elsewhere in English-speaking West Africa—and well beyond—can be regarded,
so to speak, as so many Blydenesque footnotes. This is not to deny, though,
that the differing spatial exigencies and changing temporal contexts of the
colonial also conspire to throw up original responses from those who come
after him to the problems he originally defines.

To go back to the double order of reclamation implied in the problem of African modernity encountered by the preindependence writer intellectuals: confronting them, on the one hand, was an imagining of the
"African" in some self-consistent way as a different, and in some self-centered way as an autonomous, order of being. On the other hand, this could
not preclude their seeking for the self-centered difference they so imagined
a consistency or consonance with standards and norms of an ex-centric
derivation. The former had become necessary on account of alienating
colonialist pressures registering at the frontline. These pressures compelled
the writer-intellectuals to seek and express, in that which they could imagine in a variety of "nationalist" ways as "African," a difference that would be
a contrasting identity to the "European" (or "Western"). Hence, as in Blyden's
pioneering writings for instance, the nation's Africanity in its imagining
could be differentiated by "race," a race that had its own "soul," a metaphysical quantity rooted, in Blyden's sociology of culture, in a "native" au-

thenticity. A variable interplay between racialism and nativism has been very much at the root of African self-imagining in the order of the nation.

We have heard Blyden—whose influence on Gold Coast nationalist thought was, in the first instance, mediated through his protégé Casely Hayford—protesting in 1892 that "the fringe of European civilization is violence." Blyden at the frontline—or the "fringe," as he refers to it—of the unequal European-African colonial encounter could see, in the modernity encapsulated in nineteenth-century Europe's self-given charter of an African "civilizing mission," a force that came freighted with colonialist liability for the indigenous societies of the continent. In the pioneer African nationalist's diagnosis, "Things which have been of great advantage to Europe may work to ruin us; and there is often such a striking resemblance . . . between the hurtful and the beneficial, that we are not always able to discriminate."[2] And yet both pioneer and protégé, products of European civilization, could also embrace this exogenous phenomenon which they feared. An alien and alienating modernity was a necessity to be embraced because it held within itself the promise, as Hayford affirmed in 1903, of "the practical upliftment of the native tribes in the scale of civilization."[3] And for Horton, ardent advocate of African independence in the late 1860s and early 1870s, the nationalist urge to affirm something differently African—and this is reflected in Horton's deliberately choosing the name "Africanus"—did not preclude his affirmation of "the English element . . . unquestionably the best civilizing agency."[4]

For these frontline nationalist intellectuals, therefore, the problem of a modernity that would be African emerges, as the proverbial conundrum of the Akan will have it, in how to live down the paradox of good fortune that comes inalienably bound up with a curse. The problem is structured in terms of their saying an impossible "no" to inhabiting a structure which they desired, and could not but desire.

Pressing on these intellectuals at the frontline also was the urgent task of rehabilitating an African humanity that had been indifferently done down by and under the colonial-imperial order. "The African is a much maligned man," wrote the Gold Coast nationalist J. W. de Graft Johnson, lamenting the existential burden of the African at the receiving end of European racial, cultural, and caste prejudice.[5] He continues: "Every white man that goes to the [West African] Coast seems to be under the impression that the Native has no faculties of reasoning; that his thinking is largely to be done by others" (*Towards Nationhood,* 2). As registered in De Graft Johnson's nationalist polemic, the pressure on the writer-intellectual was to rehabilitate African humanity towards a conception of "African nationality" such that the entity so rehabilitated will garner "world recognition" (7). As others of his nationalist kind had done before—and will do after—him, he entertains in this mode "great hopes, that the future will see the African better understood and appreciated, and given his due right of recognition in the Comity of Nations." Africa will step "into her rightful place as a unit in the powerful army of the human family, will . . . assume her obligations and responsibilities as a respectable and respected member of [world] society" (v). Nation and its consummation appear in a projection of Africa's "worlding," Africa's attainment, that is, of world(ly) recognition. Insofar, therefore, as Africa is seen as occupying a place "below" "the world," worlding is inscribed in a nationalist imaginary as an agenda for Africa's vertical integration within the human family.

The need to project Africa in this worldly vein meant that the frontline nationalist writer-intellectuals had to insert the entity they imagined and appropriated in *contrast* into a *complementary* domain of identification. "Ethiopia shall stretch forth her hands unto God"[6]—so went a rallying cry, resounding in African nationalist polemic, in use from the latter half of the nineteenth century to well into the twentieth. It is a cry that invokes and adapts a religious trope to a secular imagining of an Africa lifted up onto the world stage otherwise denied it under the duress of colonial imperialism. Yet what it meant for writer-intellectuals like De Graft Johnson to garner for the misrecognized humanity (or "nationality") of "Ethiopia" world recognition was that they were obliged to bring this construct into a consistency or consonance with norms of an exogenous—i.e., colonialist and modern European—derivation. In another difficult proposition, Africa of the self-centered nationalist imagining had somehow to be taken out of itself and reconciled with what, relative to itself, was ex-centric. On the one hand, for the Africa of the nationalist intellectuals to attain similarity in a worldly modernity, this construct had to capitulate to standards not of its own direct making. But this world-bound construct had, on the other hand, to be different, too, otherwise it could hardly maintain the claim of being "African."

Somehow, then, the divergent and the convergent were to be held to mutual account in the same African frame. For an illustration of how the problem registers at the frontline and how it is negotiated, we may turn to Wole Soyinka's *Myth, Literature, and the African World*. This is a work that, its postindependence status notwithstanding, is still entangled in what emerges since, and as a result of, encounter as a recurrent problem. As captured in the title, the Nigerian writer-intellectual contracts to renegotiate a modernistic basis of imagining a self-consistent and self-centered "African world." Soyinka's postindependence African literary nationalism and its precursor in the preindependence era navigate a common philosophical terrain: how to figure out "Africa" in a worldly modernity—and vice versa. The Nobel laureate addresses the problem through the writer's "secular vision," a projection which "combines a re-creation of a pre-colonial African world-view with eliciting its transposable elements into modern potential."[7] The demand placed on the writer of the secular vision appears to be one of restoring "Africa" to itself in the integrity and authenticity of a precolonial past: difference remains a desired option. Yet this restoration must also come from a place, and in terms, other than the purely precolonial. The writer's desired return to the past, it turns out, is a desire to "return" this past forward. Precolonial myth is to negotiate a middle passage through what is instituted by European colonialism, and survives in its aftermath, as a legacy of African possibility (or "modern potential," as Soyinka puts it).[8] This African possibility is colonially bestowed in literacy; and is given, also, in the agency, and the access to protocols of modern representation—i.e., "literature"—that this literacy confers on the writer. As the writer steers old-world African "myth" through the middle passage of secular translation, the aboriginal being of this myth is renovated into becoming "literature." The "African," as myth-become-literature, doubles its nature in being so rehabilitated; and, presumably, does so in the secular re-creation without forgoing its originality.

Yet the secular vision remains a paradoxical one, for its proponent imagines a structure that can be itself at the same time as it somehow supersedes and becomes other than itself. The writer is enjoined in Soyinka's projection to impossibly retrieve "Africa" in an intact selfhood at the very moment that this "Africa" must leave its intact self behind. Soyinka's derivation of "Africa" is problematic, too, for it is based singularly in the metaphysics of Yoruba ethnicity. And we have to ask of those at the frontline—a problem taken up in the next chapter—whether and under what circumstances one bird a flock makes: the philosophical problem of the relation of part to whole, in other words. What is more, the African modernity imagined in the secular vision is structured in compromise. Its agenda of thrusting a precolonial world forward, towards modern potential, also appears to leave a desired African difference captive to standards and norms of an alien imposition. Hidden in Soyinka's modernizing solution of transposing (precolonial) myth into (postcolonial) literature—"Africa's" literary nationalist warranty of worldly recognition—is the play of a residually colonial, alienating power. Modern potential for Africa, a would-be African modernity, comes double-edged, inscribed at once in possibility and liability.

It is this conundrum that confronted pioneer Casely Hayford and moved him to write in a 1914 essay, "The Future of West Africa": "No worse burden could be imposed by [European] civilization on African nationality."[9] He fulminates in his essay, also, against a middle class being afflicted, as a result of Western education, by a "double life"—the condition of being neither fish nor fowl. What is difficult in concept about African modernity and the nation folded within it, Hayford's self-diagnoses permit us to see, is compounded by a contradiction as much sociohistorical as it is ontological. The post-encounter frontline where his modern "African nationality" is imagined, he realizes, is set up by forces beyond African control to be occupied by a group with the status, on their own soil, of "native foreigners." But how and under what circumstances had this group been formed, and to what aspiration did it owe its being?

The Euro-African Middle Class: Its Sociocultural and Cognitive Formation

Historically the group referred to owed its origin to Europe's African civilizing mission as projected in the humanitarian ideology of African reform that followed Britain's early-nineteenth-century abolition of the slave trade. Humanitarian effort aimed "to convert barbarians to Western ways" at a time—the mid-nineteenth century—when the "idea that civilization meant Westernization enjoyed a special vogue."[10]

It is in this spirit, one purposed on lifting "the inhabitants of Africa [out of] the very depths of ignorance and superstition," that in 1840 the prominent British abolitionist and influential parliamentarian Thomas Fowell Buxton wrote his monumental *The African Slave Trade and Its Remedy*. Buxton noted in this work: "I lay great stress upon African commerce, *more* upon the cultivation of the soil, but *most* of all upon the elevation of the native mind."[11] In the realization of the reformist schemes laid out for Africa in Buxton's and other humanitarian projections, the agency of elevated native minds, sons of the soil, was deemed instrumental.[12] Humanitarian thinking about the mode of being of this native agency was similar to the projections made by Thomas Babington Macaulay in his "Minute on Indian Education."[13] Macaulay wrote in 1835:

> We must at present do our best to form a class who may be interpreters *between* us and the millions whom we govern; a class of persons Indian in blood and colour, but English in taste, in opinions, in morals and intellect.

To that class we may leave it to refine the vernacular dialects of the country, to enrich those dialects with terms of science borrowed from the Western nomenclature, and to render them by degrees fit vehicles for conveying knowledge to the great mass of the population. (430; emphasis added)

We may only substitute "African" for "Indian" to see the comparably similar foundations laid by the Anglo-African civilizing mission in coastal West Africa for the rise, from the 1850s on, of an African intermediary agency. The agencies of civilization, Christian conversion, and Western education would work in tandem to produce a middle stratum of natives, positioned, as one of the Gold Coast products of the process put it, "between the white man on the one side and [their] untutored brethren on the other side."[14]

This development would be in accord with the recommendations of T. J. Bowen, the American missionary operating in mid-nineteenth-century West Africa, who, in an argument about bringing its societies into conformity with the civilized world, underscored the need for exogenous agency to create an African middle class. "Thus far in the history of men," the missionary pointed out in 1857, "there has been no civilization which has not been cemented and sustained in existence by a division of the people into higher, lower and middle classes." West African societies, as they appeared to him, disclosed little vertical differentiation, and hence were civilizational aberrations in this respect. For, "With the single exception of political chiefs, themselves barbarians, the whole of the society of the Sudan rests and stagnates on a dead level, and the people remain poor, ignorant and wretched, because they have no superiors." Bowen could find "no class of eminent men whose attainments may give unity, force and direction to society; no middle class who are prepared by their attainments to receive impulses of knowledge, wisdom and power from their superiors, and communicate it to the millions of common people." The conclusion follows: "I need not say that a second and a third higher class must be added before we can regenerate African society."[15]

Imanuel Geiss has characterized the concrete result of these humanitarian projections as the beginnings of a "modern middle class,"[16] relying for this designation on the authority of the imperial British, who referred as such to the emergent neo-African group socially engineered by the civilizing mission. Yet, for Geiss to take the British—and Bowen, as it turns out—at their sociological word is to fail to do full justice to the nature and being of the new formation. "Middle class" in a purely sociological understanding, that is, does not capture the essence of what after all is a *cultural* formation intruded into indigenous (West) African societies by, and dependent upon, external agency. The emergent middle stratum is not the result of strictly internal alienation within these coastal and near-coastal societies. That is to say, its historical formation is different from, say, the *asikafo* of Asante (or Ashanti) in the hinterland behind the Gold Coast. This was an indigenous "bourgeois"—hence a sociological "middle"—class, a nouveau riche merchant class still retaining cultural Asanteness, whose mid- to late-nineteenth-century emergence is explained by processes of social differentiation more or less internal to Asante itself.[17]

In contrast to its Asante counterpart, the coastal and near-coastal middle stratum of West Africa was marked off by a qualitative cultural outsiderness, albeit complicated in the Gold Coast, for instance, by the fact that its members continued to retain their indigenous affiliations. These retentions notwithstanding, we are looking in this middle stratum at what Ray Jenkins, analyzing the Gold Coast evidence, has called "Euro-African Society,"[18] a sociocultural rather than a strictly sociological postulate. For Jenkins, this middle stratum, socioculturally understood, is nothing less than what Stuart Hall might call a "new ethnicity."[19] In the former's assessment it was a distinct "ethno-cultural formation," with a "complex symbiosis," "rather than a clear merger," between itself and local ethnic communities.

> Within the [coastal and near-coastal] townships [of the Gold Coast], "Euro-African" families maintained close family ties (and obligations) and institutional and commercial links with the local, indigenous communities. They were differentiated from them, however, in terms of ancestry (often European); education (language, literacy, and Christian affiliation); occupation (merchants, administrators, preachers, teachers, lawyers, doctors, engineers, clerks); and membership of European associations (missions, freemason, friendly, and temperance societies). ("Gold Coasters," 9)

Literally and symbolically, the Euro-Africans were differentiated in "the local vernaculars as 'Europeans,' 'white men's children' or 'white men,' and, as residents of the [local Gold Coast] townships, they were associated with distinct wards or quarters." Moreover, "it can be argued," according to Jenkins, "that their cultural reference points were . . . the European trader administrators, who had been highly visible members of coastal society since . . . the late seventeenth century" (9).

For Jenkins "class" is a problem for accounting for vertical differentiation *within* this emergent Euro-African ethnocultural formation; it is not a term that lies purely between it and others. "Ethno-cultural categories," as he writes, "would seem to be more appropriate when attempting to differentiate between members of the communities within 'Euro-African

Society' and rather less appropriate, when differentiating that 'Society' from others on the Gold Coast, namely, 'African' or 'European'" (7).

The problem with the sociocultural reading done in the manner Jenkins prefers is that it does away with the vertical differentiation of the social field implied in the use of "class." Euro-African Society, as he calls it, is not a society unto itself; nor does it, in horizontal differentiation, simply sit side by side with the collectivities he designates as "African" and "European" within colonial society. On the contrary, in the constitution of the greater colonial social formation, it is articulated with these others in a hierarchy. A sociocultural reading informed by a notion of the hierarchy that articulates the colonial cannot but conclude therefore that what Europe's African civilizing mission intrudes into the societies of the West African littoral is a modern "caste." And this "middle 'caste'" is privileged as such by its cultural nearness to an "upper" one, the "European," sharing prestige with this "upper caste" relative to a "lower caste," Jenkins's local "African." The vertical differentiation that Jenkins sees in Euro-African society, and which he denotes as the proper class phenomenon, is to be seen then as a matter, among its members, of variable degrees of access to, and relative distribution among them of, the resources of privilege and prestige. In effect, in the distribution of privilege and prestige in Euro-African society, one is bound at the high end to find a relatively highly privileged and prestigious "aristocracy" of "caste," while at the low end would be members who are relatively less privileged and prestigious. But it is the inclusive mark of prestige and privilege conferred by European social engineering of indigenous society that marks this middle stratum collectively off from the local "African," in the first place.

"Caste," as descriptive nomenclature for "Euro-African Society," is suggestive, too, since this Society, or more appropriately its "aristocratic" portion, becomes an endogamous group across urban and peri-urban, coastal and near-coastal, West Africa: Freetown in Sierra Leone, Cape Coast and Accra in the Gold Coast, Lagos in Nigeria, etc. Euro-African intermarriages across these sites, as well as Euro-African intramarriages locally, amount to a recognition and ratification by members of this middle stratum of a shared culture of distinction.

When all is said and done, however, "caste" has its special problems of usage in the sense that its ideal type is associated with the heritable and, traditionally, more or less hermetic and immutable hierarchies, associated with religious notions of degrees of purity and pollution. The sociocultural phenomenon being described here is not the same: one is not necessarily born into this middle stratum; the ticket of admission is the acquisition of

Western cultural traits through European education. Again, if culturally and occupationally, traditional castes are internally self-reproducing, with identities endogenous to the caste itself, in the case of the Euro-Africans it is an external input—the civilizing mission and its heritage—that guarantees their reproduction. This makes them a "caste" with a difference; because their modern identity is of exogenous derivation, it is a dependent identity, vulnerably so, and as such potentially a problem. It is this problem that comes to the fore with the rise of the African colonial state after the 1870s. Official racism, rising with the colonial state, threatens Euro-Africans with a loss of caste, as it were. Under the formal colonial order, as enshrined in legislation, there were two salient distinctions: European and Native. Europeans were white, natives were anything not white; and to be a nonwhite "Euro-African" was to share with the "African"—Jenkins's categorical distinctions—the same inferior exchange value as *native* compared to a superior white caste.

Imbricating notions of social-structural hierarchy and cultural identity, "caste" captures what is socioculturally distinctive about the middle stratum. The term, however, comes freighted with too much traditional baggage to capture the "modernity" of this African social stratum. What analysts prefer is to capture the flavor of this modernity, as in the case of Geiss, by making a class category out of this stratum—hence the middle stratum of Euro-Africans comprise a middle class. This study of African modernity spearheaded by Euro-Africans straddling the frontline between Europe and Africa, then, follows established usage in deploying "middle class," but with a proviso: that the use of this designation throughout its pages also carries the sociocultural connotation of "middle 'caste'" as outlined above.

To return, then, to the problem of African regeneration, as purposed in the humanitarian projections: this meant for the native fraction comprising the middle class that it found itself co-opted into becoming an imperial ancillary working to extend Western civilizational, spiritual, and commercial hegemony in Africa.[20] The vision of Africa raised to be the civilizational equal of others—the universal Africa of Bowen's rhetoric—necessarily was to come at the price of the generality of social alienation for the societies of encounter and of psychocultural alienation specifically for those co-opted at this encounter's civilizational frontline.[21]

Concerning the first generation of Western-educated coastal West Africans, Christian converts and "willing pupils of the missionaries," Rina Okonkwo notes that "the Europeans tried to transform [them] into a westernized middle-class to carry Christianity and western civilization to their countrymen in the interior." And this new intermediary, formed under similar circumstances in "Sierra Leone, Gold Coast . . . and Nigeria"—as indeed they would be elsewhere in Africa—"proudly referred to themselves as black Englishmen." What is more,

> They bore European names, given to them by the missionaries. . . . Their entertainments included horse races, fancy dress balls, cricket, musical and dramatic concerts, levees, soirees, conversaziones, and at-homes. They held elaborate weddings, dressed in plumes, stockings, gloves, fans and parasols. The wedding gifts included Morocco visiting cards and gold cheese dishes.[22]

The middle class in the late nineteenth century would appear to a contemporary observer, southern Nigeria's *Lagos Standard,* as a class at the receiving end of programmed alienation, leading the paper to write in 1896: "The Europeanized African is a geographical, a physiological and psychological monstrosity."[23]

Casely Hayford, looking back in his 1914 essay on this original scene of alienation—that is, the untranscendable and heritable contradiction constitutive of the Euro-African social fraction he belongs to—will register his existential unease in the biblical expression, "The fathers have eaten sour grapes and the children's teeth are set on edge" (*Land Question,* 100). Addressing the fractured formation of his middle-class consciousness, he would also be pointing out, at the frontline, a condition involving and jointly shared by parents and offspring, originals and heirs. This condition has been captured in the term "postcoloniality" by Appiah, a condition we are to understand as coming into being with, and in the aftermath of, the African-European colonial encounters. (Hence it does not belong only in the period following the end of formal colonialism.) That is, a native intelligentsia, under the variable forms of the African colonial order, and in its postindependence aftermath, invariably inhabits "postcoloniality" as a post-encounter condition. And to inhabit this post-encounter African condition, Appiah implies, is to occupy an ontological rift; it is to inhabit a space that is not and cannot be purely African. It is to be set apart as a member of a "Western-trained group of writers and thinkers," a group imposed upon to conduct its thinking and writing in a "Western style"[24]—in accordance, that is, with intellectual and representational protocols that are disproportionately *not* of indigenous African provenance. (The doubleness inherent in "postcoloniality" shines through, for instance, when, commenting on Casely Hayford's *Ethiopia Unbound* in 1910, Blyden, the former's cultural-nationalist mentor, writes of this work of nativist affirmation: "It is the best work on the subject that a Europeanised African can write. I mean an African imbued with Anglo-Saxon erudition." [25]) At the Afro-Western front-line, "postcoloniality" therefore, Appiah writes, "is the condition of what we might ungenerously call a comprador intelligentsia" (*In My Father's House,* 149). This intelligentsia, such as the ones represented in this book, can be seen as such because while they remain at home in Africa they are the intermediary agents of an alien culture. In spite of themselves they represent the intelligent and hegemonic medium through which Western knowledge/power and its modes of expression engraft themselves onto the "native" realities of the continent.

V. Y. Mudimbe, the Congolese philosopher and cultural critic, notes in this connection that the thought of most African leaders and thinkers who have received a Western education is "at the crossroads of Western epistemological filiation and African ethnocentrism." The "African ethnocentrism" the critic refers to is itself a near-impossible proposition since "the concepts and categories underpinning [it] are inventions of the West." Overall, the critic concludes, "Modern African thought seems somehow to be basically a product of the West," and

> the conceptual framework of African thinking has been both a mirror and a consequence of the experience of European hegemony; that is, in Gramsci's terms, "the dominance of one social bloc over another, not simply by means of force or wealth, but by a social authority whose ultimate sanction is an expression of a profound cultural supremacy." [26]

The problem may not quite be laid out in the sustained analytic fashion we find it in Mudimbe's *Invention of Africa* but the conception comes out nonetheless in Hayford's intuitions in "The Future of West Africa." The latter's mode of dealing with the problem is to proselytize, warning his youthful audience of high school students: "we miss the high mark of our national calling when we *elect* to be puppets in soul at the bidding of alien formulae" (*Land Question,* 102; emphasis added). Choice, then, of great existential moment, confronted the nationalist writer-intellectuals within this conception of the problem. On the one hand, they and their middle-class kind could elect simply to be the comprador effect of a European hegemonic narrative projected onto Africa. "Unwisely imitating and adopting the white man's style of living in every respect," as Hayford's nationalist fellow traveler, Sarbah, put it in 1906 (*Fanti National Constitution,* 250), they would be "civilized," yet in effect imposed upon to remain bastard end-products of Europe's colonialist African genealogy. On the other hand, a middle class could, from its place of Euro-African compromise at the frontline, elect to project its intermediary self standing at the beginning, as progenitor and generator, of an African narrative of renewal.

"An African nationality is the great desire of my soul," Blyden had written in this progenitive mode in 1865 in his *Liberia's Offering*,[27] and in the next chapter we will see how the pioneer nationalist explores the complications in which the postulate of African nationality is entangled. Rev. S. R. B. Attoh Ahuma, the nationalist contemporary of Sarbah and Casely Hayford, would echo this desire in 1911 in "The Gold Coast Nation and National Consciousness."[28] In this essay, Attoh Ahuma would make demands of the same existential magnitude as Hayford's to his audience in "The Future of West Africa." Implicit in the demands would be an acknowledgment that the prehistory of the consciousness of the class to which these nationalist intellectuals belonged was one in which they were programmed by a colonialist puppeteer to transmit a message not of their own sovereign fashioning. With the dawn of class self-consciousness that took on a nationalist character, that is, they stood poised to enter the lists of history to do battle as their own man, so to speak.

After 1870: Euro-Africanity in a Crisis of Consciousness

Why and how had self-consciousness arrived for these frontline nationalist intellectuals who, in now urging it on others of their own kind, were implying that it did not exist—or did only sporadically—before? Not by Pauline revelation by any means. Rather, the rise of self-consciousness as an existential and ideological problem for the middle class has its historic roots in the expansionist New Imperialism of the period after the 1870s. This was the period when British imperial ideology discarded its charter of an African civilizing mission and began to adapt itself to law and order administration under the formal colonial order. With the expansion of colonial territory from the narrow strips of coastal and near-coastal enclaves to cover the erstwhile immense hinterlands of West Africa, a hegemony-seeking colonial authority required a wider social base of power to prop up its dominion. Large populations, newly roped into the ambit of colonial rule, needed to be pacified and controlled. In the light of this the small, politically self-conscious vanguard of the educated African intermediary, long excoriated by the British on the West Coast for being untrustworthy and disruptive agitators, had nuisance value. Seen as scheming to thwart British colonial ambitions, the "intelligent Negro of the Coast" especially had become "the curse of the West Coast"; "a thorn in the side of the Govt. of the G[old] Coast"; "an embarrassing and mischievous element in the dealings of the Government with the Natives."[29] This intermediary needed to be bypassed, defanged politically, for colonial state formation, under the auspices of British Indirect Rule, to be realized. Under this scheme where the British ruled the natives "indirectly" through their colonially co-opted kings and chiefs—the so-called natural representatives—the administration would secure the expanded base of social power needed to support and reproduce colonial rule. The new alliance envisaged would be between colonial authority and an intermediary chiefly or customary authority, an arrangement under which, as Bjorn Edsman points out, "the educated elite would be left in a lurch." Regarding the new-imperialist developments on the Gold Coast, the historian provides the following assessment:

> The concrete result of the early phase of colonialism was the development of an educated elite, which had more or less been part and parcel of the ruling section of colonial society, and did to a considerable extent share its basic values. In the new situation arising after 1900 the elite was not allowed by the British to play any prominent part in the Western superstructure, and they were not easily accommodated in the traditional society . . . where the chiefs feared their claims to leadership. . . . Indirect rule threatened to deprive the educated elite of any immediate affiliation with either the European or African society. (*Lawyers,* 26)

Thus we see a middle class excluded from the apex of colonial society reserved for white power; denied meaningful political access to a social base comprised of the mass of colonized natives; and forced, under circumstances which threatened to render it a socially excluded middle, to contend in a middleman role with the supposed true representatives of native authority. Such was the condition of social and existential disfranchisement imposed upon the middle class by the New Imperialism. Sir John Rodger, governor of the Gold Coast, would note in *The African Mail* of 9 July 1909, the sorry fate of this class under a new political dispensation which continued to turn out "black and brown Englishmen" but ended up "cursing the finished article when the operation is complete" (qtd. in *Political History,* 93).

Colonial developments at the turn of the nineteenth century did not only deny a middle class its political humanity, as it were; this problem was compounded by another, also colonially engendered. A racial principle of political and cultural exclusion devalued the middle class's sense of its "cosmopolitan" humanity that came with Western education, and, if Hayford's complaint reproduced below is anything to go by, dented the middle class's "worldly" self-image. The post-1870 rise of the colonial state was accompanied by the practice of official racism in Anglo-African relations. This practice was propped up ideologically by the emergent racial science that had raised quasi-anthropological, religious, and philosophical doctrines of Negro, and interchangeably African, inferiority and incapacity to a "scientific" status.[30] In the post-1870s order, the "black Englishmen"—once accepted as full partners in the civilizing mission—would be excluded by the colonial state from a meaningful vanguard role on account of their "African race." As Okonkwo notes: "The term black Englishman, which denoted the concept that given equal education and opportunity the African could achieve equality with the European, soured to an epithet at the end of the nineteenth century" (*Heroes,* 1).

This development explains why we find Casely Hayford, speaking as a "cultured" cosmopolite, voicing this elitist complaint to his white colonial interlocutors, members of the Gold Coast Administration:

> [I]f you took mankind in the aggregate, irrespective of race, and shook them up together, as you would the slips of paper in a jury panel box, you would find after the exercise that the cultured would shake themselves free and come together, and so would the uncouth, the vulgar, and the ignorant; but, of course, you would ignore this law of nature, and . . . confine the races in separate air-tight compartments. Wherefore I preach *reciprocity.* (*Ethiopia Unbound,* 105)

Once upon a time, British imperialism defined the tasks of its African hegemony in nonracial, cosmopolitan terms: the civilizing mission, advantageously for the middle class, was to be inclusive across race. This was no longer the case. To those who had racialized colonial relations, using the "African race"—denoting fixed, immutable being—rather than "civilized African"—denoting potential to become—to determine who is deserving and who is not, who is included and who is not, Hayford in "reciprocity" announces that he is returning the compliment. The problem for him and his kind was that when it came to the question of racial dessert—and being of the African race amounted only to inferior dessert under the colonial order—the middle class was colonially constructed as undeservingly native. (Under the Gold Coast Native Jurisdiction Ordinance of 1883 the black Englishmen were legislated by race into an identity in conformity with that of an undifferentiated mass of natives.) When it came to political dessert, however, they were constructed ethnoculturally as not native enough to be deserving. Under these absurd circumstances, therefore, reciprocity for the nationalist intellectual had to mean connecting the colonial a priori of racial nativity (or Africanity) to a denied cultural nativity and imagining in both a politics of the possible for his middle-class kind.

Out of the middle-class disillusion and crisis of identity brought on by the new-imperial order, then, we see a post-ancillary consciousness, as it were, taking shape, especially within the thinker-activist vanguard of the "black Englishmen." Blyden and others, such as the Nigerians Bishop James Johnson (late 1830s–1917) and Mojola Agbebi—born D. B. Vincent (1860–1917), the Sierra Leonean Orishatuke Faduma—born W. J. Davies (early 1870s–early 1940s), spearheaded this self-consciousness by affirming the existence of what the first called "African Personality." They would exhort educated West Africans that this Personality urgently required existential validation from among their ranks lest it disappear. The post-ancillary reconstruction of middle-class self-consciousness, therefore, mandated for the Euro-Africans, Anglo-Fanti, etc., a return to "Africa"—variably imagined and constructed in the interplay between the native and the racial. And this necessary return imposed on those at the compromised frontline the task to articulate the beginning of a new, postimperial narrative of Africa. For those who had a "native" Africa to return to, foundational self-reclamation as an option was in some sense there to be taken. This was the case for the black Englishmen of the Gold Coast middle class—and the indigenous element in its Nigerian counterpart—whose members, to a greater or lesser degree, still retained their indigenous filiations and attachments. There were those, on the other hand, who could not in any unproblematic way claim Africa in a nativity, as in the case of the anglicized Creoles of Sierra Leone, and of the Creoles and other diasporic returnees who had resettled in southern Nigeria and elsewhere. For these, the elaboration of an "African" identity followed the lead of the nonindigenous Blyden, its coloring more "black Atlantic" than native, and couched therein in a Pan-Africanist idiom of an abstract racialism.[31]

In statements that reiterate the frontline theme of (im)possible necessities we have been pursuing, Kadiatu Kanneh has noted "the complicated relationship [in Africa] between colonial domination and indigenous self-understanding," and how, via the culture of imperialism, "a discourse of modernity fundamentally informs constructions of African identities" (*African Identities*, 48). The critic reminds us that the postimperial narrative which, in "Africa," would say "no" to the imperial is still hatched in the womb of the latter. Its "no" is also "yes" to the extent that its enabling categories—"race," "native," "nation," "Africa"—come from, or by way of, the cultural discourse of the imperial. Hence "reciprocity" demands of Hayford that he inhabit the *inside* of the terms operating to define African racial demerit—as furnished by colonial-imperialist representation—if he is to imagine and effect a politics to get to the "outside" of it. Reciprocity is a demand on the native intellectual to contest Empire within the terms of its own representational hegemony.

We find a parallel mode of understanding the (Pan)-African situation in Jean-Paul Sartre's paradoxical assessment of Negritude, the philosophical and aesthetic movement founded in the 1930s by French-speaking African and African-descended intellectuals, as an "anti-racist racism."[32] For Negritude to step outside racism as the latter's "anti," Sartre implies, it must be inside racism, working to alter the balance of power of its terms from within. The message of Negritude was effective, its politics effectual, as Sartre saw, in being (differently) articulated in accordance with the protocols of race, a given of representation which, as representation, was no mere metaphor but had lived, material consequences. For race was furnished in that scene where imperial anthropology and imperial politics, colonialist knowledge and power, fed off and bolstered each other in marking off human differences while assigning relative human merit and social dessert based on those differences.

It is Karl Marx who pointed out that men [*sic*], because they are constrained to make history under circumstances not of their own direct choosing, cannot and do not make history—or meaning, we might add—as they please. Human agency, always effected inside history and its constraints, is, in effect, not a pure, God-like agency. Yet, according to Marx, in spite of being constrained in the ultimate instance, men do make history in the first instance, a history of their own.[33] And they do so in the first instance because, while "given a historical situation structural constraints impose limits upon historically constituted agents," nevertheless, within these constraints "conjunctural opportunities can be enacted by these agents." And given that history is a process, "many structural constraints can become conjunctural opportunities."[34]

In search of a new African narrative, the frontline writer-intellectuals under review could come opportunistically to recover a nationalist politics and the codes of its discursive representation, within and in spite of their impossible situation, in conjunctural terms. Fanon's lament in the 1950s, "And so, it is not I who make a meaning for myself, but it is the meaning that was already there, pre-existing, waiting for me,"[35] reiterates the self-critical portion of Hayford's commentary in "The Future of West Africa." Yet what appeared at the frontline to be debilitatingly imposed categories of representation—the meaning not of the intellectual's making—also offered themselves conjuncturally for the taking. For the preindependence intellectuals, in effect, the challenge of making history and new meaning—Hayford's "national calling"—under circumstances, and within terms, not of their own direct choosing, came down to a creative rearticulation of the given. "We may be our own Architects," Attoh Ahuma exhorts his middle-class readership in *Gold Coast,* calling on this readership to muster, in a post-ancillary mode of beginning again, the force to "create something out of nothing," to "execute that which never existed before" (10, 7). Bending a non-African language, English, to his expressively African intention in *Gold Coast,* Attoh Ahuma, like others of his frontline kind and of his nationalist avocation, illustrates the conjunctural workings of agency as theorized by the great cultural critic Mikhail Bakhtin:

> As a living, socio-ideological concrete thing . . . language, for the individual consciousness, lies on the borderline between oneself and the other. The word in language is half someone else's. It becomes "one's own" only when the speaker populates it with his own intention, his own accent, when he appropriates the word, adapting it to his own semantic and expressive intention. Prior to this moment of appropriation, the word does not exist in a neutral and impersonal language . . . but rather it exists in other people's mouths, in other people's contexts, serving other people's intentions: it is from there that one must take the word, and make it one's own.[36]

The challenge, therefore, was for the frontline intellectuals to take over the categories given in imperial representation—"native," "race," "nation," "Africa," "universal," etc.—and so shifting the balance of power in them as to bring a would-be African transvaluation to them. If, in the imperial balance, say, race carried the emotive power of African denigration, its postimperial rearticulation, tipping the balance, ventures to bring the same emotive power to the term's positive African revaluation. The astute Blyden called this the "poetry of politics," by which he meant the mobilization of "the feeling of race—the aspiration after the development on its own line of the type of humanity to which we belong" (*Negro Race,* 197). We can see this political poetry at work in 1953 as Nkrumah infuses the originally imperial sign, "race," with a *particular* emotive intentionality,[37] doing so in a declamation on African political-nationalist possibility before a Liberian audience. To this audience, Nkrumah advertises the glory of medieval Timbuktu, whose people of African *race* were "versed in science, arts and learning," whose works were "translated into Greek and Hebrew," and whose teachers taught at "the University of Cordova." These achievements become racially emblematic of twentieth-century African possibility.

"These were the brains!" I declared proudly, "And today they come and tell us that we cannot do it. We have been made to believe that we can't do it. But have you forgotten? You have emotions like everybody else; you have feelings like anybody else; you have aspirations like anybody else—and you have visions. So don't let people come and bamboozle us that the African is incapable of governing himself!"[38]

On the self-conscious nationalist writer-intellectual had fallen the responsibility, then, to swerve racial Africanity, on the inside of imperial representation, from its coding as a fixed designation that imposes on the race attributes of incapacity and inferiority and that produces Africa as a metaphysical vacuum. The writer, in overturning imperial versions of Africa's being as Nothing—a "Blank Darkness"[39]—is also charged postimperially with turning this Africa over: he or she is to renew the African image for Africa itself and for the world at large. Hence, when Hayford titles his quasi autobiography *Ethiopia Unbound,* he means his reader to imagine Africa unchained from the racialist stereotypes of fixity and nullity that attach to it. Hayford's "Ethiopia" is Africa relocated in a postimperial coding as a becoming, as the beginning of a narrative that foresees a destination that yields Africa's own modern. Into this narrative of destiny, destiny's child, the middle class, is inserted as African hero, as is captured in Sarbah's vision of modern potential: "The educated African is at present like a pioneer in a forest primeval. Whatever visions he may have about the fair city that is to be, his present task is to . . . clear the ground, and prepare the site for the city of tomorrow" (*Fanti National Constitution,* 246).

The next chapter is an extended look at what Sarbah denotes as site preparation: what circumstances necessitated it; what it meant in the self-invention of the "educated African"; and what modernist cognitive tools were to hand as he set out to metaphorically cut, uproot, and clear a space for Africa's worldly emergence. The chapter gives pride of place in this examination to the philosophical thought and ideological practice of the original dreamer of the African nationalist city of tomorrow, the diasporic returnee and Liberian E. W. Blyden.

2

IMPERIAL EXCHANGES, POSTIMPERIAL RECONFIGURATIONS:

AFRICA IN THE MODERN, THE MODERN IN AFRICA

> The political and literary struggles to locate and name Africa and its
> meanings involve a range of histories needing to be read in ways that
> acknowledge the specific textualities informing them. African identi-
> ties become meaningful and politically contested within historically
> located debates and theories of race, nation, and culture.
>
> —Kadiatu Kanneh, *African Identities*

Does One Bird a Flock Make? Modernist Quasi Objectivity, or Thinking/Enacting the Whole in the Part

> [T]he African asks always not "who am I?" but "who are we?" and
> "my" problem is not mine alone but "ours."
>
> —Appiah, "The Myth of an African World"

> For the native, objectivity is always directed against him.
>
> —Fanon, *The Wretched of the Earth*

The premier Gold Coast nationalist Sarbah by ethnic identification was
Fanti; colonial legislation enacted in 1883 also classified him as a Native,
one of several million such in the Gold Coast (and beyond). We may wonder

why this "educated" author of *Fanti Customary Laws* and *Fanti National Constitution* refers to, and includes within his self-identification, a geo-racial abstraction, "African." Why not for Sarbah the relatively concrete "educated native," or the even more empirically precise "educated Fanti"? In what sense, for Sarbah, could the abstract inhere in the concrete, the universal in the singular? What gave rise to the need for Sarbah and his kind to make an Africa at large reveal itself through a Gold Coast small, the latter itself of horizontally subdivided ethnicity and of vertical class and gender differentiation? What compulsions drove the story of an intermediate class, a part, to include and mediate within its class self that of a whole? Include within itself, that is, a coherent whole that was imagined as such (a) territorially ("the Gold Coast nation"), (b) interterritorially ("West African nationality"), and (c) continentally and transcontinentally ("Pan-African supranationality")? And, to complicate matters, these constructs were also to be coherently informed by a foundational (African) "nativity."

As they engaged the problematic of African modernity at the frontline, an obligatory question of the relation between part and whole, indeed of whole displaced into part, was under perilous negotiation by the nationalist writer-intellectuals under review. For the coherently "native" and "African" forms in which these nationalists appropriated a self-identification were hardly, on historical ground, objective givens. Rather, their constructs were "fictive" objectivities, more symbolic than real. Yet these were also not necessarily false objectifications insofar as the "Africa" of nationalist idealization was consistent with a label that had a discursive, ideological, and material coherency given to it by European imperialism.

Nevertheless, that the fictive objectivity the preindependence writer-intellectuals made out of "Africa" was bound to be error-prone cannot be overlooked. For, in their time, Africa was, as it still now is, a vast continent of myriad peoples and cultures, and of heterogeneous, (differently) internally stratified societies. "One touch of nature has made the whole of West Africa kin," Casely Hayford might say out of nationalist conviction in 1914.[1] We find Appiah remonstrating in 1992, however, that "It is simply a mistake to suppose that Africa's cultures are an open book to each other."[2]

Yet Appiah reminds us, also, that a negative and durable legacy of the African-European encounters is the definition by imperial culture of "'natives' by their race as inferior" (*In My Father's House,* 76). The critic alludes to the making of a fictive objectivity—or quasi objectivity—by imperial Europeans in a wholesale abstraction that reduces Africa's variety to a singular nativity, and unethically so, since this exercise in abstraction also calculatingly projects onto Africa a negative human worth. It is this ethical contradiction that Hayford begins to negotiate as he propounds his thesis of reciprocity to his white colonial interlocutors, as we saw in the previous chapter. These are the ones responsible for denying him, on the basis of the worth they put on his racial nativity, the potential to become a political and cultural equal. Facing these white interlocutors in the Gold Coast, Hayford confronts in himself a racialized African identity qua an objectivity which is effectively so because those who have power over him make it count as such. Under the stark racial definitions of the New Imperialism, those marked indifferently as European and African must occupy, in the words of Mudimbe, their different "natural slots and social mission."[3] Hayford therefore is compelled to assume his abstractly racial African identity in the concrete circumstances of the Gold Coast as a function of this truth that Empire had made and, by the compelling force of its power, instituted socially, institutionally, and politically.

We have been accustomed recently to such titles as the colonialist *invention* of Africa, of the Orient, etc. The description above of the order Empire institutes as a fictive objectivity is meant to capture this order notionally as an invention. The term "invention" denotes the fictive, in the sense of that made to order rather than given in nature. As such, it has been raised by the critics who deploy it in questions of imperial stratagem, which includes cultural representation, in the institution of the field and relations of colonial sociality and the investment of the identities (or subjectivities) that inhabit it. Mudimbe's *Invention of Africa* and Patrick Brantlinger's "Genealogy of the Myth of the Dark Continent," in *Rule of Darkness,* are two works in this mode that examine the ways in which imperialism makes Africa to order in representation and the socioeconomic and political ends to which this invented object of knowledge is put. Mudimbe and Brantlinger imply that, insofar as Africa has been invented and an African identity invested—or Africans subjectified—by imperialism in ways that are unethical, a salutary reinvention of Africa has become a postimperial challenge for the African intellectual. Anticipating these two, Casely Hayford's "reciprocity," therefore, can also be seen as an acknowledgement by him of the challenge, in a construction parallel to Empire's, of investing "Africa" and "the African" in a fictive objectivity. And this was to be in a mode that would counter the negations of the continent appearing in the representational blueprint which has gone into the making of Empire's social order and which is lived unethically by the intellectual and his racial kind.

An alternative construction, as set out in Spivak's notion of "worlding," has been put on Empire's made-to-order objectivity. Spivak deploys the term to capture the imperial reinscription of the colonized territory of the "native" and "other" by the alien "self" of Europe, this objectifying activity proceeding on the "contradictory assumption" that native territory is "uninscribed earth." The assumption is contradictory because the presignified objectivity of a "native" world preexists the colonial encounter: before contact there is a sociocultural organization out there that exists in and for itself. Imperial worlding, however, overinscribes the "being out there," the already inscribed (or self-made), of this nativity such that its subjective reference point is no longer (dominantly) itself but comes to be that of the reshaping "in here" of the European. The European engaged in the "worlding of [the native's] world . . . anew" is therefore "consolidating the Self of Europe" in a process that necessarily "generates the force to make the native see himself as 'other.'" The native is compelled to "cathect the space of the Other on his home ground . . . [and] domesticate the alien as Master."[4]

The reinvention of Africa, as a postimperial problematic of the intellectuals who inhabit the frontline, has thus had to deal with Empire's assumption that continental peoples are uniformly worldless, occupying mere uninscribed earth. As Brantlinger points out, "The writings of literate . . . Africans such as . . . Blyden . . . Nkrumah . . . Kenyatta" show that although "Africans were stripped of articulation" in the colonial encounter, the ethnocentric discourse of [imperial] domination was not met with silence."[5] A post-encounter "African *gnosis,*" in Mudimbe's assessment, "points to the passion of a subject-object who refuses to vanish." Invested in imperial representation with the identity of "a simple functional object," Mudimbe's African has gone on from this negative identification "to the freedom of thinking himself or herself as the starting point of an absolute discourse."[6]

When all is said and done, the struggles over the meaning of Africa and the challenge to articulate its worldly possibilities, as undertaken by the frontline intellectuals, resonate within wider problems having to do with the institution of modern society, as much in Europe as on its periphery (or margin). Appiah, conveying a sense of the affiliation that the global history of Empire has made possible, reminds us that "Center and periphery are mutually constitutive";[7] and this reminder is contained, too, in Casely Hayford's "reciprocity." To understand the struggles at self-representation at the imperial-colonial frontline, and its compromises as well, then, requires that the account of an African modern be situated in the wider context of the invention of the modern itself, as has transpired in the exchanges within a globally shared culture of imperialism. What follows, without pretending to be exhaustive, provides an account of this sort. It presents the wider context in summary outline by piggybacking on some of the important critiques and debates involving the nature of the modern phenomenon. The themes broached include the questions of (a) the philosophical principles and representational means by which, and the social ends to which, the modern order inventively fashions self and other; (b) the intrication of power therein; and (c) the relation between universal and particular, also, as a philosophical-ideological question therein. These questions of power and representation lead, too, to (d) the matter of how frontline intellectuals invest (their) marginality in a critique of the modern—the modern, that is, in the aspect of the subjugating imperialism which arrives at the margin of Europe; and (e) how they invest the modern, in the form of certain post-Enlightenment humanistic possibilities, in modes of (self)-creativity at the margin.

To pick up once more in this connection the point about Empire's order as a fictive objectivity: this was so because it did not correspond to that indifferent condition of nature where there was only, as Foucault put it, "the anonymity of a murmur."[8] Foucault points in this to the condition of natural objectivity under which things and bodies exist solely in themselves, in the purity of their differences, before the power of, and behind, human representation abstracting from, and projecting onto, them articulates these differences and makes them cohere into meanings. These meanings, put into social circulation by the power that generates them, invests subjects with their identities, and, in so doing, underwrite, and more or less work to stabilize, unequal relations of power and hierarchies of social control and deference.

Foucault's sociodiagnosis and critique of European sociological and political modernity shows how the agencies of power and social authority make a knowledge of a delinquent, debased, or inferior Other as a necessary corollary to the making and identificatory marking of the Self of a *normative* European modern. This normative Self is not a naturally occurring entity; it must be "selved" as such (or constructed as a self). And this is accomplished by way of the instrumentality of the (delinquent) Other—the implication being then that the Other does not occur naturally, either, but must be "othered," that is, named and fixed in social definition as Other. As Homi Bhabha explains, "the question of identification is never the affirmation of a pre-given identity, never a *self*-fulfilling prophecy—it is always the production of the image of identity and the transformation of the subject in assuming that image." What is more, the "demand for identification . . . [is] to be *for* an Other," and this "entails the representation of the subject in the differentiating order of otherness."[9] The experiential objectivity of the Self—its self-identity—therefore is not a natural and independent given; on the contrary, it comes socially mediated by a meaning derived from and by way of the Other.

Then, again, if Self and Other are not naturally given, it is because, as Foucault concludes, it is the truth of power, i.e., truth as made in power's image, and not the power of truth, a purely unmediated meaning, that invests the objectivity of the social. The (political) implication, then, is that, in the institution of the modern social order, objectivity *is* as objectivity *does* and *accomplishes* for (modern) power. The social as an artifice of power is, above all, based on a strategic calculus of means and ends, of humans rationally instrumentalized to serve the ends of reproducing power.[10]

Foucault's critique reveals what Max Weber calls "rationalization"—a philosophico-cultural principle, normatively Western, and centerpiece of Weber's definition of Western (sociological) modernity[11]—as an accomplice of power and domination. From the former, therefore, comes a deep skepticism about the *ratio* of the European Enlightenment—that rationalist mode of appropriating the world as knowledge which comes with the ideological rationale of dominantly acting on the world so appropriated—which provides the philosophical prestructuring of, activates, and informs, European modernity. Foucault would no doubt find a basis for his skepticism in Weber's view of rationalization, for by this the latter means to imply the self-consciously systematic and strategic application of means and ends calculation to social phenomena. Under Weber's rationalized modern order, the "spontaneous" relations that obtained between humans and their socialized world in premodern forms of existence have had to give way to relations whose very social basis is the instrumentalization of human actors. With their humanity no longer an end in itself as such, rationalization has seen to the routinization of the productivity of these actors in accordance with machine efficiency, and this has happened the better to maximize the returns on capital circulating socially. From this analysis, it is but a short step to Weber's German compatriot Herbert Marcuse's humanistic critique of routinization in European capitalist modernity for producing what he calls "one-dimensional man."[12]

As has been pointed out in a number of critical studies, the Europe-centered accounts of the modern, critical and otherwise, have tended to overlook the "global society" inaugurated by imperialism.[13] They have thus been blind to the Eurocentric dynamics of othering within the imperial project in the making and institution of the modern order.[14] Hence, for instance, Spivak, is critical of Foucault for confining himself merely to the forms of internal othering that construct and authorize Western modernity. "To buy a self-contained version of the West," Spivak insists, "is to ignore its production by the imperialist project."[15] The critical proposition from the margin is that the imperial order requires analysis in its institution and function as a significant part of the rationalist project of constructing the Western Self, and of rehabilitating the West, in a reflexively modernist normativity.

One form in which the West's normativity as modern has been instituted is in the West's appropriation of a definition of the "universal" into itself. And, in that, we might see a West that, having subjugated the world imperially, acquires an image-reflex of itself that might be summed up in the catchphrase, "We are the world." The whole is displaced into the part in Western self-representation as we find in this claim by Weber:

> A product of modern European civilization, studying any problem of universal history is bound to ask himself to what combination of circumstances the fact should be attributed that in Western civilization, and in Western civilization only, cultural phenomena have appeared which (as we like to think) lie in a line of development having universal significance. (*Protestant Ethic*, 13)

Weber naturalizes the West's dominant universality, as though it were an objectivity given, not one that the West has forcefully made through subjugation of others. What he tries to repress—unsuccessfully, as it appears in his parenthetic "as we like to think"[16]—is that for the post-Enlightenment West to assume its modern self-image as normatively universal, it has had to create for itself, out of a non-West, a corollary Other. In the West's invention of non-Western subhumanity and/or subordinacy, we see the underside of the self-identity it assumes in the universal,[17] this shadow, then, supporting the reproduction of the West's dominion as universal subject. Rey Chow notes in this connection, "The production of the native is in part the production of our postcolonial [i.e., post-encounter] modernity."[18]

The native as Other and underside to Europe's Self—and in our case this native is "African"—enters Europe's instrumental construction of its imperial order, in accordance with the pragmatic calculation that objectivity is as objectivity does and accomplishes. Imperial representation—which involves the European subject of power tactically giving a name and a definition to the African Other, hence making a native, and interchangeably racial, object of (self)-knowledge out of and for this other—is therefore strategically positioned in means and ends calculation. Making the Other into a manipulable object of cultural knowledge is to ensure the preservation of the European's comparative advantage over the native and to guarantee that strategic goals are maximally accomplished at this native's expense.[19]

But what model of representation does service in a rationalist Empire's constitution of African otherness as a reality for knowledge? It is necessary to establish this, since the reinvention of Africa in the work of the writer-intellectuals under review forces us to consider, in dialectical fashion, how the representational means serving Empire's dominion encounters, at the frontline, its own contradiction. For if (imperial) center and (African) periphery are mutually constituting, then it is the same cultural logic employed by former that comes strategically to be mobilized in representation by the latter for its resistance against Empire's imposed order. The two emerge, then, in a single cultural logic, although we must add also that this logic is mobilized to different ideological and practical effects on either side.

To illustrate how "Africa," and the human subjects who appear within this domain, are displaced, according to the logic of the culture of imperialism, into objects of imperial knowledge—hence into a construction of Empire's objective order—it may be worthwhile to recall a scene from J. M. Coetzee's *Foe*. A novelistic adumbration of Empire in a racial (and sexual) allegory, *Foe* is a contemporary rewriting and critique of English author Daniel Defoe's eighteenth-century classic *Robinson Crusoe,* and in it we find the South African writer outlining a process of white-on-black projection. This involves, on the one side, the Anglo-European duo of Susan Barton, the central character, and Foe (as Defoe is renamed)—both credited with an objectifying power—and, on the other side, Friday, who lacks this power. This Friday, unlike his original in Defoe's novel who is marked by his ethnicity (he is a Carib Indian), is re-presented by Coetzee abstractly as an "African" and Crusoe's "slave," a man whose tongue has (presumably) been cut out. As a tongueless person, he has no means to objectify himself as knowledge for others; and even if he does have the means, we may presume that, as a slave, he has no power at his disposal to make his self-objectification count. About the communicative amputee and representational blank in her care, therefore, Susan Barton has this to say to her fellow white European:

Friday has no command of words and therefore no defence against being reshaped day by day in conformity with the desire of others. I say he is a cannibal and he becomes a cannibal; I say he is a laundryman and he becomes a laundryman. What is the truth of Friday? You will respond: he is neither a cannibal nor a laundryman, these are mere names, they do not touch his essence, he is a substantial body, he is himself, Friday is Friday. But that is not so. No matter what he is to himself . . . what he is to the world is what I make of him.[20]

Coetzee suggests that Friday, in a real objectivity where he is in himself alone, is unnameable—for any act of naming makes an abstraction out of, and hence violates, an inviolate objectivity. (And, in indicating this, the South African author might be borrowing a leaf from Samuel Beckett, who opines that, in the world in its pure or natural objectivity, "There could be no things but nameless things, and no names but thingless names.")[21] But Coetzee is canny enough to suggest that a natural objectivity, purely exterior to the human order and its temporality—that is, an order of objects and things as they are, unmediated and unmanipulated by human intervention—has no meaning, no utility, within the dynamic, real-historical world of power relationships. Through his novelistic mouthpiece Susan Barton, therefore, Coetzee is acknowledging power and force in the historic construction of subjects as objects of knowledge, and in the lived historicity of the labels and meanings imposed on them as such.

Coetzee's brief exemplum of white-on-black projection points to the cultural logic behind and entering Empire's making and appropriation of knowledge—of itself and of its Other. Allegory, as a number of postcolonialist and deconstructive critiques have revealed, provides the theoretical or mythological foundation of the coherence of Western, and hence derivatively imperial, knowledge;[22] it is the mechanism supporting an order of mimetic representation "in which Western rationalism preserves the boundaries of sense for itself" (*Location of Culture,* 71). And if imperial representation must preserve order for itself at the "boundaries of 'civilization,'" as Abdul JanMohamed points out, at this frontline it operates "efficiently through its central trope, the manichean allegory," which "functions as the currency, the medium of exchange for the entire colonialist discursive system" ("Manichean Allegory," 83). In the framework of imperial allegory, wholes—and wholesale and abstract attributes—are presupposed in parts; and this is to say, this mode of representation works over and confounds historical and natural differences between human entities, mapping onto and across such differences a similarity of attribution, racial, cultural, and sexual. We recognize in one pole of allegorical figuration, the displacement of the whole into a representation of the part, the operation of metaphoric condensation. And condensation, structuring imperial discourse, makes this discourse resemble, in the words of Bhabha, "a form of narrative whereby the productivity and circulation of subjects and signs are bound in a reformed and recognizable totality" (*Location of Culture*, 71).

Looking at the colonial setting as a starkly political-economic one, JanMohamed contrives an analysis of it that brings the material interests of imperial capitalism into play in accounting for the Manichean articulation, at the margin, of its allegorical discourse. He writes:

> The dominant model of power- and interest-relations in all colonial societies is the manichean opposition between the putative superiority of the European and supposed inferiority of the native. This axis in turn provides the central feature of the colonialist cognitive framework and colonialist . . . representation: the manichean allegory—a field of diverse yet interchangeable oppositions between white and black, good and evil, superiority and inferiority, civilization and savagery, intelligence and emotion, rationality and sensuality, self and other, subject and object. ("Manichean Allegory," 82)

Effectively, in colonial discourse, the critic concludes, imperial representation "commodifies the native by negating his individuality, his subjectivity, so that he is now perceived as a generic being that can be exchanged for any other native" (83). If, on an "upper" level or vertical axis, allegorical representation is transacted in terms of metaphoric condensation—a fixed relation of resemblance between whole and part, universal and particular— here JanMohamed gives us its "lower" level or horizontal axis. This is a level or axis where allegorical transaction proceeds in terms of metonymic substitution, where the mechanism of allegorical representation is capable of producing values that are diverse yet interchangeable; characteristics of attribution that are different yet, to the extent that they are substitutable for each other, equivalent. This structure of condensation and substitution in mutual play in imperial allegory that JanMohamed lays out has important cognitive implications for the modern imagining of the nation, including the African, a point that will be addressed below.

The requirements of imperial power demand, therefore, that Friday cannot remain one detached human "object" among other human "objects" in what is merely a parallel totality of humanity. Nor, we might add, does any difference presignified by and in Friday—say his ethnicity—prior to the intervention which brings him into a relationship with the imperial self greatly matter before the latter's confounding power. That is, in the cultural logic of representation Empire deploys powerfully at the frontline, individual part is not a mere independent unit in a totality comprised of equivalently independent individual parts. Friday is not individualized as *standing apart* from an attribution of blackness, the racial stereotype which imposes on him the burden of being a dehumanized cannibal and/or of being the essence of subservient humanity (i.e., a "laundryman"). On the contrary, these collective (racialized) attributes—subhumanity, subservience—are *individualized* in his person. He is at once contained in, by, and is the content of, a negative anterior sign. We are to extrapolate from Coetzee's exemplum, therefore, an order of representation where to say cannibal is to say automatically (black) African; where to see one African is automatically to see a cannibal. It is thus to see in the one all without exception, since cannibalism is a collective typology which invests each. In himself, then, Friday stands for more than just the one human entity, the singularity, that otherwise he is. Objectified in imperial representation, he is imposed upon to be one of a *kind*.

What JanMohamed implicitly reveals in his materialist critique of the imperialist sign, furthermore, is rationalization—Weber's normative attribute of European modernity—working through the operation of the Manichean allegory as it churns out imagery of the native's debasement with production-line efficiency. Empire deploys the defining philosophico-cultural attribute of the West resourcefully in the production of a simulacrum, a colonial version of Marcuse's one-dimensional humanity, to serve its profiteering agenda. The native at the margin of European modernity must undergo in image symbolic routinization if he is to serve efficiently the requirements of expansionist capitalism. On the one hand, routinized as vermin, this native "efficiently" serves expansion in his being presented as a candidate for extermination. This is the point captured by Arnold Toynbee in his critique of what Empire materially entails for those who fall under its Manichean classification as native and Other. The British historian notes:

> When we Westerners call people "natives," we implicitly take the cultural colour out of our perception them. We see them as wild animals infesting the country in which we happen to come across them . . . not as men. . . . So long as we think of them as "natives" we may exterminate them or . . . domesticate them . . . but we do not begin to understand them.[23]

To this we may add the pro-imperialist assertion in 1850 by the liberal English philosopher Herbert Spencer: "The forces which are working out the great scheme of perfect happiness . . . exterminate such sections of mankind as stand in their way. . . . Be he human or be he brute—the hindrance must be got rid of."[24]

On the other hand, routinized in image as an inferior laboring class, the native is drawn into a utilitarian relationship with the racial capitalism of colonial imperialism. Thus, for instance, there is the projection made, in 1876, by the British explorer and negrophobe Richard Burton, concerning the African's racial utility as a laborer for European capital wherever he is to be found. "I unhesitatingly assert," wrote Burton, "that . . . the world still wants the black hand. Enormous tropical regions yet await the draining and clearing operations by the lower races, which will fit them to become dwelling places for civilized men" (qtd. in *Rule of Darkness,* 183).

Toynbee (and Spencer), on the one hand, and Burton, on the other, articulate two related forms of imperial objectification here. A critical Toynbee shows that, with the "cultural colour" taken out of an Africa defined as "native," imperial knowledge produces nativity coherently across the continent—and the agents of empire relate to it in a coherence of (racist) attitude also—in the objectivity of a subhuman (or dehumanized) subjectivity. Historically, the material consequences of such objectification were the exterminist campaigns waged against African peoples as, for instance, was done by Belgian colonialism against the Congolese at the turn of the nineteenth century and into the twentieth. Congolese peoples, as happened elsewhere on the continent, were maimed, tortured, and killed by Europeans not because one group happened to be ethnic Luba and not ethnic Kongo but because both groups—and all others in territorial Congo—were indifferently (racially) "African" and "native" in being that. "Natives," in imperial designation, could not be what they were in and for themselves—a positive attribution of difference; they simply were what they *identically* were not: that is, they were non-European—a negative attribution. They could all therefore be abstracted into one category, a category which merited the special treatment, in the forms of colonial brutalization, reserved for it.

On the other hand, Burton's production of Africa in imperial knowledge—i.e., Africa objectified as the "black hand"—is a projection that articulates the continent subordinately with an expansionist imperial capital. In spite of its myriad forms of existence, African nativity is constructed, again coherently across the continent, as inhabited by an exploitable proletariat, marked as such by race. The fate that awaits this racial abstraction is to be *in* the world only in a utilitarian sense, but not to be *of* it, in a fully human sense. As Empire worlds the world in Europe's image, the black hand appears hierarchically integrated within this construction, in a mode which contrives to leave it "below" the world, in peripherality and marginality.

From the foregoing, therefore, we see Empire constructing a serviceable "Africa" in the fictive objectivity of a marginal and exploitable (sub)humanity. To this we need to add silenced humanity, too, in the way that enables Susan Barton in Coetzee's *Foe* to claim that the truth of Friday, emblem of African nativity, is what she makes of him to the world. No counterclaim is forthcoming from Friday in Coetzee's novel. It is left to Spivak, taking on the existential challenges to otherness raised by *Foe,* to claim for the frontline "postcolonial intellectual" generally that "we are natives too"; and that, unlike the silenced Friday, "We talk like *Defoe's* Friday, only much better."[25] Spivak and her postcolonial kind perform well, that is, in the language of the colonizer and in the use of his protocols of representation as afforded to them by the culture of imperialism.

That much is implied in Hayford's "reciprocity," also. And he must be seen to be talking back to his white colonial interlocutors in this mode, as it were: "If you see the Africanity of a racial and native whole indifferently in me, and falsely so, and use that in the unethical construction of your order, then I return the compliment. I accede to and claim myself in your falsehood. And, validating this claim on the highest moral ground, I fling the self I have appropriated from you as a truth, in resistance, in your face."

The sentiment accords with the reasoned assessment by Fanon, writing in the heat of African decolonization in the 1950s, that "the efforts of the native to rehabilitate himself and to escape from the claws of colonialism are *logically* inscribed from the same point of view as colonialism." Hayford's "reciprocity," then, can be seen in the light of a (planned) appropriation by this frontline intellectual of the rationalist pragmatism of Empire—the modernist cultural logic, that in Fanon's account, Empire is obliged to share with its Other. "Reciprocity" implies that Hayford finds himself enjoined to rework this rationalist pragmatism ethically into the requirements of a nationalist anticolonialism.

Both in spite of and because of the hurtful and proscriptive naming of Africa in imperial representation, then, a practical thesis emerges at the frontline occupied by the preindependence nationalist intellectuals: that their being vested allegorically by the imperially fathered common names "Africa(n)," "Native," "Negro," could prove enabling. Again Fanon, on this basis, was to proclaim: "Colonialism did not dream of wasting its time in denying the existence of one [African] national culture after another. Therefore the reply of the colonized peoples will be straight away continental in its breadth."[26]

An instance of such a reply is to be found in the volume of poetry titled *This Africa,* first published in 1928, by Bankole Awoonor-Renner, the Bolshevik and self-described "Proletarian Poet" from the Gold Coast. Titles in the volume like "My Africa," "Ode to Mother Africa," "I, too, Sing for Africa," "The Pale Face Stranger—Who Oppresses Me" reveal

Awoonor-Renner in poetic gestures of "bodily" and muscularly taking on the nativity of "Africa," in the aspect of her material suffering under colonial extermination and exploitation. In "Mutilated Congo," the poet both witnesses and commemorates:

> Twenty years thy children bled scarlet;
> That Belgian cities may be built,
> Thy huts plunder'd, thy women ravag'd.
>
> In greedy's name the Christians rush'd,
> To save the "heathens" from their gloom,
> They paved the way to heaven gold.
>
> Refusing to gather the "red rubber"
> The Congo African received, the civilization
> Of massacre, and of flogging, and of slaughter.
>
> Limbs of men, and children were cut
> Breasts of women were split in two:
> These were the works of French and Belgian rich.
>
> Nor must we e'er forget;
> That America and England gave to Leopold
> The Belgium King,—that shameful power to act.
>
> Million of ten and twenty the country peopled,
> To million of eight this number sank:
> Such is the unhealing wound.
>
> Such deeds must in the memory be fresh'd
> That to the Western rich thou owest this debt
> Africa! thy desired task'll be, to pay the holy brute.[27]

Given the death-dealing colonial circumstances Awoonor-Renner poetically vocalizes, his organizing fiction of the whole (an African "We") inhabiting the part (the poetic "I"), of a Congo and a Gold Coast (metonymically) interchangeable, through (metaphoric) Africanist mediation, for each other, acquires and transmits the force of a necessary truth. The poet reaches into the founding terms of imperial figuration wresting from there a pragmatic fiction that guarantees in the sign "Africa" the ethical foundation of a critique of imperial modernity's humanistic shortcomings. The thesis of truth that is as it does and accomplishes in this case serves an articulation of resistance to Empire, resistance that also looks, in utopian visions of the future, to the postimperial regeneration of Africa.[28]

What we can read off Awoonor-Renner's *This Africa* is an ethically anchored cognitive aesthetic, a universal grammar of African modernist representation, emergent at the middle-class frontline. This cognitive aesthetic has been captured by Simon Gikandi, following Fredric Jameson, as "national allegory."[29] Jameson—and, in his geographic and culturally unnuanced sweep, he has been critiqued for overinflating his case[30]—argues that

> All third-world texts are necessarily . . . allegorical. . . . [E]ven those which are seemingly private . . . necessarily project a political dimension in the form of national allegory: the story of the private individual destiny is always an allegory of the embattled situation of the public third-world culture and society.[31]

We can index Jameson's assessment back and give it a relevance to a time when "third world" and "first world" had not been invented but had a de facto existence in relations between colony and metropole.

To go back this way is also to recover for the rationales behind the allegorizing of the preindependence nationalist writer-intellectuals the questions that Appiah brings to bear on the literary-nationalist practice of their postindependence counterparts. Appiah addresses the relationship between African writer and his/her imagined African public in terms of the former's necessary articulation of a "We" in an "I"—the allegorical problematic (see epigraph at the head of the section). The critic goes on to ponder: "African writers are Asante, Yoruba, Kikuyu, but what does this now mean? They are Ghanaian, Nigerian, Kenyan, but does this yet mean anything? They are black, and what is the worth of the black person?" (*In My Father's House,* 76).

Out of this complex set of demands, we see in preindependence middle-class writing, as would transpire in its postindependence counterpart, strategic inventions which articulate a coherence across ethnicity as native. For instance, in his *Renascent Africa* (1937), the Nigerian Nnamdi Azikiwe ("Zik of Africa"), until 1936 a newspaper editor in the Gold Coast, insists that all who bear the racial mark of Africa are tied by nativity to the continent. He calls in a mode of nativist coherence, then, for the "realization that an African is an African no matter where he was born, whether at Kibi or at Zungeru, Navrongo or Cape Coast, Bathurst or Accra, Brazil or Manyakpowuno, Patagonia or Tuscaloosa, Mepom or Kukuruku, Nairobi or America" (*Ideologies,* 421).

Azikiwe's made-to-order nativity of yore, as is the case with the nationalists under review in this study, foundationally underwrites a transitional subject-object, a popular narrative, which is articulated as, and in the name of, the "African nation." If the intellectual imagines the givenness of this nation in a prior nativity he also imagines it in modernistic terms as *still to come*, the nation thus projected as a goal. In middle-class self-invention, moreover, it is the intermediate class self in which the future nation finds its objective incarnation in the transitional present.[32] Middleness, therefore, figures as the intermediate starting point of an imagined community—"the people," "the nation," "the race"—greater than, but included and expressed within, the middle-class self. This construction activates the middle class, to the extent that the objectivity of the nation is presumed to be incarnate in its subjectivity, as the central character, the *primum mobile*, of the national allegory. This premise underlies Awoonor-Renner's *This Africa*; and it structures, too, Casely Hayford's earlier *Ethiopia Unbound* (1911), as it does again Kwame Nkrumah's later *Ghana: The Autobiography of Kwame Nkrumah* (1957).

About the writers at the post-encounter frontline who are inhabited by the condition he resolves as "postcoloniality," Appiah tells us that they "mediate the trade in cultural commodities of world capitalism at the periphery" (*In My Father's House*, 149). One such cultural commodity, put in global circulation by imperial capitalism, is the nation-form. We will recall Anderson in *Imagined Communities* averring that the character of the modern world emerges in the fact that in it not *one* uniquely but *every*one alike will have—or is deserving of—nation. By this, Anderson means to show nation-ness as a global measure, a universal standard, of calibrating human equivalence. When we translate this thesis into Appiah's terms, we see that nation has historically come to acquire the trade, exchange, and representational status of a General Equivalent; it is *competitive* cultural-political capital in a worldly sense and acknowledged as such by a truly global public.

Africa, systemically incorporated into the world as peripheral by Empire, and constructed as marginal and in the image of an undeserving otherness in imperial representation, was in these ways refused a competitive share and stake in the world as mediated through nation. The words of Martin Delany, the early African American Pan-Africanist, to his West African hosts in 1859, bear repeating here: "The claims of no people are respected until they are presented in a national capacity." There is a penalty for lacking cultural-political capital of world-significance, Delany was telling his Yoruba hosts; and, if so, his axiom sums up why it becomes necessary to articulate "African nationality" at the African periphery of imperial modernity. The effort then was, as it still is, to rehabilitate Africa properly within the General Equivalent (or the Universal). Nation, a shimmering object of middle-class desire, becomes the notation of Africa's rise into a worldly universality.

If "Africa shall rise"; if "Ethiopia shall stretch forth her hands unto God," therefore, she is obliged to do so by way of the intermediation of a desiring middle class. The allegory of nation is disposed by its frontline creators also, to come in a form wherein its central character, the middle class, is invented as a class-for-the-world. And this class invents a popular "Africa" in an image of its class self, too, and gives this back to Africa in terms in which it carries the former with itself on its world-bound mission. And so we find Sarbah chiding his kind for their failure to lay "stress on the necessity of levelling-up of the masses."[33] Sarbah must enjoin his middle-class kind to bring the native "masses" up with itself because he foresees the warranty of the worldly destiny of the former in a nationalist mobilization of the latter.

For some of or all the reasons laid out in the foregoing, the preindependence Ghanaian writers felt obliged to address themselves to a postimperial task of *African* revisionism and transvaluation as a part of, through, and in spite of, the local concerns that preoccupied them. We find this "we are in this together" mode on display, for instance, in De Graft Johnson's *Towards Nationhood in West Africa*. He takes on a continental identification as a "Young African" as he makes a particular anticolonial case, addressed to an audience at the imperial center characterized as "Young Britain," for African nationality.

De Graft Johnson is aware that addressing Africa in a comprehensive objectivity is impossible. He is enjoined "to take the case of some particular country," his own Gold Coast in this case, "In order to deal definitely with concrete facts and figures, and to present a true and uncoloured picture of the political appeal" (*Towards Nationhood*, v). Yet at the same time that speaking as African is concretely impossible for the nationalist, historical and ideological necessity demand that he does so. The implied premise informing this necessity could be put this way: since what was negative for and about Africa—the whole—in imperial discourse necessarily held true for the Gold Coast—the part—what was positive for and about the Gold Coast ought also to hold true for Africa. The two-in-one mechanism of metaphoric condensation and metonymic substitution, operating at the allegorical heart of imperial representation, is appropriated by De Graft Johnson to make a postimperial case in which the small and the large, and the side-by-side, entertain ethical relations of mutual accountability. The fiction that the Gold Coast is Africa, and that this one African unit may substitute for all others, remains, given the vicissitudes suffered by a continent in an imperial history, a "tolerable falsehood."[34]

As for the story coming out of the Gold Coast, according to Johnson, it was good, because the Gold Coast "has built up one of the greatest romances of modern industry and is very much at the forefront at the present time" (*Towards Nationhood*, v). A modernizing Gold Coast in itself ideologically and ethically represents Africa in the image of *possibility* in Johnson's rhetoric. Where before she was weighed down by negative stories that made her the epitome of human incapacity, Africa stood poised to be rehabilitated in the salutary image of the Gold Coast, in the latter's proven "progressive" capacity.

Johnson's polemic has greater ambitions, for in pointing out, via the Gold Coast, the progressive capacity of the African, he is also claiming that the movements of a world spirit are dynamically manifest in his Africa. If, as indicated above, Weber claims the universal exclusively for Europe, Johnson's answer to this, as it were, is an inclusive "We are the world, too— the universal inhabits us." Again, to make an ethical case, Johnson travels the route of metaphoric condensation, where this time it is a worldly universality that inhabits an African particularity, this particularity as specially mediated by the Gold Coast. The problem Johnson, the Young African, addresses to Young Britain may, then, be put this way: "If we are the world, too, then African nationality must be our worldly dessert in the same way that your worldliness guarantees you European nationality as your dessert." In short, while metaphoric condensation is demonstrable in Johnson's polemic, the problem is that metonymic substitution fails, under circumstances where the Gold Coast is not (yet) interchangeable with Britain, where Africa and Europe are not substitutable for each other, where Young Africa and Young Britain are not equivalent. And it is colonialism—a datum of unethical power—that is responsible for the state of affairs in which African worldliness is thwarted in its nationalist completion.

In 1943, we find the leading Gold Coast nationalist of the interwar years, J. B. Danquah, imbricating the anticolonial demand for power in an ethics of worldliness. Mounting the political platform in the name of Gold Coast Youth, Danquah demands: "We must have power, and must adequately fill in that power to give us world citizenship."[35] Johnson's argument for nation is, as it were, completed by Danquah; what appears in the measured tones of a *plea* in the rhetoric of the former becomes a radical *demand* in that of the latter. And demand will be radicalized further when Nkrumah, taking the mantle of leadership from Danquah, proclaims his agenda of "self-government now!" Donning the garb of the Gold Coast/ African "we," as we find in these representative nationalist figures, the middle class inventively decks its assumed representative self out ethically as a class-for-power. If one dimension of middle-class self-definition is mediated by access to the world—hence a class-for-the-world—the additional self-understanding is that in (sovereign) power a middle class will be at home in the world—and make the world at home. Only in political power, secured at home, will the national allegory, impelled forward by its popularly informed allegorical protagonist, the middle class, consummate its worldly destiny. In the end, modernist representation, wherein whole is displaced into part, in an interplay of metaphoric condensation and metonymic substitution, comes ethically to underwrite the urgencies of African anticolonial struggle.

Insofar as "falsehoods" are tolerably mobilized to construct pragmatic quasi objectivities in an Africanist domain of modernist representation, the question remains to be posed about the limits of tolerability of such falsehoods. Stuart Hall has reminded us that "Practices of representation always implicate the positions from which we speak and write—the positions of enunciation."[36] In that case we may not ignore the class marking of De Graft Johnson's rhetoric appropriating Africa by way of the Gold Coast for his nationalist polemic. The Euro-African Johnson's "Africa" is enunciated from within a social-structural and cultural rift, a class rift between himself and those native masses who he assumes speak through him. While the width and depth of this rift must not be exaggerated, it may not be minimized either. The thoughts Young Africa addresses to Young Britain, through the medium of *Towards Nationhood,* comes from one political and cultural elite—colonially deprived of power, but an elite nevertheless—talking to another in whose elite image it sees its African self-reflection. Johnson's rhetoric may be read critically, then, as Gold Coast/West African elite representation exploiting "Africa," qua the political image of the native body of the masses, to further narrow class interests. This is the contradiction Lewis Nkosi captures in part in his observation that

> in asserting their right to self-determination Africans had to employ the language of their colonial masters. . . . [T]he rhetoric of political demand they employed was better understood in Europe among rulers and the common people, than among the African masses for whom, presumably, the demands were being made.[37]

Inasmuch as a middle-class rhetoric of nation appears to Nkosi more or less as self-serving, what may we make of what for Nkrumah was a truism of anticolonial struggle: that "a middle class elite without the battering ram of the masses, can never hope to smash the forces of colonialism"?[38] Could that be the datum of a middle class cynically manipulating the masses on whose backs it bolsters its claim to nationalist representativeness?

The question of how far the tolerable falsehoods of political mythmaking are tolerable has never been an easy one to answer. The current postnationalist haste to deconstruct such mythmaking, however, can learn to curb its excesses from the wisdom of the South Asian postcolonial critic Asha Varadharajan. She opines: "The propensity to error and to self-interest does not destroy the potential for change; rather it exists in tension with that potential and, indeed, produces hope for a better world. . . . [A] philosophy incapable of error is also incapable of truth."[39] For this critic, therefore, simply collapsing the politics of knowledge-as-resistance back into, and regarding it as no different from, the politics of knowledge-as-domination is an ethically and politically untenable move. We may take with only that moderate skepticism which is healthy, therefore, Casely Hayford's claim that: "Whatever the Gold Coast man becomes in the struggle for existence, whatever position he attains, he generally remains a Gold Coast man who loves his country dearly . . . he remains at heart a Gold Coast man, ready to serve his country at any moment."[40] And Sarbah gives this example of Gold Coast middle-class patriotism an all-African imprimatur: "the African dwells here, this is his home. His interest in its welfare is not transitory but permanent" (*Fanti National Constitution,* xii). Middle class these two may be, but even as we acknowledge with Hall that representation is always situated and reflects its situatedness, we must take care not to rob the rhetoric and self-representation of them and their kind of a situationally transcendent existential dimension. And this lest we water down a necessary—but by no means always virtuous—politics of nationalism, transforming it into a mere ungainly "politics of narcissism," as has become fashionable in certain poststructuralist-inspired forms of reading encounter and its aftermath.[41]

It is in the spirit of taking the politics of African nationalism seriously in spite of the positionality of its enunciation, and of its sometimes grossly intolerable falsehoods, that, below, this study examines the certainly error-prone ideation of the precursor of it all, Blyden. And this is thought situated at that juncture, the frontline, where, with a "metropolitan culture [defining] the 'natives' by their race as inferior," the native intellectual is imposed upon to make cognitive and political virtue, in the mode of an African modern, out of wrenching existential necessity.

"Liberia's Offering": African Nationality vis-à-vis Universal Humanity in Blyden's Thought

> No nation is coterminous with mankind.
> —Benedict Anderson, *Imagined Communities*

> Internationality is a style of thought and global social organization
> that tries to generate a plurality of nations. . . . Internationality, you
> might say, is the tendency for the global imposition of the nation-
> form.
> —Jonathan Rée, "Internationality"

> The pact of humanity cannot be signed by individuals, but only by
> free and equal peoples, possessing a name, a banner, and the con-
> sciousness of a distinct individual existence. If you desire that people
> should become such, you must speak to them of country and nation-
> ality and impress in vivid characters upon the brow of each the sign of
> their existence and baptism as a nation. . . . Nationality is destined to
> give its name to the [nineteenth] century.
> —Mazzini, "Principles of Cosmopolitanism" (1834)

Comparing Horton's and Blyden's use of "African nationality," one finds
with the former that the qualifying "African" is a polemical, incompletely
theorized category. Horton, in this regard, more or less falls in with the
early West African intelligentsia, about whose southern Nigerian branch
Zachernuk reports that "they were more preoccupied with promoting the
civilizing mission than questioning it, and it is not clear that the meaning of being 'African' was deeply probed [by them]." For these the "immediate need was to establish a new social order and a place for themselves," and this desire made them supporters and apologists of European expansion, seeing in it the means to bring about the order that
they assumed would be beneficial to themselves. In the expansionist aspect of their thinking, Horton was of course unlike them in that he cast the
new society he advocated in terms of an independent African political order. Nevertheless he shared the attitude of the early intelligentsia generally
of looking "upon things African with a different attitude,"[42] maintaining
with conviction, in *West African Countries and Peoples,* that "It is impossible for a nation to civilize itself; civilization must come from abroad."[43] If
Africa, in the relationship the black Englishmen imagined they had with
it—before the rise of official racism in the 1870s—was "not to be discarded
wholesale," as Zachernuk remarks, it was nevertheless only "relevant [to

the extent that] it marked what had to be improved." Africa remained an entity that was to be "judged according to external standards" (*Colonial Subjects,* 45).

As brilliant theoretically as he was in drawing up a program of institutional renewal for the societies of West Africa, the technocratic Horton could address the philosophical question of African difference only in terms of an abstract Pan-Negro racial conception. The Creole medical doctor who adopted the name "Africanus" could relate to Africa on the basis that its color was not European. That is, the affective basis of African identification for Horton, deep though it may have been, was more or less a matter of external form and appearance—albeit these externals, over the span of an imperial history, had been, and continued to be, even as he was writing in the 1860s, fraught with psycho-existential consequences for people of African descent. And, in that sense he, like other early occupants of the frontline, could "assert a special relationship with the continent that diasporan Africans might share, but which Europeans could not" (*Colonial Subjects,* 45). The externals of appearance that made him African—and the histories of slavery, brutalization, and denigration staged on these externals by Europeans—could thus enter a political calculus of difference in Horton's nationalist polemic.

Yet in his vindication of the African race, carried out at length in *West African Countries and Peoples,* Horton was also insisting that externals hardly mattered where "cultural color"—i.e., civilization—could be seen, as he argued in diffusionist terms, as general human property and capacity. This was an argument directed against the orthodoxy that "civilization" was synonymous with Europe, was Europe's essence. Cultural integrity, culture in the relativist proposition, in effect, could be only an obscurantist myth in Horton's Promethean thought. In the name of African nationality, therefore, Horton was advocating that African societies could, indeed had to, overcome the presumably adventitious differences that marked them off culturally from "civilization" and appropriate for themselves this universal whose ownership has never been, and could not now be, exclusively European. And what this way of reasoning amounted to was a sophisticated nationalist restatement—Africa politically independent but civilizationally assimilated—of the tenets and projections of Europe's African civilizing mission. It has to be said for Horton, then, that if, in his proto-Promethean nationalist posture, he dreamt of Africa recovering itself in being assimilated, this was to be an assimilation into the universal. And it was assimilation to be negotiated *through* but not *tethered to,* "the English." For if, in his diffusionist assessment, the English among the Europeans came out as "unquestionably the best civilizing agency," the former were merely agents, not owner-proprietors, of "civilization."

It is in the question of what assimilation entails for "African nationality" that we find a divergence in the thinking of the two West African nationalist pioneers, Horton and Blyden. For where the former accepted the philosophico-cultural premises along with the modern substance of the civilizing mission, the latter rejected those premises in accepting the self-same modern substance. In Horton's nonrelativist thought, African *modernity* in essence would be no different from the European, except in the superficial matter of racial externals and geographical location. For the Orphean Blyden, on the other hand, African modernity characterized this way, without reference, in some form, to an inner racio-cultural "essence" of Africa, would not really be *African* modernity.

In the work of Blyden, therefore, the problem of "Africa" and "the African"—those questions of difference and cultural integrity pushed into irrelevance in Horton's Promethean advocacy—moves to the center of philosophical meditation. The Liberian contrives to bring a relativist cultural nationalism to a mediation of questions of race and humanity, difference and universality. Blyden's copious writings, as well as his exhortations from pulpit and podium, spanned the last half of the nineteenth century and the first decade of the twentieth. These endeavors would be instrumental in generalizing the desire for *his* kind of African nationality among educated West Africans who were increasingly feeling the raw bite of the new-imperial culture of racism as the nineteenth century drew to a close.

Blyden had emigrated from St. Thomas to Monrovia, Liberia, in 1851 as a teenager after American racism had thwarted his efforts to attend a Christian seminary on the American mainland. From his Liberian and Sierra Leonean bases in West Africa, Blyden would go on to become *the* "Black Spokesman,"[44] winning wide recognition in the anglophone Atlantic world as the leading Pan-Negro public intellectual of the last half of the nineteenth century. In this capacity he would influentially work his *African* voice into the otherwise one-sided Victorian humanitarian projections and debates about how to "improve" Africa and the African.

As noted previously, humanitarianism's most monumental statement, combining projections of economic and cultural, material and spiritual, imperialization of the continent, is to be found in Buxton's 1840 *The African Slave Trade and Its Remedy*.[45] With the demise of the dehumanizing Atlantic slave trade, so Buxton and other humanitarians projected, African peoples needed to be repositioned in new relations, ethical and mutually profitable, with their former enslavers. Africa was thus not to be abandoned to her helpless and demoralized fate; on the contrary, European intervention would bring Africa the know-how and the ethic that would encourage continental societies to enter profitably into legitimate commerce with Europe. The rhetoric of African uplift was thus centered on curing what was seen as a continent of culturally aberrant peoples, spiritually sick communities, and institutionally defective societies.[46] Commerce, Christianity and Civilization—the so-called three Cs—would be the engines of an Anglo-African missionary narrative which foresaw, at its culmination, Africa brought up to be on a par with Europe.

Yet, the way Blyden saw it, at precisely that moment of parity, Africa, sporting a thorough alien makeover, would also have ceased to be "African." That is, if in the humanitarian design Africa was to be modern, the continent was projected as such in what we might call a "modernity of the excluded middle." Two exclusive terms, on the one hand, Africa, on the other, Europe, stood at the inception of the narrative of the civilizing mission. Only one term, however—the alien European—would remain at the conclusion because by then the second term—the African, on its own soil—would have been obliged by European political, institutional, and cultural power to be absorbed into the first. Under the all-or-nothing terms of the modernity of the excluded middle, the humanitarian goal of African similarity (or parity) was unthinkable outside complete assimilation as its means.

This negative perception was to be the basis of a critical point made by Blyden, in his "Study and Race," an 1893 lecture given West African publicity by the *Sierra Leone Times*. "Some have revelled in the prospect of hearing some fine morning of the last of the Negroes,"[47] Blyden noted, adding:

> It has been said that the fringe of European civilization is violence. All the agencies at work, philanthropic, political and commercial, are tending to fashion us after the one pattern Europe holds out. Society is calling upon us to be like the rest of its worshippers. All the books and periodicals we read—all the pictures we see beguile us. Everything says to us, "Efface yourselves."[48]

Responding to the projections of the Anglo-African civilizing mission, therefore, Blyden would vigorously insist that Africa was not a civilizational and institutional blank sheet, waiting to be remade in the image of Europe. "The mistake which Europeans often make in considering questions of Negro improvement and the future of Africa," Blyden protested, "is in supposing that the Negro is a European in embryo—in the undeveloped stage," and that "when, by and by, he shall enjoy the advantages of civilization and culture, he will become like the European."[49]

Nevertheless, Blyden did partially acknowledge what he called a "stagnant barbarism" in Africa and therefore concede that "civilizing" improvement must come to the continent from outside agencies—including, controversially, the agency of American Negro colonization.[50] However, if "The African at home," as he wrote, "needs to be surrounded by influences from abroad," he needed these influences "not that he may change his nature, but that he may improve his capacity" (*Negro Race,* 277). From around 1870 to the end of his nationalist career, Blyden insisted stridently, as a corollary to an argument about Africa's aboriginal cultural wholesomeness, that this improvement had to be worked out on Africa's own terms. "What we want," wrote Blyden, "is that the foreign information introduced should . . . be so assimilated as to develop, and be fertilized by, native energy" (281). To have anything less, he argued, would be injurious to the integrity of what Blyden famously labeled African Personality, conceived by the pioneer nationalist and put forward in "Study and Race" as a God-given "race individuality."

If Western civilizational modernity remained a desirable African option for Blyden, therefore, this modernity served Africa well only insofar as it was remade conservatively as, through, and in an African difference. Not the modernity of the excluded middle, therefore: there had to be room and opportunity in between Europe and Africa in encounter for a both/and— hence a negotiated—"African modernity." Africa could say "yes" to similarity as a projected goal of the civilizing mission but say "no" to assimilation as the means. Africa could, in the last instance, desire the universalist premise of parity contained in the rhetoric of improvement while somehow making this desire, in the first instance, accountable to "Africa" as a particularist premise of purity.

Blyden, in effect, wanted to hold purity and parity, difference and similarity, together in the representation of Africa in modernity. But by what stratagem did one think this purity in and towards parity; how did one proclaim a self-validating difference without giving up on demonstrating the similarity of this difference to others? Blyden was aware of movements in modern thought in Europe regarding these very questions. As he acknowledges in *Negro Race*:

> Within the last thirty years, the sentiment of race and of nationality has attained wonderful development. Not only have the teachings of thinkers and philosophers set forth the importance of this theory, but the deeds of statesmen and patriots have, more or less successfully, demonstrated the practicability of it. (122)

Blyden is moving with the nationalist spirit of the times, therefore, when he confesses in 1862, in *Liberia's Offering*, that "An African nationality is the great desire of my soul" (v).

The extent of Blyden's debt to European nationalist thinkers and political developments has been traced by Abiola Irele (and also by Blyden's biographer, Hollis Lynch, whose observations about the African pioneer appear shortly below). Irele notes that in Blyden's time was to be found "the culmination of the movement of ideas set in motion in an earlier age by men like Herder and to which the French Revolution and Napoleonic wars were later to give historical impetus." The African pioneer, Irele notes further, was familiar with the activities and writing of the Italian Giuseppe Mazzini, the personality in whom, "in the mid-nineteenth century the nationalist principle was perhaps most fully embodied."[51]

What must have been revealed to Blyden was how, in the category of nation, the thinker-ideologues of Europe, discarding the excluded middle from the structure of their thinking, had negotiated an inclusive and democratic reconciliation of cultural difference and human similarity. For instance, Mazzini's assessment of "the character of the epoch," the European nineteenth century, was that it enjoined "the mission . . . to harmonise the idea of fatherland and nationality with the idea of humanity."[52] In other words, piety to native "purity," a fatherland, could coexist with, and be ratified in, a humanistic idiom of international parity, or Humanity. If "the object of our aim is Collective Humanity," as Mazzini proclaims further, he adds in qualification, "For us the starting-point is Country" (*Writings*, vol. 3, p. 7). For Blyden, in whose work the same principle appears, Race is Country, and Country is the nativity of "Africa." Mazzini's point—as it would be Blyden's, too—is directed against "*soi disant* cosmopolitans" whose "*aim* may be Humanity, but [whose] starting point is Individual Man" (3:10, 7). For the Italian, such cosmopolitans, excluding the middle ground between Individual and Humanity in their thinking, "deny the special mission of the different races, and affect contempt for the idea and love of nationality" (3:10).

Pure abstraction that it is, then, the unmediated universal of the so-called cosmopolitans will not do. In Mazzini's critical rethinking, therefore, the negotiation of a passage from the concretely lone Individual towards the collective abstraction, Humanity, had necessarily to pass through Nation, an intermediate "third space," as it were. Nation as such emerges in Mazzini's thought Janus-faced. It is a paradox of an embodied (or grounded) abstraction, upon which the universal converges and is concretely differentiated from itself; where collective or wholesale attribution is individualized in and for a self or part.

What the inseparability of abstract and concrete meant for Mazzini, too, was that how morality was organized, and law defined, in the realm of the abstract, had repercussions on and within the realm of the concrete. "The law of the individual can only be deduced from the species" (3:6), he wrote. And the implication was to make it a moral-political challenge for the individual, whether conceived in the singular or as a corporate body, to target the species (or Humanity) for revolutionary transformation if the law it gave to the individual (or Nation) did not wear a human face. And this is where Mazzini's definition of the "special mission of the different races"—a postulate that recurs in Blyden's writings, as it does his fellow late-nineteenth-century Pan-Negroists[53]—is critical. For this mission waged by each aims ethically at bringing a human face to a common law of nations—or international law. And by this the Italian aims to point to an overarching morality that harmonizes human differences—as conferred by, and lived through, custom, culture, language, race, etc.—without abolishing these differences, as wishful cosmopolitanism of the kind he critiques would want to do. "Nationality and humanity are . . . equally sacred" (*Writings*, vol. 5, p. 274), Mazzini insists in "The Holy Alliance of Peoples," and in saying this he foresees that "underlying all the competing nationalisms of the modern era [there should be] a fundamental . . . [humanistic] vision of the international."[54] "The ruling principle of international law," Mazzini notes in this vein, "will no longer be *to secure the weakness of others,* but *the amelioration of all through the work of all: the progress of each for the benefit of the others* (*Writings,* vol. 3, p. 14; emphases in the original). An internationalist thesis of equity that articulates national differences in a structure guaranteeing equal dessert for each: this is the mainspring of the Italian's thought.

Mazzini's envisioning of nation-ness in his 1849 piece "The Holy Alliance of the Peoples" restates these principles by inserting the category into a definition of a global democracy interlinking national-popular sovereignties. His humanist internationalism confers on each nationally identified people the right to world citizenship:

> Without the nation there can be no humanity, even as without organization and division there can be no expeditious and fruitful labour. Nations are the citizens of humanity, as individuals are the citizens of the nation. And as every individual lives a twofold life, inward and of relation, so do the nations. (*Writings,* vol. 5, p. 274)

In all of this Blyden would have found a liberal crusade on the Italian's part to collapse boundaries and hierarchies in the cooperative name of hu-

man similarity while yet conservatively defending the construction or retention of boundaries in the competitive name of particular human collectivities. "*You are the true masters of your native soil; you are the sole interpret-
ers of your own law of life*" (5:267; emphasis in original), Mazzini had
written in endorsement of what he read as national-popular awakenings
against intra-European imperialism and monarchical tyranny in the early
nineteenth century. If nation was a third space, it was also incarnated in a
conception of a movement of a "third force"—the people—in Mazzini's
thought.

Nation in the European thought of Blyden's acquaintance gave itself,
therefore, as a category able to mediate his imagining of a modernity—
occupying a liberal-universalist pole—that would answer to the designation "African," taking up a conservative-particularist pole. He was to write,
after stating his desire for African nationality in *Liberia's Offering*, that the
pure liberal universalism of "Cosmopolitism," the one that leaps straight
from Individual to Humanity, "has never effected anything, and never will,
perhaps, till the millenium." It may be true that "God has 'made of one
blood all nations of men.'" However, Blyden will insist, in the manner of
Mazzini, that God "has also 'determined the bounds of [men's] habitation'"
(v). It was an important polemical move on Blyden's part to claim a Janus-
faced third space in what he referred to as African nationality. On the one
hand, this African nationality conservatively faced inward towards the "race
individuality" of African nativity; on the other hand, it was (to be) liberally
oriented outward towards a worldly universality.

As in Mazzini's terms, then, nation as Humanity served Blyden as a
General Equivalent: through this universal equivalent the differential values identifying an African particularity were to be worked out in a modernist convertibility or translatability into the Universal. To convert African
difference this way was important: it identified for African nationality its
peculiar moral mission—what Blyden called "Africa's service to the world."
If, again, nation for the Italian was Individuality, then in this aspect, for
Blyden, it was unalienable particularist value. The conservative case for the
preservation of an African essence could be made by the pioneer nationalist
at the same time as he made the liberal-universalist case. And, for Blyden,
making the latter case was not just about Africa's service to the world. It
was also about the world giving Africa its moral due: the *recognition* of the
human basis of Africa's difference, recognition long withheld in Western
representations of, and attitudes to, peoples, things, and qualities African.

When, therefore, apropos his critique of cosmopolitanism, Blyden
states his conviction that "I believe nationality to be an ordinance of nature;

and no people can rise to an influential position among the nations without a distinct and efficient nationality" (*Liberia's Offering*, v), he is to be seen making two humanistic assertions. First, that there is a natural law ("ordinance of nature") which imposes a moral equivalence on all human beings without distinction; and, second, that, in its universal reference, this moral law left all equally deserving of the particular distinction of nationality. The case for African nationality is thus made by Blyden on behalf of a special existential form of humanity which is deservingly different and equally deserving.

In making these claims Blyden was contending with the formidable forces that had exiled the portion of humankind to which he belonged from a universal humanity. Even Mazzini's datum of universal dessert in nationality appears Eurocentrically placed in this regard. Mazzini reads history in the motions of a world spirit incarnating itself epochally in different forms with the nineteenth century furnishing a "social epoch" for which "Humanity is the soul, the thought, the Word" and whose "programme is God and Humanity" (*Writings*, vol. 3, p. 65). Yet if the appeal to godhead is made in the name of Humanity, the national-popular third space which the humanistic world spirit was clamoring for as its epochal incarnation was a pan-European affair. It turns out that if a humanist internationalism was the "unknown quantity of the new epoch," as Mazzini wrote in 1834, "The school in which the equation was to be solved was Europe." It followed therefore that "the organisation of Europe must of necessity precede every other" (3:16). The universal spirit grants Europe sole priority, in the new epoch, of making its movements concretely manifest in the world. We find lurking at the heart of the Italian's liberal-democratic thought, therefore, a Manicheism. Non-Europeans may at best be delayed and derivative subjects of History, History already made in (the image of) Europe.

Mazzini was not the only prominent European liberal whose generous humanism was infected with a Manicheism. Blyden would have been aware—as his Liberian compatriot and Pan-Negroist collaborator Crummell certainly was[55]—of the opinions held by John Stuart Mill, the acclaimed "sage of mid-Victorian liberalism." Mill's argument, as paraphrased by Henry Wilson, was that "to hold that the normal rules and customs between one civilised nation and another would apply 'between civilized nations and barbarians is a gross error.'" For "barbarians have no rights as a nation," and moreover, "Independence and nationality, so essential to the due growth and development of a people . . . are generally impediments to theirs" (*Origins*, 25).

Wilson notes that Mill's "clinching epigram, about barbarians having no rights as nations, turned on an ambiguity in the meaning attached to the word 'nation.'" The point had been reached where "fashionable Western usage was . . . beginning to play a cruel trick on educated, aspiring Africans." Where "nation" had before "possessed a handy imprecision, allowing it to serve any more or less identifiable group of peoples," now it was "becoming increasingly precise and normative in its connotations. . . . A notion of what was a typical and proper nation was emerging that tended to embarrass African aspiration in that direction" (25). Even in liberal thought, with its broadly humanistic implication that all are called, it turns out that only some are chosen. And if educated Africans found in this Manicheism cause to despair, it was because its polarized definition of dessert and nondessert, modern European and nonmodern Other, operated on the principle of the excluded middle, and as such left them no possibility to see their African faces reflected in the Universal.

To Mazzini's ideas, Blyden's biographer Lynch adds that of Herder, Hegel and Fichte to constitute the constellation of European nationalist and racialist thought that the pioneer African nationalist "seemed . . . to have been profoundly influenced by" (*Pan-Negro Patriot*, 60). Herder especially is to be singled out, in Lynch's estimation, for if we substitute his "'Nationality' for [Blyden's] 'Race,' we find a striking similarity in their ideas."[56] As a Race Man, Blyden would have found, too, Hegel's idealist metaphysics, which underpinned the latter's raciology, both inspiring and insultingly provocative—inspiring for the potential built into it for thinking the world in terms of a humanistic ecumene; provoking for the Manicheism that severely qualified this ecumenicity.

In *Phenomenology of Spirit*, Hegel had affirmed of "the Absolute" that "*of its own volition*," and "all along," it is "with *us*, in and for itself."[57] Hegel meant by "us," however, not the human race at large but specifically (western) European humanity: in effect the humanistic entitlement of the Absolute, or what the philosopher renders "World-Spirit" elsewhere, is reserved for the European race. Hegel's world-historical drama of incarnate Spirit, Blyden would have found to his dismay, did not admit a part for Ethiopia stretching her hands unto a humanist godhead—stretching, that is, in the effort to receive this godhead into her racialist self-realization.

Hegel lays out the justification for Europe's world-historical entitlement in *The Philosophy of History* where he argues that a part of the world, by the nature of its geography, has been hospitable to humanity in its cultural career of peoplehood and its culminating political expression in statehood. Statehood for Hegel is both the precondition and embodiment, in its mature form, of what he calls "Freedom." This Freedom is not the absence of constraint but a notation of human self-realization, negotiated precisely through the social presence of constraint—as embodied in institutions of Law, State, and so on. What the philosopher means can be garnered from this citation: "The History of the World is the discipline of the uncontrolled natural will, bringing it into obedience to a Universal principle and conferring freedom" (104).

Conformity with a "Universal principle" in Hegel's thought, then, belongs (variably) within Eurasia. On the other hand, "Africa proper," by which Hegel means the black and sub-Saharan portion of Africa, is excluded (as are the aboriginal Americas and aboriginal Australia). Geographically and geo-culturally, therefore, the world divides itself up into world-historical areas and peoples, on the one hand, their non-world-historical counterparts, on the other.

Hegel also proposes that the Spirit of World History expresses itself in developmental or evolutionary stages in the particular careers of the world-historical peoples. "In the History of the World," Hegel writes, "the Idea of Spirit appears in its actual embodiment as a series of external forms, each one of which declares itself as an actually existing people" (79). Thought in terms of development, then, Freedom's being is relative along axes of time and space. It becomes possible for Hegel, therefore, to trace a narrative of History—an allegory of the World Spirit, that is—as a movement in Eurasian space-time. World History moves from infancy to maturity, from ethereal potential to material actualization, from inaugural promise to final consummation. That said, however, Hegel points out that even within the Eurasian theater of true History, a racial geography of West and East is warranted to divide those favored by Spirit off from those who were merely used by it as it sought the scene of its culmination. "[T]he Orient quarter of the globe [is] the region of origination. . . . In Asia arose the Light of Spirit, and therefore the history of the World" (99). This notwithstanding, "The History of the World travels from East to West, for Europe is the absolute end of History" (103). The European West becomes the geo-racially favored offspring of the universal Spirit; it is modern Europe, therefore, standing in a fully self-conscious relation to Freedom as elaborated in its institutions of State, Law, Rights, etc., that shows the developed essence of the world historical.

But what is the case of Africa? The assertion that "geography is fate" is attributed to Greek philosopher Heraclitus. Hegel is clearly operating according to this procedure as he weds space, traced through time, to anthropological knowledge as the principle organizing his rhetorical staging of the World. For him physical geography absolutely determines the time of culture for those areas that fall outside the space of the world historical.

Thus it happens that, to the extent that Spirit is partial to one geography and not another, "Africa proper" is culturally sunk by its geography, a geography forsaken by Spirit.

> Africa proper, as far as History goes back, has remained—for all purposes of connection with the rest of the World—shut up; it is the Gold-land compressed within itself—the land of childhood, which lying beyond the day of self-conscious history, is enveloped in the dark mantle of night. Its isolated character originates, not merely in its tropical nature, but *essentially in its geographical condition.* (91; emphasis added.)

Physical geography is not the only thing that is determining; there is a compulsion in Hegel's argument for this geography to be racialized. Spirit in willing its consummation has been discriminating racially in favor of the European West. The allegory of Spirit, as we read between the lines, is to be resolved also as an allegory of Power, with the philosopher making global power racially manifest as the western European subject's historical entitlement. In Hegel's geo-raciology, therefore, Europe emerges in Spirit-endorsed mastery and authority as *deserving.* The rest—Asia, Africa proper, the aboriginal Americas and aboriginal Australia—are named and devalued in subordination; they are shown to be *un*deserving, that is, in proportion as Spirit has been stagnantly present or completely absent in their respective geographies.

Hegel additionally maps a psycho-anthropology—"character"—onto his racialized geography in order to further justify his assignments of deserving Europe and undeserving Others. Thus this characterological portrait of black Africa emerges: "The Negro . . . exhibits the natural man in his completely wild and untamed state" (93); "want of self-control distinguishes the character of the Negroes." What is more, Africa (proper) and the Negro are locked into a condition that is "capable of no development or culture, and as we see them at this day, such have they always been." Two broad implications follow from this, the first a practical justification of the subordination of black to white in slavery: "The only essential connection that has existed and continued between the Negroes and Europeans is that of slavery. . . . [W]e may conclude *slavery* to have been the occasion of the increase of human feeling among the Negroes" (98; emphasis in original). The second implication has to do with knowledge and representation, of the kind, say, that would arise with the questions: "Who is the African/Negro?" "What is his ontology?" "Is an accounting of the African and his world to be done in terms of the same representational categories by which the European is understood?" Hegel responds thus:

> The peculiarly African character is difficult to comprehend, for the very reason that in reference to it, we must quite give up the principle which naturally accompanies all *our* ideas—the category of Universality. In Negro life the characteristic point is the fact that consciousness has not yet attained to the realization of any substantial objective existence—as for example, God, or Law—in which the interest of man's volition is involved and in which he realizes his own volition. This distinction between himself as an individual and the universality of his essential being, the African in the uniform, undeveloped oneness of his being has not yet attained. . . . The Negro . . . exhibits the natural man in his completely wild and untamed state. We must lay aside all thought of reverence and morality—all that we call feeling—if we would rightly comprehend him; there is nothing harmonious with humanity to be found in this type of character. (93)

By his own admission, for his African information, the armchair geo-historian relies on the "copious and circumstantial accounts of missionaries" (93). These "facts," as they appear in *Philosophy of History* are meager, to the extent that they are limited to a few observations about the conquest states of Ashanti and Dahomey and a vague "Guinea" (i.e. West Africa). They nevertheless provide enough "evidence" for Hegel to abstract all of black Africa into a timeless representation that puts this portion of the continent geo-spatially below the world and geo-temporally before "universal" time. Still "on the threshold of the World's History," Africa, "is no historical part of the World; it has no movement or development to exhibit." Hegel concludes: "What we properly understand by Africa, is the Unhistorical, Undeveloped Spirit, still involved in the conditions of mere nature." (99). Black Africa emerges in Hegelian speculation as Nothing compared to white Europe's Everything.

Hegel's rendering of "Africa proper" amounts, therefore, to an "unworlding"—i.e., removing from the sphere of a humanist universal and its rights and desserts—of the continent's racially Negro sub-Saharan portion. Insofar as Blyden was acquainted with Hegel's thought, it presented the pioneer with the challenge of inventing an Afrocentric Africanism, one that would world Africa in opposition to its Eurocentric counterpart. Producing Africa in a geo-racial cultural consistency, making Something (worldly) out of Nothing: this is the path that Blyden's intellection would traverse in response to the intolerable falsehoods of Eurocentric Africanism.[58]

From these samples of nineteenth-century European nationalist and raciological thought, then, we see the strands that went into framing Blyden's intellection; the ontological and existential postulates therein regarding race, geography, and dessert that he was enjoined to challenge; and the styles of thinking that he had to redefine for his own Africanist purposes.

For Mazzini in Europe, the people had emerged in self-consciousness, ready, in and for themselves, to step into history. In Africa, let alone the territories of West Africa, however, no such national-popular self-consciousness was to be observed as Blyden was writing. Was this not enough justification for Mill's Eurocentric exclusion of what he deemed unmodern Africa from the norm of national peoplehood? Not for Blyden this perception, however, for in his conception the modernist means were to hand by which the popular self-consciousness of racial Africanity could be represented. From the 1870s on, the West African middle class emerges strongly for Blyden as the (potential) proxy of the people, realizer within itself of the pioneer's conception of African nationality.[59] Mazzini's idealism finds an African modernist adaptation as Blyden launches a pioneering nationalist crusade from his Liberian and Sierra Leonean bases. And this crusade projects an African middle class occupying the third, Janus-faced space of Nation, thus falling between the corporate Individuality of a racial Africanity and a human Universality, and containing within itself the germ-plasm, the concrete abstraction, of African peoplehood.

A number of Blydean propositions follow from this. Foremost was the task of maneuvering a middle class into a nonnegotiable commitment to occupying as its "natural" slot the third space Blyden assigns it, where it would be and act as the nationalist custodian of the self-consciousness or Individuality of a racial Africanity. For, as the pioneer nationalist had come to see, the consciousness of his addressees, the black Englishmen and the diasporic returnee-settlers of West Africa, was cast by the humanitarian philanthropy of the civilizing mission in a false, because racially self-deprecating, cosmopolitan mold. It was consciousness oriented away from, and not towards, a natural self; a false consciousness. Hence we find the task of recalling the ancillary consciousness of the middle class to itself placing on Blyden the burden of inventing his racial nationalism in and as a naturalistic quasi theology, complete with notions of original sin and redemption from such. For Blyden, preaching to awaken the middle class, sinning against one's own nature was the sin of sins. Rejoining oneself with one's nature and keeping faith with one's Individuality was the path towards racial self-redemption.

But what was the "nature" of racial Africanity in this case, and what was its "natural" determination? Insofar as Blyden was acquainted with Hegel's work, he accepted and worked with its Heraclitean thesis, "geography is fate." According to this "law," the externals of physical environment are racio-culturally determining; hence the internal character of geo-racial groups reflected the imprint of an environing objectivity. But for Hegel, as it will be for Blyden, the humanist Spirit operating through a people's racio-cultural character guaranteed that this character, qua their cultural subjectivity, reciprocally or dialectically registered an imprint on geography. In its own self-serving image, the racio-cultural Personality "worlded" a world, in other words. For Hegel the imperial apologist, of course, Europe's worldly fate in its dialectical eventuation needed not to be exclusively confined to the particularity of European geography. As Spirit realized its career and mission through the European racio-cultural character, Europe appeared inevitably as world-historically fated to absorb a universal geography into itself. All possible geographies and the Individualities whose expression they enable are cancelled out by and into a dominant European one whose reflexive Personality emerges triumphant in encounter.

In comparison to the Hegelian one, Blyden hands us a modest postimperial proposition. In his conception, geography and cultural originality, in a dialectical interplay, constructed African nativity. And by this nativity we are to understand an African world stamped or "worlded" in the particular racio-cultural image of its inhabitants, and which particular accomplishment authenticated their humanity. Reading against the Hegelian grain, Blyden affirms that Spirit has neither remained stagnant in "Africa proper" nor bypassed this geo-racial region of the world completely. On the contrary, Spirit realized itself in the African setting in the form of a racio-cultural character which, keeping faith with its nature, had been able to transform itself within the enabling constraints of a God-given geography. Blyden elaborates this naturalistic, nativist, historicist and developmentalist thesis in the centerpiece of his last works, *African Life and Customs* (1908), executed for the purpose of "unfolding the African, who has received unmixed European culture, to himself, through a study of the customs of his fathers" (3). This undertaking had become necessary, he points out, because "Those of us who . . . witness the result of European influence along this coast have many . . . misgivings . . . and anxieties about European civilization for [Africa]." For, "in our indiscriminate appropriations of European agencies and methods in our political, educational, and social life, we are often imbibing overdoses of morphine, when we fancy we are only taking Dover's powders!" (*Black Spokesman*, 237).

Insofar as Blyden interpreted Europe's African civilizing mission in terms of the Hegelian dialectic of European geo-racial Personality absorbing and canceling out the African Personality, this negative existential insight explains his fervent Africanist quasi theology, based on the doctrine of the divinity of "Race Individuality." Inaugurally publicizing his concept of African Personality in his 1893 "secular sermon," "Study and Race," Blyden would exhort the thinking youth of the race in these terms:

> [F]or everyone of . . . us there is special work to be done—a work of tremendous necessity . . . and importance—a work for the Race to which we belong. . . . [T]here is a responsibility which . . . our membership in this Race involves. . . . [T]he duty of every man, every race is to contend for its individuality—to keep and develop it. . . . [T]o give up our personality . . . would really be to give up the divine idea—to give up God—to sacrifice the divine individuality; and this is the worst of suicides. (*Origins* 249, 250, 252)

The Absolute wills itself to be, and must already be, in and for itself with us: in Blyden's exhortation to the middle class, we see the Hegelian phenomenology of Spirit recast, as an article of humanist faith, in African nativist form. African race individuality is sanctified and marked off as a special province of Spirit in Blyden's idealist metaphysics. And this makes it a cardinal sin for his addressees of the educated middle class not to choose to live in continuous awareness of, and to be duty bound to continue to *realize* in worldly form, this virtual, and would-want-to-be abiding, African self-presence.

Fidelitas in Blydean quasi theology, the morality he imposes on a middle class endangered in alienation, reads as a matter of conserving African Personality in and through the class self. Its racio-cultural responsibility becomes a guarding of the native soul of the African race against corruption, a preservation of this soul inviolate in the midst of the destructive gale-force winds of so-called civilization buffeting it from without. As he exhorts another audience in 1881, on the occasion of his inauguration as President of Liberia College,

> The true principle of mental culture is . . . to preserve an accurate balance between the studies which carry the mind out of itself, and those which recall it home again. When we receive impressions from without we must bring from our own consciousness the idea that gives them shape, we must mould them by our own individuality. (*Black Spokesman*, 238)

It is a matter of a middle class staying in touch with a divinity-informed natural self, while continuously realizing its soul-Personality, bodying it forth into the world, in accordance with its own native idiosyncrasies. "[I]f we are to make an independent nation," Blyden exhorts further, "we must listen to our unsophisticated brethren as they sing of their history, as they tell of their traditions" (244). The essence of the pioneer's message was: modernize, don't Westernize; middle-class nationalism in his sermonizing was enjoined to contrive to make the modern go native. Inasmuch, then, as Blyden desired, and tasked a middle class with, a modernist *originality*, as conferred by the Western *techne,* this had to be subject to African racio-cultural *priority,* as furnished by a native *logos.* For, as he argued, "We must not suppose that the Anglo-Saxon methods are final. . . . There is inspiration for us also. We must study our brethren in the interior, who know better than we do the laws of growth for the race" (236).

The challenge for Blyden, however, was not only the Orphean one of a middle class returning to a source in a native popular. It was also to give, in Mazzinian terms, this racio-cultural looking inward, towards the divine African Individuality, an expressive dimension oriented outwards, towards a worldly Universality. The formula "Ethiopia shall stretch her hands unto God" is to be understood also in the form of a third space "gone native" which must draw the challenge of "going worldly" with this nativity into its intermediate self. Blyden advocates an African (nationalist) internationalism negotiated on a nativist basis. This we see in his projection, out of Africa, of essays such as "Africa's Service to the World" (in *Negro Race,* 113–29) and "Study and Race" as important internationalist manifestoes. "If you are not yourself, if you surrender your personality, *you have nothing left to give the world*" (*Origins,* 250; emphasis added), Blyden cautions in the latter essay, adding, "We were made for the highest of all glory, which is service to Humanity" (251). He contrives to work out middle-class *fidelitas* to African (native) Individuality in these essays also as a sacrilegious class responsibility to be a medium of this Individuality's *translation,* and a guarantor of its modernist *convertibility,* into the worldly.

For Hegel, as we have seen, "Africa proper" is pure Individuality and nothing else. Blyden's response to this in his metaphysical idealism is resolved as a conservative quest to make Africa intelligible in a worldly ontology as a special province of Spirit. Preserving the African Personality that Hegel and others disparage in misrecognition was to preserve this Individuality not merely for itself; it was to preserve it for the world as well. The middle-class return to the native was thus to be negotiated as a world-bound return to source. What is more, this internationalist aspect of Blyden's thought involves turning the tables on Hegel. For it is Europe, sunken in materialism and given to exterminatory excesses in her imperial dealings with "aboriginal races," that Spirit had abandoned. Africa—figured by

Blyden as "the spiritual conservatory of the world" (*Negro Race,* 124)—
would be, through middle-class nationalist intermediation, on a world-
bound civilizing mission, a postimperial spiritual civilization that will re-
charge the exhausted moral batteries of European and international
humanity. For, as he affirms in faith in "Africa's Service to the World," "the
promise of that land" is that "'Ethiopia shall *suddenly* stretch forth her hands
unto God'" (124, 129; emphasis in the original).

In 1899, a letter addressed to "European-educated Africans" by the En-
glishwoman Mary Kingsley was published in the *New Africa,* a Monrovia
(Liberia) paper. Kingsley, who had traveled in, and was a commentator on,
West African affairs, was a critic of political developments in this region as
dictated by the economic, social and cultural imperatives of the British
New Imperialism. What she saw and reported, in her *West African Studies*
(1899), about British policy in West Africa was that it was proceeding on
the assumption that this part of Africa was "uninscribed earth." Hegel's
symbolic "unworlding" of Africa was thus being rendered literal in material
and practical political expression. The West Africa Kingsley saw therefore
was rapidly being overtaken by imperial worlding, in an imposition on
nativity of an alien legal system, mode of rule, and structure of social and
cultural relations. Kingsley called this "interference," criticizing her
imperializing countrymen for "proceeding to alter African institutions without in the least understanding them" (*Fanti National Constitution* [app.], 261).

Kingsley was Blyden's friend; the two were ideological bedfellows also
in that they shared a conservative concern about preserving the aboriginal
integrity of native lifeways.[60] Fine polemicist though he was, Blyden has
been described as "impractical" when it came to a defining a concrete middle-
class politics in a West Africa. He was not "the type of nationalist dreaded
by the colonial administration."[61] It is in the inter-imperial conjuncture,
where Blyden's Orphean idealism intersects with the Victorian Kingsley's
practice, that this idealism gains a concretely political validation. Kingsley,
taking on Empire on behalf of the peoples of West Africa in her books as in
her public lectures in England, provides a modular image of the engaged,
oppositional public intellectual, speaking out against an imperial policy,
under the Crown Colony system, of governing without politics, as it were.
Hers, then, as the encomiums given her by West African intellectuals show,
was an inspiring example to these intellectuals of a practical politics of the
possible within the new-imperial colonial theater. Thus it is that Sarbah
not only speaks approvingly of Kingsley's writings, finding it "a pity her
books have not been generally read and studied by educated West Africans

as they deserve to be" (*Fanti National Constitution,* xiii); but he also reproduces her hortatory letter to the *New Africa* as an appendix to his 1906 work. For Hayford, on the other hand, Kingsley is "A greater than any who have, of late prated about Africa," and her name is one "at mention of which sensible Africans are wont to rise, as our manner is, in token of respect and gratitude" (*Land Question,* 6).[62]

"The African is not living as a mere horde" (*Fanti National Constitution* [app.], 260), Kingsley would remonstrate in personal correspondence to Sarbah, in a phrase which sums up her efforts to educate a British public which believed the contrary. And she would argue that for African development to be meaningfully African, it would have to take into account the "natural idiosyncracies" of this African. As a matter of Britain's moral accountability to the native, Kingsley would advocate in conscientious appeal to her countrymen that the modern element, as wielded by British agencies in Africa, should be enjoined to preserve in improving. These agencies should be employed to protectively nurture and further the growth of African institutions rooted in native soil, and not to uproot and destroy them.

A conscientious British agency, however, could preserve in improvement only that whose idiosyncracies it understood. But how was the cultural gap between alien and native to be negotiated for this cross-cultural understanding to take place? And who was to do the suasion that would correct the political and moral line of vision of Britain such that, as Casely Hayford put it, it would "bear manfully its responsibilities"? (*Native Institutions,* 5). In these questions lay the moral and political injunction laid on European-educated natives by Kingsley in her letter. Kingsley wrote:

> The white race seems to me to blame in saying that all the reason for its interference in Africa is the improvement of the native African, and then proceeding to alter African institutions without in the least understanding them; while the African is to blame for not placing clearly before the Anglo-Saxon what African institutions really are. . . . The stay-at-home statesmen think that Africans are all awful savages or silly children—people who can only be dealt with on a reformatory, penitentiary line. This view . . . will remain so until you . . . who are educated in our culture, and who also know African culture will take your place as true ambassadors . . . between the two races and place before the English statesman the true African. . . . There are . . . Englishmen . . . who would not destroy native independence and institutions if they but knew what those things were; who would respect native laws if they knew what it was, and who would give over sneering at the African and respect him if they knew him as he is really and truly. (*Fanti National Constitution* [app.], 261, 262, 263)

For Kingsley, therefore, the bicultural makeup of the educated native spelled the potential for the true translation of his nativity into "universal" understanding. "Only the Negro will be able to explain the Negro to the rest of mankind" (*Negro Race,* 263), Blyden had asserted. Kingsley is in agreement with him if she also cuts his grandiose theme of explaining to mankind to politically manageable size. For she renders it as a project and responsibility of a frontline African middle class within the confines of the colonial theater to endeavor by its own (courageous) efforts to creatively forge into being that which is stillborn under the Crown Colony system, a properly dialogic—hence oppositional—public sphere.[63]

If Kingsley enjoins a "universalizing" translation of the native, with the doubly disposed middle class as its medium, therefore, this translation had directly political implications. The middle class as a frontline agency of translation, had necessarily to find and adapt the native to the imperative of survival. The politics of translation, as advocated by Kingsley, amounts then to a worlding of the native from below, hence the native rising in worldly opposition to what Ania Loomba has referred to as imperial "overworlding."[64]

In sum, with Kingsley, the Orphean problematic of African modernity, idealistically laid down in Blyden's cultural nationalism, gains a directly practical anticolonial function—albeit we should be reminded that her conception of middle-class anticolonialism was reformist rather than radical, agonistic rather than antagonistic. The political in her work is about curing systemic wrongs; it remains, like the politics of Gold Coast and West African nationalism up to World War II, subserviently tethered to a humanistic datum of imperial cooperation. The upcoming chapter, "'Worlding' Nativity," in part traces, in the work of figures for whom Kingsley was exemplary, an early Gold Coast outline of this development. In that chapter, we will see the middle class beginning the task of inventing the native; and, also, attempting to bridge the class rift by inventing its class self aboriginally in the native. Additionally, we will see a middle class that begins to imagine figured on its role as universalizing translator of the native the lineaments of the nation. Why else would Sarbah's 1906 work of politically motivated cultural translation be titled not "Fanti Ethnic," nor even "Fanti Native," but *Fanti National Constitution*?

3

"WORLDING" NATIVITY

EARLY GOLD COAST CULTURALIST IMPERATIVES AND NATIONALIST INITIATIVES

Here on the Gold Coast, you have to deal with an aboriginal race with distinctive institutions, customs and laws, which . . . European writers may attempt to portray, but which they can never fully interpret to the outside world.

—Casely Hayford, *Gold Coast Native Institutions* (1903)

The life of a people grows . . . it absorbs the thought of other nations into its own forms, and gives back the thought as new wealth to the world; it is a power and an organ in the great body of the nations. But there may come a check, an arrest; memories may shrink into with-ered relics—the soul of a people—whereby they know themselves to be one, may seem to be dying for want of common action. But who shall say "The fountain of their life is dried up, they shall forever cease to be a nation"? Who shall say it? Not he who feels the life of his people striving within his own. Shall he say, "That way events are wending, I will not resist"? His very soul is resistance, and is as a seed of fire that may enkindle the souls of multitudes, and make a new pathway for events.

—Attoh Ahuma quoting George Eliot, in *Memoirs of West African Celebrities* (1905)

To Be or Not to Be Native: Navigating the Problem of "Thrown-Togetherness"

> When did we become a people? When did we stop being one? Or are we in the process of becoming one? What do these big questions have to do with our intimate relationships with each other as well as with others?
> —Edward Said, *After the Last Sky*

> The residual anomaly of tribal exclusiveness has the regrettable tendency of evolving unhappy antagonisms against those called of and qualified by God to harmonise the disorganised interests of our Country. . . . We are in sore need as Africans of an expansive horizon . . . broad as the heavens.
> —Attoh Ahuma, *The Gold Coast Nation and National Consciousness* (1911)

> Unhappy are the people who cut themselves off from the past.
> —Sarbah, quoting Gladstone, in *Fanti National Constitution* (1906)

In 1895 the first edition of Rev. Carl Christian Reindorf's *History of the Gold Coast and Asante,*[1] treating events from "the origins of the different tribes to the year 1856," appeared. That Reindorf had long unsuccessfully sought an English publisher for his manuscript—he completed it in 1889—accounts for why the *History* was published in its first and second editions in Basel, Switzerland. This was the logical alternative considering Reindorf's lifelong career as an agent of Basel Mission evangelicalism on the Gold Coast.

Reindorf was the pioneer among Gold Coast indigenes of the country's *literate* history, the "indigenous-traditional" variety.[2] He was born a Ga, the ethnonym of the group whose traditional capital, Accra, was situated on the eastern littoral of the Gold Coast.[3] Accra, at the time Reindorf was born (1834), was divided by European imperial interlopers, British, Danish and Dutch, into protectorates and spheres of administrative control. From these protocolonial centers each maintained links of trade with, and of informal political and military dominion over, the diverse surrounding coastal and near-coastal ethnic polities of the eastern Gold Coast. The European settlements also provided the bases and logistical support for the furtherance of confessional and cultural relations, as in the activities of the Christian missions, notably the Basel and Wesleyan, with these surrounding communities. The Danes held sway over Christiansborg (Danish Accra), the British over Jamestown (British Accra), and the Dutch over Usshertown (Dutch Accra). (In the case of the latter two, Cape Coast and Elmina respectively, on the western littoral of the Gold Coast, were centers of greater significance for their mercantile, diplomatic, and political activities.) It would be a while yet after Reindorf was born before the Danes would turn their settlements and spheres of influence over to the British (1850), a process to be repeated by the Dutch in 1872, circumstances that would leave the British the sole European power in the Gold Coast. In 1877, three years after the Gold Coast became a formal British colony, the administrative seat of the country would be transferred from Cape Coast to Accra.

Accra was therefore, as were Cape Coast and Elmina, a zone of significant commercial activity, with trade and maritime routes converging on it from the near-coastal interior and the seaboard. The routes ran coastward, too, from the hinterland behind the few tens of thousands square miles that the Europeans had, in an imprecise geography, designated the Gold Coast, a hinterland dominated by the imperial kingdom of Asante. If European merchant capitalism, centered on towns dotted all over the Gold Coast littoral, exerted a magnetic pull, it was a pull to which the territory's different ethnic groups responded alike as participants in, and joint beneficiaries of, the legitimate commerce that had succeeded the slave trade's abolition. Before and briefly into the nineteenth century, the dominant trade in slaves had favored the rise of conquest and mercenary states in West Africa whose belligerent slave raiding had disrupted many ethnic communities. As the nineteenth century unfolded, however, commerce in palm oil and other produce was transforming a now relatively settled Gold Coast and its Asante-dominated hinterland into a broad transethnic emporium of European-African trade and exchange.

If Asante and the Gold Coast were thinkable in an "identity," this was because the geopolitics of ethnicity and trade involving these two areas were singularly focused on the economic advantages deriving from a common coastal area, falling more or less between "5th degree of west longitude and 2nd degree of east longitude."[4] Asante could not be overlooked in Gold Coast commercial calculations. Its great wealth in gold, ivory, and forest produce; its large (consumer) population; its military might, repeatedly proven against the British, were crucial to the success of the coast-centered trade.[5] It made practical and ideological sense, therefore, in what we might term a mercantilist, populist and Christian "coastal imaginary," to think the Gold Coast and Asante in convergent terms. It is this imaginary that we find operative in the eastern-littoral-born Reindorf's *History.* Eight years after the *History* appeared, we find the same imaginary at work centrally also in the western-littoral-born Casely Hayford's *Gold Coast Native Institutions.*

Within a supervening imperial sphere joining European and African in commerce, what one might call an Atlantic interest had emerged. Margaret Priestley has captured this as a "working relationship" between indigene and expatriate in her study of West African coast and trade society.[6] But this reading is incomplete if we do not see within this commercial "ecumene" the emergence of Gold Coasters in a particular light as potential wielders of an interest identified more or less competitively against the European one as *native*. The distinction was routinely made in the nineteenth century between "native" or "African" traders and European. And, as revealed in nineteenth-century commercial history, the activities of so-called native/African traders disclose the knitting together of the Gold Coast and the Asante-dominated hinterland in mercantilist interdependence.[7]

There was an ethnically transcendent native interest, then, to which inappropriate imperial policies could prove injurious. This matter is given clear articulation in 1903 by Casely Hayford, in his *Native Institutions,* where he ropes Asante, recently conquered and annexed to the Gold Coast by Britain, into a pan-Gold Coast defense of free trade. The mercantile pressures causing the Gold Coast and hinterland to converge into a common market area, a transethnic zone of symbioses and mutual survival, could make room for a Gold Coast of oftentimes fractious ethnicity to be read as a "subecumene," a proposition that arguably informs Reindorf's *History.*

From Accra, too, which formed one corner of a Gold Coast coastal and near-coastal triangle of Euro-Christian acculturation—the other corners were Cape Coast and Akropong, the capital of the ethnic Akan polity of Akuapem—mission routes radiated into the surrounding country and interior. If commercialism, based on the economy of material exchanges between interloper and indigene, and between indigene and indigene, was making for the objective emergence of a corporate pan-Gold Coast interest as native, evangelism, in the economy of confessional and cultural exchanges, may be seen as also tracing a similar path. For evangelism on the territory circumscribed as the Gold Coast promised an ecumenicity of faith that transcended ethnic affiliation. In the eastern Gold Coast, Gas and Krobos (subsets of Ga-Adangme ethnicity), Akuapems, Akyems, Kwahus (subsets of Akan ethnicity), Krepes and Anlos (subsets of Ewe ethnicity) would come, as European missionary activity took off from the 1820s on, to indifferently tag onto their different ethnic "confessions" the common denominational confession Presbyterian. Another ethnic overlap would take on the label Wesleyan (or Methodist). Yet another would become Catholic, and so on. Beyond denomination and faction, however, all converts within the confines of the Gold Coast would profess a belief in a singular Judeo-Christian divinity.[8]

The career of Christianity as a cosmopolitan interfaith in the Gold Coast shows that a drawing of ethnic difference out of itself into modes of confessional sameness has not been a negligible part of the Gold Coast/Ghanaian experience. (The same could be said of the career of Islam in the northern hinterland, which, from 1901 on, would be a part of the country's British-dominated colonial history.) It is not altogether implausible to see how, under these circumstances, the mission to convert, entrusted to mission-educated natives like Reindorf, could also be converted into a visionary and patriotic vocation to integrate, a challenge to sublimate in a local narrative the sameness coming by way of the cosmopolitan interfaith. The production of a native "interfaith" to which belong different ethnic "denominations" or "confessions": we might see this, then, as Reindorf's challenge of historicizing a local Gold Coast/Asante ecumene. And, in what might be seen as a secularization of the historiographic imaginary informing the Bible—which traces time from Genesis to Revelation—the ends of this vocation would be a revelation of Gold Coast/Asante ethnic variety in a common popular destiny, one that it is predestined to commonly share. Christianity, mission education, and the interdenominational composition of the Church arguably provide the cognitive tools, image structure, and ideological referents which Reindorf adapts to knit the Gold Coast and Asante together in his *History.*

The transethnic mutualities and interdependencies emergent in the Gold Coast would have been a central part of the experience of Reindorf growing up. This after all was the time of "great trade which sprang up in the [eighteen] thirties . . . between Ashanti and the Gold Coast," and which would reach its "meridian in the sixties . . . a trade based on good-will and mutual confidence between merchants on the Gold Coast and their friends . . . in Ashanti" (*Native Institutions,* 98). The mutual connections were certainly his experience over the course of his career, first as a youthful trader, subsequently as one of the important (Euro-African) indigenes who helped to lay the foundations of Presbyterianism in the Gold Coast.

The future missionary was born the son of a trader who was himself the son of a Danish settler at Christiansborg who married a Ga woman. The Reindorfs were part of the "intricate network of African Christian trading communities which had emerged in the towns of the Gold Coast littoral during and after the 1820s."[9] The necessities of making a living as a trader had compelled *père* Reindorf to take up residence in coastal Prampram, a non-Ga (albeit Ga-Adangme) town. It is here that the son was born to parents whose trading activities took them on eastward journeys as far as Krepe, a matter of crossing some three linguistic, if not ethnic, divides. Carl Reindorf's Euro-Christian education started in Danish at the Castle, Christiansborg. Subsequently, around 1846, he attended the newly opened school of the Basel Mission where the pedagogy was conducted in the Ga language.

Young Carl, we are told, left school early to start trading on his own. He would have had to negotiate linguistic and ethnic borders as his trading activities took him to the easternmost districts of the Gold Coast littoral, deep into the country of the Anlo-Ewe. Forced to return to the Basel Mission school, he qualified in 1855 to become, so to speak, one of the prominent native laborers in the Lord's Gold Coast vineyard. In his many years of missionizing, he was stationed in and/or worked in the districts of Krobo, Akuapem, as well as closer to home among the Gas and their Guan neighbors to the west of Accra. For all his devotion to the Mission and to its rhetoric denigrating heathenism, Reindorf was also adept in the arts of healing native to the Gold Coast. We see in his posture a figure who maintained an unswerving allegiance to his Ga ethnicity. Nevertheless, as we find in his *History*, he insisted on a "we" and "ours" that was pan-Gold Coast and Asante, hence native, in reference. Being a local Ga patriot, it seems, did not preclude his being a "confederate" Gold Coast patriot.

That the Gold Coast as a site of "crossings" would come in the future to give itself as an intellectual and ideological problem to Reindorf can be read off the churchman's biography. It is a matter that appears in the prefatory justification he provides for the *History*. The problem may be stated thus: the Gold Coast and Asante, in the exchanges between outsider and insider, had come to be knitted together in a material objectivity: a pan-Gold Coast *in itself* could appear in the mind's eye. Hence, in the Preface to the *History*, Reindorf nominates a "we" of the Gold Coast and Asante as he readies himself to give this "we" the attribution of "our history" (viii). There *was* for him, then, a Gold Coast/Asante ecumene to speak of, a country whose differently ethnic inhabitants commonly confronting the European Other in encounter and exchange were similarly native. But could this transcendently native similarity be seen then as not merely fortuitously tied to the differentiating presence of the Other? Could a common nativity be demonstrated to have its own internal derivation, consistency, and necessity? History is the challenge for Reindorf of narrativizing the Gold Coast as a confederate existence *for itself.*

In the Preface, Reindorf addresses this appeal to the Gold Coast "educated Community": "The sole object of this publication is, to call the attention of . . . my . . . countrymen, to the study and collection of our history, and to create a basis for a future more complete history of the Gold Coast" (viii). This endeavor has become necessary because "a history of the Gold Coast written by a foreigner would most probably not be correct in its statements." Indeed, claims Reindorf, several accounts by foreigners of the Gold Coast must be deemed "comparatively worthless" since they were not "witnesses personally" to what they wrote. It is "most desirable," he concludes therefore, "that a history of the Gold Coast and its people should be written by one who has not only studied, but has had the privilege of initiation into the history of its former inhabitants and writes with true native patriotism." Reindorf could claim this native patriotism, for "[i]t is no egotism when I say I have had the privilege of being initiated into, and also possessing the love for, my country" (ix). As he points out, not only had he been raised as a child on his grandmother's lore, but he had also interviewed for his historical undertaking, as a mature adult, "more than two hundred" living sources "of both sexes" (x).

Reindorf's complaint sounds against what he sees as foreigners' distortions of a historical memory that ought to be pan-Gold Coast/Asante in breadth and scope. In that respect he situates his work as the first native intervention, in essence political, in the modes in which what he calls "my country" was being rhetorically worlded (i.e., produced as a mode of being in the world). For what was out there was the interloper's historiography, which was counter-patriotic insofar as it could not be identified with a transcendent Gold Coast interest. Nineteenth-century European histories of the Gold Coast, as Kimble notes, were "written from a European point of view, from outside, and the argument for Empire runs through [them]."[10] One kind of European history, for instance, was focused on Asante as a conquest state. This Asante-centered history produced a narrative of imperial coverage in which all other Gold Coast groups became insignificant tributaries emptying into an Asante mainstream.[11] Another kind of expatriate history was ethnocentric. This was the case, for instance, of the ethnohistorical work of A. B. Ellis, whose concentration on the Gold Coast's majority Twi-speaking Akan— in *Tshi-speaking Peoples of the Gold Coast* (1887)[12]—excluded other ethnicities making up the colonial territory. The elevation of the few in colonial representational estimation could only mean the deprecation of all others; such historiography divided rather than integrated. A patriotic nationalist history, for Reindorf, therefore, was one that did not confuse the history of one (ethnic) denomination with the history of the (native) ecumene.

It was true that a dominant Asante had to be given its imperial due. Reindorf concedes:

> I may . . . state briefly my object in connecting the history of Asante with that of the Gold Coast. There must be a starting point in writing a history of a nation. If the [Ga] kingdom of Akra, which appears to have been the first to be established on the Gold Coast, could have continued and absorbed that of Fante, or been absorbed by the latter, I might have easily obtained the starting point. But both kingdoms having failed and the kingdom of Asante having become the leading and ruling power, a Gold Coast history would not be complete without the history of Asante, as the history of both countries are so interwoven. (xi)

A thesis of two histories "interwoven," for that reason not standing in pure opposition to, nor (only) in a stark hierarchical relationship with, each other; two tributary histories, therefore, Gold Coast and Asante, emptying into a common mainstream. This is the ideological and affective conjuncture that the patriotic native wishes to tease out of the history of his country. From Reindorf's point of view, what was required was an interdenominational history, one disclosing, as in the history of the Church, different creeds and confessions bound by an ecumenical faith, and sharing, as a wellspring of their different life-trajectories, a common divinity.

As Reindorf brings his coastal Christian imaginary to the vocation of proving that the past ratified the necessary existence in the present of the Gold Coast/Asante as a pan-ethnic federation, what problems had to be negotiated? For one, the past did not disclose Gold Coast origins in a monogenesist form but in a polygenesist one. The various groups of the country had different myths or traditions of origin. "If the Akras and Adangbes emigrated together . . . from Same in the East, between two large rivers," they came to meet

> [t]he aboriginal race all along the sea coast and inland [who] were nearly all of the Guan, Kyerepong, Le and Ahanta tribes. . . . In the interior were the Akan or Twi and Fante tribes who more probably, "when the Moslem invasion of Western Europe was stemmed, and the Christians reassorted [*sic*] their superiority in Sapin [*sic*], were driven by the Moors from Central Africa into the low-lying countries between the Kong mountains and the river Pra." (21–22)

That which would become the Gold Coast, then, begins as a veritable Babel. Reindorf's historiography, however, is disposed, in post-Babelian fashion, to tell a story of ethnic merger and not of self-perpetuating difference. He labors to show, in his ethno-genealogical reconstructions falling between 1660 and 1680, how origin is traced over by dissemination, how initial adjacency of groups becomes later interjacency. Consider, for instance, "the people of La" who "were originally a part of the numerous tribe who seem to have been the first settlers on this Coast, known as the Les" (41). The career of the La, however, reveals this group in a series of reconfigurations of their ethnocultural identity. Having "entered into alliance with [the Akan and Twi-speaking] Akwamus," the La later turned against their allies and united with the Gas to drive the Akwamus onto territory beyond the river Volta in the eastern Gold Coast. We are told that the La people pursuing the Akwamus "had to stay several years at Krobo" where they "intermarried." Subsequently, they "removed to Adshimanti on the Akuapem hills" (Guan/Akan territory). In conclusion, Reindorf informs his reader, this group which in present-day Ghana is Ga-speaking, "[b]y their connection with the Akwamus . . . acquired much of the Twi [or Akan] character, hence it was said the Labades [i.e., La people] are Twis" (42).

The historiographic principle of interweaving is in evidence again as Reindorf relates the stories of the developments taking place around the European comptoirs as peoples fleeing conflict sought the relative safety of these areas to regroup. "The forts of the Dutch, English and Danes at Akra, during the days of dissension between the Akwamus and Akras, invited the latter to flee to the Coast for protection from the Akwamus" (38). The Akras are joined by the "Aseres and Aboras," this group of migrants added to by people from Dankera (or Denkyira) which in 1700 had been newly conquered by Asante. The Dankera group, Twi-speaking Akan, would arrive in Akra from Elmina by Dutch mediation. This latest immigrant group, we are told, "Being free and intelligent trading people, they acquired and enlarged their quarter very rapidly with refugees from Dankera, Akwamu, Akyem, and Akuapem [all Akan subdivisions]" (39).

Reindorf demonstrates therefore that there are exigencies and emergencies that recurrently throw the different Gold Coast groups together. The *History* tells about war; about Gold Coast groups negotiating mutual defense and offense pacts, political alliances, territorial space for settlement, intermarriages; it tells about these groups' joint dealings, partnerships, and collaborations with, as well as antagonisms against, the European interlopers, etc. Reindorf is to be seen demonstrating that these historical and existential conjunctures have made for a commingling and merger of Gold Coast ancestral bloodlines. As in the three-personed Divinity (God the

Father, the Son, and the Holy Ghost), whose tripartite plurality is singular, so it would seem with the Gold Coast/Asante. In the missionary's historiography, the latter's multipartite ethnic personalities have so worked themselves into each other as to appear to have confounded for the historian any retrospective distinction, in strictly purist terms, between Self and Other. Superficial observation of the country, of the kind Reindorf accuses foreign historians of the Gold Coast of, can only reveal its apparent ethnic discontinuities as irreducible, and hence confine its ethno-genealogies to a linear plot. His practice, on the contrary, shows us the plotting of a "spatial" history, in which ethno-genealogy, unfolding in time, does not preserve the boundaries of its coherence in "pure" space. This is so because as Reindorf continually resolves the Gold Coast/Asante as a scene of ethnic definitional spaces folding into, and unfolding out of, each other; of currents of consciousness merging interethnically into, and emerging postethnically out of, one another.

The construction more or less of fluid coherence across Gold Coast/Asante space—the interjacency that Reindorf calls "interweaving"—appears very much to be a main organizing ideological principle of the *History*. Reindorf's Gold Coast/Asante is bounded in being a shared nativity. Hence, we discover that the war bands of the Ga-speaking Akras have Akan designations—"Asonkofo . . . Apagyafo . . . Akomfode . . . Amferefo . . . Atuafo . . . Ntiafo . . . Kyiramimfo . . . Ohwirammirifo . . . Ampotifo . . . Apesemakafo . . . Piankofo . . . Ankobeafo" (112)—and the polyglot Ga historian renders for his reader the drum language of each of these military companies in the Akan original. Yet, lest this be seen uncritically as Akan hegemony over the Ga, Reindorf reminds his reader also that, "When in the asssembly of kings . . . a display of nobility, heroism . . . [is] extolled, the horn of [Ga] King Taki sounds in a deep broad tone: 'Kpo avuwo, po avuwo to me!'" (114–15). And this language assimilated to Ga ceremony is (non-Akan) Ewe. Making the *History* a demonstration of the intermingling of ancestral consciousnesses and bloodlines, Reindorf is to be seen establishing therein the basis of a secular interfaith of the Gold Coast/Asante ecumene—this interfaith being what he terms "native patriotism."

Reindorf reaches also in his nativized history for that which coheres in time. In his account, we might tease out one other organizing principle: that the comminglings and mergers of the past laid out before the reader have made for the inception of a corporate Gold Coast/Asante protoself-consciousness. Hence the history being recounted is not simply of the order of random happenstance. The *History* has, of necessity, to end up being the story of this protoself-consciousness, a Gold Coast/Asante Genesis (time before), retrospectively discovering and recovering itself in Revelation (Reindorf's time now), and doing so at a juncture of prospective imagining (a nation in the making). This would be a juncture, then, which marks a (new) beginning for the career, a nationalist one, of this self-consciousness.

To this end, it is important for Reindorf to show that in spite of the numerous conflicts that he recounts—the *History* is full of them—a coherent and abiding basis of a confederate "we" and "ours" has been present in the conjoint biography of the Gold Coast and Asante. If we understand the *History* in this mode, then the many conflicts, quarrels, and wars come out as less interethnic than *intranative,* i.e., within a variously dispersed native Self recurrently in fratricidal conflict with itself. And what this may very well mean for Reindorf, then, is that this Self is conflicted because it is not yet fully present to itself.

If this interpretation be conceded,[13] then the claim being made by the pioneer historian is that in its ethnocultural cross-insemination, Gold Coast/Asante history has been pregnant with a protoself-consciousness all along. As such it has been bearing within its womb a child awaiting the auspicious future occasion for its wholesome birthing, nurturing, and maturation into a fully fledged self-consciousness. If so, it is the middle class which the *History* constructs as the midwife, the agency for the birthing of Gold Coast/Asante self-consciousness, which, as it looks to its maturation, must *now* begin over again as nationalist. "If a nation's history is the nation's speculum and measure-tape," writes Reindorf in this regard,

> then it brings the past of that nation to its own view, so that the past may be compared to the present to see whether progress or retrogression is in operation; and also as a means of judging our nation by others, so that we may gather instruction for our future guidance. . . . Keeping this in mind, we shall more clearly understand the necessity of collecting materials for a complete history of the Gold Coast from every source within our reach. (x)

The archival work of the educated native cannot remain in the order of pure folkloric research; beginning over again, it has necessarily to be a political activity, according to the pioneer historian. Reindorf's reading in pan-Gold Coast terms of the historical institution and evolution of a native "Constitution," the basis of precolonial Gold Coast self-government and social organization, is illuminating in this regard. "The Constitution," he assesses, "has run out its three stages: the prophet stage, in which the prophet priest held the reins; the priest stage, in which the high priest of the national fetish had power; and last the king stage" (109). If this is a narrative of progressive enlightenment, then the highest stage of enlightenment will have been reached when "the educated community," beneficiaries of "[t]he introduction of Christianity [which] has so much enlightened the people," contracts to "reorganise the whole system of government on christian [*sic*] principles." And it is imperative that this should happen, for only "then we shall be recognised as a nation" (109).

The biblical John the Baptist was the herald of Christ's messianic kingdom in the context of Roman-imperialized Palestine. So it would seem a Gold Coast middle class, in the context of British imperialization, has become for Reindorf the herald "messianically" working towards the institution of the secular kingdom of the Gold Coast/Asante nation. A nationalist middle class emerges idealized in the image of an enlightened secular priesthood serving the "divinity" of Gold Coast/Asante nativity—a "divinity" erected in the nativist interjacency and consanguinity resulting from the ancestral intermingling of bloodlines. With Christianity as its progressive ally, this middle-class secular priesthood is poised to bring a Gold Coast/Asante native-popular protoself-consciousness—a people's memory to which Reindorf insists the middle class, as archivists, must stand in a custodial relationship—to modernist maturation in nationhood. The class in the middle is imagined and invented in the *History* as the intermediate starting point of the confederately native Gold Coast/Asante nation.

Reindorf includes the following apology and exhortation in the preface to the *History*:

> The title chosen for this publication, "History of the Gold Coast and Asante," may be deemed to promise more than I was actually able to give. . . . Still I venture to have the book so named in the hope that our brethren and friends on the Gold Coast . . . may possess better sources of information . . . and may, laying aside all prejudice, be induced to unite to bring the history of the Gold Coast to perfection. (x)

The premier Gold Coast historian entreats his colleague educated Fantis thus: "I trust, my friends in Fante . . . will cooperate with me in revising, if need be, what I have written" (x).

Concerning the collaboration that Reindorf solicited from educated Fantis it will not come in a form bearing directly on the pioneer's call to expand the *History*. What emerges out of Cape Coast—consolidated in the 1890s as the literary and political center of Gold Coast nationalism—rather will come to augment what the *History* stood for, the ideological vision that sought to invent, out of the many, one native ecumene. It will be the nationalist exertions of Wesleyan-educated Fantis—preeminently Sarbah, Hayford, Attoh Ahuma, Sekyi—that will substantially carry forward the vision of Reindorf. As for the acknowledgement of Reindorf's monumental pioneering effort, it will come in 1930, in J. B. Danquah's nationalist tribute to the man. "Reindorf has been dead for many years now," Danquah points out while lamenting that "not a single voice has been raised to recall our inestimable debt to this most admirable prophet of Gold Coast nationality" (qtd. in *Political History,* 521 n. 3).

Among the important publications to come out of the Cape Coast school is Hayford's 1903 *Native Institutions,* written in response to a "national" emergency, a political crisis, in the Gold Coast at the turn of the nineteenth century. Reacting to apparent colonial chicanery on the part of the British, the treatment *Native Institutions* brings to its political subject matter is confrontational of colonial authority, hence somewhat different in middle-class conception compared to Reindorf's *History.* For the latter is imagined in part as a (middle-class) effort to cement a compact with "Christian England," for whom "we are very glad and thankful that Providence has placed our country and people under" (*History,* 274). In Reindorf's interpretation, colonialism, qua the imposition of Pax Britannica on the Gold Coast, was justified in the name of nativity and imperiality in encounter sharing, and working out of the principles of, a common Atlantic interest. Empire is resolved as the enlightened ally of a progressive middle-class nationalism. This view of Anglo-British goodwill informs the paean dedicated to the colonizer as the concluding item on the very last page of the *History*:

> Rule, supremely rule, Britannia, rule
> Thy newly acquired Colony on the Gold Coast!
> . . . .
> Let justice, love, and peace prevail!
> . . . .
> The Danes and Dutch, on profit bent alone,
> Thy rivals were, with equal power.
> But now Britain stands alone
> To bless and save!
> Two mighty foes impede her way,
> Ignorance and blood-stained superstition.
> To rule and not fight such deadly foes,
> Is not Britannia's way.
> To lift the nations which she rules:
> to educate, and leave the gospel free. (335)

By the 1890s, however, such romantic imaginings would have soured considerably as colonialism revealed its true face as the pursuit of a paramount British interest wholly at the expense of a native one. What the developments since 1874 boded for Gold Coasters can be seen in an 1895 complaint protesting against a government in the appointment of whose members "no native of the Gold Coast has a voice and over whose policy and conduct the people of this country have no control whatever."[14] The crisis Hayford was responding to in writing *Native Institutions,* then, had been induced by a series of undemocratic colonial diktats. Most drastic of them was the attempted legislative passage of a bill, in 1894 and again in 1897, that would vest control of the lands of the colony, hitherto subject to traditional laws of land tenure, in the Crown.

The Gold Coast in late-nineteenth- and early-twentieth-century crisis may have been comprised of groups bearing different ethnic labels. Nevertheless, the category "native" in Casely Hayford's title amounted to an explicit claim that it was possible, had indeed become mandatory, to recover the Gold Coast across this variety in a coherent transethnic and intercultural objectivity. It made nationalist sense, in a time of crisis, for Casely Hayford therefore not to produce a knowledge of Gold Coast *ethnic* (or tribal) institutions, the notation of differences within his colonial country, but of *native* (or aboriginal) institutions. For he was seeking therein a politically effective articulation of a commonality and organic solidarity across these differences.

Hayford's work followed on the heels of his Fanti (and Euro-African) compatriot Sarbah's 1897 *Fanti Customary Laws,* written to provide empirical demonstration of the existence and functioning of a "native law." With a history and genealogy, this native law in Sarbah's demonstration was a *living* one, seeded and transmitted as such in a popular memory. Sarbah's book was the first comprehensive Gold Coast response in print to the crisis alluded to. In it he presented a sustained exposition of the customary whose aim was to reveal to an uncaring colonial power that "the African is not living as a mere horde"[15]; a power apt to forget, in Casely Hayford's words, that "on the Gold Coast, you are not dealing with a savage people without a past" (*Native Institutions,* 128). "Today we are being ruled," Sarbah would vehemently protest in 1889, "as if we had no indigenous institutions, no language, no national characteristics, no homes"[16]; the Gold Coast had been colonially reduced to a political and cultural *terra nullius.*

It is in these circumstances, therefore, that we find Sarbah expounding the general principles of a native law from case studies drawn mainly from the Fanti. He will offer these principles as a starting point of cross-ethnic comparison that will in time elicit a shared, hence native, Gold Coast jurisprudence, a homegrown common law. Sarbah justifies his endeavor and his conviction about the native as a datum of comparative similarity thus:

> I have made a selection of cases bearing on the local Customary Laws, and I hope that by grouping and classifying decisions together, facilities will be afforded for ascertaining what is really the *general* Customary Law with re-spect to which, it is well known, the natives are tenaciously attached, the principles underlying it, and how far it is qualified by any special local or tribal custom. And now that comparison is rendered possible, and the lines of inquiry as it were placed before them, this is a field of investigation which should engage the close and studious attention of every educated native. . . .
> . . . if by my efforts other natives of the Gold Coast, acquainted with the several local dialects, and trained in the English Inns of Court, are induced and stimulated to enter the hitherto unexplored field of *our* Customary Law, I shall not have laboured in vain, for I am certain, that it is only by patient investigation and intelligent study, that the Customary Law can be well de-fined and consolidated. (*Fanti Customary Laws,* x, xii; emphases added)

Hayford and Sarbah were claiming, in response to a critical emergency, that there was something singular about and across the Gold Coast that merited the choice of "native"/"aboriginal" over "ethnic"/"tribal," the comparably similar over the incomparably dissimilar, to capture its mode of being. "We" have a nativity of "our" own grounded in shared institutions, including a common law, their works were protesting, against colonialist perceptions and claims to the contrary. For them, in effect, the politically charged premise was that a Gold Coast (native) whole inhabited and could be teased out of an (ethnic) Fanti (or greater Akan) part.

For the colonial apologists the homogenizing claims of the nationalists could hardly appear to be justified if the disposition of the relations between the inhabitants of the British colony was looked at in the light they preferred. The Akan-Fanti subethnicity Sarbah and Hayford belonged to, for one, was hardly a politically unified group; its own intragroup rival-ries had divided it over the course of the nineteenth century. Then, again, the Fanti were marked off as one distinct division among others of a larger Akan ethnicity that occupied a considerable portion of the British Gold Coast (and spilled over into the neighboring French colony of the Ivory Coast). Even though the Akan were a cultural federation speaking, to an appreciable extent, mutually intelligible dialects of the same language and having near-identical institutions and social organization,[17] they were grouped into and organized as different political units. The histories of these units had evolved differently and often antagonistically. The Gold Coast on the whole, the preponderance of Akan populations within it notwithstanding, was comprised of politically and ethnoculturally disparate peoples. It was these peoples whose sovereignties the British had usurped, untidily cobbling them together and bringing them under their colonial domination.

British domination had been exercised informally and on a restricted scale from the 1830s on. During this period, the jurisdiction of the Crown, variously negotiated by treaty with several traditional authorities whose sovereign rights the Crown recognized, had been extended to cover judicial protectorates confined for the most part to the Gold Coast littoral. With the launching by the British of the aggressive expansionism of the New Imperialism after 1870, the coastal, near-coastal, and hinterland territories of the Gold Coast would be brought together and roped into the ambit of a jurisdiction formalized and exercised by the Crown as colonial. The confederate Asante who, unlike the Gold Coast colony proper, had been conquered militarily by the British, would be annexed to the Colony in 1901. The non-Akan Northern Territories lying beyond Asante—and sizeable portions of which had been part of the Asante empire—would also be annexed in the same year. The Gold Coast would thus emerge with one coherent political identity as a colony of a subject people, under one governor, the representative of the Crown. And yet for three and half decades into the twentieth century, in a self-serving effort to limit cross-territorial communication between the inhabitants, the British would pursue a policy of maintaining separate administrative and legislative identities—under one executive—for the Colony, Ashanti, and the Northern Territories.

The justification for this illogical state of affairs would be laid out explicitly in 1919—albeit we can index this justification back to the foundation of the colonial state—in an address before the Royal Colonial Institute by then governor of the Gold Coast, Sir Hugh Clifford. According to Sir Hugh these were the "facts" on the ground:

> The Gold Coast and Ashanti . . . could not be regarded as a single State. . . .
> At Cape Coast and Anamaboe [two Fanti communities], situated something like Somersetshire and Devonshire, the inhabitants regarded themselves as mutually strangers. Away from the Fanti country, in Ashanti, the difference was greater still; and in the eastern part and in the Volta the people were widely separated as the French and Italians. (qtd. in *Political History,* 530)

Clifford's observations could hardly be disinterested. The governor had overseen the introduction in the Gold Coast of formal indirect rule, the policy of making the several ethnic and subethnic rulers functionaries of colonial rule, in the early teens of the twentieth century. A Gold Coast severally divided into enclaves of tribal rule under customary law, the tribal unit defined in terms of watertight customary borders, only went to secure politically the reproduction of the central colonial state. It is only to be expected that Clifford would be an apologist of a policy amounting to what Sarbah characterized in *Fanti National Constitution* as "*Divide et impera,*" "one of the principles of Crown Colony rule," with a "tendency to sow and disseminate amongst the inhabitants distrust and suspicion of each other" (230). Sarbah's complaint against Crown Colony administration was that its production, policing, and perpetuation of division and difference below the colonial state was deliberately aimed at blocking the emergence of a corporate native identity and interest.

In Clifford's ideological argument, therefore, the Gold Coast did not add up to a coherent political territoriality. It found the logic of such coherence not in itself but in the colonial state appearing above, and bearing down on, it. The Gold Coast, that is, was native only insofar as it had become colonial. The country's nativity found its necessity outside itself, in the element imposing itself from without.

If nationalist wisdom rose to challenge this view, it did so in the fact that the mélange of territories acquired, and peoples subjugated, by the colonial overlord had come under the unified address of the name the Gold Coast. This wisdom could not remain stuck in Clifford's question of what Gold Coasters are in what they were. And this would be the differences, enshrined in ethnonyms such as Asante, Fanti, Ga, etc., that Gold Coasters had brought with them from the past and which gave themselves in colonially exploitable form in the present. Rather the question had come to be the difficult one of imagining what the apparently horizontally discontinuous peoples could *be* in what they have always been, and could *become* in being this always-have-been. Hence, in a state of colonial emergency, a political one, the project of culturally construing one native people and, on that basis, one (potential) nation had become imperative. An uncompromising Attoh Ahuma takes up this challenge, declaring, "If we were not [a nation], it was time to invent one."[18] He will go on to argue a transethnic— or native—basis of the coherence of Gold Coast political territoriality: "We own a Political Constitution, a concentric system of government, of one Race, born and bred upon our own soil." He adds, "With the Akan language one can cover a seaboard 350 miles in extent, and an area of 105,900 square miles, more or less. The so-called languages [of the Gold Coast] may perhaps be simply regarded as so many dialects, often mere Provincialisms" (*Gold Coast,* 1–2).

"*We are all one, and natives of the same colony,*" was the response journalists in Accra used to greet the appearance of Sarbah's newspaper, *The Gold Coast People,* when it first appeared in 1891.[19] However, these middle-class intellectuals waving the banner of a Gold Coast that was singularly native were also less and more than native. Formed biculturally as Euro-Africans, these were men who on that account wrote and proclaimed their nativity from within a culturally referenced social rift, as it were, a rift between their privileged selves and the masses with whom they would make common cause in the name of a shared nativity.

Hayford, for instance, insisted on the distinction of being "cultured," a cosmopolitan distinction which, as we have seen, he unfavorably opposed to "the uncouth, the vulgar, and the ignorant." Yet, under the social and political order of the New Imperialism, power, firmly in the hand of the colonizer, had become a winner-take-all proposition, and official racism divided the social and political field starkly into deserving white and undeserving black (indifferently native). The ability to derive political value from the distinction they wielded in the name of "culture" had become a dubious existential proposition for Euro-Africans. In circumstances where the Gold Coast was part of a "West African system [of Crown Colony administration which] has been as much as possible to rule the country as if there were no inhabitants in it,"[20] this contrivance left "cultured" middle-class Euro-Africans and the "vulgar" masses similarly disenfranchised.

Not only that: the Euro-African merchant aristocracy—and Sarbah, Hayford, Attoh Ahuma, and Sekyi were scions of Cape Coast "merchant princes"—which had thrived in the era of free trade before colonial imposition, had awakened to the realization that the economic playing field was no longer level under the new-imperial order. What was worse, the colonial state was a referee in a Gold Coast commercial game in which British interests were players; hardly a situation where the referee will bind himself to rules of fair play and impartiality.[21]

The social upheavals and unfavorable political and economic developments in the Gold Coast in the dying years of the nineteenth century, then, conduced to the growth of a middle-class sense of existential "thrown-togetherness"; a sense, that is, of a pan-Gold Coast "We" undifferentiated in facing "our common ruin." What is more, under the colonial order, it was the fate of this Euro-African middle class to be at once native by colonial racial prescription and to be politically alienated from nativity by colonial proscription. Taken together these developments had made it urgent for Euro-Africanity to grasp Gold Coast (and generally West African) nativity, in a material-economic and sociocultural geography, as inalienably and coherently its own. Thus Attoh Ahuma will claim, "We are *ab origines*," "lineal descendants of the Aborigines of . . . the Gold Coast," in his 1897 essay "Colony or Protectorate" (*Native Institutions* [app. B], 326, 325).

Attoh Ahuma's claim is made from within the ranks of what had by this time become the Cape Coast and Fanti nationalist vanguard of the Gold Coast middle class. It was this vanguard which would come to capitalize on widespread Gold Coast discontent—brought on by the colonial attempt to wrest control of Gold Coast lands from its natural custodians—to begin to articulate an oppositional politics out of the predicament of thrown-togetherness. And, in doing this, the lawyer-dominated Cape Coast vanguard would seek to draw for its political agency on a native below, as it were. The political articulation of nativity—that is, the making of a politics out of culture, deemed a people's culture—begins in earnest in 1897, then, with the formation in Cape Coast of the Gold Coast Aborigines' Rights Protection Society. The A.R.P.S. was and would remain over its lifetime an alliance between the educated natives of the middle class and the so-called chiefly natural rulers. In conception the A.R.P.S. was a frontline organization defending what it articulated as a corporate Gold Coast interest, mobilized in the rhetoric of its leading spokesmen as "native"/"aboriginal" or "national," against colonial encroachment. Attoh Ahuma, the first secretary of the A.R.P.S., explained its *raison d'être* thus: "The Society . . . shall always stand for strenuous efforts to ensure combination of the scattered interests and the unity of our natural rulers; the establishment of harmonious relations one with the other and the cohesion of forces which make for the safety of the public and the welfare of the race."[22] Self-described as "the mouthpiece of the nation" (as qtd. in *Political History*, 350), and idealized by Casely Hayford in *Ethiopia Unbound* as a people's parliament—"prototype of the kind of African National Assemblies which must be called into being . . . for the solution of African questions" (183)—the Society would function as an unofficial opposition to the colonial government.

The A.R.P.S. would also be a launching pad from where the legal luminaries in its leadership would hurl incendiary devices into the judicial and administrative arenas of the popularly unrepresentative colonial state. Thus it is under the auspices of the oppositional A.R.P.S. that the legal arguments challenging colonial land and social reform would be conducted from 1897 on. The Society's activist model of popular advocacy would project it into the frontline organization defending what it fashioned as the

Gold Coast public interest. The colonial attempt to vest control of Gold Coast lands in the British Crown would be interpreted from the society's populist legal stand, founded in a would-be coherent native law and constitution,[23] as threatening to deprive the inhabitants of the colony of their sovereign and exclusive rights to their ancestral patrimony. In a Gold Coast nativity, so the arguments of the legal luminaries of the A.R.P.S. went, collective ownership of land mediated in fundamental ways the institutional relations within and between family, community, and state. It mediated also metaphysical conceptions in which identities—and the roles, functions, rights, and responsibilities bound up with these identities—in these interlocking spheres rested. Now, so the A.R.P.S. argued, without exception Gold Coasters stood absurdly to be reduced by colonial fiat to mere settlers on their own land, as such owing their tenancy to an alien landlord. This threatened disruptive development needed to be countered urgently by the projection and defense of the Gold Coast as *one* in being identified in a cultural commonality as much as in conjoint territorial ownership across both its horizontal and vertical divides. The memorable Attoh Ahuma may be quoted again: "every inch of ground is ours and ours irrevocably. . . . We are the undisputed masters of the soil." And he would exhort his countrymen and women, "Let unity of thought and unanimity of purpose prevail, and your love for the Motherland, its institutions, its traditions, be without dissimulation" (*Native Institutions* [app. B], 326).

"His very soul is resistance," Attoh Ahuma, quoting George Eliot in the epigraph reproduced at the head of the chapter, affirms of his activity. We may acknowledge this without however exaggerating the radical quality of his and the A.R.P.S.'s politicization of the native. For Attoh Ahuma also reminds the auditors to whom he addresses his appeal for unity that they should "Above all, strain every nerve to remain loyal to the Queen, our Protector" (*Native Institutions* [app. B], 326). If we see this ambivalent play in Reindorf's nationalist history, too, this must return us once more to the matter of the "no" uttered in impossibility because it comes out in spite of itself also as a "yes." This, as has been pointed out, is the paradoxical condition inhabiting a post-encounter frontline class sharing the culture of imperialism, a class voiced, therefore, in the colonial setting by its joint possession, with the colonizer, of the protocols of representation and prestige forms furnished by this imperial culture. How, then, stands the claim of political resistance when its nativist articulation, because it is given in imperialist prestructuring, appears fatally flawed; when the resister taking a stand *against* the colonizer does so only to reveal his desire to share the grandstand *with* the latter?

Unflatteringly dubbed "co-operationist,"[24] A.R.P.S. middle-class politics is perhaps better understood in terms of Ross Chambers's notion of "oppositional behavior," which he proffers in a book suggestively titled *Room for Maneuver.* Chambers, bringing literary representation to the examination of the sociology of power and resistance, notes:

> Oppositional behavior consists of individual or group survival tactics that do not challenge the power in place, but make use of the circumstances set up by that power for purposes the power may ignore or deny. It contrasts, then, with revolution, which is a mode of *resistance* to forms of power it regards as illegitimate, that is as a force to be opposed by a counterforce. . . . [R]evolutionary materialism . . . in correctly diagnosing oppositional behavior as ultimately conservative (in that it helps the existing power structure to remain in place by making the system "livable") . . . fails to see that . . . oppositional behavior has a particular potential to change states of affairs, by changing people's "mentalities. . . ." This potential derives from the mysterious phenomenon of *authority,* whereby anyone, given the opportunity to speak, may so use words as to change situations. Although it derives its power initially from preexisting power relationships . . . "oppositional authority," once gained, has the extremely tricky ability to erode, insidiously . . . the very power from which it derives.[25]

Chambers adds that, in all social situations, "There are those who are denied the right of speech," and for these, "oppositional discourse can sometimes be seen to have an 'on behalf of' function, using its own power of speech vicariously, so as to represent the voices of those condemned to silence" (*Room for Maneuver,* 3).

A.R.P.S. anticolonial politics, then, may be seen as "oppositional behavior" in these senses outlined above.[26] Looking at the late-nineteenth-century West African setting, Henry Wilson observes the political in this negotiated sense. He notes that "outgunned and commercially outclassed," denied "individual assimilation, promotion and political sovereignty," the nationalism of the middle class had to "become a cultural nationalism and their politics a politics of survival."[27] Yet early Gold Coast cultural nationalism was more than a nationalism of culture, if by this Wilson means a purely symbolic nationalism. This is the kind about which Fanon wrote that it takes us back to "some very beautiful and splendid era whose existence rehabilitates us both in regard to ourselves and in regard to others."[28] For in reaching for the cultural symbols and institutional forms of a Gold Coast nativity, A.R.P.S. functionaries were attempting to *materialize* a politics of homegrown culture as a force within a colonial realpolitik that would exclude it (or suffer its inclusion only in a distorted, self-serving form). Hardly a matter of locking their nationalism in a past threatened by obsolescence, theirs was to enliven this past, and giving it contemporary colonial currency, work it decisively as political intervention into the order of the New Imperialism. The politicization of the native becomes the middle-class way of saying and meaning "no" to coloniality in spite of having been heard to say and mean "yes" in desiring its positively transforming modern possibilities. The politics of survival Wilson alludes to as that fated to be practiced by the middle class under the new-imperial dispensation comes thus to involve making a virtue out of necessity. We see a colonially excluded middle, as it mobilizes the native, seeking out, as in Chambers's construction, "room for maneuver[ing]" itself into an included middle, an intermediary third force within colonial sociality.

The previous chapter mentioned the 1899 letter of the Victorian Afrophile Mary Kingsley to the "European-educated natives" of West Africa. In that letter, Kingsley sets out what it was that had to be "maneuvered" into place by the middle-class fraction of nativity if it was to gain ontological utility and existential validation inhabiting its third space and constituting a nationalist third force between colonizer and masses:

> [T]here is [a] factor . . . I wish you to consider carefully . . . the factor of nationalism. I believe no race can . . . advance except on its own line of development; and it is the duty of England if she intends really and truly to advance the African on the plane of culture and make him a citizen of the world, to preserve the African nationalism and not destroy it. *But destroy it she will,* unless you who know it come forward and demonstrate that African nationalism is a good thing, and that it is not a welter of barbarism, cannibalism and cruelty. . . . The [British] public . . . has been taught that all African native institutions are bad; and unless you preserve your institutions, above all, your land law, you cannot . . . preserve your liberty. . . . [D]o your best to prevent this fate falling on your noble race. I believe you can best do it by stating that there is an African law and African culture, that the African has a state form of his own. I believe if you do this thing fairly and well, that England, at any rate, will not destroy the African nationality. (*Fanti National Constitution* [app.], 263–64; emphasis added)

To her African auditors, Kingsley was implying something like this: Empire is Power that in assuming its worldliness correspondingly assumes your Nothingness and can effectively act on this assumption because it is Power. Confronted by an uncomprehending and destructive Power, your politics of survival can only mean one thing: to image and speak your endangered native being in the very power-laden language of worldliness wielded by Power, the language it understands and which you also, fortunately, understand because you are European-educated natives. You are uniquely placed, then, to piggyback on the (representational) power of Empire, turning its worldliness to the purposes of negotiating a reversal of the absolute defeat of your nativity that the New Imperialism presages. Henceforth, for your nativity to (continue to) be is for it to be *in* the world (i.e., for you to make it gain intelligibility and recognition, even as you work to preserve it, in a worldly frame); for your nativity to become is for it to be *for* the world (i.e., Kingsley's thesis about advancing "the African on the plane of culture and mak[ing] him a citizen of the world").

"[T]he oppositional," writes Chambers in what could be a gloss on Kingsley's counsel, "always necessarily fights on terrain it has not chosen" (*Room for Maneuver,* 5). What is more, "a rule that defines oppositional behavior . . . is the rule of using the characteristics of power against the power and for one's own purposes" (10). Conceived in these terms of capitulation and compromise, then, a middle-class politics of survival from the turn of the nineteenth century on is to be seen as a scene of negotiated defeat. It should be borne in mind, however, that, unlike absolute defeat, a negotiated defeat is a form of victory, victory in the sense that it preserves for its negotiators initiative and agency and, in that, the power to go on the offensive. Reading the oppositional in early Gold Coast/West African nationalism, therefore, is to acquaint oneself with the paradox of a politics of *offensively* negotiated defeat.

Kingsley, counseling and setting out the terms of a politics of survival for educated West Africans of the middle class, is full of praise for Sarbah for having anticipated her counsel. "Mr. Sarbah," she writes, "is at present the only man who has worked on that question [i.e., demonstrating 'African law,' etc], in his book 'Fanti Customary Law'" [*sic*]. "That book has done a great deal," Kingsley concedes, and for this reason, "Mr. Sarbah deserves well of his countrymen, who wish to be free citizens and not slaves, *however cultured in European culture*" (*Fanti National Constitution* [app.], 264; emphasis in the original). And indeed Sarbah had done a great deal considering the substantial imperial and intercolonial recognition accorded his pioneering *Fanti Customary Laws.* If this recognition came from his being able to carry the native with him in world-bound translation—thus making the native intelligible to *and* in Power—it also reveals his work in the light of the victorious politics of negotiated defeat of early Gold Coast and West African nationalism. What comes below looks, as this registers in the pioneer Sarbah's work, at the paradox of worldly translation of nativity—hence this nativity's transformation, its makeover—as in fact the only valid mode of its "preservation" in view of the corrosive colonialist modernity impinging on it.

As with Reindorf's before him, Sarbah's will also be a representative tale of a frontline navigating African modernity—navigating between this modernity, in a predicament-sense, as a problem given; and, in its offering of transformative potential, as a problematic to be taken. As an original contribution to the problematic of African modernity, a matter recognized by his West African peers and others wider afield, his work reveals an engaged attempt to work through the dilemma captured by David Scott. Scott notes "the transformations effected by modern power, the consequence of which is that the old, premodern possibilities are not only no longer conceptually approachable except in the languages of the modern, but are now no longer available as historical options."[29] In these terms, what was available as a historical option for Sarbah and his frontline kind, in the transformation scene that was Africa in the grip of the New Imperialism (qua modern power)?

It was the activity of breathing life into the old order of nativity as a matter of its material and conceptual transmogrification into, and of guaranteeing its intelligibility within, the new modern-colonial order. The old had to capitulate to the very medium of its alienation, the literate standards and rationalist protocols of a colonialist modernity. Nativity's existential warranty, its political valency, had become a matter, therefore, of the doubly disposed middle class letting it live in modernist transcoding—from oral to written—and translation—from conceptually and cognitively Akan-Fanti (or "native") to Anglo-Western. It was either this or, what with this nativity subject to a Darwinist New Imperialism, leaving it to atrophy and/or die.

To Let Live or to Let Die? Sarbah, Worldly Translation, and the Necessity of "Thinking in English"

> Here on the Gold Coast the people have shown that they do not mean to go under.
> —Casely Hayford, *Ethiopia Unbound*

> The secular vision in African creative writing . . . combines the re-creation of a pre-colonial African world-view with eliciting its transposable elements into modern potential.
> —Soyinka, *Myth, Literature and the African World*

In his preface to *Fanti National Constitution,* Sarbah, explaining why he has "attempted to avoid as much as I can, the habit of using the word native in connection with men and things African," records:

> I remember once examining a [European] witness in the Concessions Divisional Court . . . sometime in 1902. After he had spoken of *native* bush-path, *native* canoe, *native* watercourse, *native* river, *native* mines and *native* gold, I asked him to explain...in what respects *native* gold and the other *native* things particularly differed from those found in other parts of the world, but he could not; for the absurdity of always describing in Africa everything non-European as *native* had dawned on him by that time. (*Fanti National Constitution,* x; emphases in original)

The problem addressed by Sarbah is that of colonialist representation which, mediating "Africa" and "the African" in the category "native," has conspired to produce this category as irreducible. African nativity is incommensurable with the Universal, in other words; and, in what can only swerve this nativity from recognizing itself sharing in Humanity, its difference is mobilized in colonial discourse as untranslatable. This is Hegel and his "Africa proper" all over, that Africa which is purely itself—a Singularity—and nothing else. For, as we have heard Hegel argue, there is "a peculiarly African character" which is "difficult to comprehend" and which has "nothing harmonious with humanity" in it. In reference to Africa, therefore, "we [Europeans] must quite give up the principle which naturally accompanies all our ideas—the category of Universality."[30] For Hegel as for the apologists of colonial imperialism, then, Africanity was no competitive principle, and could have no force as such, in the world.

To be "native" in the terms understood by Sarbah's European witness, therefore, was to be bereft of a world worthy of recognition by those who would claim a universal identity exclusively. Thus, it is the burden of uncreated Africa, the image of a continent imposed by imperial-colonial discourse, and materialized in colonial practices that treated his Gold Coast as a cultural, and withal politically invalid, *terra nullius,* that in a general way Sarbah sets up his two major works to address. *Fanti Customary Laws* and *Fanti National Constitution* are together assertions that the difference of Africa termed "native" is translatable, and that nativity is commensurable with the Universal. Insofar as the colonial comes representing itself in and to the Gold Coast in the image of an exclusionary Universal, therefore, they are works aimed by their author to achieve for the category "native" politically effective recognition as partner, and to project it as morally deserving, within the domain of the Universal.

Sarbah's political agenda, born, according to Hollis Lynch, out of a "desire to obviate the worse aspects of an increasingly felt British administration," was and would remain modestly "oppositional." In this regard, Lynch notes further: "he was no anti-British revolutionary: he recognized and admitted that the British could be a force for good . . . if they respected the indigenous Fanti culture, and cooperated fully with the traditional rulers and educated elite."[31] In this light, Sarbah's translation of the native into worldly intelligibility came premised on intelligent cooperation between educated native and alien ruler. "Co-operationism" as cultural translation—what Kobina Sekyi would come to fear as the liability of "thinking 'in English'"[32]—was understood by this early nationalist father-figure as the best way to promote the conservative interest of the Gold Coast. In his terms, the concession of making the native intelligible "in English"—not just in the language but through Anglo-Western cognitive protocols as well—promised the payoff of protecting native institutions, and of developing them along their own lines. The Sarbah who desired the rationality of what he called "scientific colonization, in which the guiding spirit is sympathy" (*Fanti National Constitution,* xx), could appreciate as well the material and social progress of his country premised in the modern element impinging on it (albeit in an undesirable colonial form).

Sarbah was born in Cape Coast in 1864, the eldest son of the wealthy Fanti/Euro-African merchant prince John Sarbah and his wife Sarah. After completing his education at the local Wesleyan Boys' High School, he proceeded to England, where he was enrolled at Taunton School, matriculating in 1884. Refusing to enter commerce as his father had planned for him, the younger Sarbah got his father's permission to return to England to study law. There, entering Lincoln's Inn, he was called to the Bar in 1887. After his father passed on in 1892, Sarbah combined the running of the former's commercial enterprise with his law practice in Cape Coast. He had also by this time developed a keen interest in native law and custom and would embark on the archival research that resulted in the groundbreaking *Fanti Customary Laws.* Generous with his money and time, the civic-minded Sarbah was at the forefront of activity in the 1890s and 1900s to enhance public education in the Fanti area of the western Gold Coast. Sarbah's dream was of independent schools "which . . . would foster study and understanding of indigenous institutions and initiate an indigenous literature" (*Fanti Customary Laws,* xiii). His efforts led to the consolidation of Mfantsipim School in 1904 (the Wesleyan institution founded under a different name in 1876), then, as today, a leading institution where many of the prominent names in Gold Coast/Ghana nationalism were trained.[33] After using his legal skills and diplomatic savvy to successfully lead the reaction against the Crown's attempts to take over control of Gold Coast lands, Sarbah emerged as the leading Gold Coast public figure. In 1901, the same year in which he started his second paper, the *Gold Coast Weekly,* he was appointed an unofficial African representative to the Gold Coast legislature. Sarbah held his tenure as legislator until 1910, the year of his premature and much-lamented demise.

Sarbah dedicates his preface to *Fanti Customary Laws* to the lawyer G. E. Eminsang of Elmina, a friend of his father, whose "patriotism is well known." He does so on account of "how often you have encouraged me to . . . persevere in the task I had set myself, to reduce into writing the Customary Laws and Usages of the Fanti, Asanti, and other Akan inhabitants of the Gold Coast" (ix). If his inspiration comes from a patriot from the generation before him, the goal of Sarbah's literary activity is a patriotic one also. It is executed to bridge a yawning communicative gap between English colonizer and native, a gap whose existence is proving detrimental to the latter. Sarbah explains in this regard: "newly arrived European officials . . . having no intelligent person to explain things to them would fain say there were no Customary Laws" (ix).

The need felt by Sarbah for an "intelligent person" to explain the customary by *transcoding* it from orality to literacy, and *codifying* it as law therein, has its urgency in the historical developments of the turn of the nineteenth century. Under the old imperialism of the pre-1870s, influenced by the post-Abolitionist liberal ideology of Anglo-African partnership-for-progress, the British, as Edsman arguably points out, had "contented themselves with a kind of guiding mission" (26). The treaties the Crown negotiated with the various Gold Coast polities under this rubric of guidance did at least point to a recognition of the latter's nativity as a legitimate political quantity in the sphere of imperial relations. What is discernible under the old imperial order is the effort to evolve an Anglo-African political and diplomatic framework that more or less balanced multilateral interests. The new times after 1870 would however witness a change in "[t]he character of colonialism . . . from a civilizing mission to full-scale [law and order] administration" (*Lawyers,* 26). The New Imperialism thus marked the advent of colonial unilateralism, with an overbearing British presence increasingly dangerously exerting "a solvent influence over native rule which falls to pieces by mere proximity" (*Crown Colonies,* 75).

Effective African dispossession was the goal of the new-imperial juggernaut, as Sarbah points out:

The new Imperialism of recent times [has declared West African] territories undeveloped estates, to be specially exploited with all expedition . . . for the benefit and profit of Great Britain. While the policy was in vogue, much harm was done to British West Africa, for there were not a few Government officials . . . who thought it good policy to ridicule and try to break up aboriginal institutions of the people, to undermine the authority of their natural rulers, and to subordinate everything possible to the paramount claims of what they called Imperial uniformity. In the minds of such persons, the doctrine of the individualism or distinct characteristics of each nation or race had no existence; to introduce English laws wholesale, abolish what is peculiar to Africans, and to treat them as subject races saved them much trouble, patient study, and the effort of thinking. (*Fanti National Constitution,* 226)

Where colonial power conceded that there was a "native law" at all, the latter, on its own soil, was defined relative to English law as *foreign* law. "Native law," as a Gold Coast Supreme Court judge argued in 1891, "must stand on the same footing as foreign law and must be proved by the evidence of expert witnesses" (*Fanti Customary Laws,* 137). English law, which was written—the visible sign of its rationality—and could quote precedent, therefore, took precedence over native law. The latter, orally expressed, could only give reason for doubt as to whether it had the status of anything properly codified—whether, that is, it disclosed any inherent rationality and had any historical memory of its own.

In short, the English colonizer had law—recognized himself as such in the Universal—while the colonized Gold Coast native had, at worst, no law, at best, a not-yet-law—a mode of colonialist interpretation that left Gold Coast nativity locked in a past tense mode of political and sociocultural irrelevance. If the customary, and the native institutions which ratified and were ratified by it, were to be suffered by the colonizer to exist at all, then this was only insofar as they could be made accountable to an Anglo-British priority, a gesture that condemned them to certain distortion.

With Akan-Fanti custom, institutions, and the oral tradition of their expression under assault, not a few in the educated community of Cape Coast had come to feel at the turn of the nineteenth century a grim foreboding that the customary order was threatening to go under. For those who experienced the times this way, it had become crucial, therefore, to attempt to shore up local defenses against the destructive new-imperial flood. Sarbah, in this connection, informs his reader in the preface to *Fanti National Constitution* about the founding by the Cape Coast educated community in 1889 of the *Mfantsi Amanbuhu Fékuw* (Fanti National Political Society). The *Fékuw,* having become "dissatisfied with the demoralizing effects of certain European influences, determined to stop further encroachments into their nationality" (xvii). *Fanti Customary Laws* was the first outstanding contribution to the *Fékuw's* program of social conservation.

The *Fékuw's* aspirations, as Kimble points out, were not immediately political. What with this organization's metamorphosis in 1897 into the A.R.P.S., however, "social and political aspirations [were] fused" as the latter took on the task to "defend land rights and the social structure based upon them" (*Political History,* 331). Comparing the *Fékuw* and the A.R.P.S., Kimble characterizes the latter's activity as the properly "political" one. His notion of the political is unsatisfactory, however, for containing this category narrowly within a relativist defense of culture. The politics of culture of the A.R.P.S., then, appears in the light of a (Cape Coast) educated middle-class vanguard and its chiefly allies organizationally closing ranks and adopting at the frontline a protective stance towards custom. This reading sees frontline activism as simply polarizing: it casts the vanguardist politics of the A.R.P.S. in the image of a wall built to stay the new-imperial siege.

Yet locating "the political" at the frontline in a purely defensive cultural relativism tells only a part of a fascinating story of the complex navigation of this category in *Fékuw*/A.R.P.S. cultural nationalism, as demonstrated in Sarbah's two major works. Sarbah's works, written in English and not in the Fanti in their titles, show us the political at the frontline not in the image of a defensive wall but of a *bridge,* making the politics of culture amenable to being read, then, as a matter of a defensively positioned strategic offensive. For Sarbah shows us that what he defends, a customary nativity, is paradoxically defended in his ability to translationally project it in the terms furnished by, and into, that against which it is being defended.

Looking at Sarbah's works, therefore, one sees a nationalism obliged to politically negotiate its culturalist claims between relativist purity (difference) and universalist parity (similarity). One sees a nationalism striving to reconcile the romance of past essence—the *priority* of a native heritage—and a rationalist pragmatism. He notes in this regard: "One has already thought proper to remind the educated inhabitant of the Gold Coast . . . to review his mental equipment, and settle down to solve the hard task of adapting all the best features of his national institutions for use in the inspiring work of good government" (*Fanti National Constitution,* 245). What urges itself on the middle-class intellectual as a contingently practical necessity is finding by way of the *ratio* of the colonial-modern present the *originality* required to transcode and translate a native priority. In other words, this intellectual is called upon to effect at the frontline, as a political matter of defensively guaranteeing its survival, nativity's modernist transvaluation.

Regarding the matter of the political as bridgework, as cultural translation, then, two major conceptual-cum-ideological propositions, one "spatial" the other "temporal," define it in Sarbah's oeuvre. In the first and spatial sense, Sarbah must labor to make customary nativity leave its confinement in Nothingness, the nonplace where, and the nonpresence in which, a Eurocentric discourse of Africanism had immured it. Customary nativity must "cross over" in order to stake a claim to a share, stage its full presence, and demand its recognition, in the "space" of the Universal.

The second and related endeavor, the temporal one, discloses a double order of negotiation at the frontline which requires Sarbah to bridge (or mediate) time past and time present. On the one hand, he must repackage the homegrown vintage of old time in bottles of new mintage, bearing an alien stamp, in order, as it were, to guarantee the continued saleability of this native vintage. This task amounts to bringing the essential precolonial past forward, rehabilitating its substance in the forms of the colonial-modern present—forms whose normativity is underwritten by colonial power—and thus invest it with the political relevance importunately demanded by this present. Sarbah must *nativize* the modern, an aspect of his work that accords with Soyinka's notion of the secular vision, which, as we have seen, labors to combine "the re-creation of a pre-colonial African world-view with eliciting its transposable elements into modern potential."

On the other hand, Sarbah is enjoined to *modernize* the native. And that is to say if the (native) past must cross over in a forward-linkage with the (colonial-modern) present, so also must this present, in a reverse crossover, inhabit the past in a backward linkage. In this aspect of his work, Sarbah seeks the infusion into customary nativity of borrowed modern elements for the ends of this nativity's auto-effective constitution. The thesis of "auto-effectivity" is elaborated below.

As Sarbah addresses the first goal of making the native visible in the Universal, we find him contesting the nineteenth-century narrative that produces the European-African encounter as the story of Europe the Universal, or full Self-Presence, in creative contemplation of Africa the full Absence before it. This is Europe, then, determining after the fashion of the biblical God of original creation, "let there be light," in relation to the blank darkness that is Africa. Encounter however, Sarbah insists, was not the story of (European) Presence, endowed exclusively with creativity, happening upon (African) Absence: it was a meeting of two human Presences, both similarly endowed with the powers of (self)-creation. And this claim, in *Fanti Customary Laws,* is made by way of "ancient [European] authors," Africa watchers of old represented in the 1665 work the "Golden Coast of Guinney," who were presumably free from the prejudices of their nineteenth-century counterparts. A study of the works of the former "abundantly proves that when, in 1481, the Portuguese navigators and other European trading adventurers first appeared on the Gold Coast, they found an organized society having kings, rulers, institutions, and a system of customary laws" (v).

The claim here must be that the ancient European observers of the African scene recognized their humanity reflected in Gold Coast nativity. This nativity may have been different in specifics of form and detail from the world they knew as people from another part of the planet. However, it was comparatively similar to what they knew—was intelligible on that basis—in showing evidence of popular relations regulated by institutions of government and law. Gold Coast nativity, in short, accorded for these observers with universal norm; its native worlds, in this humanist-universalist sense, were substitutable for their own. The Europeans acknowledged in other words that the relationship between the Self and Other of encounter was a metonymic one.

The contemporary problem Sarbah has to deal with standing at the colonial frontline, however, is the (threatened) abrogation by the Anglo-European of the warranty of humanist recognition vouchsafed Gold Coast and African nativity by the ancient writers. For in the matter of the Law, imperial representation, backed by power, has turned England as metonym into England as metaphor, reducing the whole to a (mere) part. This reduction has made the ethnonym "English" and the Universal into an equivalence: English law in its colonial application has "lost" its Englishness and become Law as such—the sole embodiment of the General Principle. Under the circumstances, the customary which should co-occupy and compete with Englishness in the space which it occupies as Law-as-such has become "foreign." Recognition for the customary, in the field traversed by colonial law, has thus come to mean the customary being made beholden to English forms of legal intelligibility and procedure.

For Sarbah, however, to concede that the customary as law must find its intelligibility strictly according to the interpretive canons and procedural protocols of English law amounted to sanctioning the absorption of customary law by, and not its equally valid coresidence in the Universal with, English law. "It cannot . . . be correct to say," he opines, "that the native laws and customs are foreign matters which, unless proved, cannot be recognized or noticed by a judge" (18). Arguing against this tendency, Sarbah points out further:

> A learned writer has recently said, in discussing Indian topics, it cannot be too strongly asserted that there is great danger in too indiscriminately apply-ing the technicalities of the English Law to a country like India, whose insti-tutions, popular traditions, and prejudices are so entirely different from those of England. Indian customs are not to be tested by the arbitrary rules pecu-liar to English law, but rather . . . by the rules of universal applicability. (16)

Universal applicability in the domain of the law for Sarbah, then, is not a matter of substituting the imperial One for the imperialized All—what Sarbah decries as a stifling "imperial uniformity"—on the basis of the pre-tense that the former's rationality is exhaustive. Rather, it is a matter of working out, on an egalitarian basis, a comparative jurisprudence.

There is a counter-argument confronting Sarbah, however, the one that says that two systems are comparable only if they are similar in certain respects. Could the orally mediated customary be considered law, its ele-ments amenable to comparison with those that obtain in what is consid-ered law proper, that is, statute (and written) law? Sarbah offers this an-swer:

> [J]urists . . . have always felt a difficulty in so defining the term Law, as would make it comprehend not only the express enactments by a sovereign legislature, which Austin and his disciples alone admit to be law properly so-called, but also those rules regulating conduct and usages, which are habitu-ally acted upon in the ordinary affairs of everyday life, in communities hav-ing no regular political organization, without at the same time confusing mere notions of abstract morality which do not even possess the essentials of what Austin calls positive morality. (20)

But the difficulty of the jurists appears to Sarbah to be an academic one. For "it is universally admitted that wherever there is an assemblage of per-sons united for common purposes or ends, there must be some notion of law; for mankind have, as Cicero observed, a genius for law" (20). Looking at the communities of "the Gold Coast, Asanti, and neighbouring states," Sarbah finds operative in them "pre-existing rule[s] sanctioned by the will of the community, [that] which in the history of every nation is found to be long anterior to the more formal written law" (22–23). "'Law is every-where built on usage'" (22), Sarbah quoting an English authority, argues, and this universal truism applies to the African communities he has mentioned. These, as *human* communities, display

> much of those positive rights and obligations constituting that Austinian
> Positive Morality, which may be called the Customary Law, and which each
> person can enforce against his neighbour, either by means of the village council
> sitting and acting judicially as a local tribunal, or by invoking . . . the silent
> force of popular sanction according to an [*sic*] usage long established or well
> known, all of which more or less possess an imperative attribute, and there-
> fore . . . partake of the character of law. (21)

Sarbah's argument ultimately is that, attuned to the specific circumstances and conditions of its own place, Gold Coast customary law is *cus-*
tomary and is different in being that. But the defensive argument is one
that has also to step on the offensive. For this reason, Sarbah is obliged to
carry this difference into the heart of the Universal in a demonstration that
this customary law is, and shares the normativity of, *Law*. Therein, it is on
a humanistic par with, and comparably similar to, English law.

Sarbah's offensively mounted defense, engaging the adversary on universal terrain, reconfigures the same inclusively such that it ceases to be one
of exclusive habitation by this adversary. If his ends are "cooperationist," as
Langley rightly has it, this cooperationism in fact is built on a paradoxical
principle. His work, in proving that the Different (i.e., in the form of the
customary) is Similar (i.e., as Law), successfully inserts customary law into
the colonial order (as in the postindependence order which succeeds it) as
a principle, and in the form, of a *competitive* complement. Sarbah's cooperation has competition self-consciously built into it. It is this point that
Attoh Ahuma, praising Sarbah's pioneer endeavor, raises in his review of
the second edition of *Fanti Customary Laws* (1903):

> [*Fanti Customary Laws*] was the very *Deus ex Machina* in those sad days of
> promiscuous and indiscriminate legislation, when the ordinational feats of
> our Star Chamber were assuming proportions out of all cess with the genius
> of progressive history, and in direct antagonism to the spirit of advancing
> light and thought of the day. . . .
> 　　[Sarbah's] codification of our Customary Laws has . . . put the Legislature
> on its guard, and enabled it to proceed in the multiplication of ordinances
> with a cautiousness born of higher intelligence, practical sympathy, and happy
> discrimination, coupled with conspicuous desire for the conservation of peace
> and justice among the people of the Colony and Protectorate.[34]

Sarbah's success may indeed be praiseworthy; however, as real as the
victories of a politics of negotiated defeat are, they are also always precari-

ous. And, under the colonial order, Sarbah's victory would not be an exception to this rule. With the consolidation of indirect rule by colonial power in the Gold Coast, Sarbah's success will turn out to have been something of a Pyrrhic victory. For his modernist delineation of the customary, as much in substance as in its making available a precedent, will come to be expediently misappropriated by a manipulative colonial power and its local chiefly functionaries. Against Sarbah's own best intentions, the operatives of colonial power will fall back on his precedent as authority to ratify, not mollify, the domination of British colonialism.[35]

The customary would be rendered competitive not with respect to relations between colonizer and colonized but, in a stratagem of divide and rule, with respect to relations within nativity itself, between the educated middle-class native fraction and the chiefly elite. For a long time, to block the emergence of a transcendent anticolonial consciousness, the British would employ "custom" as a weapon against those with a coherent nationalist consciousness, the educated middle-class elite. In the name of the sanctity of Tradition, the influence of this elite would be kept away from the many watertight tribal domains British colonialism had invented, and to whose "sovereign" laws and customary authorities it had bound—in a "decentralized despotism"[36]—the divided masses of a Gold Coast nativity.

An oppositional politics such as Sarbah's cannot help but fight on terrain it has not chosen, as Chamber's points out, and this paradox renders such a politics also vulnerable to misreading. Thus with an intent more or less to undercut Sarbah's nativist project, Edsman approvingly reports that "When Sekyi invited the opinion of Justice L. E. V. M'Carthy [on *Fanti Customary Laws* in 1938], the latter expressed doubts about the purity of Sarbah's traditionalism" (*Lawyers,* 191). Sarbah's endeavor is flawed in the Sierra Leone–born M'Carthy's view—a view endorsed by the apparently uncomprehending Edsman—because he "uses English legal terms in describing Fanti customs [and] he at times confuses the past with the present." Additionally, "he does not always distinguish the original customary law and the law as administered in his day, even though it may have been affected by modern influences" (qtd. in *Lawyers,* 191).

M'Carthy and his latter-day historian-supporter Edsman are blind to the element of negotiation—the simultaneous "yes" and "no"—that drives Sarbah's endeavor. The two are guilty of overlooking the politics in the pioneer nationalist's translation, a politics which seeks self-consciously to make "Fanti" convertible into, and thinkable in, "English"; and, in that, to institute the competitive interchangeability of the former with the latter. What an invalidation of Sarbah's endeavor amounts to, however, is an endorsement more or less of the colonial will-to-power registered in the imperious declaration in 1922 of the then Attorney General of the Gold Coast. This colonial functionary definitively dismissed the argument for the parity of English law and Gold Coast customary law in the following terms:

> [T]he law of this colony only recognises . . . native customary laws . . . insofar as they are consistent with the enactments of the Colonial legislature and with such of the enactments of the Imperial Parliament which apply to this Colony. These limitations already make considerable inroad into any fanciful doctrine of the absolute sacrosanctity of native customary law in the Gold Coast Colony. (qtd. in *Lawyers,* 50)

Colonial stratagem reveals itself in these pronouncements as one of keeping *behind*—as inferior—customary nativity, a stratagem whose political effect in the here and now of the colonial order is to keep this nativity *down,* as subordinately subservient.

It is in terms of this colonial manipulation of the temporality of nativity that we must gauge the motivation of, and the effects sought in, the navigation conducted by Sarbah as translator. His aim was to change the time of the customary, bringing it forward so that it would share the same temporality as the colonial modern. And the conduct of this aspect of Sarbah's navigation—inventing the native in an overlapping temporality with the modern—appears very much in the terms we find Blyden philosophically laying out, in 1881, in "The Aims and Methods of a Liberal Education for Africans."[37]

Blyden may have been an ardent apostle of African purity, but we have seen his nationalism, engaged on a quest to institute Africa as a competitively worldly power, as equally ardent about African parity. Blyden confronts a problem that he must philosophically navigate in that he had come to see that his would-be competitive institution of Africa is obliged to seek its ontological intelligibility in the terms of the authority and power, cognitive and cultural, undeniably wielded by the imperial European Other. In other words, for Africa to be like Europe in authority and power required that it must image its passage towards this competitively worldly being-like-Europe in the very model of the competitive available to itself— which was no other than Europe. The desire for parity mandated for Africa that it speak its being otherwise, in the paradox of European-mediated self-translation. But did not speaking Africa otherwise compromise the very competitive principle this was intended to accomplish? How, that is, did one make Africa over by way of European translation without giving this principle away?

For Blyden, mulling over the African relevance of the European liberal heritage, the answer that returns is that what is contained in this heritage has a human priority. In other words, this heritage is neither a priori nor exclusively European; rather through and beyond European cultural expression is to be perceived something transcendently human(ist). Blyden argues the point on the basis that "culture is one, and the general effects of true culture are the same" (240). In effect, while there are cultures—culture as a relativist and pluralist postulate—they all tend towards a humanistic point of convergence. Blyden the relativist does not identify this convergence, however, as a point where cultures would have lost their essential differences. This postulate appears in his argument rather as a thesis about developmental potential built without exception into all cultures, a potential given to them in their relativity to *similarly* attain worldly "elevation," as he puts it. Blyden is contending on this basis that the progressive *ratio* identified with the European Enlightenment is not in fact Europe's sole property but a property of culture universally, immanent in all.

A historicist and evolutionist postulate follows in Blyden's argument in which the progressive *ratio* realizes itself developmentally in different forms of human cultural expression.

> The special road which has led to the success and elevation of the Anglo-Saxon is not that which will lead to the success and elevation of the Negro, *though we shall resort to the same means of general culture* which has enabled the Anglo-Saxon to find out for himself the way in which he ought to go. (240; emphasis added)

Blyden advances two claims here on behalf of the Anglo-Saxon. First is the relativist postulate that he is exceptional; and, second, that this exceptionality following its own "special road" *as such* has arrived at a consistency with the general, a consistency that conferred on it competitive authorization in the universal. The competitive Universal—Blyden's state of "elevation," which apparently coincides with "general culture"—is that potential always already in the Anglo-Saxon self, which, over developmental time, this self has found, cultivated, and come to embrace as itself *otherwise*. The pioneer African nationalist hands his audience a thesis in which cultural difference is competitively *convertible* over time, and apparently without self-loss, into humanistic consistency. In the exception, it would seem, the general rule is proved.

On this thesis of convertible difference then is borne Blyden's logic of the exceptional Negro who must find his way as such also into competitive authorization and recognition in the Universal. If the Negro needed to use the "same means" as the familiar Anglo-Saxon, this is so to the extent that the latter's culture, in its elevation, pointed in a similar direction in which others, following different paths, might go. In the Anglo-Saxon is to be found the *identical means* by which the *different ends* of the Negro's elevated—because it is competitive—convertibility can be attained. For Blyden, then, if it is not to be the Negro borrowing the substantive Anglo-Saxon robes themselves, then it has to be a discriminating appropriation of their pattern, their informing blueprint, that element which he grasps as transcendently humanist. It is this transcendent blueprint, acquired by way of Europe's Anglo-Saxon representative, that was to be put by Blyden to the "translational" work of rehabilitating the African body in substantively different robes as it competitively looked towards its own universalist elevation.

The Negro remade *through* the Anglo-Saxon in the universalist *likeness of*, but not remade *as*, this Anglo-Saxon: bristling with paradox, the philosophical negotiation of partial concession and partial withholding going on here is a most difficult one. But it is also necessary if Blyden is to win some cognitive and ontological space—room for maneuver—wherein the relativist purity and competitive parity he desires in his conceptualizing of a Negro/African modern may be reconciled. If he concedes that the Negro is behind the Anglo-Saxon in time, how to negotiate the forward linkage that brings what is behind into the same temporality as, and on a competitive par with, what is ahead? Thus it is that Blyden has to capitulate to the necessity and compromise of construing that which is behind, his Negro/ Africa, in the likeness of that which is ahead, a Europe which as such already wears the competitive crown of the Universal.

We may draw on Blyden's difficult philosophical negotiation for a model to account for Sarbah's practice. Sarbah, too, must conceive nativity in a politics of survival, a politics which will guarantee that this nativity lagging behind coloniality is not left behind in obsolescence but is forwardly linked in potentiation with the latter. But to be competitive, Sarbah's customary order, the nativity of yore, is enjoined to derive its potency in the present in a translational piggybacking on the English Other. And for Sarbah, in thinking itself otherwise—i.e., in (English) translation—a nativity lagging behind may enact this empowering catching up with a colonial modern inasmuch as its mode of being is *demonstrably* in cross-cultural conformity with "English" rationality. Sarbah appears to see that his case is a stronger one if proof for this demonstration of conformity came from the other side; that is, if he could bring someone English forward who would acknowledge that in the customary order of yore he saw a reflection of (his)

"English" rationality. The merit of such an acknowledgement would be in its surrender of the notion that "English" rationality is exclusively English property. Very early in *Fanti Customary Laws,* therefore, Sarbah calls to the stand an expert witness, a Sir J. Smalman Smith. This Englishman "in the Full Court held at Cape Coast Castle on October 24, 1887 . . . stated, 'I have found the native laws and customs always founded on very good and intelligible reasons, which are perfectly rational and consistent'" (xii).

Smalman Smith's concession that the native laws of the Gold Coast are rational comes from one who belongs on the side of English colonial power—a power otherwise adamant that it would concede to the customary no such rationality. The Englishman provides a small opening for the customary to get its foot in the colonial door. That is to say, he offers an opportunity for a competent authority to step forward to demonstrate how the overpowered customary may more or less cohabit with colonial power in a shared temporality. We might in this regard see Sarbah, the native intellectual, taking advantage of Smith's opening and invading the colonial mansion, so to speak, by making his nativity comprehensively "go English" in a book-length demonstration. He is able to appropriate, in his "going English" with the native, the rationalist procedures and methods wielded by power, bringing them to the task of cultural translation. He is to be seen mounting this translation in a search for competitive similarity, under the colonial order, on behalf of the native difference.

Taking a defensive look behind at nativity is for Sarbah a turning of the visage of this nativity to face ahead; the backward turn has to lead to a necessary return forward. What this forward linkage entails in Sarbah's work is that the Gold Coast customary order, as viewed through "Fanti," sits alongside the colonial-modern order, as viewed through "English," in a temporality of competitive equivalence. Hence it is not so much that Sarbah "confuses the past with the present," as M'Carthy and Edsman will have it, as that he strategically con*flates* the (living) past with the present. For an aware Sarbah, the political necessities of the Gold Coast situation at the turn of the nineteenth century required a nativity of yore—whose temporality is *then*—to leap across the gap of time to accommodate itself to present political exigencies, inhabiting a colonial-modern temporality of *now.*

Nor, finally, is the purist view that Sarbah's enterprise is irredeemably flawed because he uses English legal terms in describing Fanti customs a valid one. For that argument requires of Sarbah's enterprise that it remain a purely defensive one—this in a colonial situation where confining oneself as a native intellectual to an unreconstructed relativist view of culture was to help colonialism along in confirming the obsolescence and political irrelevance of nativity. As in Blyden's example above, therefore, Sarbah, negotiating the transition that will bring the *ratio* immanent in African customary nativity forward, to an elevated state, must navigate between confirming the relativist exception and appropriating for this exception, beyond a reductive relativism, what Blyden calls the "same means of general culture." Like Blyden, whose "Negro" must in paradoxical necessity appear otherwise in the likeness of the "Anglo-Saxon," Sarbah is enjoined by the exigencies of his colonial situation to find the similar-in-the-different by way of rationalistically "going English" with the native.

The expression "gone Fantee" is a pejorative invented by the British in colonial West Africa. It evokes the horror of sinking below culture and civilization, defined as the property of Europe, and regressing into "savage" and "barbarous" African ways. The expression in Sarbah's hands takes on a new value, however: not the negativity of civilizational backsliding, but the positivity of the frontline intellectual linking his (cosmopolitan) modernity backward with nativity towards the end of the latter's renovation. Sarbah thus presents himself in *Fanti National Constitution* as "[f]ully convinced that it is better to be called by one's own name than be known by a foreign one" and states "that it is possible to acquire Western learning and be expert in scientific attainments without neglecting one's mother tongue" (xvii). He reminds his reader that "the African's dress has a closer resemblance to the garb of the Grecian and Roman," ancient cultures "the acquisition of whose languages and philosophies is still promoted in modern European Universities, [with] the knowledge of them [having become] the standard of liberal culture" (xvii-xviii). African dress, therefore, "should not be thrown aside even if one wears European dress during business hours," for has not non-Western "Japan since shown it is possible to retain one's national costume and yet excel in wisdom and knowledge"? (xviii).

A pseudonymous writer, "Lux," writing in the *Gold Coast Leader* of 18th March, 1905, concurs with Sarbah about the Japanese. The man of Japan "having dealings with a European house will appear in the white man's office in European clothing; but you would not know the same man, if you saw him in the bosom of his family." If the Japanese have been able to learn "the methods of the European [and] improve . . . upon them"; if they "assimilated and assimilated well to the purpose," then "Lux" could only conclude that "The bedrock fact in connection with national development that we, as a people, must recognize is that you can assimilate without losing your identity."[38]

Japan as an example of non-Western modernity in an *achieved* form, after its Meiji Reforms in the 1860s, has persisted as model for frontline

African intellectuals in their imagining of African modernity. Thus what Sarbah and "Lux" wish for along the lines of Japanese modernity in the 1900s reappears in Achebe's 1980s essay "What Has Literature Got to Do with It?" And for Achebe, as for his preindependence frontline counterparts from the Gold Coast, what Africa can learn from Japan is translation accomplished in a backward linkage, a reverse crossover that has made the modern "go native." Dwelling in meditation on the unfulfilled problematic of the African modern in this reverse crossover mode, Achebe recalls the words of a Professor Kinichiro Toba:

> "My grandfather graduated from the University of Tokyo at the beginning of the 1880s. His notebooks were full of English. My father graduated from the same university in 1920 and half his notes were filled with English. When I graduated a generation later my notes were all in Japanese. So . . . it took three generations for us to consume western civilization totally via the means of our own language."[39]

Achebe provides this gloss:

> If Professor Toba's story is at all typical of the last 100 years of Japanese history (and we have no reason to believe otherwise), we can conclude that as Japan began the countdown to its spectacular technological lift-off it was also systematically recovering lost ground in its traditional mode of cultural expression. In one sense then it was travelling away from its old self towards a cosmopolitan, modern identity, while in another sense it was journeying back to regain a threatened past and selfhood. (*Hopes and Impediments*, 160.)

It is a mark of Japan's spectacular genius, in Achebe's view, to have "comprehend[ed] the dimensions of this gigantic paradox" and to have "coax[ed] from it such unparalleled inventiveness." (160)

The modern may have come to Japan in the first instance as Western-flavored vintage, useful but alien. However, it has been a matter, after the encounter with the West, of Japan, in a superlative act of creative alchemy, so steeping this vintage in essences of its own ancient native manufacture as to have stamped on this foreign vintage a more or less authentic Japanese flavor. Modernity has lost its quality of otherness in Japanese transsubstantiation—or "cannibalization," as Professor Toba's use of "consume" suggests—and has become, in this qualitative transmogrification of Other into Self, an extension of Japanese nativity, at once preserving and enhancing the survivability of its difference. This, then, is the datum of auto-effectivity wherein one culture, obliged to borrow from another, has so managed this liability, in self-creating alchemy, as to have transformed it into a relative enhancement of the borrower's own possibilities.

Appendix XII of *Fanti Customary Laws,* the last item in the book, comes as something of a surprise to the reader, for after three hundred pages of English text, Sarbah hands him a "Deed of Conveyance in the Fanti Language." Yet the scriptural form which bears and preserves the Fanti substance is not Fanti-derived but Western. The frontline intellectual "going Fantee" with the modern obliges "Fanti" to scripturally wear a borrowed garb, a circumstance that may be seen as robbing Fanti of a self-produced and self-perpetuating authenticity.

Might this point to ontological uncertainty at the frontline, a problem not so much of being neither fish nor fowl but of the fish inauthentically wishing it were a fowl (or vice versa)? Not if we read this frontline navigation in terms of Sarbah's, "Lux's," and Achebe's accessing the example of a consummate Japanese modernity, authentically Japanese, as a model of cultural auto-effectivity pointing towards what African modernity might achieve for itself. On the one hand, then, we have the forwardly linking exercise by Sarbah of converting native orality to English literacy. On the other hand, we see the pioneer nationalist performing the reverse crossover, the backwardly linking work of bringing modern literacy to the preservation, enhancement, and maximization of the life-chances of this orality. Sarbah, experimentally displacing a borrowed literacy into native orality, was dreaming the modern in a locally cannibalized form. He was willing a transsubstantiation, in accordance with the tenets of auto-effectivity, of modernity's otherness into the authentic self-reproduction of Gold Coast nativity.

The patriotic vocation of building an auto-effective national culture entailed, therefore, a disciplined modernist "going Fantee/native." But was the European-educated middle class equipped with the alchemizing (self)-consciousness and originating (self)-will adequate to the nativist task of transsubstantiating the otherness of its heritage of Western modernity? Sekyi is doubtful as he mulls over this question in his "Education with Particular Reference to a West African University." Sekyi remonstrates in this piece against "how our countries have been flooded with a new type of African . . . understand[ing] neither what European teaching has left it as a heritage of its subservience nor what ancestral Africans had bequeathed as the legitimate inheritance of the sons of the soil."[40] Sekyi's diagnosis, Blydean in essence, was one that he shared with his nationalist fellow travelers of the early twentieth century. And for these aware nationalists it was a diagnosis that mandated a crusade to cure the middle class of its colonially imposed false consciousness, and redirecting this consciousness restored to its native or African self towards the institution of nationalist auto-effectivity. What follows below examines this dimension of early Gold Coast nationalist thought and ideological practice.

Nation's Call: Meditations on a Post-Ancillary Middle-Class (Self)-Consciousness

[T]he despotic and overruling method which has been pursued in [the Negro's] education, by good meaning and unphilosophical philanthropists has…entirely mastered and warped his mind. . . . All educated Negroes suffer from a kind of slavery in many ways far more subversive of the real welfare of the race than the ancient physical fetters. The slavery of the mind is far more destructive than that of the body.
—Blyden to Pope Hennessy, Governor of Sierra Leone, Dec. 11th, 1872

[T]he adoption of European names was a result of the introduction here of Christian ideas. . . . [There has been a] Europeanising of Akan-Fanti names resulting in the strangest medley of syllables wildly joined together into dreadful hybrids such as Aikins for Ekyin or Kyinbua, Hayfron for Afuna, Ackinney for Akyin, or Brookman for Budukuma etc. . . . Now, those who think "in English" on the subject consider it unbecoming the status of "civilized" man to encourage his children to bear names which they call "barbarous" because they are not "Christian."
—Kobina Sekyi, "The Meaning of the Expression Thinking 'in English'"

Breathes there a man with soul so dead, / Who never to himself hath said, / This is my own, my native land!
—Attoh Ahuma quoting Sir Walter Scott, in
Memoirs of West African Celebrities

And so, it is not I who make a meaning for myself, but it is the meaning that was already there, pre-existing, waiting for me.
—Fanon, *Black Skin, White Masks*

In 1914, Kobina Sekyi's play *The Blinkards,* a tragicomic satire lampooning the Anglo-Fanti as mimic men and women, was performed in Cape Coast. "The George Bernard Shaw of West Africa," as Sekyi was nicknamed, was born into a Cape Coast Euro-African (or "Anglo-Fanti," as Sekyi precisely dubbed it) family in 1892. His paternal grandfather's surname, Sackey, was an anglicized version of Sekyi; the grandson, in a gesture of re-Africanization, reverted to the latter spelling with his grandfather's permission. Sekyi's mother, Wilhelmina, to continue to detail the Euro-African connection, was the daughter of the wealthy Cape Coast merchant W. E. Pietersen. Between 1903 and 1909, Sekyi attended Mfantsipim Boys' School. After Mfantsipim, Sekyi moved on to the University of London, where he gained a degree in Philosophy. He returned to England in 1915, after a two-year stint at home as a teacher and commentator on social and literary issues, to study law. Sekyi qualified as a barrister in 1918, with an M.A. in philosophy and a membership in the Aristotelian Society also under his belt.

Ayo Langley, in his 1974 introduction to *The Blinkards*, has noted that Sekyi was raised "as an Anglo-African in a society whose educated members were brought up to believe that all things African were retrograde and were to be despised, and that thorough anglicisation (and Christianisation) was the passport to 'civilisation' and 'progress.'" And the "evidence . . . indicates that Sekyi accepted these values. . . . Up to 1910, therefore, when Sekyi sailed for England to study he was, as he later confessed . . . an 'Anglomaniac'" and "ashamed of most things African."[41]

England had, however, turned out to be a disillusioning experience for Sekyi. Victim of English racial prejudice, Sekyi, the black Englishman, had lost his innocence, and was forced, in his early twenties, to turn the searchlight of the question "Who am I?" on himself. Events that took place on his second trip to England deepened this psycho-existential crisis. The boat on which he was traveling, as Langley reports, had been torpedoed—World War I was raging—and Sekyi had managed to scramble onto a lifeboat. A European "started shouting at him to get off, as . . . a black man, had no right to be alive when whites were drowning" (introd. to *Blinkards*, 7). How much Sekyi's lifelong uncompromising nativism—which saw him vigorously campaigning against "denationalisation" and for racial "self-respect"—owes to this incident is worth some speculation.

The Blinkards features characters with names denoting generic types. There are the risible (and memorable) Mrs. Brofusem, "a Leader of Fashion," and her merchant husband Mr. Brofusem, "been-tos"[42] both; and there is also Mr. Onyimdzi, the magus figure of the play. If "Onyimdzi" in Akan-Fanti means "knowledgeable," a name conferring on its bearer a quality of inner spiritual grace, "Brofusem" literally means the affectation of "European ways." Hence the two characters bearing the latter name are to be seen as standing for those middle-class Euro-Africans who, affecting embourgeoisement, had modeled their lifestyle, dress, thought, and behavior along Anglo-European lines. The damning irony of the playwright contrives to show us the discrepancy between the artificial ways of these hybrid civilizational converts and the tropical setting. There is no objective fit, *The Blinkards* insists continually, between the mentality, almost wholly alienated, of these Anglo-Fanti and the "natural," ancestrally made-to-fit Akan-Fanti cultural environment in which the actuality of their bodily being lives, breathes, and moves.

It is the vitiation of an organic connection between self and place, between the imaginary order that confers an identity on the bourgeois aspirants of the middle class and the objective sociocultural order of the Akan-Fanti, therefore, that Sekyi is at pains to point out in his drama. And his absurdist thesis is that people like Mrs. Brofusem—the accusation of cultural (self)-betrayal falls heavily on this self-described "lady," less so on the henpecked and weakly resisting husband who is forced to do her Anglomaniacal bidding—live in an "as if" mode. Their identity is a shallowly worn pretend identity; they live, that is, as if they are in England and are English. For these of bourgeois pretensions, therefore, England, in a distant elsewhere, has cast a long spellbinding shadow over their Fantiland; and, worse, the shadow is usurping the reality, the Fanti substance. There is an unnatural inversion here, for, absurdly, the English shadow, pervasive, has become "real" on Fanti and Gold Coast soil, while that which should be the substantive Fanti/Gold Coast reality, increasingly denuded of its substance, is fast becoming a shadow of the shadow.

Underlining this theme is the attempt by Mrs. Brofusem, herself an imperfect English clone, to convert Miss Tsiba—the daughter of the wealthy but unlettered cocoa magnate, Mr. Tsiba—from her unspoilt native ways into an equally imperfect clone of her Anglomaniacal self. Sekyi works a near-tragic subplot out of this. Mrs. Brofusem, abetted by Mr. Tsiba, worshipper at the shrine of all things English, flouts traditional sanction by working out an English-style liaison, illegitimate according to customary law, between Miss Tsiba and Mr. Okadu, a half-baked Anglo-Fanti youth. A shotgun marriage between the two, complete with an English-style wedding, must follow to conceal the scandal of Miss Tsiba's having been made pregnant by her beau. Ultimately, though, native law annulling the marriage prevails as the young barrister, Mr. Onyimdzi, wins an important battle on its behalf in the colonial court.

These antisocial developments, as Sekyi reads them, account for the lone crusade carried out by the magus figure in the play, Mr. Onyimdzi. Onyimdzi, the self-conscious bearer of a normative nativist knowledge, is in the drama the representative of the critical voice of the playwright. At the end, happily, Mr. Onyimdzi, preaching his nativist philosophy, is able to reconvert an educable Mrs. Brofusem to the wholesome ways of Akan-Fanti tradition.

Part of Sekyi's delineation of a Gold Coast absurd is that the Brofusems and other imitators of English ways, laughably copying the superficial, have missed the true essence of Englishness. No more at home in what they copy than they are in the local traditions from which they have distanced themselves, they are at once distorted (English) copies and denatured (native) originals—existentially speaking, neither here nor there. This is tellingly illustrated, for instance, in scene two of the third act of *The Blinkards,* which makes the audience privy to a meeting of the Cape Coast Cosmopolitan Club. One of the members of the Club reads a treatise on "How to be a Gentleman," his reading punctuated by words of assent and encouragement from the floor. Below is a portion of the proceedings:

> READER "In conclusion of this treatise on 'How to be a Gentleman,' I must embrace opportunity to impress force on you to say that without tailors and hatters and shoemakers, gentlemen, we are nothing."
>
> 1ST MEMBER Well said!
> 2ND MEMBER Praise God!
> 3RD MEMBER A Daniel come to judgement!
> VICE PRESIDENT Amen!
> PRESIDENT (*Gavelling sharply*) Order! Silence in court! Continue, brother.
>
> READER (Bowing to president, then to members) I must express to you my thanks and gratitude, gentlemen, for your most vociferous ovation. (*Reading*) "To continue my dissertation, I say, without tailors and hatters and shoemakers, we will be savages."
> 1ST MEMBER God forbid!
> 2ND MEMBER Heaven forfend!
> 3RD MEMBER *Deo* not being *volente*!
>
> READER "Without these people, we sill [*sic*] walk barefoot. We will wear native dress. Our feet and arms will be naked, and indecent. But with the help of these useful workmen we have mentioned, and I must add, with the help of European merchants, who have given us ham and bacon and milk and sugar and—"
>
> 1ST MEMBER Marmalade
> READER "—and marmalade and jam and lemonade and beer and stout and champagne—ripe, mellifluous, elevating champagne, and—"

2ND MEMBER Good old fizz!
READER "—brandy and whiskey—"
TREASURER And soda
READER "—and gin and rum."
3RD MEMBER And vermouth.

READER "Without European drinks we have only palm-wine to drink, which only bushmen drink. No scholar who wants to be a gentleman must drink palm-wine. It is better to be placed in a state of obliviousness of surroundings and circumstances and environments by European drinks than by palm-wine: it is more gentlemanly. In August, when it is too cold, there is nothing like whiskey or vermouth to keep you warm. And on Sundays, before going to Chapel, or Church, which is more fashionable, it is good to take a little gin and bitters as an appetiser, in order to relish the sermon. One word more: to be a gentleman, we must imitate Europeans." (*Sits amid loud cheers*). (91–93)

As the solecisms and malapropisms of the mimic men proliferate, Sekyi underlines the relevance for the Gold Coast of W. E. B. Du Bois's absurdist analysis of the situation of the Negro in America. The black person's existence at the diasporic frontline, according to Du Bois, "yields him no true self-consciousness." He is left inauthentically "measuring [his] soul by the tape" furnished by another, the white world, which "looks on in amused contempt and pity."[43] The epigraph to *The Blinkards* is Robert Burns's "O, wad some pow'r the giftie gi'e us/Tae see oursel as ithers see us," and in that Sekyi captures a sentiment similar to that of Du Bois.

Sekyi would go on in 1918 to finish *The Anglo-Fanti*,[44] the fictional autobiography of Kwesi Onyidzin, "Onyidzin" literally meaning "Nameless"—in effect, he who possesses only a shadow self, and hence no true self-presence in the world to speak of. This time it would be a tragic study in Western acculturation and African alienation. The existential theme of the African whose being is neither here nor there is given a much darker treatment by Sekyi compared to the tone and mood he brought to the same in *The Blinkards*. If in the latter, being neither fish nor fowl is the laughable—and potentially curable—problem of shallow mimics, in the former it is the problem of the highly self-aware and preternaturally sensitive Anglo-Fanti intellectual, the question of a cure a highly uncertain one. Sekyi, in *The Anglo-Fanti,* prefigures many of the themes of the postindependence Ghanaian novelist Ayi Kwei Armah, as set out in his second novel *Fragments.*[45] As in the case of the latter, we see Onyidzin as a been-to who returns home after his legal studies in England disillusioned in Western civilization and resolved to keep faith with the authentic lifeways of his people. But in his *fidelitas* to the old Akan-Fanti ways, he encounters only resistance from the loved ones around him. These glory in their own alienation and impose false demands and expectations on him, false because they are derived within the alien Anglo-European norms, and therefore seek to force his soul to inhabit the Anglo-Fanti selfhood he has learned to reject. No longer at ease in his inauthentic Anglo-Fanti self, and finding his path to true self-consciousness blocked by the deadening Anglomaniacal weight of the familial heritage of middle-class social convention, the only alternatives left for the hero, Onyidzin, are madness and death.

What Sekyi illustrates in the disillusioning career, dementia, and demise of Onyidzin is the truism of Blyden's thesis that for the assimilated frontline African to be himself is to be nothing. Blyden is worth recalling if only because Sekyi was traveling on the nationalist trail of psycho-existential critique insightfully blazed by the former. In "Christianity and the Negro" (1876),[46] we find Blyden lamenting the misfortune of the Negro assimilated into Western ways which he finds are, by their very nature, designed to leave him displaced from a purposive knowledge of and toward himself.

> The Negro in Christian lands, however learned in books, cannot be said to have such a thing as self-education. . . . [H]e is taught from beginning to end of his book training . . . *not to be himself, but somebody else*. . . . From the lessons he everyday receives, the Negro unconsciously imbibes the conviction that to be a great man he must be like the white man. He is not brought up . . . to be the companion, the equal . . . of the white man. To be himself in a country where everything ridicules him, is to be nothing—less, worse than nothing. To be as like the white man as possible—to copy his outward appearance, his peculiarities, his manners, the arrangement of his toilet, this is the aim of the Christian Negro. . . . The only virtues which under such circumstances he develops are, of course, the parasitical ones. (*Negro Race*, 37)

Here and elsewhere in his extensive writings, we find Blyden reflecting on the modern predicament of the Negro at large as a comparative nonentity. And this is especially the condition of the Negro, Blyden underlines, standing in the first line of assault by the assimilationist agencies—Euro-American Christianity, the philanthropic enterprise, and Eurocentric education—of what we have heard him declare a "dogmatic and insurgent" Western civilization.

The Negro in the first line of assault is a comparative nonentity for Blyden because in relation to the white man he has no exchange or competitive value, and advantageously for the white man, therefore, the Negro exists solely as manipulable use or instrumental value. His contact with the white man has been for the Negro an overwhelming experience, one that has left him enslaved in desire to, and locked him in body and soul inside, an alien value system. The frontline Negro is not self-representative: in himself he represents that which is not his true self; he represents absurdly only that which has taken the place of the true self.

Writing in this mode, Blyden registers the first far-reaching existential analysis of the "black skin, white masks" syndrome, the syndrome of the enslaved and colonized black psyche so-named in the middle of the twentieth century by Fanon. The frontline Negro, for Blyden as for Fanon after him, is wedded to a Western structure that does not give him back a genuine self-image—and such a genuine self-image would be one that relates the self to the world on its own terms. Since in himself, the Negro's place is taken (over) by another, ontologically he is not his own origin. "What we call the black soul," Fanon concludes therefore, "is the white man's artefact."[47] The skin that encloses the Negro soul may objectively be black, but the essence subjectively contained within it is not. Like Blyden, therefore, Fanon laments, as in the last epigraph reproduced above, the unknowing racial self that may not invent purposes that are authentically its own since its self-knowledge is held captive in another's meaning system. On this basis, Blyden concludes some eight decades before Fanon, "Every intelligent Negro"—and "intelligent" is another way of saying "existentially self-aware"—"must feel he walks upon the face of God's earth a physical and moral incongruity" (*Negro Race*, 37).

What does this moral incongruity come to mean for the "intelligent Negro" of West Africa, the frontline intellectuals of Sekyi's kind who follow in Blyden's footsteps? To turn to the latter's disciples in the Gold Coast setting is to see them making the spectacle of existential horror he conjures—the Negro programmed into living in a self-confirming mode of Nothingness—comparable to their own predicament. And it is to see emerging in their work, therefore, diagnostic analyses, along Blydean lines, of the psycho-existential sort. These analyses produce a Gold Coast, and generally West African, middle-class affect and imaginary distorted by the philanthropic and spiritual agencies of Empire. Hence we find Attoh Ahuma in the 1900s charging in his piece, "The White Man and His West African Understudy":

Histrionism is undoubtedly the special forte of the educated West African; he is a copyist to the pitch of profane excellence. . . . As [the white man] lands in the latest things in vogue, his echo takes full notes, and, in less than seven weeks, like a puppet or marionette he sports the identical fashion. . . . If [the West African's] lord and master holds a cigar in a peculiar manner, it is copied; his gait, mode of expression, his expletives, smiles, laughter . . . are all taken in wholesale, and reproduced with the fidelity of an Edisonian Phonograph. (*Gold Coast,* 37–38)

Attoh Ahuma concludes: "It is never to the credit of any West African to strive manfully to become Anglo-African, Europeanised or Anglicised in anything. A Black Whiteman is a creature, a freak, and a monstrosity" (40).

Attoh Ahuma would know, having undergone an African awakening and recovered for himself his authentic native name. He was born Samuel Richard Brew Solomon into a Euro-African family in 1864. Attoh Ahuma attended the Wesleyan High School in Cape Coast and subsequently trained for the ministry at Richmond College in London. After a stint in America, the churchman returned to the Gold Coast. With two unsuccessful attempts at running a school behind him in the 1890s, Attoh Ahuma turned his attention as writer, journalist, and polemicist to the great social and political issues of the day. The Wesleyan Mission put him in charge of *The Gold Coast Methodist Times,* the paper it founded in 1896. Attoh Ahuma, who would in the following year become a secretary of the A.R.P.S., refused to confine the paper to reporting and commenting on confessional and spiritual matters. Until he was removed as editor late in 1897 for meddling in politics, the paper's position was an exemplary anticolonial one, having been the leading public voice against the efforts by the Crown to take control of Gold Coast lands. It is no surprise that Attoh Ahuma earned high praise from Casely Hayford for "the greatest effort in journalism in . . . the last decade of the [19th] century" (*Native Institutions,* 176).

As editor of the *Methodist Times,* Attoh Ahuma had in late 1897 initiated a debate in its columns on "the advisability of a general resumption of Native Names in the case of persons . . . who had assumed European Names" (qtd. in *Political History,* 518). His own response was to change his name during the same period from Solomon to Attoh Ahuma, a move he justified thus:

[T]he greatest calamity of West Africa that must be combated tooth and nail...is the imminent Loss of Ourselves. . . . Rather let men rob our lands if possible, but let us see that they do not rob us of ourselves. They do so when we are taught to despise our own Names, Institutions, Customs and Laws. . . . The days are coming, however, when not to stand by the nation and its true life shall mean the eternal forfeiture of all claims to respect and reverence. (*Celebrities,* 2–3)

He would exhort in conclusion, "[L]et us sound the Bugle-Call to wake up" (3).

Attoh Ahuma in exhortation echoes Blyden's lament in "Study and Race," where the latter notes:

> It is sad to think there are some Africans . . . who are blind to the radical facts of humanity as to say, "Let us do away with the sentiment of Race. Let us do away with our African Personality and be lost if possible in another Race."
>
> This is as wise or as philosophical as to say, let us do away with gravitation, with heat and cold and sunshine and rain. . . . [W]hen you have done away with your personality, you have done away with yourselves. Your place has been assigned to you in the universe as Africans, and there is no room for you as anything else.[48]

Blyden challenges educated West Africans to recognize in their acculturated makeup the sin of sins of existential bad faith, of lapsing into a state of moral infidelity in respect of their authentic Africanity. Thus Hayford, summing up Blyden's teachings in a eulogy of the pioneer in *Ethiopia Unbound*, points out that its challenging essence to his West African and wider Pan-Negro audience was the Socratic injunction, "man, know thyself" (*Ethiopia Unbound*, 165). And for Hayford, as for Attoh Ahuma and Sekyi, a critical knowledge of the self at the frontline, as enjoined by Blyden, was a knowledge of a self that has lapsed from righteous ways, as it were. Oriented away from itself, and directed towards furthering the purposes of an alien other, the career of the self at the frontline was a falling off from true first, or foundational, principles. Thus Blyden makes the ancillary consciousness of the middle class, its existential endowment as the assimilationist product of Europe's civilizing mission, morally untenable.

Making thinking educated West Africans aware of the moral incongruity of their bastard selfhood—of their black visages overlaid in bad faith by white masks—therefore, Blyden had come to impose on them a postlapsarian challenge of moral rearmament. This moral rearmament was to be invested in an existential crusade whose theme Hayford lays out, in his *Ethiopia Unbound*, in a foundational, orientational, and self-creative thesis: "self-consciousness [which] obviously depends upon self-revelation after which comes self-realisation" (180). The diagnosis of the middle-class self as the bearer of a consciousness misaligned in bad faith with the nativity that ought rightly to be its own nurturing sphere becomes the starting point of a quest to recover a nationalist authenticity. And, as it looks to reinvent at the frontline the "intelligent" (West) African who genuinely represents himself, it is this Orphean quest which appears in the Gold Coast anchored, in accordance with Blydean specification, in moral and phenomenological referents of authentic self-consciousness and necessary self-creation.

It is in this mode that we find the spirited nationalist sermonizing of Attoh Ahuma in *Gold Coast* where his central demand is: "But if we are a Nation, are we self-conscious?" And this is especially addressed to the "rising generation" of "cultured West Africans" on whom has fallen the "birthright, privilege, duty, destiny and honour" (vii) of creating the "Gold Coast nation." As he outlines the matter in the chapter "The Difficult Art of Thinking Nationally," the problem militating against the rising generation's adoption of its birthright vanguard role is that, "We have ceased to be a THINKING NATION. . . . Western education or civilisation undiluted . . . has . . . enervated our minds and made them passive and catholic. Our national life is semi-paralysed; our mental machinery dislocated" (6–7). The churchman must exhort and warn from the nationalist pulpit therefore that creative "Ideas cannot germinate" when "emergent novelties of a foreign strand absorb the energies of mind and soul and strength" (8, 7). And to an unthinking rising generation he must drive home the point about its existential Nothingness thus: "Existence is a mere parody unless embroidered with the flowers of the intellect and the fruitage of the soul" (7).

For Attoh Ahuma, "want of real, vital and solid thinking has its moral dangers" (8). In that case, a middle class must be under moral suspicion insofar as it neglects to see the fulfillment of the prophecies "Ethiopia shall stretch out her hands" and "Africa *shall rise*" as an unavoidable task entrusted to its class self. Placed advantageously as an intermediary, the middle class has lamentably not become conscious of itself as a third force that may step into history, assuming therein the burden of making a modern Gold Coast, West African, and Pan-African destiny. It has not thought "the thoughts that galvanize and electrify into life souls that are asleep unconscious of their destiny" (9). And this is why the nationalist must raise (self)-consciousness as a question of the highest duty and moral obligation and bring it to what he sees as a twin challenge confronting the middle class at the frontline—the challenge of existentially affirmative self-founding and representative self-fashioning.

We find Attoh Ahuma in *Gold Coast,* therefore, looking to invent, in a self-consciousness that will be true to the nation, the true self of the nation. The questions directed at the rising generation by him might be: "How, *in ourselves,* might we find the characterological resources to position ourselves as the sovereign foundation of the nation?" "In what characterological bearing ought we to appear, and how do we find and (hegemonically) secure our nomination therein, as the authentic representative of the national people?"

Toward nationalist purposes, then, we find Atto Ahuma espousing to his middle-class audience a notion of self-consciousness which, as in Blyden's quasi theology, was moral insofar as it posited itself as nothing less than intrinsically and irreducibly *original*—that is, as a foundational power, *in* itself. Flowing complementarily from this originality, this self-consciousness had to be for Attoh Ahuma also radically *originating*—that is, *for* itself, a founding power. What the latter signifies is that, in relation to what is outside itself, consciousness is that which is able to induct itself into an "out there" and vice versa. This is consciousness, therefore, thought as project-making, its projects endowing its inner creative logic—i.e., its originality in itself—with representative status in the objective world "out there." This is exactly what is proposed in Attoh Ahuma's early nationalist projection of representative self-fashioning.

Attoh Ahuma puts the question of self-consciousness—the founding of a foundational and founding self, that is—in terms of a cultivation of an original and an originating will in his essays. In its terms, he goes on to spell out the moral foundations of the Gold Coast nation in a refashioned self of patriotic duty, of civic obligation and responsibility, of heroic sacrifice, and so on. "Have we the outward and visible signs of the inward and spiritual graces of Cohesion, Concentration, Continuity of purpose, and the dynamic of self-sacrifice—so highly distinctive of other nations?" (3), the churchman ponders. And he must ask rhetorically of the rising generation, "Are the people—our own kith and kin—cultivating a national consciousness, a national conscience, national affection, national passion, and national vigilance?" (2–3). To the extent that the answer appears to him to be negative, Attoh Ahuma must take the middle class to task for lacking the nation-making requisite of originality. "Origination cannot be predicated of us as a rule" (7), he points out, and this is because the middle-class self is merely "tailor made." And "Tailor-made men," who in their artificiality are no organic and necessary outgrowth of a native soil, "do not constitute a State" (10).

We may characterize Attoh Ahuma's deepest intuitions on the question of self-consciousness in terms of a radical quasi-existentialist phenomenology. In its terms, authentic being could come only from a middle class ready to choose and project its being for and towards something—those purposes and ends represented in the ideal projects of nationalism. As he exhorts, "We may be our own Architects. Beneath the debris was a marble out of which Michael Angelo liberated an imprisoned seraph" (10); and he foresees in that a class being able to will itself into self-consciousness and mustering the force to "create something out of nothing . . . [and to] execute that which never existed before" (7).

These points are further clarified in two other essays in *Gold Coast*: "I am, I can"; "I ought, I will" (20–25; 26–31), which address a need for the "I"—the self-consciousness in the middle—to assert a radically original creative will. Inasmuch as Attoh Ahuma's thundering "I am" makes the "I" irreducibly original, what follows the auxiliaries "can," "ought," and "will" is the predicate of origination, those nationalist projects and projections wherein the "I" acquires a worldly attribution and ratifies the force of its originality. For, as he asks, "[O]f what earthly use are the supreme consciousness of ourselves, the cognizance and realization of our Powers, Faculties . . . forces which are heaven's own investiture—what shall it profit if with the comprehension of our obligations and responsibilities nothing else ensues" (29).

Thus, preaching his morality of self- and national consciousness, Attoh Ahuma gives us a conception of power that must be mustered from within ("I am; I can"): hence a self-reliant power. Additionally, in a dialectic involving part and whole, Attoh Ahuma presents this self-reliant power as one that fulfills itself as such only by being able to project its self-will outward to embrace a communal will at large. And this communal will was to be found in "Backward Movement," "Back to the Land"—in a return, that is, to the living legacy of "our [native] progenitors" (vii). A middle-class endangered in alienation still has the existential option of rooting itself in an organic consciousness, the organic being captured in the back-to-the-land metaphor. Linking itself backward, the middle class will be at one with the people, "our kith and kin," albeit exercising this option requires that, first, "We must lay violent hands upon ourselves . . . and break the heart out of those things . . . which seek to crush the soul of our nation" (10).

In Attoh Ahuma's heroic existential phenomenology, then, there must be a middle-class will to die to a decadent consciousness in order to be wholesomely reborn in the image of another whose living necessity is rooted in the native land. His moral injunction to the rising generation ("I ought") to cultivate a consciousness at once inward-looking—the self-reliant "I am"—and outwardly self-projecting—"I will"—demands of the middle-class self that it put itself under the obligation of a contract. The middle class must voluntarily contract to relate to the native in a form of mimesis; it must rediscover and embrace a native whole from which it has been divided and induct into its refashioned self-consciousness the will of this nativity. With self-will and native will reconciled such that one is (mirrored in) the other and either is both, this will of the self-native (or nativized self-will) is then to be inducted into the worldly projects of the middle class, endowing these projects with representative nationalist force.

Attoh Ahuma's call to root consciousness organically in the land, his exhortation to return to the native, must in fact read as a return *of* the native: it is a matter of the middle class appropriating and turning the native towards its nationalist and worldly purposes. This conscientious formula, wherein a post-ancillary middle class commits itself to return the middle to the native as a return of the native to the middle, stands out, as we shall see, in Casely Hayford's figurations of national allegory in *Ethiopia Unbound,* reviewed below in chapter 6. Hayford's own practical commitment to working out the return of the native had seen him founding in the early teens of the twentieth century a public interest research group, the Gold Coast National Research Association. The conservative mandate of the Association, in the words of Sekyi and J. C. de Graft Johnson (brother of J. W.), two of its leading members, was "the elimination of the white man's standpoint from the black man's outlook," and the restoration of "national respect and self-confidence." And what this imposed on intellectuals of Sekyi's and Johnson's kind was the task of reconstructing nativity in its institutional authenticity "before the disintegrating foreign element intruded or insinuated itself into it" (qtd. in *Political History,* 525).

The call for the emancipation of the middle class from the shackles of mental slavery, and a restoration of itself to authentic African ways, therefore, sounds loud and clear in early Gold Coast/West African nationalism. Sekyi, above all, will bring to his stepfather Attoh Ahuma's post-ancillary proposition of middle-class homecoming the completest philosophical expression, systematic exposition, and ideological justification. A *detailed* analysis of Sekyi's radical conservative philosophical and political thought lies beyond the scope of this present study. The reader may, however, refer to Ayo Langley's "Modernization and Its Malcontents: Kobina Sekyi . . . of Ghana and the Re-Statement of African Political Theory" for an insightful review and analysis of the thought of the foremost ideologue of the A.R.P.S.

In conclusion: even as they utilize Blyden's diagnostic for middle-class autocritique, the Gold Coast nationalists must be located in a political context different from his. They may confirm the quasi-theological and racial abstractions of Blyden's cultural nationalism, but their analyses are also importantly rooted in political calculation in the concrete. For them, in addition to a worlding of the Negro race, the project of "worlding" the middle class as a political class, a class-for-power, urges itself also in the Gold Coast/West African setting. The search for a post-ancillary self-consciousness is also about the making of a political affect that will found a class-for-power. "But if we are a nation are we self-conscious?" we have heard Attoh Ahuma demanding, as he charges the rising generation to seek out the bases—as in their self-rehabilitation within, and effective political mobilization of, a people's culture—of conceiving and birthing the nation out of the colony. In Attoh Ahuma's wake-up call, nation is the projection of a middle-class destiny, that destiny succinctly captured by J. B. Danquah in 1943: "We must have power, and must adequately fill in that power to give us world citizenship." The projections by Attoh Ahuma and Danquah of that ultimate nationalist and worldly destination, the contradictions and pitfalls in these projections, provide the stuff of analysis in the following chapter.

4

ON THE ROAD TO GHANA

NEGOTIATIONS, PARADOXES, PRATFALLS

Horton's Pragmatism and After: The "Gold Coast Nation" in Attoh Ahuma's Rhetoric of Political Demand

> Even the Awoonahs who have been our enemies for the past twenty years have now joined us and have agreed willingly and joyfully to join the deputation movement.
> —Tackie, King of Accra, to Kwame Fori, King of Akwapim, 1886

The epigraph is taken from the context of late-nineteenth-century inter-ethnic diplomacy in colonial Gold Coast. The letter of the ethnic Ga, King Tackie of Accra, to the ethnic Akan, King Kwame Fori of Akwapim (or Akuapem), in which the former urges the worthy example of the ethnic Anlo-Ewe on his addressee, is produced here as an instance of the anticolonial solidarities which, mobilized at the time, were making for the incipient "nationalization" of the Colony.[1] King Tackie's letter is issued in the context of widespread native protests against the heavy-handed usurpation by the British Crown of the sovereign rights constituting the legitimate basis of the indigenous polities of the country.

The King of Accra would likely not have seen the conclusions contained in a memo written by one Sir Edward Cust in 1839. Nevertheless it is a memo worth recalling since the goals that Tackie and others in the

1885–87 Gold Coast Deputation Movement stood for were directly opposed to its conclusions. Titled "Reflections on West African Affairs," and addressed to the Colonial Office, Cust's piece foretells the shape and direction British policy on the Gold Coast would take, especially in the last few years leading up to, and those following, the promulgation of the Colony in 1874. Cust then wrote:

> It is out of season at this time of the day, to question the original policy of conferring on every colony of the British Empire a mimic representation of the British constitution. But if the creature so endowed has sometimes forgotten its real insignificance and under the fancied importance of speakers and maces and all . . . has dared to defy the mother country, she has to thank herself for the folly of conferring such privileges on a condition of society that has no earthly claim to so exalted a position.[2]

For Cust, therefore, the conclusion was a very obvious one: "A fundamental principle appears to have been forgotten or overlooked in our system of colonial policy—that of colonial dependence." Hence, "To give to a colony the forms of independence is a mockery; she would not be a colony for a single hour if she could maintain an independent station."[3]

Cust's argument for Empire, as it stands, founds its defense *implicitly* in natural law, and its corollary, natural right—the former a law of universal humanistic application, the latter of universal humanistic dessert. However, as he deploys them, the authority of these two founding notions undergo subtle shifts so that the imperial enterprise, otherwise an indefensible principle of violent, inegalitarian power, discovers its indemnity in them. Empire discovers its universality—earthly exaltation—to the extent that, as Cust implies, might confers universal right. As for the weak, the dictate of natural law requires them to be dominated by those, such as Britain, on whom might has conferred such universal right. Britain's haste to grant subordinate colonials, weak peoples all, an unearned right to an "independent station"—and an unearned dessert, too, to the symbols of British national strength, "speakers and maces"—therefore, goes contrary to the dictates of nature. It is only those who, backed by, and because of, their might, have seen their national visages reflected in the Universal, Cust implies then, who are naturally entitled to self-determination and the institutions expressive thereof. For colonials in subordination whose faces as such do not appear in the Universal, self-determination was thus a most unnatural right, hence a "mockery," a parody, of the authentic thing.

If Cust's naturalism and universalism supply defensive theses to cover the offensive nationalism of Empire, the political-intellectual road to

"Ghana" begins in the encounter between colonialist apologetics of his kind and the pragmatic spirit of the colonized native, that spirit exhibited in King Tackie's urgent letter. The African counter-arguments, when they began, would be based, as Anderson remarks in *Imagined Communities,* on the "*inner* incompatibility of nation and empire" (88–89). For Empire, as it appeared to the native in its colonial expression, was clearly a principle of power, not nature; as such, its claim to universal right could not be legitimately defended on humanistic grounds.

This, indeed, is the mode in which we find Blyden arguing, not long after Cust's reminder, bending the latter's thesis of nature towards the anti-imperialist call for a "distinct" "African nationality." Blyden appearing to abjure, too, a "cosmopolitism" which would in practice see the weak enfolded by the mighty, wrenches universal right from the imperial coding and transfers it to the sovereign, free-standing particularity of the nation. For Blyden, nationality is "an ordinance of nature," and this, as pointed out previously, was an assertion that natural law imposed a moral equivalence on all human beings without discrimination. This conferred on all equally—and not some exceptionally, as the belligerent Cust would have it—the universal dessert of the particular distinction of nationality. Access to nationhood was a human right, a right of each to distinction and sovereignty conferred indifferently by "the ordinance of nature" (i.e., natural law). Deserving to be different and equal in dessert: Blyden having hammered home this point, this will be the essence of what a pragmatic Attoh Ahuma will substantially advance in his polemical claims on behalf of Gold Coast nationality. The discussion of Attoh Ahuma's argument comes shortly below; it is preceded by a brief nineteenth-century Gold Coast sketch of the historical and political context of its articulation.

Stripped of its accretions of naturalism, Cust's defense of colonial imperialism rests simply on the long-lived cliché, "might is right." In his nation's relations with the others it had confined to subordinate colonial status, it was power, not natural law, which spelled the limit of political rationality. And as for this unnatural imperial principle, the opportunities for its clear demonstration would come in the years after 1844, in the context of changing relations between Britain and the native polities of the Gold Coast.

The watershed of the modern constitutional history of the entity that would become Ghana in 1957, it is commonly agreed, was the ratification of the Bond of 1844. This was a treaty between the British Crown and traditional rulers representing the loose agglomeration of polities comprising Fantiland in the western Gold Coast. At the basis of the agreement by the chiefs to transfer rights of suzerainty to the Crown, with regard to the exercise of specific judicial functions, lay the fact that British mercantile interests, since the late 1820s, had enjoyed and exercised considerable prestige in this part of the Gold Coast. The astute George Maclean, President of the Council of Merchants, had, out of the British settlement of Cape Coast Castle, pursued a policy of constructive engagement with the so-called adjacent areas, managing to secure the exercise of irregular jurisdiction over them. The Fanti signatories to the Bond, therefore, were giving legal sanction to a jurisdiction that Maclean's Pax Britannica, generally advantageous to trade, had established de facto. And if these native signatories were transferring certain rights in exchange for the Crown's protection, the Bond committed them also to a radical "modernization" of their native institutions. In the wording of the Bond they were accepting the principle of "moulding the customs of the country to the general principle of British law."[4]

The late 1860s would see Africanus Horton—to whom "belongs the credit of having been the first to voice national aspirations in the Gold Coast"[5]—concluding in his two major works that commitment to institutional reform in the Gold Coast Protectorate pointed in the salutary direction of African self-determination. Writing as an advocate for the modernization of the "political condition of the Gold Coast," Horton proposed in his works that if certain changes of a politico-legal nature were to be introduced and suitable adaptations implemented here and there, the country he had worked in and observed firsthand could become two modern self-governing entities.[6] Horton would not have felt that his unofficial recommendations were unique. Indeed, he made them as an adjunct to an 1865 resolution by the Select Committee of the [British] House of Commons that seemed to endorse a policy of gradually transferring institutional power to Africans in British settlements on the Gold Coast and elsewhere in West Africa.[7]

Nevertheless, appearing between 1868 and 1870, in tandem with the protonationalist agitation that was then shaking the country,[8] Horton's proposals sounded urgently against a backdrop of official paternalism and insouciance, increasingly on display in the arbitrary exercise of British power over the very Gold Coast polities the Crown had contracted to protect. And, if anything, the arbitrariness of British power was being helped along, as Horton saw, by petty rivalries between these already relatively disadvantaged native polities. For Horton, then, only a will towards nation-statehood by these rivalrous polities, by which he meant a disciplined delegation or cession of power by them to a central representative body, could have hoped to secure them an equitable deal against the otherwise gratuitous impositions of British imperial might.

The optimist who was thinking and writing these things in 1868 and 1870 could not have foreseen that the political homogenization he wished and worked for would come in a colonialist, rather than a homegrown nationalist, form. Six years after Horton first ventured his policy recommendations towards a self-determining Gold Coast, the country would lapse from the status of a Protectorate to a de facto colony, administered as a Crown Colony. (It would not be until 1901 that the colonial enclosure of the Gold Coast would be given full legal backing by the British). It would be left to Attoh Ahuma, accusing the Crown of a breach of faith and trust, to give a vigorous statement of what Horton would have felt, following the disappointing conduct of Britain, to be the height of imperial chicanery. Thus Attoh Ahuma in his "Colony or Protectorate" (1897):

> Our rulers are our friends and nothing more—valuable acquisitions, friends in need and in deed, true friends, good friends . . . and being friends, and nothing but friends, to seek insidiously to enslave us, to brand us with the hall-mark of conquered subjects, is to outrage good faith and commit a breach of confidence.[9]

If "Punic faith is impossible to the genius of the British Constitution," as Attoh Ahuma reminds his interlocutors further, then colonial imposition was a confidence trick. It was an artifice that went against the principles of natural right and justice enshrined in a constitution from which the people of the Gold Coast were deriving "our budding ideas of British jurisprudence . . . fraught with peace, fair play, and justice—especially justice" (*Native Institutions*, 316–17).

It is with "justice" on his side therefore that, in "The Gold Coast Nation and National Consciousness," Attoh Ahuma proclaims the natural and other rights of his "people." These were rights that the British presence, by ungenerous colonial default, had shown could repose constitutionally *only*, as it were, in the idea of nation-ness. If it is nation that frames the contest, then Attoh Ahuma opens his argument by directing a salvo at and against the "rash and irresponsible literalists" who would deny the nation-ness of the Gold Coast as a tactic to sanction her oppression under the colonial yoke. These are the ones asserting "strenuously" that:

> [T]he Gold Coast, with its multiform composition of congeries of States or Provinces, independent of each other, divided by complex political institutions, laws and customs, and speaking a great variety of languages—could not be described as a nation in the eminent sense of the word. The term, it is urged, presupposes in its connotation, the existence of a homogeneous

community included in or bounded by one vast Realm, governed and controlled by one potent sovereign, and possessed of one constitution, one common tongue.[10]

The argument for nation as a seamlessly homogeneous constituency, though, is one that appears to Attoh Ahuma to be "purely academic"; making a case against the Gold Coast this way was certainly to pay insufficient regard to the "practical considerations" that attended her unique, pluralistic situation.

Yet if homogeneity as a datum of nation-ness must be insisted on, then, presenting what amounts to his tongue in his cheek to the proponents of this view, Attoh Ahuma advances a gallantly paradoxical line of reasoning that is also consistently rational in its own terms. In a counterargument which at once rhetorically concedes his opponents' point, to his nationalist advantage, *and* withholds it from them, to his anticolonialist advantage, Attoh Ahuma points out that the longevity of colonial duration alone has imposed and imposes, as if from above, the nation-making prerequisite of homogeneity on the Gold Coast's variety. He notes:

[F]or more than sixty years there has been established within our territories an *imperium in imperio*—the highest organized form of government in creation, which binds us as an integral part of an empire over which the sun never sets. We are being welded together under one umbrageous Flag—a Flag that is the symbol of justice, freedom, and fairplay. [11] (*Gold Coast*, 2)

He concludes: "The Gold Coast under the *aegis* of the Union Jack is the unanswerable argument to all who may incontinently withhold from us the common rights, privileges, and status of nationality" (2).

What Attoh Ahuma appears to be saying in the passage is that both *through* and *in spite of* the colonial presence "We are a nation." He is affirming in other words that, in themselves, the acts by which colonial power imposed homogeneity on the Gold Coast did not make her a nation so much as that the *essence* of the colony's nation-ness was being revealed through and in spite of these acts. As a contingent fact, that is, colonial duration did not and could not encompass Gold Coast nation-ness. Hence it is that in response to those "wiseacres who would fain deny us, as a people, the inalienable heritage of nationality," Attoh Ahuma "dare[s] [to] affirm, with sanctity of reason and the emphasis of conviction, that—WE ARE A NATION" (1).

From here Attoh Ahuma's nationalist counter-argument on behalf of the prerequisite of homogeneity, it would seem, is compelled to rely on an understated metaphor of natural osmosis to carry its paradoxical point. If he saw homogeneity imposing itself on the Gold Coast from "above," it came not so much from the will of a colonial imperialism as it came from somewhere *beyond* this will. On a positive side, the colonial will carried as a latency within itself certain "God-given" rights, truths, and values felt to be coextensive with the idea and status of nationhood. Hence the sixty or so years of living in a "contiguous" mode with what the Union Jack *really* represented—the political and value-ideals enshrined in the language of post-Enlightenment civility—already conferred on the Gold Coast, by "natural," if also willed, osmotic transfer, the status of a nation.

Against a reductive literalism, therefore, Attoh Ahuma takes a position—and Horton would have endorsed its practicality—that argues that a nation is not an inert fact of being so much as it is a matter of the willed actualization of a human latency. Nation being a matter of will, then, according to Attoh Ahuma, since "any series of States in the same locality, however extensive, may at any time be merged into a nation," it is only reasonable to suppose that, "If we were not [a nation], it was time to invent one" (1).

All nations, Attoh Ahuma appears to be arguing, are (f)acts of symbolic constitution. Nation is the incarnate expression of a preconstitutive *and* pro-creative Idea, Spirit, or Will. For this reason, even though his "nation," the Gold Coast, smarting under the colonial yoke, "may be 'a miserable, mangled, tortured, twisted *tertium quid*,' or . . . a Nation 'scattered and peeled . . . a Nation meted out and trodden down,'" it nevertheless was "still a Nation." For his emphatic assertion is that the pro-creative *Geist* of nation-ness is abundantly manifest in the Gold Coast. Attoh Ahuma's name for it is the past: not only do "we have a nation," as he argues, but "what is more, we have a Past—'though ungraced in story'" (1). To the explicit demand to invent a political nation, therefore, he adds the equally explicit demand to invent a foundational culturalist national allegory, a narrative whose "story" will express the unfolding of an immemorial *Volkgeist*.

In what location does Attoh Ahuma find the potential for the *Geist* of the Gold Coast nation to reach its most developed form? Where does he find the perfect vehicle for that spirit which, moving towards self-consciousness, wills the invention of a transcendent community—"a people"—beyond the Gold Coast's otherwise merely "multiform congeries . . . of States . . . independent of each other"? (1) In what sociohistorical matrix, that is, does it appear as an imperative to subsume the fragments and the differences comprising the colony in a higher rationality: that of modern nation-state-hood?

The answers lie in the situation of the "rising generation" of the middle class, Attoh Ahuma's addressee in *Gold Coast,* a generation left in an existential lurch as its rise was thwarted by the advent of British colonial policy under the New Imperialism. For all the class prestige it still enjoyed relative to the "masses," the political and social reality for the middle class was that it had been shunted aside, pushed into a peripheral and inconsequential role in the affairs of the Gold Coast. The colonial alienation of power from the middle class was the special predicament of the rising generation referred to in 1909 by Sir John Rodger, governor of the Gold Coast. Rodger, as we noted earlier, pointed out the contradiction inherent in the colonial policy of turning out "black and brown Englishmen" but "cursing the finished article when the operation is complete."[12]

It is lack that hollows the human and social being into desire. Such a description, it must be understood, captures the relational nature of lack and desire: one can only desire that which one can visualize but which an obstacle perforce deprives one of. In this sense, then, the account Rodger gives shows us a colonial relation that had "hollowed" power out of the very being of a native middle class. It is not unreasonable to assume, therefore, that if the class being had been emptied into desire, its desire thenceforth was for power. Hence, in the facts of the immediate colonial relation, we see a launching of a middle class, rendered socially peripheral in colonial affairs, into a consciousness of itself as a class-for-power.

Then, again, the intellectual vanguard of this Gold Coast class-for-power—figures such as Attoh Ahuma, Casely Hayford, and Mensah Sarbah—would also be aware that the protocols of imperial worlding have included the invention of substantial cultural pasts for Europeans. As in Hegel's *Philosophy of History,* these were speculative histories or allegories of a group *Geist* unfolding towards its worldly consummation. The competitive value of such inventions would have been evident to the frontline intellectuals in the successful blacking out of Africa achieved by the consummate European *Weltgeist;* an Africa thenceforth induced to appear only as Europe's negative foil. Thus Attoh Ahuma's invocation of a national past deliberately inserts his nation into the very protocols producing the European *Geistesgeschichtes.* As he factors a culturalist agenda into the political one, we see a class-for-power inventing itself as a class-for-the-world, too.

Looking at a socially peripheral middle class at the turn of the century, then, we find the burden of powerlessness—created by the colonial alienation of power, and the burden of worldlessness—created by the wholesale alienation of Africa by imperial worlding, pushing it to discover its desiring narratives of empowerment and worlding in the same plane, that of nationality. And as middle class nationalism looks towards the worlding of a Ghana-to-be, we get an intimation of a class characterology beginning to be shaped in its ambit. The worlding of the nation opens up a speculative dimension in which to frame characterological questions about a collective destiny, about the moral and other agencies that should commit to the realization of this destiny, and so on. Hence we have seen Attoh Ahuma interrogating the rising generation of his class, indicating that only in a self-consciousness, defined above all by and in terms of a nationalistic imperative, would the touchstone for a responsible morality be found to undergird the ascendency of a middle class unto power.

A turn of the century Gold Coast class-for-power—a generation on the rise—thus comes to seek in national consciousness the authority to proclaim its social and political legitimacy. Attoh Ahuma anticipates the arrival of his kind in a nationalistically served morality, a morality bearing enough suasive power to give a rising generation representative—that is to say, hegemonic—force over the sociohistorical field comprehended by its members as their own. Like Sarbah, Hayford, and Sekyi, Attoh Ahuma does not forget where such legitimacy would come from. In the foreword to *Gold Coast,* he addresses the rising generation thus: "Intelligent Retrogression is the only Progression that will save our beloved country. This may sound a perfect paradox, but it is, nevertheless, the truth" (vii). Given the plurality within which Attoh Ahuma advances Gold Coast nation-ness, the crucial term in that declaration has to be the adjective "intelligent." The point will be picked up shortly below.

Attoh Ahuma emerges, then, as one who had found it pragmatically necessary, as he looked to figure one nation out of the multiform cultural and political organization of Gold Coast nativity, to invent an essential national past. However, he gives us a hint that it would be necessary to temper essence with the kind of critical attention that would bring it into line with the contingent demands urgently imposing on a native world. For Attoh Ahuma, therefore, if the rehabilitation of the middle class in a national character took account of what came from "below," drawing on it as the repository of an immanent native *logos,* the rationality of political and cultural modernity that he desired this essential *logos* to assume obliged it to take on an auxiliary character. And this was in the "osmotic" sense of the middle class, inventing the nation and national character, drawing on "help" arriving solvently from "above," in the form of the discursive protocols and politico-legal structures of Empire.

Such are the relativist implications to be drawn from the gallant paradoxes polemically advanced by Attoh Ahuma, paradoxes which one might construe and recuperate in the light of Bakhtin's discussion of "stylization" in *The Dialogic Imagination*. The great Russian theorist produces this as one of the constitutive elements of the "mutual illumination of languages"— or "dialogism"—that he finds at work in all human culture as a scene of invention, of making newness enter the world by way of a recombination of elements of difference. Bakhtin writes in this mode: "Every authentic stylization"—as is Attoh Ahuma's "stylization" of the "Gold Coast nation"— "is an artistic representation of another's . . . language." It is "only in a stylized language, one not his own, that the stylizer can speak about the subject [at hand] directly."[13] Yet for Bakhtin, this sense that making the new requires a falling back on precedent models is not a debilitating but enabling truism; it is not the notation of reductive liability but of *negotiated* possibility. For the stylizer comes to the precedent model as a "free," originating agent, more or less, endowed with the power of recombination as such. Wrested from the old, the precedent, "[the new] stylized language is . . . exhibited in the light of the language consciousness of a stylizer contemporary with it." The old is sublimated into the new inasmuch as "contemporaneous language casts a special light over the stylized language," wherein it "creates a free image of another's language . . . by carrying into it its own interests" (*Dialogic Imagination,* 362–63).

Read in a Bakhtinian light, therefore, Attoh Ahuma is to be seen appropriating British precedent in a way that makes it function in spite of its imperial self as a useful auxiliary for a nationalist reinvention—or stylization, if you will—of a colonized nativity. For, after all, Empire's institutions, including its discursive protocols, are invested with prestige and power. And the frontline intellectual, confronted by the "impossibility" of his postimperial location within these power-laden forms, has at least the option of wresting this power, diverting it towards his own oppositional and creative ends. It is in this sense that, for Attoh Ahuma, the imperial formation could be usefully tapped into to fashion out of an otherwise ethnically plural, uncreated Gold Coast, nationally speaking, a sense of a transcendent, imagined community.

As negotiated possibility, the "Gold Coast nation" of Attoh Ahuma's stylization emerges in a two-in-one articulation: in between what is below and what is above—in the middle, that is—an enduring principle of nativity finds the moral and political purposefulness that will augment and consummate its self-creating impetus. The call made by Attoh Ahuma to a rising generation to awaken to national consciousness is thus a call to revive and reactivate a submerged but otherwise continuously living past of nativity. It is a call to do so within and in spite of the contingency alienating this past into a colonialist modernity. Indeed, in Attoh Ahuma's argument, as we have seen, Gold Coast nativity, even in its contingent alienation, showed itself compatible and continuous with the humanistic and nationalistic presuppositions inherent in—but needing, as it were, to be extracted osmotically from—the very medium of its alienation, the imperial-colonial state appearing above it.

Attoh Ahuma's *Gold Coast* presents one more early literary example of a middle-class intermediary embarked on a by no means easy quest, based in the idea of nation, for the creative rubrics that will legitimate and further its self-definition. In this endeavor we find Attoh Ahuma affirming that he is able to muster a nationalist self-presence from his middle location. This self-presence was what was needed to mediate between, on the one hand, the claims of a continuous, past-legitimated aboriginal essence (embodied in what Attoh Ahuma and Sarbah refer to respectively as "the people" and "the masses"); and, on the other hand, the claims of a future-driven contingency. As for this contingency, it was that into which the Gold Coast's aboriginal essence, in colonial time, had found itself willy nilly displaced. These might be the questions confronting the intermediary: "Who are we?" "What is our being?" "And if we must become, what, and how, shall we become?" What Attoh Ahuma thus reveals is a middle class compelled, within its reflexive idea of *becoming* a nation in *being* native, to seek the means towards this paradoxical end of becoming-in-being by negotiating a continuity out of the colonially enforced rupture between nativity and the forms of an impinging modernity.

When all is said and done, however, the author who makes a paradoxical continuity between nativity and modernity thinkable in the name and creative endeavor of an "osmotic" (or absorbent) intermediary leaves us with the merest hint of an answer to an outstanding question. The question may be construed thus: if a middle class, osmotically drawing on the alien auxiliary to invent the nation, had come to deem the past necessary for a present conception of a future to come, what constituted a viable definition of such pastness? Here viability must mean above all the question of how the past was to receive a qualified insertion into nationalism's progressively imagined present. And if the hint of an answer given by Attoh Ahuma appears in the crucial adjective "intelligent," qualifying what he calls "retrogression," it would seem then that, for him, what was at stake was not just an antiquarian "what was our past?" What the adjective does at a stroke, then, is to bring (ethno)historical reconstruction to the center of early Gold Coast nationalism's political and moral purpose as the quest, in its here and now, for a responsible *mediation* of the past.

We may infer in that case that Attoh Ahuma's point is made not so much about an eternally "pure"—i.e., univocal—past, simply available to be retrieved, as it is made about the contingent presentness of the past. "History," according to Mudimbe, "is a legend, an invention of the present. It is both a memory and a reflection of our present."[14] The past in this wise is a site where libidinal investments are to be, have been, or will be made by a present containing decidedly plural interests; a present which, as a consequence, rendered the past a mediate site reflexive of its immediate concerns and contentions. "Intelligent retrogression" might therefore be read, given Attoh Ahuma's demonstrated awareness of Gold Coast plurality, as a caveat.

But if so what kind of caveat? This question is a relevant one as we move on to examine the forces that will come into play in the early to mid-twentieth century to transform the "Gold Coast nation" into its successor "Ghana." As we step below onto the discursive road leading from a Ghana of the ideal "past" to its modern counterpart, Attoh Ahuma's caveat should be a reminder for our own time. The point then is that, regarding the question of the past and its present uses, a consideration of the contentious variability of interest—a consideration lying at the productive heart of the questions: what kind of "people," ideally, were we? and, based on that, what kind of nation might we, ideally, be(come)?—is precisely that which we are not at liberty to overlook.

The time has come, therefore, to turn to the (historical) production of, and subsequent struggle over, "the people of Ghana." It is an occasion also to place this contest where it relevantly belongs: within the nationalist characterology of a middle class, a characterology inscribed on that functional modification of the modern which yields the middle-class and front-line problematic of African modernity. It is from within this matrix that below and in subsequent chapters, this study submits "Ghana," in its various idealizations (or stylizations), to the test, as Appiah will have it, of the interest-relativity lurking at the heart of any and all such idealization.[15]

Imperial "Auxiliary," Native Understudy: From the Akan Geistesgeschichte of Rev. Balmer to the Akanized "Ghana" of Danquah/Meyerowitz—and Beyond

> This meeting with Europeans on the coast of Guinea is destined to be the most decisive event in the history of the Negro peoples and, if

rightly used by them, will enable them to recover once again a position of power and influence among the nations of the earth, not only equal to that which they held in the far-off days of the vanished kingdom of Ghana, but one which will far exceed it in all that is worthy of esteem. The right use of their present opportunity will depend upon their learning how to avoid the fatal cause which ruined them as a people in the past.

—Rev. W. T. Balmer, *A History of the Akan Peoples of the Gold Coast*

By Mr Balmer's conspectus the Akan people themselves are for the first time enabled to see themselves clearly in relation to mankind in general.

—C. W. Welman, Secretary for (Gold Coast) Native Affairs, Preface to Balmer's *A History of the Akan Peoples of the Gold Coast*

The Gold Coast, April 15, 1948: this day could be read as one of those dotting human history that tell of a watershed when the slow evolution of a colonized people's psychology, finding itself coalescing around a congenial, transcendent symbol of self-definition, suddenly reaches a heroic consciousness of destiny. On this day, from the leadership ranks of the respected vanguard intelligentsia of the Gold Coast middle class, Dr. J. B. Danquah publicly proposed that the name of the colony be changed to "Ghana." The latter was a name that had been in limited circulation in the coteries, circles, and clubs of a nationalist vanguard since 1928, when Danquah had professed in writing that there were historical links between the Akan of the Gold Coast and the medieval western Sudan empire Ghana.[16]

In the build-up to and following Danquah's 1948 proclamation, as Jack Goody notes,

the Ghana theory [had] became an established part of nationalist ideology. Private schools were named Ghana Colleges, the motto "Ghana Boy" was painted above the cabins of innumerable mammy lorries. . . . To the populace the use of the term meant a rejection of the colonial status implied by "the Gold Coast."[17]

What had taken place was a successful engineering of mass revulsion against the infelicitous colonial "trademark," the Gold Coast. First imposed on a strip of the coast of Guinea by European mercantile interests, this was a name later adapted to suit the convenience of the British Crown as a common reference to all the territory coextensive with this portion of the West African coast covered by its colonial administration and jurisdiction. It is to Danquah's credit that he mooted "Ghana" again, and, giving it wide-ranging acceptance in the colony, invented the most efficacious symbol around which the anticolonial struggle would come to articulate its purposes, and out of which it would draw its moral and political meanings of nationalist authenticity.

Danquah was the nationalist leader of note to emerge in the period intervening between the demise of Casely Hayford in 1930 and the ascendency of Kwame Nkrumah in the late 1940s. He was born in 1895 to a Basel Mission evangelist father and a mother who were both of Akyem (or Akim) Abuakwa stock. Akyem was one of the Akan subethnicities, located in the interior of the eastern Gold Coast. Danquah attended mission school among his people, and left at seventeen to become a law clerk in Accra, the colonial capital. He had a close relationship with Nana Sir Ofori Atta (1881–1943), the powerful Omanhene (or paramount king) of Akyem Abuakwa. Under the system of indirect rule, which was premised on the British ruling the inhabitants of the Gold Coast through their natural rulers, the brilliant, politically shrewd Ofori Atta became, in the teens and the twenties of the twentieth century, easily the most dominant native political figure in the Colony. Danquah served at the court of Ofori Atta—with whom he shared Abuakwa royal blood—as his secretary from 1916 to 1921. It is not surprising, given this collaboration and cohabitation between the middle-class intellectual and royalty, that the ideological leanings of the most important Gold Coast intellectual after Casely Hayford would have a conservatively royalist flavor. "I believed," Danquah confessed, "in chiefdomship and democracy. The intelligentsia believed in democracy. I thought the chiefs and intelligentsia could come together. I did not think we could get anywhere by destroying the chiefdoms."[18]

In late 1921, Danquah arrived in London, on Kobina Sekyi's advice, to study for his B.A. He obtained this from the University of London in 1925. Two years later, with a John Stuart Mill Scholarship in the Philosophy of Mind and Logic under his belt, he was a Ph.D. A member of the Inner Temple since 1922, he was called to the Bar in 1926. Danquah returned to Accra in 1927 to begin a career as a lawyer and to continue one as an illustrious Gold Coast scholar and nationalist politician.

Danquah was a prolific writer who continued in the ethnohistorical and ethnolegal tradition of Sarbah and Hayford. If initially he shifted the ethnographic focus from Akan-Fanti to Akan-Akyem, he managed also to enlarge this focus into an inclusive Akanness in his major writings. The assessment of Danquah that follows dwells on his invention and codification of "Ghana" and the paradoxes and pratfalls therein. What it does not do is pretend to offer an exhaustive assessment of Danquah's monumental writings, or of the range of his thought, or of what might be seen as his chameleon politics. If Danquah remained politically conservative—like Sarbah and Hayford before him, he was one of those liberal constitutionalists that Langley refers to as "co-operationists"—his conservatism, compared to Sekyi's, for instance, was not hidebound but adaptable. As Edsman, the historian of colonial Gold Coast politics "from Mensah Sarbah to J. B. Danquah," assesses the man, "Danquah is not easy to analyse." For "[d]uring his long public career he managed to express almost every conceivable opinion on every conceivable topic, which probably contributed to making him a rallying figure in the complicated and heterogeneous colonial setting."[19]

The assessment following also does not look at Danquah, who died in a medium security prison in 1965 as Kwame Nkrumah's political prisoner, as a postindependence moral icon. This is the Danquah whose memory has become a patriotic rod with which to chastise Ghanaians for suffering their country to lapse into a one-party dictatorship under the autocrat that Nkrumah became in the early 1960s. This is the Danquah, then, whose name has become synonymous with the liberal-democratic value of "liberty of the subject," which is also the title of one of his publications.[20]

As a leading spokesperson of the youth of the Gold Coast, Danquah had been prominent in 1929 in the founding of the organization known as the Gold Coast Youth Conference. This organization, in the hyperbole of a sympathetic observer, was "the only militant organization [from 1930 to1946] preparing the minds of the youth towards eventual self-government."[21] Lapsing into inactivity soon after it had been convened, the Youth Conference would be revived by Danquah in 1938 and, subsequently, metamorphose into the vanguard nationalist movement the United Gold Coast Convention. It is the U.G.C.C. that in 1947 would initiate, and itself be one of the leading actors in, the final act of the drama (although it would, so to speak, have faded from view by the final scene) culminating in the independence of the Colony in 1957. On this occasion the Gold Coast would take on the seemingly endogenously derived name Ghana.

But whence this symbolic "Ghana," this ideal mooted and popularized by Danquah as a replacement of the tag of colonial convenience "the Gold Coast"?

To tell the story of the invention and subsequent "academicization" and popularization of the myth-ideal "Ghana" is to recapitulate not only the genealogy of a contestation but also that of a collaboration, a compromise even, acted out between black and white, native and auxiliary, in the colonial setting. It is an endeavor that must first bring us to what native agencies on the frontline, like Danquah, starting out as absorbent, would-be middle class types in close contact with the auxiliaries of the white colonial establishment, could be tutored to become: native auxiliaries in their turn. In the relationship between the bright native youths of the Colony and European mentors that defined the field of formal colonial pedagogy, the former represented potential middle-class types waiting to be appropriately molded, thanks to the prestige a European education had come to wield in colonial African space, into representative mouthpieces of, and role models for, the Gold Coast youth.

An observer of the 1950s Gold Coast scene, the African American writer Richard Wright, noted in this connection that, "From the point of view of British mentality, an education was a guarantee that the educated young would side with the British, and, what is more, many of them did."[22] If the youth of the Gold Coast needed to be so mentored, we might suppose that it was because the powers-that-be had projected correctly the inevitability that the European-educated rising generation would come to occupy influential leadership roles in the future of the Colony. This rising generation could thus be seen potentially as providing the malleable material that, shaped by an appropriate pedagogy, might be relied upon to provide the small but vital spark which, characterologically speaking, would induce the generality of the youth into "spontaneous" reform of the kind approved by power. And so Wright found it unsurprising that "the British had never suppressed nationalist feeling per se"; by colonialist contrivance, "they had merely shunted it into ineffective channels" (*Black Power*, 65).

That a calculating, interventionist colonial enterprise of this nature, aimed at reforming the native character, was a historical reality is what I have attempted to capture in the two epigraphs I have juxtaposed at the head of this section. Both are taken from Rev. W. T. Balmer's *A History of the Akan Peoples of the Gold Coast*, first published in 1925, but based on material the Methodist educator had tested on his students at Mfantsipim school, Cape Coast, between 1907 and 1911. In the two epigraphs is to be found a statement of a white colonial complicity; a complicity which the native son Danquah's "Ghana," when it came, would more or less participate in and perpetuate.

The epigraphs are set up, then, as a preliminary to investigating why two agents of Empire, the Christian missionary and educator, Rev. Balmer, and the colonial administrator, C. W. Welman, would have found a common ground from where to assume an apparently "disinterested" pedagogical responsibility for rehabilitating the Colony in an appropriate past. On this ground where religious and secular orders meet and overlap, where metaphysical and political eschatology are reconciled, the stage is set for the white man's burden, organized around the *topos* of pastness, to be given a classic, peculiarly Gold Coast performance. And since, in this performance, Balmer's insistence on what he calls the "right use" of the past is one that already presupposes a potential for its wrong use, it is only proper that we interrogate Balmer's history and its promoters about what exactly the *appropriate* past might consist in. With what pedagogical stakes, in effect, did Balmer invest his history in the present of its conception? And, as he was aided and abetted by Welman, what political stakes did Balmer's history carry for the future?

Posing the questions this way amounts to a refusal to take the performance of the two white expatriates at face value; instead these questions demand that we read with a healthy skepticism between the lines. For between the justification of Balmer's endeavor at historical reconstruction and Welman's endorsement, what we have is a manifesto of a reformist colonial pedagogy in which a Gold Coast "Spirit," a metaphysics of abiding selfhood, produced and wrapped in attractive Hegelian packaging, finds itself poised for a long-term collaboration with colonial political goals.

Balmer writes of the Akan of the Gold Coast in his preface: "there has been a definable purpose at work moulding the career of these people." Quoting an authority who writes in the mode of the Hegelian *Geistesgeschichte*, Balmer concludes therefore:

> It will always make for better history to generalize the soul of [such] a people and regard it as a uniform striving towards self-realization amid continual change of circumstance, than to detail the endless circumstances without reference to the controlling purpose that utilizes or resists them.[23]

Indeed, for Balmer, imparting the lessons of the past to his students at Mfantsipim School, if an educated native elite, the "*present representatives of the chief actors in* [the] *drama* [of the past] could be led to grasp that purpose, make it more spiritual and follow it loyally then assuredly there would be a future for them *as a nation*" (*Akan Peoples*, 14; emphases added). For an otherwise multiform colony, then, the future held the potential of a "real unity," but this would be so only insofar as history could be pedagogically enlisted to "set forth plainly the desirability and worthiness of, and the way to this goal" (15).

The motivations behind Balmer's inspiration to be an auxiliary, a midwife assisting in the birth of a wholesome Gold Coast national character, invite comparison with the better known anthropological exertions made, as it were, on behalf of the natives of Africa by yet another missionary, the Belgian Fr. Placide Tempels. Tempels's quest, like Balmer's, was for an undifferentiated Bantu principle, an African essence worthy of insertion into the civilizational course of mainstream History. The result of his ambitious effort to produce one, based on his (amateur) ethnographic researches conducted among the peoples of colonial Belgian Congo, appears in his landmark work *Bantu Philosophy*, published in 1949.

Balmer valorizes the colonial encounter positively as the most decisive event, civilizationally, to have happened to the peoples of West Africa, preparing the way for the Negro to be revealed to himself. In much the same spirit, Tempels claims the salutary discovery of *the* "Bantu ideal," a vital element, alas, lost to the decadent Bantu themselves. That the Bantu were unremembering is precisely what would lead Tempels to deny their ideal any possibility of immanent self-fulfilment. Instead, the idiosyncratic conclusion he reaches is a self-serving, Eurocentric one: "It is in Christianity alone," Tempels writes, "that the Bantu will find relief for their secular yearning and a complete satisfaction of their deepest aspirations. . . . Christianity . . . is the only possible consummation of the Bantu ideal."[24]

In time and space the English missionary and his Belgian counterpart may have operated in different colonial locations, but the prescriptions made by the one in British West Africa are interchangeable with those to be made later by the other in Belgian Central Africa. Both, in fact, read themselves not only as working in native space but *on* it as well; and they see themselves as doing this ideally on behalf of *la mission civilisatrice européene*. As such we need to make their endeavors resonate relevantly within a larger problematic: that characterized by Mudimbe as the (European) invention of Africa. As spelled out in Mudimbe's own investigations, an attention to this problematic, coming with postimperial hindsight, is one that must necessarily invite the question of how, and for whom, (colonial) Africa came to be constituted as a reality for knowledge.

In Tempels's reconciliation of the spiritual and secular yearning of the Bantu, we find a remarkable concurrence between the missionary's position and that of the colonial administration: Christian mission is self-consciously positioned as the cultural-spiritual arm of the politics of Empire. The earlier collaboration in the Gold Coast between Balmer, the missionary, and Welman, the colonial administrator, in *Akan Peoples* tells a similar story. It would appear from this collaboration that the ideology of Empire had reached a stage where it scorned the trick of naturalizing and justifying the belligerent Darwinism which enforced, as we saw above, Sir Edward

Cust's radical separation of dominant superior and subordinate inferior in the colonial relation. Empire could now, from the turn of the century on, feel the need to present itself, in a guise of social meliorism, as the intimation of a global commonwealth. In this cooperative guise, Empire reads itself into a reinterpreted metaphysics of history: a suitably retooled *Weltgeist*, now proposing an ameliorative objective in the colony, does the ideological work of justifying and securing in the long term Empire's political, economic, and cultural goals.

It is evident, in the hopeful prognoses, in 1908, of Evelyn Baring, Lord Cromer, that by the early twentieth century these goals had come to require explicit redefinition and justification in the ideology of Empire. Astute colonial governor of India and Egypt, and above all a diligent servant of Empire whose words carried weight, Cromer's prognoses concerned those fortunate enough to have fallen under British imperial tutelage. These were "Egyptians, or Shilluks, or Zulus . . . these people who are all, nationally speaking, more or less *in statu pupillari*." He concludes on behalf of these subject peoples:

> There may then at all events be some hope that the Egyptian will hesitate before he throws in his lot with any future Arabi [prominent early-twentieth-century figure of Egyptian anticolonial resistance]. . . . Even the Central African savage may eventually learn to chant a hymn in honour of Astraea Redux, as represented by the British official who denies him gin but gives him justice.[25]

The national ideal is not to be denied the colonies here; even the lowliest savage, according to Cromer, may be taught to aspire and, aspiring, become a candidate for the higher humanity of nationhood. However, what Cromer gives with one hand he is also obliged to take away with the other. Since the colonies, as it turns out, were merely *in statu pupillari*; since colonials were children needing to be tutored into majority, it was only by remaining in Empire's cooperative embrace after all that they, Empire's diligent pupils, would be raised to, and maintain, the stature of nations.

Cromer's prognostication addresses, among other things, the question of how the colonies are to be *subcanonized*, as it were, in cultural and political cooperation with an enfolding imperial canonicity. If so, the generous allowance he makes for the incorporation of the colonized into the modes of British civility—made with an authority deriving from his impressive background of imperial service—has not a little to do with the rhetoric of Balmer, the missionary historiographer of the (Akanized) Gold

Coast Soul. And, moreover, if nation enters Cromer's polemic as the bearer of the canonic idea (of which Empire and the imperial official—who denies the native gin but gives him justice—are but the transcendental embodiment), it does so as a window opening onto a space where questions of the disposition, taste, and appreciation of the native in the colony—questions of what is appropriate behavior for him/her and what is not—are to be decided. In short, inserted into a demand to invent the appropriately pro-imperialist subject, Cromer's and Balmer's pedagogy-unto-nationhood (abetted by Welman) underwrites a self-serving colonial characterology.

In the idealization that foresees a future filled with grateful ex-savages chanting to the Astraea Redux, metropolitan culture—at the service of imperial political economy—expands and secures its canonicity further in a give-and-take. Just as tributary feeds mainstream and just as the former may be said to feed off the glory of the latter, it is the modes of subcanonicity imparted by the center at and to the periphery that Cromer imagines will return to feed the center in a virtuous imperial circle.

The foregoing must prompt us to examine closely what Welman could have intended when he floated the thesis that the strength of Balmer's history was in its permitting the Akan to see themselves *for the first time* in relation to "mankind in general." Why for the first time—an expression carrying the unmistakable hint of initiation? And why do we have the sense that he speaks from the position of a supreme guardian who is now able to give his benighted wards permission, withheld before, to see themselves in the light of day? And yet this light of day for which the Akan are supposed to be grateful does not come gratis. For the thesis "mankind in general" is hardly a "free" one; on the contrary it is bound to and euphemizes what we have already seen as the long-lived process by which Europe had usurped the universal, the general, into its self-constitution. The matter of retrieving a history of the Akan peoples of the Gold Coast may be read, therefore, as an exercise in imperial self-reference, an exercise on the colonial periphery calculated to further the ambitions of British imperial worlding.

Reading the Akan then as possessing an illustrious imperial pedigree of their own, as Balmer does when he adduces historical "evidence" locating their origin in the medieval western Sudan empire of Ghana, was to fit the Gold Coast into the ideology of an imperial commonwealth of nations so eloquently articulated by Cromer. Thus, in the hands of Balmer and Welman, the Gold Coast nation receives its civilizational subcanonicity all right, but it is invited to do so in accordance with the standards canonized and specified by the imperial overlord.

And what were the operational terms of the standard? Let us consider the writ of comparative European raciology as it circulated within Europe itself in the nineteenth century (and well into the twentieth). In the distinctions of hierarchy made between the white "races," the Anglo-Saxon, on whose Empire the sun never set, came out on top by his own measure as approaching God's ideal human type. In the words of Cecil Rhodes, the Anglo-Saxon race was "the finest race in the world . . . the best, the most human, most honorable race the world possesses."[26] Charles Kingsley—and other leading Victorian intellectual lights, like John Ruskin and Carlyle—articulated what most Victorians accepted as axiomatic: "The reign of world peace, order, and morality was to be established by the Anglo-Saxon-Teutonic Christians, and if necessary it was to be founded on the bodies of inferior races."[27] What is important for us at this point though is how the heritage of Anglo-Saxonism lies athwart Balmer's effort. The member of the self-defined aristocracy of races, finding both colonial motive and opportunity, makes to order a parallel aristocracy of tribes, the Akan, in the West African setting of the Gold Coast. Out of that will issue the heritage of "Ghana," a heritage standardized originally in accord with the new, cooperative design of Empire.

This study has recurrently advanced the thesis that any consideration of the modernist invention of Africa by Africans at the frontline of encounter must be fundamentally prepared to grapple with contradiction and paradox. In effect, for this study—and we have seen something of this in Attoh Ahuma's argumentation—African modernity gives its predisposition in a paradoxical play of possibility in liability, of constraint in opportunity. As a subtheme in the invention of Africa, Balmer's "Ghana," then, must be seen as straddling both terms, at once proffering possibility and liability; and its resultant thus requires to be engaged in those terms.

With this critical consideration before us it is now time to give attention to the influence of the missionary historian. We must consider how the history of the white auxiliary, considering that it went through fifteen printings (with sponsorship coming, no doubt, from the colonial establishment), must have been hugely successful in tapping deeply and directly into the worldly desire of a Gold Coast class-for-power seeking the normative basis of its nationalist characterology.[28]

More likely than not Balmer's work, directly and indirectly, provided topics for discussion in the agencies operating on behalf of a Gold Coast middle-class nationalist characterology. These were the Literary, Youth, and Social Clubs that brought the youth together, providing channels for informal education networks to be formed, and forums for discussing affairs of note in the Colony. Today these Clubs are largely forgotten, but from the turn of the nineteenth century to the middle of the twentieth they were agencies that actively disseminated a pedagogy whose avowed aims, couched in a rhetoric of self-improvement and upliftment, were, in essence, nationalist.[29]

It was Danquah, a stalwart of the Clubs who, on the native side, as has already been noted, would be the first, after Balmer, to stake the Akan claim to origin from Ghana in his *Akim Abuakwa Handbook* (1928). In so doing, Danquah would go one step further than Casely Hayford, who, in a manner not unlike Balmer, had also waged a conservative campaign in his *Ethiopia Unbound* on behalf of a normative African soul-principle that might be thought to reveal itself as a "uniform striving towards self-realization amid continual change of circumstance" (*Akan Peoples,* 14). *Ethiopia Unbound,* whose exploration of an "Ethiopian" metaphysics is based on its author's Fanti lifeworld, appeared in 1911. By 1925, when Balmer's history appeared in monograph form, it would seem from its title alone that the area of ethnohistorical and metaphysical enquiry was being broadened from an original, parochial Fanti base into a more generally "Akanized" invention of the Gold Coast nation.[30] And in the new native endeavor, the discursive Akanization of Gold Coast nationalism starting in the late 1920s, the figure of note was surely Danquah.

In a series of writings on the Ghana connection, Danquah, scion of the royal house of Akyem Abuakwa, was concerned to show—and his royal background had to have been a strong factor in his demonstration—that his country could claim an imperial genealogy. And this was a genealogy, moreover, whose civilizational pedigree could be thought to parallel that of the ruling house of the British colonial overlord. In effect, if in Danquah's work the past and imperially oriented Akanization of the Gold Coast translated into the salutary worlding of "Ghana"—as approved in Balmer's essentialism—this was a construct that was constrained to come dressed in the garb of the very colonial imperialism it was designed to "overthrow." *Sankofa*—or return to source—in Danquah's "Ghana" could thus be read as a cooperative, homegrown version of an imported conservative, centrist, and elitist discourse, a model and style of nationalist articulation routed through, and rubber-stamped by, the artifices and protocols of colonial-imperial prestige.[31] A subtheme in the agenda of attributively writing African modernity, Danquah's "Ghana" was a construct that suffered itself to be hijacked into the agenda of colonial-imperialism.

This finally, it seems, is the understanding we must bring to the productive collaboration, regarding the Ghana connection, between Danquah and Eva L. R. Meyerowitz, one-time art supervisor at Achimota College, the premier institution founded in 1927 by the colonial government to train the elite of the Colony. Meyerowitz, as Goody informs us, is on record as having declared Danquah to be the "inspirer of her researches, and he on his part has applauded her discovery of the connexions [of the Akan] with the 'ancient heliolithic cultures which once flourished in the Mediterranean and the Ancient East'" ("Myth," 468). In the 1950s when Danquah had to reiterate "The Akan Claim to Origin from Ghana" (1955)—a thesis that he had advanced in an appendix to his 1944 work *The Akan Doctrine of God*[32]—Meyerowitz would not be far behind him. She would present her defense of this claim in "The Akan and Ghana" in 1957. Both endeavors would be directed against the skeptical contrary claims made by commentators like Raymond Mauny in "The Question of Ghana" (1954).[33]

The fruit of Meyerowitz's amateur ethnohistorical researches—the earliest such research conducted among the Akan in 1945–46 was underwritten, suggestively enough, by the Colonial Welfare and Development Fund—began to appear in the 1950s. Her first monograph is *The Sacred State of the Akan* (1951), which sacralizes Akan statehood in an unmistakable royalist effort. In this and subsequent works she would seek concurrently to imperialize, "whiten," and "Orientalize" her recurrent subject—the Akan (ruling aristocracy) and Ghana. All these pseudohistorical moves may be read in retrospect as feeding into the late ideological quest by imperial Europe at the colonial periphery for auxiliary, self-serving modes of (ethno)centrism, a quest incorporated in the project I have identified as civilizational subcanonization.

Take, for instance, these "discoveries" that Meyerowitz makes about the Akan in her researches: "Akan civilization," she writes, "is *essentially* pre-Arab North African in character, and the claim of some of the Akan that their ancestors had been of a white race and originally came from the Sahara is unlikely to be fiction."[34] Or, again: "Akan culture and civilization is *not* Negro-African in origin but can be classed, *on the whole,* as Libyo-Berber, *more precisely perhaps* as Libyo-Phoenician or Carthaginian . . . a civilization which owed *almost everything* to the Near East and Egypt."[35] Or, yet again: "One can safely deduce . . . that the ancestors of the *present Akan aristocracy* were Saharan Libyan Berbers."[36] Here, in the revelation and dissemination of the elite white origins of the Akan genius to the, perhaps, unremembering Akan themselves, we find the Balmer-Tempels wish-fulfilling complex working itself out once again through the agency of yet another European auxiliary. (It does seem that, for Meyerowitz, claiming for the Akan kinship with, let us say, St. Augustine, a pre-Arab North

African Berber, patristic luminary of the Roman Catholic Church, and one of the central cultural icons of Western civilization, was to achieve a satisfactory insertion of the Gold Coast into the Occidental problematic of worlding—as given in Hegel's speculative *Philosophy of History*).

Little wonder, then, that a skeptical Goody has this to say of Meyerowitz's "insights": she "sheds little light and considerable confusion."[37] Still, the element of confusion notwithstanding, Meyerowitz disposes in such a fashion what Danquah first successfully proposes that we cannot but see her as usurping the original endeavor of the native into becoming a tributary. And this is a tributary obedient to the pull of a cultural-political discourse reinvented by and for the imperial mainstream. Thus it is that Danquah's success at cultural name-making—and its effect was not an inconsiderable one—was fated to come already framed and contained by an advance guard of impressive, mutually reinforcing formations emanating from the imperial metropole. We might number among these the elitist intellection characteristic of the Victorian era (as seen, for instance, in the moralism of Matthew Arnold's *Culture and Anarchy*), a jingoistic Anglo-Saxonism, and the classic civilizational historicism underwritten by the conservative Occidental idealism founded by Hegel.

Still, to be fair, any assessment of Danquah's culturalist achievement must credit him with having given shape in and through "Ghana" to a general structure of feeling, as the late Raymond Williams might have put it. And in the arena of anticolonial contestation in the Gold Coast, this affective aspect of myth-making and social idealization, this finding of an appropriate symbol around which attitudes might cohere, finally mattered.

But there needed, it seems, to be more than an invocation of a symbolic past, however glorious. Reading Danquah's achievement shows us that if a compatible structure of value must needs accompany and inform a structure of feeling as the latter's sustenance, then his "Ghana" was lacking in this important respect. It is not enough, therefore, for Goody to put matters the way he does when, in summarizing the Ghana connection, he suggests that the "adoption of the name of an ancient kingdom legitimises the status of [the] newly founded nation" ("Myth," 473). That must remain an incomplete reading of what happened in the case of the entity that would become Ghana in 1957. For it is only insofar as, following the proclamation of 1948, the myth-ideal of "Ghana" had been displaced into a sensuous programme; only insofar as an active human symbol had intervened to incarnate the ideal as the possibility of secular transformation; only then would the different peoples of the Gold Coast come to discover in "Ghana" the foundations of national—as opposed to merely ethnocentric—legitimacy. And for this momentous shift in value, as I hope to demonstrate in my reading of Kwame Nkrumah's autobiography in chapter 7, Danquah's elitist, backward-looking, and neo-royalist Akan-centrism could hardly have sufficed.

Continuing boldly in the tradition of radical anticolonial contestation introduced into the Gold Coast in the 1930s by the Sierra Leonean labor activist I. T. A. Wallace-Johnson and the Nigerian journalist Nnamdi Azikiwe,[38] it is Nkrumah who will bring a new brand of nationalist politics to postwar Gold Coast. In the process he will appropriate and successfully insert a popular past into a competitively redefined—as opposed to Danquah's more or less cooperative—characterology of a nationalist middle class. Wresting "Ghana" from Danquah, Nkrumah will translate the name from idealist myth into concrete program. Thus, on the road to Independence, it is in Nkrumahist ideopraxis, finally, that "Ghana," considered from the standpoint of short-term success at least[39]—for Nkrumah will also be seen to have compromised the ideal—discovers and seals its consummation.

Afterword: Reviewing "Ghana," "Africa," and the Black (Man's) Burden of Creativity in (a Colonialist) Modernity

> We were created and are not creators; recipients at the point of a gun, not givers, at the point of an assegai [spear].
> —Kofi Awoonor, Ghanaian writer

To the British poet Dame Edith Sitwell goes the credit of penning the following lines about Africa in her poem "Gold Coast Customs" (1929). In them the customs of the Gold Coast are put to poetic work on behalf of an "Africa" that

> . . . is the unhistorical,
> Unremembering, unrhetorical,
> Undeveloped spirit involved
> In the conditions of nature—Man
> That black image of stone hath delved
> On the threshold where history began.[40]

By its clearly Hegelian wording, Sitwell's poem establishes the conviviality of its message with a longstanding rhetorical and philosophical tradition.

This is the European tradition that had *created itself* by *un*creating Africa, rendering the latter as Nothing to its Everything. If the *topos* of the white man's burden shapes itself by drawing for credit on the readily available fund of this uncreated entity, it is this same fund of Nothingness that will impose itself on the black man as the burden of liability that alienates him into worldlessness.

Perhaps, nowhere is this corollary of credit and liability more in evidence than in the pedagogical circuits of exchange involving black and white in the, by definition, unequal colonial relation. If the pedagogical relation can be imagined as that between white analyst and native patient, then it is the case that the former draws disproportionate credit by both speaking the latter's illness and shaping a cure for it. And this is because the lowly native is thought to be imprisoned in the liability of not knowing, let alone having the ability to diagnose, his own sickness (i.e., the sickness derived for him by the knowing analyst). The diagnosis of Sitwell's poem, if it perpetuates a tradition, is nothing more and nothing less than a restatement of the place of sickness, the created worldlessness, from where Balmer's pedagogy for the Negro and Tempels's for the Bantu (and for that matter the "revisionist" politics of Cromer and Welman) begin to shape a cure.

For, as we have seen, what both missionaries read as Africa's human failure to remember translates into the moral infirmity of her peoples; and moral infirmity, in a further extension, translates into a history of fatality, which, as such, finally is no history at all. Indeed, we may surmise in the case of Balmer, operating in the Gold Coast, that the evidence of such fatality was there before him in what his own experience would render to him as the Babel of disunited peoples of the polyglot country. The fact of the matter, then, is that in Balmer's conspectus it is not Europe that had self-servingly created the uncreated Negro. It had to be the Negro himself onto whom the responsibility, and hence the burden, of worldlessness—his Nothingness, that is—was shifted. Since it was he who had been heedless of his own creation, it followed that it was he who had to be rendered blameworthy for the fatality of his lowly colonial estate.

Balmer, in his foreword, is thus the knowing analyst anatomizing the psyche of the race, establishing the ambient flaw in the racial character, and complementarily bringing to it the gift of the cure that will restore it to history—and hence humanity. Cured into remembrance, the racial patient, Balmer's Negro, could only thenceforth assume moral responsibility for itself; and, as the missionary prognosticates further, an educable elite's assumption of such responsibility translates salutarily into nation-ness as a retrieval of historical continuity out of otherwise meaningless fatality. This, ultimately, is the Creator entrusting an auxiliary creativity to his creation with a vengeance; and thus we are to understand Danquah's "Ghana," as an articulation given in the unfolding of the *mythos* of the white man's burden in colonial Gold Coast. Reading his "Ghana" the way I have, then, is meant to reveal how such auxiliary creativity proceeds directly out of the worldless condition of alienation imposed on the black man; how this, subsequently, becomes his burden of worlding.

Taking a critical, retrospective look at the white auxiliary's gift of "Ghana" to his native understudy and collaborator, as we have done, can only remind us, finally, of the injunction to "beware of the Greeks when they come bearing gifts." The paradoxical implication carried by the saying should remind us, then, that such a thing as Balmer's gift never was free. In the pedagogies promising an amelioration of the burden of worldlessness alienating Africa into a colonialist modernity, the intention may have been to shape possibilities for the native at the receiving end. However well intentioned such thought may have been though, in the unequal relations of power and representation obtaining between auxiliary and understudy in colonial Gold Coast, the possibilities sponsoring and underwriting the invention of "Ghana" were such that they were more or less to power's advantage. In the circumstances, "Ghana" was not given to the native in advance as pure becoming; rather, it was fated to come already entangled problematically in liability, the liability of being uttered by the interested giver from without.

Must that then leave us with nothing other than Awoonor's rather grim conclusion, as cited in the epigraph above?

Not necessarily, although the epigraph is a sobering reminder that in the worlding of the African nation, liability is never far behind possibility. To think African modernity as possibility at all—and it is within this possibility that nation accompanies a middle class in the rising—we need first to recognize the imposed liability of worldlessness in which this possibility is inscribed as its own structural and semantic precondition. As it detaches itself from this precondition, in a heroic quest for its own possibilities, African modernity presents itself in a manner not unlike Soyinka's reading of the Yoruba god-figure Ogun in the trammels of the "fourth stage" or the "abyss of transition." Here, in what might be called Ogunist paradox, the god-figure admits within a single frame both life-affirming possibility and death-dealing liability. If he is the creator-redeemer of what—until he exerts a questing, creative will—remains an uncreated world, Ogun also possesses impressive blind spots that make him an unthinking destroyer of the world of his own effort. And in destroying—i.e., compromising—what he has created, Ogun might be thought (in somewhat Sisyphean terms) to represent heroic creativity finding itself repeatedly subject to perdition, or as the will-to-become forever shadowed by the worldless, alienated condition of its beginnings.

I invoke this reformulation of Soyinka's Ogunist problematic of worlding Africa—and I have given it an interpretative twist that makes it partial to my own project of reading the modernist problem(atic) of the African nation—to provide a *partial* analogy for the two error-prone, would-be heroic middle class types whose narratives provide the subjects of discussion in the next chapter. William Narh Ocansey and George Ekem Ferguson are the names of these two. Natives both of the Gold Coast, they did some of the earliest anglophone writing to come out of the country at the beginning of the colonial era.

In Ocansey's *African Trading* (1881), as we shall see, he is the Kafkaesque naif almost, his story that of the native attempting, from the injustice of the colonial periphery, to beat a path to the unknown but thought-to-be-righteous heart of Empire. The theme of the quest for economic justice at the center of *African Trading* we would certainly recognize as an early statement of the recurrent crisis afflicting an Africa displaced into a colonialist and lately neocolonialist modernity. If so, one merit of Ocansey's story is that, however uncomfortable its resolution, it refamiliarizes us with the pursuit of equity in a forgotten era.

Ferguson's 1890s narratives for their part describe the expeditions of a native colonial servant into what was then the unincorporated hinterland lying behind the Gold Coast Colony. The author hands us narrative descriptions of the series of scientific surveys and mappings he conducted of this "unknown" space. In relation to his "own" native territory, we see a Ferguson who gauges his mission generally in terms of what would be called, in today's language of postimperial uniformity sponsored by the Bretton Woods Institutions, "structural adjustment." If his narratives depict a black man in the role almost of a civilizational demiurge, Ferguson reads himself in this role as a bridge in the middle. He is a native auxiliary drawing on the pulse of an imperial modernity, and conducting its immense vitality to rejuvenate and recreate the enfeebled heart of a "savage" and "barbarian" country.

Between naif and demiurge in the middle—both starting from, and attempting to negotiate, the created burden of uncreated Africa—the next chapter draws a composite sketch of resolution and compromise as a theme which haunts that frontline scene of becoming designated in this study as

African modernity. To this end, reading between the narratives of these two enjoins the performance of a delicate negotiation. This negotiation will have to establish the gesture of the *then* of the nationalist writing the nation—and the *now* of the critic reading this nation—as an activity that proceeds more or less affirmatively in spite of being compromised. And reading *in spite of* has thus to be a critical interpretive activity that attempts to construct (nationalist) possibility in the interstices of (colonial) liability. Hence, in spite of the fact that Ferguson and Ocansey were error-prone, I can hardly claim to speak this from an Archimedean point of view. On the contrary, rendering them as problematic studies in paradox is to measure the contemporary dilemmas of Africans—dilemmas that come with occupying a post-encounter frontline—against, and to show them as flowing from, theirs.

Thus the next chapter, drawing on narratives representing two facets of the native auxiliary, the outbound messenger (Ocansey) and his inbound counterpart (Ferguson)—archetypally representing what Ngugi wa Thiong'o, the Kenyan writer and critic, refers to as an African *messenger class*—steps back and forth in time to configure a genealogy. And this genealogy self-consciously traces the paradoxes going into the making of African modernity, that problematic configuration in which the African nation is entangled and out of which it strives to name its own possibility.

5

FAUST IN AFRICA

GENEALOGY OF A "MESSENGER CLASS"

Tyger Tyger burning bright
In the forests of the night,
What immortal hand or eye,
Dare frame thy fearful symmetry.
    —William Blake, "The Tyger," *Songs of Innocence and Experience*

Let us help one another to find a way out of Darkest Africa. The impenetrable jungle around us is not darker than the dark primeval forest of the human mind uncultured. We must emerge from the savage backwoods and come into the open where nations are made.
    —Attoh Ahuma, *The Gold Coast Nation and National Consciousness*

[In 1977] I told [my third year English class at the University of Nairobi] . . . "I want to attempt a class analysis of Chinua Achebe's fiction from *Things Fall Apart* to *Girls at War*. I want . . . to trace the development of the *messenger class* from its inception as actual messengers, clerks, soldiers and road foremen in colonialism as seen in *Things Fall Apart* and *Arrow of God*, to their position as the educated 'been-tos' in *No Longer at Ease*; to their assumption and exercise of power in *A Man of the People*; to their plunging of the nation into intra-class civil war in *Girls at War*."
    —Ngugi wa Thiong'o, *Decolonising the Mind*

174

Sons and Fathers; Or, Locating the Present in the Future Anterior of the Past

Introducing the Picador collection of his first three novels in 1988—the collection goes by the title *The African Trilogy*—Chinua Achebe steps back for one reflexive moment to make a candid observation about his relation to his father. Recalling that the man was "a devout evangelist," Achebe reveals a father whose wholehearted devotion to the brave new white dispensation, introduced by the colonial encounter, was matched by an iron resolution to make a clean break with his traditional Igbo past. As far as the novelist can recall, he "never divulged to me before he passed on" the "sensational masquerade dancing" that he did "before he renounced the devil and all his works" (xi). The devil and all his works: this language we will surely recognize as one whose inscription and meaning appear in the very order of colonialist diagnosis, which, as divulged in the last chapter, contrives to impose on Africa her burden of worldlessness.

Achebe, looking at this scene of fatherly alienation, is moved to acknowledge that there might be a "great story in [the] generation (his father's) that navigated the perilous crossroads [brought on by the colonial encounter]" (xi). Yet, in spite of the positive acknowledgement, the novelist suggests that he might not after all be the person to write this story. Its ambivalent implications, it would seem, impinge too powerfully on his present to allow him to give this story the "objective," clear-sighted treatment it deserves. As he surmises: "why rush into it and perhaps get things (*if not yourself*) tangled up?" (x). A father's deliberate oversight in the past strikes a contemporary responsive chord, an equally deliberated oversight, in his son.

As we read the literal detail of a personal oversight in a father's relationship with his son, then, it is to watch the scene of biographical confession disposing itself into an allegory of trepidation and unresolved guilt. This is the overwhelming impression we get when, in a moment haunted by a necessary failure of creative nerve, the novelist writes:

> The major problem was this: my father's generation were the very people after all who, no matter how sympathetically one wished to look upon their predicament, did open the door to the white man. But could I, even in the faintest, most indirect, most delicate allusiveness, dare to suggest that he may have been something . . . of a . . . traitor? (x)

Not surprisingly, as he tries to account for his difficulty, Achebe takes the soft option:

[I] don't mean this [refusal to call my father a traitor] in a sentimental, soft-headed, filial-duty sense at all, but in relation to concrete things I knew about the man. So *the only permissible* interpretation had to be that I was not old enough, or simply did not know as much as I should have when it happened. (x; emphasis added)

Contrary to what seems to be a deep-seated wish of the novelist to avoid the allegorical interpretation, we perceive in his account two individuals whose relationship is written over by a heritage bigger than either and encompassing both of them. This heritage is the frontline one, the frontline being what Achebe poetically refers to as the "crossroads." Originally conducted through the position occupied by the father once upon a time vis-à-vis the "white man," the frontline heritage is that which is bequeathed to his similarly positioned son. Like father, like son: the original sin of the former, it appears, is condemned to perpetuate itself.

Ngugi, in the example of the third epigraph above, gives us a clue as to why Achebe insists as he does on the "concrete things"; as to why the latter must manage a larger sense of existential unease by deflecting it into the merely literal detail of a sensuous relationship. To read Ngugi reading Achebe is to understand why the Akan have observed proverbially that anyone who insists on peering into the eyes of a corpse renders himself liable to the unnerving experience of seeing a ghost. Yet this is precisely what Ngugi would commit his African audience to doing. For, as appears in his understanding of Achebe's *oeuvre,* giving the past relation—the buried corpse of the self, so to speak—an allegorical reading, of the kind given the scenario of Achebe *et père* above, is to usefully read the present relation symptomatically.[1] Such a procedure, it is to be understood, shifts interpretation away from a manifest relationship—Achebe's concrete things—such that it points to a latent or residual one: the proverbial "ghost" that, lying (obscured) behind those concretely manifest things, threatens to jeopardize and contradict their reassuring, "fleshly" meaning.

Thus it is that reading symptomatically, Ngugi's allegorical presentation of Achebe's writings from *Things Fall Apart* to *Girls at War* invites us to link these works in one continuum of paradox, furnished in that frontline positionality occupied by an African leader middle class. In Ngugi's assessment the colonially alienated beginnings of this class leaves it the actively residual function of an Other's messenger. His class-reflexive reading, furthermore, obliges us with the radical implication that, as exemplified by Achebe's *oeuvre,* since the creativity of a messenger class terminates in its self-consumption in war,[2] the beginnings of this creativity may be thought to be based on, as it were, an inaugural Faustian compact.[3]

Going by Ngugi's style of interpreting Achebe, then, is to see in the detail of the latter's biographical confession a sense of fatherly liability that impels forward a history that can only displace from a middle class a self-possessed sense of African belonging. Where the generation of the fathers—the originals, as it were—are responsible for "letting in the white man," beginnings shape themselves not in originary purity but in a situation of genealogical "miscegenation." Such a reading, in effect, throws the continuities that follow from those beginnings—i.e., the nationalist and postindependence progeny of the fathers—into relief as an astonishing chiaroscuro. The open door of fatherly liability means that the modernist project of "African" self-attribution that comes in its aftermath takes shape in a continual quest to resolve black from white; to coax endogenous (African) authenticity out of an exogenous (European and colonialist) overlay, and so on. It is in these terms that, whether he wants to admit it fully or not, Achebe, seeking to contain his immediate past in a critical narrative frame, finds himself also, in a reflexive doubling, immediately containing himself in the uneasy consequentiality of that past.

The suggestion at the end of the last chapter was that the present one was going to be a reading of the paradoxical genealogy of African modernity, and that this would be done in a manner that brings into view retrospect conceived on the prospect. Genealogy, in the simplest sense, is about who begat whom. There ought to be more to it, however, than this reductive account if we consider that genealogical reconstruction traces a dual movement: it preserves in one continuum the movement of past in present and present in past. In such reconstruction, that is, the past is brought forward and preserved as present memory, and present memory itself reaches back towards and into the past for an investment of its own future possibility. Past and present are thus inscribed in each other, and the genealogical exercise reads as an attempt to capture both in a continuum whose points it defines always as the *creative* or *original* moments of a future anterior.

What was meant at the end of chapter 4, then, was an exercise of this nature: to configure in a mutual relation the postindependence present reading (itself in) the preindependence past, and the past reading the future that is our present; hence a past reading itself (its present, that is) as a future anterior. Hence this chapter has begun with a critical reading of one of the central icons of African originality in the postindependence era doing a keenly present-minded reading of his relation to his fatherly past, an investigation that revealed the symptomatic presentness of the past in Achebe's present. What now remains to be done is to complete the circle by reading the presentness of our present in the preindependence past, that past which endows the future-oriented projects of African modernity.

This mode of reading is justified if only because the subjects of this chapter, Ferguson and Ocansey—but, in an outstanding sense, the former—present a huge interpretive challenge. What are we to make of the ambivalence, the fearful symmetry, that inscribes the relation between the concrete things—in our postindependence situation, we might think this concreteness in terms of palpable achievements in the projects of African modernity—and the residual element which, although it may not manifest itself immediately, nevertheless shadows and insinuates itself (as Ngugi reminds us) into the workings of the former?

As we shall see, while resolving the challenge of reading Ferguson may not vindicate Achebe reading his father, it cannot also be a question of, as it were, unproblematically choosing Ngugi over Achebe either. For, as should be obvious, Ngugi, the symptomatic reader of Achebe, cannot *logically* claim to occupy a pure space outside the one which he reads the latter as operating in. Ngugi may claim ideological exemption but he certainly does not have the benefit of existential exemption from the condition he describes. It is this logical difficulty that necessitates the ambivalent reading brought to Ferguson. And, having said that, for pragmatic reasons, it will become necessary to suppress this same difficulty with Ocansey's *African Trading*, reserving, as in Ngugi's demonstration, a symptomatic reading for his narrative. Read this way, the latter's agonized self-presentation furnishes what might be thought as the traumatic pre-text that paves the way, in the structure of this work, to present the at once reactive and proactive nativist nationalism of Casely Hayford. Following the unself-critical *African Trading*, then, we arrive at *Ethiopia Unbound* as the earliest literary example of the self-critical reaction of an African middle class discovering, relative to its own native sphere of belonging, its alienated messenger status.

Before we get to *Ethiopia Unbound* in the next chapter, however, in order to assist us to square the circle of past in present/present in past, we will have to revisit Hayford's important reflections in 1914 concerning "The Future of West Africa." Structured around the theme of fatherly liability, Hayford's reflections find an uncanny echo in what Achebe will come to write about his relationship with his father in 1988. If Hayford in this essay finds himself grappling, like Achebe, with the problem of reading the fathers, the future anterior of his reading, as denoted by the title of the essay, also foresees the problem in terms of the Faustian compact of alienated creativity that Ngugi gestures at. Insofar as Hayford is compelled beforehand, as it were, to read his situation towards Achebe and, beyond that, towards Ngugi, it is because he had arrived at an awareness that he had inherited a dubious "burden of the double life."[4] This is a reference to the oxymoronic selfhood (or subjectivity) that the ambivalent currents of a colonialist modernity had elected to shape for his kind. Thus it is that, drawing on the ageless poetry of Old Testament prophetic utterance, Hayford is moved to indict the immediate past: "The fathers have eaten sour grapes, and the children's teeth are set on edge." Acknowledging this unpleasant truth, the he asks rhetorically "who shall deliver us from the body of this death?"[5] Hayford shows that not only are he and his kind saddled with a deathly heritage—we might translate this as a colonialist Unconscious— but that this is something they are powerless *not* to pass on.

Hayford's reflexive lament about grapes gone sour on the children goes particularly for a middle class whose European education had trapped it, so to speak, in implements of colonialist devising. To be sure, the situation in which "The Future of West Africa" was conceived, and the language in which it was composed, English, bear the uneasy symbolism of fatal compromise. Written to be delivered within the walls of a colonial school by one of its prominent native products,[6] it is a presentation that, compelled to take a critical look at its own prehistory, "confesses" to a complicity—that its own premises depend, more or less, on the conveniences of a colonialist modernity. For Hayford, then, all who come after the fathers, that generation which "did open the door to the white man," are heirs of the terrible burden of fatherly liability. Forever threatening to go sour on their descendants, the acts by which the fathers partook of the grapes of Europe thus become the very notation, as it were, of original sin.

It is on the basis of this Hayfordian conception that the will of the sons to original creativity appears subject to a Faustian compact (the self-same "compact" from which Achebe, coming much later, would much rather avert his gaze). "No worse burden," Hayford concludes in his piece, "could be imposed by [European] civilization on African nationality" (*Land Question*, 101). His lament shows a keen awareness of how the desire of a native African middle class, his kind, has been alienated into an Other's desire. If this desire originates in the burden of worldlessness imposed by the latter, then Hayford registers this as the mode by which Europe, handing down the language and dictating the terms that structure the burden, holds "Africa" captive to her design.[7]

Reading in the future anterior of colonial time, Hayford dramatizes the impossible situation of his kind: he shows the dilemma of the alienated subjectivity that has arrived at knowledge of the ultimate sort about itself. Just as in the allegory of the Faustian soul, Hayford, pondering creative originality—or a would-be sovereign, self-impelling principle—from the standpoint of an African middle class, must confront the ultimate genealogical paradox. Middle-class creativity finds itself, if not wholly mortgaged to the purposes of the far-ranging power of a Mephistophelean—i.e., imperializing—Other, then, at the very least, alienated into participating as a secret sharer in the structures put in place by this power.

As for this predicament, the dubious Faustian compact of an African middle class, the postindependence Senegalese author Cheik Hamidou Kane, has given it a tragic and, perhaps, in all of African letters, the most moving, rendering in his allegorical novel *Ambiguous Adventure*. Kane powerfully dramatizes the theme of self-loss, doing so within the larger ambit of the major "upheaval in the natural order" grounding the cultural practices of African societies that came after the colonial encounter. Resolving the encounter in a frontline allegory of "the [black] man" and "the [white colonial] school," Kane proposes:

> [W]ithout either of them wanting it, the new [black] man and the new [modern-colonial] school come together just the same. . . . The man does not want the school because in order that he may live—that is, be free, feed and clothe himself—it imposes upon him the necessity of sitting henceforth, for the required period, upon its benches. No more does the school want the man because in order to survive—that is, extend itself and take roots where its necessity has landed it—it is obliged to take account of him.[8]

What Kane renders here is a mode of retrospective paradox where, at the African frontline, post-encounter Freedom (the notation of possibility) is obliged to be inscribed in, and therefore impossibly wrest itself out of, colonial Necessity (the notation of liability). In *Ambiguous Adventure,* Necessity possesses a sense of ultimacy: the tragic self-loss of the hero read in these terms translates the situation of Africa coming after the colonial encounter into the harsh Experience of unfreedom (or, lately, a postcolonial delusion of freedom). It is a liability that, so to speak, leaves African nativity robbed forever of the sovereign repose of its pristine Innocence (for Kane, an unidealized Innocence, equally rigorous and harsh).

Thus the paradox of modernity's colonialist African genealogy; and it is to examine some of the implications of this paradox that this study turns to the expeditionary narratives of Ekem Ferguson in the next section. If Ferguson provides the occasion to illustrate the problem of doubling (or ambivalence), then the discussion of Ocansey's *African Trading* which follows reads out the colonialist Unconscious—or the secret original sin, if you will—of a middle class. And reading the two figures is done to sound not so much the pastness of the past as the future anterior that necessarily structures a problematic colonialist past within present African endeavors.

Innocent Zealot or Glorious Fool? Notes on a "Paradoxical Patriot"

The discussion of the expeditionary narratives of Ferguson that follows is meant to resonate within: (a) Hayford's preoccupation in "The Future of West Africa" with thinking a way out of the impasse of a double consciousness; and (b) what Achebe's retrospection, as we saw, has to admit by default. For the latter, the way out of the impasse would hardly seem to be one that required a closing of "the door"—as if this is possible at all—through which, in the first instance, the generation of the fathers had let in the modern *and* colonialist civilization of the "white man." Still, Achebe's evasiveness concerning the ultimate question of fatherly liability does indicate the unpalatable condition this moment imposes on the (genealogical) future, the present which is the originality of our future anterior. Thus his reservations can only leave us the startling problem of what to make of an "African" consciousness that appears in a modality of doubling, that very ambivalence which Hayford had put his finger on a half-century or so earlier.

Inasmuch as the inaugural act of the door's opening is irreversible, therefore, going back to read fatherly types like Ferguson poses a by no means easy challenge. For those who would read and write about the narratives that occupy the colonialist beginnings of modern African nationality, then, Achebe's hesitation before the ultimate admission of original sin (or fatherly liability) can only be an uncomfortable reminder that, in these narratives, it is by no means always possible to tell the collaborator from the resistor, the traitor from the true patriot.

Such, perhaps, is the meaning of the strange ambivalence we find in the description of Ferguson, the youthful technocrat and loyal native servant of Her Majesty's colonial government, given by Kwame Arhin, the Ghanaian historian. In Arhin's assessment, Ferguson emerges as a clearly "extraordinary" personage, although Arhin is quick to add that "one may, in retrospect, disapprove of [Ferguson's] assiduous and devoted service to an alien (i.e., colonial) government."[9]

By any measure it is true that Ferguson was extraordinary. Born in 1864, he started work in the colonial civil service at seventeen. After taking a course of instruction in astronomical observation and map-making, he had by age twenty already compiled for the colonial government a map of the divisions of the Colony. The first of his expeditions took place when he was twenty-five, after his return from the Royal Normal School of Mines in Britain, where he had studied surveying, among other things, between 1889 and 1890. At age thirty-two (January 1897), in the course of another expedition, Ferguson would meet an untimely death in what is today's Upper West Region of Ghana.

In Ferguson, then, we are looking at a native son—he was of Fanti extraction—who impressively brought the combined roles of political agent, diplomat, surveyor, geologist, cartographer, draftsman, explorer, historian, linguist, and ethnographer to a colonial administration which, by all accounts, was grateful. Nevertheless, Arhin cannot help but admit that, for all his "support for colonial rule," this was a native African who was "paradoxically patriotic" (*Papers,* xi). What are we to make of Arhin's paradox of a patriot? What of a "patriotism" fated, as it would appear, to perform dual service: as much for a colonial regime, whose ends it furthered in the past, as for a present reaching back to look for an enabling archetype of national beginnings? These questions point still to another: in obedience to the genealogical logic described above, what value must the present invest in Ferguson's past if it is to retrieve this past for itself as its own possibility?

On the one hand, looking back, the "father" who gave an unquestioned dedication to a colonial administration could be read in a positive sense as one who played the exemplary role of a pioneer, spearheading a process of modernization that today's Ghana pridefully inherits. On that score Ferguson is Arhin's "extraordinary" figure. To the extent that he shows himself able to traverse, chart, and point a way ahead, a way out of and beyond the limitations revealed to nativity about itself by an all-conquering imperium, he represents a figure of utopian possibility for the present-day national formation. It is Ferguson's literal groundwork, after all, that made it possible to imagine the actualization of Atto Ahuma's nationalist desire for a postethnic Gold Coast/Ghana, complete with the "rights, privileges and status of nationality."

If, however, on the other hand, serving as the instrument of colonial power,[10] Ferguson appears to be guilty of furthering the territorial and cultural alienation of a hitherto self-accountable sphere of nativity into a colonialist modernity, then a problem arises. In this problematic mode, Ferguson presents a liability which we must factor into the African nation as a part of its modernist heritage. The question is then: is Ferguson, the man who more than any other *native* bestowed upon modern Ghana her physical configuration, a glorious fool or an innocent zealot? A categorical interpretation of the man's career is snagged by the fact that today, if a people know and live their existence daily as Ghanaian, their consciousness of an imagined community redounds in large part on the personage and work of Ferguson. And yet this technocrat's valuable work—work on which succeeding generations are compelled to place a national significance—was enabled by the conveniences of a European civilization he accepted and unqualifiedly revered as such, its colonialist implications notwithstanding.

Again, it would seem that to arrive at a comprehensive sense of African modernity at all, we are required to maintain a posture of reading between liability and possibility. In the circumstances, our African situation is not unlike that captured in the proverbial Akan conundrum about the *santrofi* bird, which might be read as thematizing the dilemmas characteristic of the twilight zone of historical transitions. The nature of the *santrofi* bird, we will recall, is such that to take it from the wilds and bring it home with you is to impose a curse on yourself (and, it would seem, on generations to come). And yet a failure to claim this bird is to unwisely deny yourself (and, by implication, your posterity) a great fortune.

We may substitute modernity's *colonialist* dispensation in Africa for the troubling otherness of the *santrofi* bird and, in that move, locate in the Akan proverb both a salutary imperative and an ominous warning. If the proverb resounds as the difficulty, in our situation, of distinguishing regenerative potential (the promise of a rationalized modernity) from deathly liability (colonialist alienation), still, we may tease from it the implication that if the regenerative possibilities introduced by the strange element are to be realized, then this requires that domestic space be urgently reoriented.

This is where Ferguson's expeditionary work yields a *mythos* of beginnings. For he makes us see African agency transformatively working on its native world in an active quest to align it productively with an outer world, that novel world so importunately bearing down on the old Africa. His accounts of his travels from coastal Gold Coast into an "unknown" interior posits the possibility, then, of reconciling an "inner" with an "outer" world. And this possibility is precisely what we observe in the extraordinary drive of the native surveyor who traverses, charts, maps, records, and prognosticates on the native space in hopeful preparation for its infusion by a rationalized—in the Weberian sense—and, in his own account, "civilizing" modernity.

Ferguson was sent by the Colonial Government on a series of expeditions into the hinterland of the Gold Coast between 1890 and 1897. He recorded these journeys dutifully in accounts addressed to the Governor of the Colony and representative of the Crown. These accounts furnish us with a series of astounding travel narratives which frame meticulously prepared histories, ethnographies, and comparative cultural and linguistic-anthropological data relating to the several peoples Ferguson encountered as he traversed the then Gold Coast proper and the hinterland beyond. If Ferguson's accounts also provide sophisticated, historically engaged analyses of the contemporary political economies of these peoples, these analyses are accompanied by speculations on their potential utility in relation to the overall colonial political economy. Towards this end, he provides an impressive cartographic and statistical survey and furnishes geographical and geological details and maps, among other vital items of information, about both Colony and its hinterland.

Ferguson's projections, in relation to what he saw as the fragmentary patchwork of weak ethnic enclaves in the interior, are inscribed in his expeditionary narratives as a vision of a sustainable postethnic world. If we get an obscure intimation of nationality—a uniform community, that is—in this postethnic world of his imaginings,[11] we must also acknowledge the fact that Ferguson consistently saw its sustainability in terms of its being engulfed by a stabilizing British imperial-colonial power. This theme is of a piece with his measurements, classifications, diagnoses and prognoses. In them we might see the techniques of science and instrumental reason objectifying themselves in colonial power—this power, then, being projected in advance, through the mediation of Ferguson, as the requisite normative principle that will homogenize and stabilize an otherwise "chaotic" native sphere.

The career of Ferguson, this great believer in rationalization, must recall another, the one that saw Horton earlier advocating a rationalizing of the political condition—in reality the political economy—of the Gold Coast. However, unlike Horton—whose writings, appearing before the inception of formal colonialism, uncompromisingly sought African independence— Ferguson, the servant-beneficiary of the new colonial dispensation does not, indeed cannot, give explicit expression to a politics of self-determination. This crucial difference notwithstanding, these two, for being native men of science—Horton, we will recall, was a medical doctor—were not too far apart. The rational reorientation of nativity that Horton committed himself to exploring in thoughtful action (if we can describe his reflections this way)—that same rearrangement which Ferguson would come later to commit himself to actually sketching on the ground—these commitments represent both to us as conduits of the same force: modernization.

What most identifies the two, then, is that they are middle-class ideologues of the same—a rationalized modernity. If this is reflected in a certain unwavering pursuit of a principle of standardization found in their writings, in this "obsession" lies the common "political" ground occupied by the generality of their class.[12] Here, on this ground of desire, we might think of a middle class projecting itself, in the name of science, as a standardizing or equalizing norm over the hotchpotch of more or less rivalrous ethnicities comprising a native African sphere.[13] With Ferguson, as with Horton and others, this idea of the middle as equalizing standard translated into more than a dream of a horizontal fraternity of native peoples, however. In its terms a middle class could also imagine itself in representatively modernist terms as the equalizing bridge between the native peoples and the exogenous sources of a "civilizing" modernity.[14] It is in respect of this that, as one of the first actuations of the modernist desire of a middle class to reorient ethnic discontinuity in the Gold Coast and its beyond, the groundwork of Ferguson finds a place in the anxious genealogy of this class. The drive, then as now, was to reshape nativity into a unitary entity that would thereafter recognize itself as a more or less standardized sphere of politically, if not culturally, shared values.

But what were these values for Ferguson and his "co-religionists" of the modern, and what system of valuation empowered them and assigned them their validity? In Ferguson's writings they fall under the Enlightenment and Eurocentrically defined themes of "civilization" and "progress," both terms deriving their authorization from the power and prestige of Empire. Backed by this magisterial imperial guarantee, Ferguson presents his relation to a native sphere in terms that permit us to read his role as that of an emissary of light bringing a dark and inchoate interior progressively into a measurable relation with a radiant center. Hence, as we see him negotiating treaties of friendship and protection with the chiefdoms, states, and polities of the Hinterland, Ferguson's instrumentality is invariably produced in an enlightened language of amelioration. His task is to bring an "unknown" Hinterland into the ambit of the known: that which, by his account, is a "civilized" and "progressive" British colonial ambience. We can hardly fail to notice that in his self-descriptions in his reports, he belongs to a circumscribed world of "us," the world of the "civilized mind" represented by the colonial administration, to which he opposes "them," the "rude" world of "native minds" (*Papers*, 60, 129).

Within the problematic binary of "us" and "them," the centrality of imperial Anglo-Europe is insistently proclaimed by the dedicated messenger in passages where he ventures his "civilized" and "progressive" opinions. Thus, for instance, concerning the depredations visited by Asante on her neighbors, Ferguson notes ruefully: "It is a pity that, in these days of civilisation, a savage and unreliable country like Ashanti should be recognised and respected as though it was one of the great Powers of Europe" (61). With colonialist belittling of this kind going on, there is little to be surprised about in the following observation where Ferguson comments on colonial education and the language question: "With regard to secular education, I am of the opinion that as long as the instruction . . . is confined to the native languages—languages which have no literature and no *ulterior utility*—there will be but little progress" (24; emphasis added). Throughout the account of his travels, a language that identifies him with the "ulterior utility" of Europe—and nativity's lack of ulteriority here advances Europe's claim to be the outermost limit of the "universal"—fixes the native surveyor within the symbolic centrality of a European universe. And it is in relation to this assuredly secure universal symbol that, through Ferguson's instrumental mediation, the Gold Coast and its hinterland were to be progressively surveyed, sketched, mapped, and, finally, drawn into the political economy and geography of the universe of "civilized" nations.

Reading Ferguson in our paradoxical genealogy, it would seem, then, that to arrive at an awareness of itself (and its modern potential) at all, a Gold Coast/Ghanaian nationality, sponsored by a middle class, had first to undergo the fatal compromise of seeing itself with and through the eyes of the colonial Other. The narratives of the native surveyor, cartographer, and political agent provide a sustained account of this process. His own demise in the hinterland in 1897, at the tender age of thirty-two, in the service of his colonial masters, lends a symbolic dimension to this element of fatality.

Fatality notwithstanding, returning to the moment of the paradoxical patriot as a present self-consciously reaching for an enabling archetype of national beginnings means reminding ourselves of one thing: that it is in the nature of the idea of nationhood to achieve a transformation of fatality into continuity. For Anderson, whose observation this is, the imagined community of the nation proffers a mythopoeic solution to fatality in which time's liabilities, the orts and fragments of history, pass into a progressively meaningful genealogical narrative.[15] Thus, like any other, in the *mythos* of his nation, Arhin may turn Ferguson's literal staking out of physical and political territory for a colonial dispensation into a patriotic staking out in advance of imaginative territory for a unified native constituency. It is this constituency that, with time, would come, more or less, to imagine a singular selfhood within and in spite of the fatality of both colonial imposition and its own internal diversity.

As for Ferguson himself, when he quotes a European source, E. B. Tylor's *Primitive Culture* (1871), he appears to approve, with regard to the relations between colony and native constituency, a language of fatality. He writes:

> With regard to progress "year by year the influence of traders and missionaries is *breaking down* the old native life and substituting European ways. This change is *inevitable,* indeed it exemplifies in an extreme form those movements in civilization which in every tribe has gone on from remote antiquity by neighbouring tribes bringing in new arts and improvements at home taking place by slow degrees." This is what Dr. Tylor says, and is true as representing the general progress of the people of the [Gold Coast] Protectorate. (*Papers,* 23; emphases added)

In this representative quotation, we observe a Ferguson who has succumbed to the fatalistic logic of borrowing and utilizing the cognitive tools, symbols, and signs of a European civilization to break down and assimilate what this civilization represents to him as a "savage" and "barbarous" native sphere.

Still, even though he feels himself operating within the same cultural ambience of a European and Europeanized "us," this "civilized" native enacts the beginnings of his project in an "eccentric" manner that, in Anderson's terms, we can turn to imaginative nationalist account, seeing in it the ghost of a possibility that he was working with a logic in view different from the colonial one. Far from an admission of fatality, therefore, we can rescue a sense of continuity-in-prospect from a Ferguson who demonstrates an intuition that, rather than serving a colonial *end* in an Anglo-European Empire at large, his project may stand at a *beginning* in relation to a nativity at large.

The evidence is in the revealing self-presentation in which Ferguson gives an account of how, before he starts his journey, he orients himself in relation to Accra's James Fort. In this first account, submitted to the Governor in 1892, James Fort might be a symbol of the standard universal, the centrality of Anglo-Europe itself. Ferguson reports:

> For the purpose of my mission Your Excellency was pleased to cause to be issued to me . . . an 8 in. sextant, a false horizon, a 5 in. aneroid barometer for ascertaining heights, a pedometer and an Abney's level . . . your field glasses.
>
> Before my departure I made certain preliminary observations. The first was to determine the latitude of James Fort, Accra, so as to be able to compute the positions of places by "dead reckoning," should I be unable to fix them by celestial observations—a foresight which I had no cause to regret (5).

Ferguson grants the "foresight" to the Anglo-European structure; yet, within that prior structure, he introduces his own foresight, a self-serving foresight that modifies the original. Thus he is not to be understood in any simple fashion as one who cooperates with the structures defining an Anglo-European priority. On the contrary, working within those structures, he shows a remarkable display of initiative, which is competitive because it is adaptive. When the borrowed tools he wields prove inadequate, the servant shows himself perfectly capable of using this adaptive initiative to reinvent their priority towards his own moment. Consider:

> Though for rapid military surveying [the false horizon] may be very serviceable, yet for fixing the positions of places, such as was suggested by Your Excellency, it proved unsatisfactory, and in the absence of a mercurial horizon I had to substitute for it Stephen's blue black ink used in a wooden trough. In sheltered positions (which I selected) I was satisfied with the results obtained. (5)

Ferguson's figurations of self and role in his expeditionary accounts are by no means simple. Arhin may have cause, therefore, to paradoxically heroize Ferguson for the reason that in the face of necessity he showed ample demonstration that he could hold his own. Here was a figure who could literally and figuratively take on the world, determined and prospective, and do so, in however compromised a fashion, on his own premises.

It is in this adaptive posture towards modernity—a modernity that Ferguson valued for its techno-scientific and bureaucratic rationality, for its civilized order, and for its promise of a progressive amelioration of "backwardness"—that our paradoxical hero gives us a spirited performance of native initiative. And this is initiative that anticipates by several years the denial in Conrad's *Heart of Darkness* (1902) that any such thing could come from Africa. The comparison with Conrad is called for if only because Ferguson's stewardship in relation to the implements of modernity that had been handed him nullifies the skeptical vision in the former's novel of an Africa capable of authoring and directing itself in modernity. In Conrad's novel, this prejudice appears in the portrayal of the fireman and the helmsman, the African fellow travelers with Marlow, the hero of *Heart of Darkness*, on his journey up the Congo.

Conrad's portrayal of his African figures is done in a mode of irony—in the author's reductive biologistic language the fireman is an "improved specimen . . . to look at him was as edifying as seeing a parody of a dog in breeches."[16] Not only that: in what only renders him laughable, the vessel of modern European design the fireman finds himself on appears to be of an order of inscrutable witchery. As for the helmsman, being one who lacks both initiative and discipline, he cannot hope to control the boat without Marlow's (or European) supervision. Read as an emblem of the modern, the European vessel, which has taken the two Africans on as fellow travelers, casts them into a journey that represents for both a sort of technological, managerial, and existential cul-de-sac. Conrad's Africans, in short, are conceived in a composite of fatality.

That reading is confirmed when the author causes the helmsman to be killed by a spear pushed through his heart (of darkness) by one of his own "savage" kind. This event rebounds on the "Dark Continent" as an image of a disabling atavism. It carries the presumption that, since he is bereft of a capacious understanding, the "savage" at the helm of the European machine represents the *reductio ad absurdum* of the idea of an Africa able to initiate and actuate itself in a forward-driven modernity.

Rendering the modern as a genealogical cul-de-sac for Africa, Conrad's parodic account appears in the very colonial era that produced Ferguson. Inasmuch, however, as we wish to rescue from this same era not fatality but a sense of continuity-in-prospect, it is necessary to enlist and uphold Ferguson in a nonparodic reading of beginnings. Such a reading should challenge Conrad's dispiriting portrayal, taking back for Africa the modernity that he (and the ideology he represents) would deny us. It means, just as Arhin does in his assessment of the man's work, acknowledging his heroic, forward-looking initiative. It means shaping possibility in the past in a manner that enables the present of the imagined community of the nation to place itself positively in a relation of continuity with this past of adaptive initiative.

Still, to read the folding of liability and possibility into each other that characterizes the paradoxical genealogy of African modernity means we cannot ignore the crassly utilitarian element in Ferguson's thought. The enthusiasm with which he presents the ulterior utility of Europe in relation to a domestic nativity cannot always be justified. For instance, Arhin quotes him as writing:

> Now it is only by extending our influence northwards and introducing the luxuries of civilization to them that we can hope to create a necessity for our goods. Powder, guns, kola-nuts, rum, gin, brass and copper rods, flint, beads, will sell well. Cotton goods must be produced thick in texture, good in quality, and low in price, to replace native manufacture. (*Papers,* xii)

As Arhin observes, Ferguson was recommending a policy that would and did in time reduce the native to total dependence on Europe "even for tools and utensils" (xii). He is guilty of the original sin of envisioning his brave new world from the all-encompassing perspective of Anglo-European scientific and commercial imperialism. Within the terms of that vision, we find him judging the material culture and the symbolic securities of a native sphere and pronouncing them inferior on the whole to the European. In his projections, he foresees the substitution of these Old World securities by the new insurance of "civilization," which means the European.

A Ferguson in this mode, standing in a brave new world of triumphalist science, commerce, and progress sponsored by his imperial mentors, may have envisioned his role of spreading *Pax Britannica* in terms that would create a confraternity of black and white, native African and European. However, to the extent that this vision also sought a progressive customizing of the native to acquiring "a taste for European goods," his dream of bridging a native sphere and the sources of a civilizing modernity was a colonialist one. It sought, in a mode of dystopian liability, to bind nativity over to a dependent relationship. If, therefore, Ferguson's work registers the utopian possibility of a transethnic fraternity of a national people, it is also not altogether easy to tell this transformative work apart from his shadowing of this imagined community in terms that leave it beholden to the colonial imperatives of Britain. Conceived as a common market for British goods, the greater Gold Coast he envisions appears in a supplementary and dependent relation with the metropolis. And this is what is tellingly revealed, as we saw, in his apologetic citation of Tylor to the effect that "year by year the influence of traders and missionaries is breaking down the old native life and *substituting* European ways" (*Papers,* 23).

But could such substitution as Ferguson imagines be as benign as the passage he cites makes it sound, especially in the era in which he wrote? What, we might ask then, are the colonialist implications of civilizational substitution for a colonized nativity? For an adequate answer we need a form of understanding that works *risk* into the political economy of the unequal colonial encounter, one able to show how, in the era when Ferguson wrote, substitution entailed precisely how such risk was to be managed and contained. The dependent status presupposed for the native by his work needs to be read, therefore, in a mode of liability, towards what we might refer to as *substitutive risk*. By this is to be understood the manner in which a colonialist modernity bears into and onto nativity new conditionalities of risk; how this conspires to shape the colonized native into a docile vessel, a "substitute," who as such conducts, in the distant setting of the periphery, the real commercial (and bodily) risk of Europe away from the latter onto his own person and onto a nativity at large. Substitutive risk, the mechanics of whose working on the native psyche is demonstrated shortly below, remains the *unthought* element in Ferguson's unqualified veneration of a rationalizing, modern European civilization.

Conceived on the genealogical prospect by the children, as it were, the retrospect on the archetypal father, Ferguson, reveals the ambivalent beginnings in which a would-be African modernity, the future anterior, inscribes its possibility. The momentum of his creativity is revealed only insofar as he has more or less endorsed his "own" Nothingness—as shown by those comments that detach him from what he sees as an obsolescent and in itself useless nativity. As we saw in the paradox of the creator-destroyer Ogun, Ferguson's originality, therefore, has a blind side of compromise: it is shaped in an oversight. As such it is originality that is to be understood in terms of the parable of the fatherly sour grapes, which, according to Hayford, imposes a deathly burden on the children—that is, the Unconscious of colonialist liability. To his own question as to who shall deliver his kind from the burden of this "death," Hayford foresees a middle class absolving itself from a participation in its own "death" only in the motions of original creativity. From traitorous liability, then, creativity, looking towards patriotic possibility, foresees its own absolution. Thus Achebe, contemporary creator of the "African," seeks absolution for himself and/in his father; and thus Arhin, middle-class heir of Ferguson, in designating the latter as a paradoxical *patriot,* appears to absolve him and a class heritage of fatherly original sin.

Yet, depending on how we read, on how we position ourselves in relation to, the heritage of the fathers, absolution must appear to a greater or lesser degree. Ngugi, *contra* Achebe, inclines to the latter, and pronounces in no uncertain terms the guilt of a messenger middle class; he sees the gesture of absolution faking an innocence in an inability to fully acknowledge a middle-class unthought and its unspeakable, that domain in which the Unconscious operates. If so, what we need to shadow forth more fully is the unthought element of middle-class Innocence. And of the Gold Coast writings of the turn of the nineteenth century none, perhaps, obliges us with a full account of the archetype of guilty Innocence—Innocence that complements the theme of substitutive risk—more than John Ocansey's travel narrative *African Trading,* which is examined below.

The Political/Poetic Economy of False-True Security: Colonialist Symptoms in Ocansey's <u>African Trading</u>

> The phantoms formed in the human brain are also, *necessarily,* sublimates of [men's] material life process.
> —K. Marx and F. Engels, *The German Ideology*

But now our African markets are failed and the only business we can transact is commission business, because lot of Europeans firms has been established here who sell their goods invoicely and also give 10% commission to all buyers who buy from one pound upwards, so there is no profit at all in our works here when we order.

—I. H. Caesar, Gold Coast native trader, to Edward Challinor and Company, 1889

[O]ne could from the records of the Law Courts show to what extent the simple African merchant has had his confidence in the rectitude of the European merchant abused to his undoing; and when such things are exposed in the course of a trial Court, the excuse given is either in Gold Coast, "they do not understand these things," or, "it is customary."

—J. M. Sarbah, *Fanti National Constitution*

Published in 1881, seven years after the promulgation of the Colony, John Ocansey's *African Trading* survives as the first full-length Gold Coast "been-to" travel narrative. In this work we can observe, through the author's defective analyses of self and world, a key illustration of the consequences of Africa's emptying into a colonialist modernity. As Ocansey's self-presentation reveals, this liability, as we have described it, registers in a marked psycho-affective dependency, a condition referrable to nativity's loss of a self-accountable power as it fell under colonial subjection. To take one example of how this problem registers in *African Trading*: if Ocansey takes his existential measure within a community that he imagines as different—notice the "African" in the title *African Trading*—he nevertheless presents himself naively as one among a dependent population of "British subjects," and his home territory, Addah (Ada in today's Ghana), as a "British possession" (92). We only need to relate the "innocence" that presents itself in this substitutive mode to objective historical process to realize that there is nothing spontaneously natural about Ocansey's innocence. It is, as we shall see, an invented innocence: "Britannia ever, ever shall rule the waves" is writ large, if in disguised form, over *African Trading*.

Reference has been made in earlier chapters to critiques of Empire in historical and cultural studies—and this will include the pioneer nineteenth-century work of Blyden—that reveal the ways in which nineteenth-century British mercantilism masked itself in an ideology of philanthropy. In this mode it marched to the rallying cry of improving Africans and making them self-sufficient through Christianity, Commerce, and Civilization.[17] Such was the language of Buxton, of David Livingstone, and many others whose work, performed either in or on behalf of Africa, straddled the grey zone between British imperial commercialism and Christian evangelism. Reading between the lines of Ocansey's narrative in *African Trading*, it is not difficult to demonstrate through it the ways in which the ideal of suffusing Africa with the supposedly mollifying influence of a Christian civilization could and did in fact play Africa false. *African Trading*, as indeed its mercantile title-theme suggests, is thus read in this demonstration as a fragment within the larger narrative of the capitalization by Europe of the spaces on its periphery, of which the African coast formed a part. This is the narrative which went hand in hand with, but is usually represented as, the account of the global march of Christianity and Western civilization.

To acknowledge the linkage between the march of capital and the march of a Christian civilization means peering beneath the romantic rhetoric adorning the latter and acknowledging what counterfactual truth is disclosed there. We will see in this disclosure that the unequal power relations that favored the creation of colonial dependencies like the Gold Coast were directly reproduced in commercial relations. As for these unequal relations, as we have seen elsewhere in this work, they had led to the progressive dislocation and weakening of African coastal polities and the maximizing of British control over them. From the status of "Protectorates," these territories would lapse into "Possessions" with the advent of full-blown colonialism.

This process of maximizing control—which is what direct colonial relations are all about—can only point to an effort to minimize the risk to British commercial capital in the colonial "Possessions." In effect, with its material and symbolic supports of the gun, the school, the law, culture, and ideology—also the instruments of modernizing social change—the commercial power of Britain, having reached a stage of colonial expression, contrives to secure capital an advantageous hold over the Gold Coast as over other territories falling under its dominion.

This is the backdrop against which the narrative of *African Trading* unfolds. John Ocansey is the European-educated son of W. N. Ocansey, an unlettered African trader seeking a foothold in a commercial game controlled by and from the European metropole. The educated native son retells the story of his travels to and within England, giving us an account which shows him as an African successfully interpellated in a dependent colonialist mode. Given his insistent self-characterization as one who is subjoined to a power greater than himself, it is not altogether surprising that his narrative is achieved by and large in a form and mood that is subjunctive. As such, it is a narrative that achieves an extraordinary effect of guilelessness. Ocansey observes without penetration; or, perhaps, it would be more appropriate to say that his observations are already accounted for by the circumambient Christian symbolism in which his thought operates and which substitutes for any penetration he might have of his own. Hence in metropolitan England he is the real innocent abroad, showing a child-like trust and reverence before the symbolic heights attained by English civilization, and doing so in an awed register that reveals the effects of a missionary upbringing that had inculcated deeply in him habits of subservience.

In John Ocansey's fulsome praise, his father has "natural qualifications [that] would lead people to say that he was a born merchant." And "though he can neither read nor write, he is so quick, shrewd, and sagacious that he can trade in any way in native fashion as well as any learned man" (5). However, by the time Ocansey's narrative opens his father's business has undergone a series of upheavals, not least among them the loss of a substantial sum he was forced to pledge to the colonial authorities on behalf of the people of Ada. A pall of insecurity hangs over Ocansey's narrative from the beginning; it is fully realized in the Jobean trials of father and son, especially regarding their business dealings.

What occasions the son's trip to England—the trip which the bulk of the narrative is about—is a breach of trust by one Hickson, an English trading partner of W. N. Ocansey. For the native trader, England is the distant unknown. Still, the force of circumstance has caused him to place "full confidence" in this Englishman, and to rely "on his word, and on his honesty as a white man" (17). In the event, this white man fraudulently misappropriates the substantial figure of nearly three thousand pounds belonging to Ocansey, money meant for the purchase of a launch to facilitate and secure the firm's business on the Gold Coast. Hickson, when his own England-based business runs into trouble, is compelled to sacrifice the trust of the African. The object of the trip of John Ocansey, the educated native son, therefore, is to deliver the burden of an African father's grievance onto, and seek a redress for it in, the justice system of the all-powerful metropolis.

If there is trepidation as Ocansey embarks on his voyage, there is also hope that the coverage of the distance between the Gold Coast and England by the native son will end in a retrieval of a father's security pledge (which is also his children's patrimonial guarantee). There is the faith that such a pledge is redeemable in an assumed universe of shared trust underpinned, from an innocent native perception, by the rationality of the ruling symbols of the "white man": his government, his schools, and so on, but especially his religion. That the voyage takes place at all leads us to see that the native trader trusts that the law of the metropolis, expressing this rationality, will be hospitable and sympathetic to his cause; that it might provide an infallible medium of security for native and metropolitan equally. For that to happen, however, it is the son in the middle, the son learned in the symbols of the white man, whose "bridging" role has come to be deemed indispensable.

Thus, we might read in *African Trading* the "prefiguration" of a new mode of securing nativity. What Ocansey's middle passage points to as a larger significance is nativity making a compact with its own, reorienting itself towards a new center—the educated middle—after being newly decentered (and hence made insecure) by the "distantiating"[18] impact made on it by the power of colonial Europe.

Yet, if these assumptions and intuitions accompany the messenger-son, finally, the native trader in fact fails to get the kind of justice he desires. In the resolution of the case, the English defendant gets off with a light prison sentence, and the money of the African trader, for all the expense he incurs to recover it, is irretrievably lost. Behind and beyond fact, however, the wasted voyage of *African Trading* needs to be made to carry a certain logic of interpretation: that of the native son who had been programmed to fail. Ocansey is the African who, in himself betrayed and incapacitated by the symbols of Europe, finally represents an ironic failure to bridge and secure that distance which nativity expects of him. And how could this not be so when *African Trading* shows us a native son who has lost his own ground, his identity usurped by and into the mythologies rationalizing the white man's symbols—white mythologies which, as we shall see, shape and speak (through) his innocence? Ocansey's innocence turns as much on a problem of imposed misprision (and hence a problem of self-knowledge) as on misplaced trust and hope; and to understand the objectivities behind this imposition we need critically to implicate *African Trading* in the larger mercantile and colonial framework to which it alludes. In this larger critical framework we will see the educated native posing a security risk to his own nativity.

Within the larger imperial-colonial framework, then, the parody of justice the native receives is hardly surprising. In a glance *African Trading* shows us how British mercantile interests had been guaranteed a relatively secure base of operations in the Gold Coast by the powerful presence of a colonial agency. In that sense Ocansey unwittingly gives us an aspect of the *raison d'être* of colonialism itself which, as already observed, was to reduce the element of hazard and risk accompanying British venture capital in a peripheral African location. This reduction was possible only to the extent that risk and hazard could be successfully transferred to a subject people, directly through methods of coercion, and indirectly through a colonial pedagogy and its supporting media. We might say, in other words, that the success of the colonial venture was predicated on the extent to which a subject people could come to substitute themselves, as literal and symbolic containers, for the colonizer's risk. This is the meaning of colonial dependency that Ferguson, overly obsessed with "civilization" and "progress," never considered. Turning to the opening pages of *African Trading,* however, is to see a crudely literal, but instructive, picture of how British power, as a colonial surrogate of mercantilism, worked directly to effect a transfer of risk to the native.

By 1875, as a consequence of Britain's proclamation of the Gold Coast Colony, Ocansey's home district, Ada, in the general loss of sovereignty across the country, had come under the jurisdiction of the Crown. In the early part of that year, as he reports it, the people of Ada were found guilty under colonial law of looting cargo from a ship belonging to a British firm, F. A. Swanzy, a ship that had foundered and was going down anyway. Adjudged to be in the wrong, they were ordered to repay F. A. Swanzy "5,000 dollars" (8). To enforce this order the colonial government deployed its military apparatus in a show of force that left the King and people of Ada grovelling before the might of its authority. In the sequel to this historical confrontation, after the King and W. N. Ocansey had pledged their money to pay the "debt" on behalf of the natives of Ada and its environs, a great number of them subsequently abandoned their homes and fled in order to avoid paying the money back. What might this dispersal indicate? The authority of the King that once came with a native sphere's being internally self-accountable is severely attenuated: the greater fear of the native is of a greater power.

It is not too much to assume that before their contact with the European, native African peoples like the Adas had a sense of self-sufficient power in the sense that their material and symbolic cultural forms could be relied on to make hazard relatively manageable in their own terms. Here, in Ocansey's brief account, we can see the threatening and possessive symbolism of an Other, whose power appears near-absolute and unmanageable. And for the natives, what the impinging power of this Other meant was a fairly radical transformation of their lived experience. If a modernity they experienced in a colonialist form reformed natives as "British subjects," within the same procedure, they must be assumed to have experienced a compromising breach in the secure moorings of their nativity. A colonized nativity becomes insecurely decentered in relation to the workings of a directly felt but still "distant," and hence unfathomable, metropolitan power.

Ocansey's self-presentation in *African Trading* shows us how this "present-absent" temporal power of the colonial Other is transmogrified into a captivating poetry of "absent-presence." We see it occurring within an ideological transfer mechanism whereby the new rationality of substitutive risk imposed on the native is managed in such a way that it effects a reproduction of his subjectivity as "British." It is "Christianity," with its grand poetic theme of the inscrutability of Divine overlordship, which performs this transfer in a colonial setting. In the putatively Christian language of submissiveness which Ocansey recites, we thus approach the colonialist, dependent modality of his innocence.

In *African Trading*, then, we must read colonial power as that which is displaced by a mechanism of transference into the language of reassurance that allows the native son to put himself through his self-abasing substitutions. And if these substitutions are reassuring, this is so to the extent that they guarantee him an imaginary stake in a puissant Christian God. The implication throughout Ocansey's narrative is that if a self-determining power eludes him in a this-worldly dispensation, this sense of worldly loss is reconcilable with the unfathomable workings of a divine will, a will to which it is his Christian duty to submit. Ocansey recites a Christian hymn—and his writing is characterized by fairly extensive recitations in this mode—that is instructive in this regard:

> The past no longer is in my power,
>   The future who shall live to see?
> Mine only is the present hour,
>   Lent to be all laid out for Thee.
> Now, Saviour, with Thy grace endowed,
>   Now let me serve and please my God.
>
> Why should I ask the future load
>   To aggravate my present care;
> Strong in the grace to-day bestowed,
>   The evil of to-day I bear. (7)

There is more going on here, and elsewhere in *African Trading*, than an innocent protestation of faith by the son of the African merchant. We might seize this native son, for whom the past is forfeit and the future uncertain, as an emblem of the decentered ontology afflicting nativity, but more keenly its educated portion. What his rote recitation reveals, however, is that this decentering is already taken care of pedagogically, through a mnemonics of substitution. Recitation, that is, functions as a validating mechanism: its mnemonics act in advance to "resolve" a problematic consciousness of insecurity (what has been called the burden of worldlessness elsewhere in this study) in the native son. And it does so by permitting a projective displacement of the colonially "emptied" native self, leaving its place to be taken by the supposed plenitude or fullness of an all-powerful dispensation.

What Ocansey's account shows, then, is the magical working of a colonial affect. This affect subjects the native to explanations that magnify temporal power and renders a mystified account of its workings. This mystified power, in proportion as its authority usurps and exerts control over past and future, "distances" Ocansey's hold over his subjective present. In that respect, it fashions for him a subjectivity that knows itself as completely dependent, at a distant Other's mercy and living by his gracious power.

In keeping with our theme of colonialism as an administrative and symbolic management of risk and hazard, therefore, Ocansey's pieties may be read as the affects of a native subjectivity reformed by a pseudo-Christian education to function as a substitute for the exported risk of distant Europe. The language of Christian humility and duty taught to the insecure son of the African trader—a merest cog in a mercantile machine whose controls are in distant Europe—reads as an efficacious exercise in symbolic management. By rendering nearly invisible the objective reality of the ugly Darwinian struggle going on in a process of British capital accumulation—as recorded in a native trader's complaint in this section's second epigraph, and Sarbah's in the third—it papers that struggle over and transforms it, in the exercise of faith, into nativity's "free" acquiescence in its own domination. When we come to Casely Hayford's unillusioned account of colonial power and "Christian civilization" in the next chapter, we will see that he understood this dimension of the colonial project only too well.

If Ocansey's account first shows us a transformation of the visible hand of colonial power into a dependable "God," as we read between the lines we might see this "God" also as incarnating the invisible hand of metropolitan capital. The "word of God" and the imperative of Mammon are hardly distinguishable in this formulation by the author:

> Oh! that [Africans] would consider and be wise, and rise up like the prodigal son, and say, "I will arise and go to my Father, and will say unto him, Father I have sinned against heaven. . . ." And God will in no wise cast us out; but He will instead of servants, make us his dear children. I have had conversa-

tions with many intelligent, high-minded Christian people in England, and they all say that the improvement of the white man is derived from nothing but the word of God. Africa, I hope, will not cast away this most sacred, precious Word, which is now being preached among them in very many places by white men. . . . Oh! may the knowledge of the Lord spread over Africa as the waters cover the great deep! Then shall Africa find out her great wealth and riches,—then will the earth yield her increase, and God, even our God, shall bless us. (37)

The repleteness of the white man's world makes him "Foremost of the sons of light! / Nearest the Eternal Throne" (41). Ocansey's Africa, by contrast, is bereft of light, a "great deep," whose vacuity needs to be filled with the light of a Euro-Christian God under whose dispensation "poor Africans . . . may also enjoy the benefits, advantages, and pleasures of knowledge and civilization!" (36–37).

Godhead for Ocansey, then, makes itself manifest through the manifold splendors of a rich and replete Europe. His England is captured in a register of wonderment in an account that juxtaposes church and cathedral, the symbols of European technological advancement, and the spectacle of British imperial might indifferently as objects of religious awe and veneration. St. Paul's Cathedral and the railway train; the sight of Cleopatra's Needle and the spectacle of a pyrotechnic enactment of the imperial Battle of Navarrino, designed to show off the "Commerce and Naval Power of Britain" (49): all these excite in our innocent abroad feelings of "astonishment" and wonder. Having covered the distance from the Gold Coast to England, the mighty unknown, Ocansey, in terms of the substitutions that the colonialist apparatus of a Christian education has taught him, is enjoined to reproduce faithfully his colonized ("British") subjectivity.

Yet, inasmuch as he appears to show a wondrous fidelity to everything English in *African Trading,* perhaps a reading of Ocansey's narrative is incomplete if it does not see, however dimly, the chiaroscuro effect of light playing on shadow, and shadow playing on light. This is the ambivalence of the middle we identified earlier in the chapter. In that paradoxical respect, it too is an anticipation, however obscure, of the projects of cultural attribution that would go into the nationalist problematic of African modernity. To take, first, the native son's song of innocence:

Not many years back, and but few Africans came to Europe. . . . But now native traders and their sons . . . come on their own business; and the kindness shown to them is so great that they are filled with pleasure and gratitude. They are taken to see anything that is useful or profitable, and they are improved and not spoiled. When they return . . . they have very much to say, and are listened to with respect and confidence. Then their people are proud and pleased that the English have respected them; and they are far more ready to accept English ways and customs. And thus little by little, Africa will be changed as England was changed; for she too has come out of the darkness into God's marvellous light. (37–38)

Ultimately, however, this is an arrested song of innocence. For an Ocansey lost in the attempt at finding a secure grounding in imperial power's distantiated omnipotence, a return home is shadowed as the possibility of a different mode of empowered belonging. The desire for homecoming anticipates obscurely a mode of self-ownership: home reads as the location where one is empowered to belong *in* a world of one's own, not *to* an Other's as his dependent. Here, then, is the native son giving us a balance sheet summation at the end of his account: "And now I felt my business in England was done. I should have seen all its wonders with different eyes and sensations if it had not been for this agitating, disturbing business" (87). In the event,

My mind dwelt very much on *my home* and friends. . . . [M]y mind wandered away to my *own* dear home, and I *remembered* all *our people* come down on the beach, waving their handkerchiefs and bidding me adieu; and I prayed that the good Lord would preserve me in health and strength, that I might return safely and give them the pleasure of welcoming me back again amongst them. (87; emphases added)

Thoughts of homecoming notwithstanding, Ocansey's final word is still given in an idealized Christian language. This language shows itself only too ready to elide the imperatives of resistance that European colonialism had conspired to impose on the particular affiliations and identities it had (in part) created to serve its dominion.[19] Turning the other cheek, so to speak, he speaks instead a language of universal brotherhood that anticipates a magical egalitarianism beyond earthly inequality:

"Where friend holds fellowship with friend;
Though sundered far, by faith we meet
Around one common mercy seat." (88)

Such persistent otherworldly rhetoric, it goes without saying, only leaves an innocent Ocansey in an ungrounded universalism—it leaves him, that is, beholden to a noncompetitive idea of the universal, not so much his own as it is held ideologically captive in the *competitive* white European mythology of worlding.

In the circumstances, he is not unlike Blake's innocent child-persona in the poem "The Little Black Boy." We will recall that in this poem the little black boy foresees a future in which, the clearly disabling tag of his blackness abolished, he is resolved into a communal brotherhood of white, angelic souls. The projection is that in shedding his black identity—which, in the course of the history of Empire, has become an existential burden displacing him into the deprivation of earthly Nothingness—the black boy will then become like "the English child." He will be co-opted as such into full participation (i.e., on equal terms) in the white universality whose fantastic representation is, and in which symbolically reposes, God's sovereign dispensation. We need only to run this poetic fantasy by this section's first epigraph to realize its foundations in the imperial-colonial political economy. And inasmuch as Marx and Engels are right, and the "phantoms" that arise in the human brain have a basis in a material existence, the narrative of *African Trading* can read only as the enactments of a native psyche overwritten by an entrancing poetry, poetry whose beauty traps it in a false consciousness of colonial materiality. Little wonder then, that, after Ocansey, the post-ancillary theme of authentic self-consciousness, as represented prominently in the writings of Attoh Ahuma, Sekyi, and Hayford, will come center stage in Gold Coast nationalist writing.

The chapter has sought, by way of the central examples of early narrative self-presentations by two middle-class Africans, to sketch the paradoxical beginnings and continuities of a class genealogy. The aim has been one of sketching a knowledge, on the basis of a frontline ontology, of African modernity in its problem mode. To this end, the chapter has tried to illustrate with the Faustian archetypes, Ferguson and Ocansey, the more or less insidious ways in which a colonialist modernity impinges on and reforms the African consciousness. Both figures show how this consciousness, having responded to the pull of the Other of European civilizational modernity, is pressured towards a reconstitution of its physical and mental lifeworld, in a substitutive mode of dependence and a world-depriving mode of self-abnegation.

In just such terms the chapter has tried to draw out the ambivalent resonances of the ideological baggage carried by Ferguson. On the one hand, we find a native "salutarily" defined in, and marching to the tune of, an ideology whose implications are rationalist, evolutionist, and which promises Africa a progressive amelioration of her backwardness. Yet the unexamined Eurocentrism of this ideology means that we see Ferguson's mission as a colonizing one, this to the extent that it involves him in plotting and realigning nativity along the merely supplementary lines of Anglo-European modernity. The implications, as we saw further, turning to *African Trading*, were that the brave new world imagined by Ferguson could be only insofar as nativity was denied any originality, any world-defining attributes, of its own. In Ocansey, we encounter the native reformed into representing an existent "past" to himself as a backward and spent force. Ocansey—and many others before and after him[20]—reveals how this could and did leave the educated native, newly produced at the problematic confluence of the colonial and the modern (Achebe's "crossroads") at the mercy of an exorbitant power. It is an Ocansey caught at this bewildering juncture, therefore, who is compelled to turn again to examine the eventuality of going back home at the end of his narrative. Finally, contemplating the possibility of recalling himself to himself, so to speak, he effectively reveals, in nativity, the latent reality of another pull, the affective pull of a sphere of "natural" African belonging.

An innocent Ocansey in this mode of emergent awareness, however, could not but foresee an organically defined home only dimly. However, as we have seen, within the same period that *African Trading* appeared, Blyden had embarked on his crusade to project a nativized Africa as a worldly force. Blyden had abjured "cosmopolitism," the ungrounded universalism whose Euro-Christian espousal we find in the language of Ocansey, for its dangers to the weak—and such was the condition of imperialized Africa. In the circumstances, maintaining cosmopolitism of Ocansey's kind could result only in the absorption of Race Individuality, the assimilation of African Personality, in a universal bearing the ethnocentric imprint of strong Europe. Ocansey's ungrounded universal, therefore, amounted to giving Africa unselfconsciously away, confirming its Nothingness—as proclaimed in the negations of European Africanism—by denying it a world of its own making. What was needed, in Blyden's reformulation of Mazzini, therefore, was the working out of a nationalist third and in-between space, one that would give a grounding to the Universal in the Individual. It is from this third space that the universalist projection, the worlding, of a *présence africaine*, in Blyden's thought, was to be accomplished. If this required a third force, as we have seen, Blyden had found the potential for this intermediary force in the European-educated middle class. On this group he had come to impose the double nationalist vocation of *being* the embodiment of native African Individuality and *becoming* this Individuality's projection onto the world stage, into the domain of the Universal (i.e., Mazzini's Humanity).

In defining the African modernist problematic, Blyden had, as noted already, come to stamp his influence decisively on the Gold Coaster, Casely Hayford, whose *Ethiopia Unbound* comes up in the next chapter. This work is a Blydean demonstration by one in the awakened middle-class vanguard that he is intellectually and politically capable of taking on the challenges of occupying the third space, of being the third force able to transform an African "home" into a nativity universally resurgent. In *Ethiopia Unbound* we encounter a Hayford who seeks to press a colonially emptied nativity into service as a secure foundation of African (self)-knowledge, this on the very competitive ground—the Universal—which Ocansey, trapped in an imposed innocence, had been forced to abdicate to a white godhead. Thus this many-sided Orphean classic marks a beginning, an attempt by a front-line intellectual to navigate, within the problematic configuration of a colonialist modernity, a middle-class passage from ancillary Innocence to post-ancillary Experience.

As we pass in the next chapter from *African Trading* to Hayford's quasi autobiography, *Ethiopia Unbound,* therefore, it is to attend, in part, to the matter of a middle-class figure going through the difficult motions of shedding a guilty Innocence. Insofar as Hayford is aware that in its ancillary Innocence, a middle class is guiltily complicit in colonialist modes of knowing and being, we will find his autobiographical persona in *Ethiopia Unbound* projected in a postcolonial quest for authentic self-grounding in a (racial) nativity. Hayford will sound the possibility of giving a worldly (i.e., competitive) grounding to the blackness and the nativity which Ocansey, drugged by the power-laden symbolism of Europe, forfeits in his unselfconsciousness. Where the latter defers the tutelary guidance of a dependent and subservient nativity to Europe, it is left to the former to remonstrate with post-ancillary conviction: "What, indeed, can be more certain than that the African . . . has need to unlearn a good deal? But the unfortunate part of it is that the way out is as yet dimly dawning upon such as would otherwise be qualified to lead the masses." For Casely Hayford, therefore, "it thus becomes the sacred duty of those who can see a little more clearly ahead to point the way."[21] *Ethiopia Unbound* presents, then, a representative work of early middle-class nationalism whose author commits himself, albeit not without shortcomings, to begin and to lead this exercise in reorientation and path-finding; this, in essence, Orphean/*sankofa* project of cultural-nationalist map-making. The autobiographical Hayford, moreover, is able to sound some of the first strident notes of a reformist anticolonial nationalism.

6

BLACK ORPHEUS, OR THE (MODERNIST) RETURN OF THE NATIVE

J. E. CASELY HAYFORD'S *ETHIOPIA UNBOUND*

Mr. Hayford . . . has now cast his ideas on the subject of racial problems more or less into the form of fiction. We say "more or less" because some of the chapters . . . break quite away from the slender thread of story on which most of the episodes are strung.
—*Journal of the African Society,* London (1911)

Of *Ethiopia Unbound* I wish to say that no book, in my judgment, of the present century holds greater interest to the thoughtful and observant Negroes of Africa and the world than it does. It . . . discusses with masterful ability the great world question—the relation of the darker races to the dominant races. . . . *Ethiopia Unbound* is a remarkable book . . . a profound analytical study of present racial and sociological conditions as seen through the eyes of an African scholar and thinker. It is bound to create a favourable impression in America among Negroes who read it, especially those who think, as well as to excite surprise among white men that a Negro has given such a faithful and accurate description of their methods in adding field to field "by tricks that are vain and ways that are dark."
—N. Barnett Dodson in the *Freeman,* Indianapolis (*c.* 1912)

Some of the chapters [of *Ethiopia Unbound*] evince indebtedness to the masterly influence of Edward Wilmot Blyden, but [Mr. Hayford]

is not a servile imitator, for he is a master of his subject.
—announcement of book just published, J. Bruce, Yonkers, N.Y. (*c.* 1911)

Ethiopia Unbound: Autobiography of the Nativist-Modernist Concept

[*Ethiopia Unbound*] is . . . written by one whom education has not lured away from sympathy with his own race and people.
—*Jamaica Times,* Kingston (*c.* 1912)

Mr. Casely Hayford, an African of unimpaired instincts and European scholarship . . . has written from the European and African standpoint.
—*African World,* London (1911)

With *Ethiopia Unbound,* we come to the quasi autobiography—"quasi" because it is cast in a fictional form—of J. E. Casely Hayford, the nationalist who emerged as "an 'uncrowned king' of British West Africa."[1] Born in 1866 into a prominent Fanti (and Euro-African) coastal family, Hayford was educated at the leading Cape Coast Wesleyan Boys' High School, later Mfantsipim. Subsequently he attended Fourah Bay College in Freetown, Sierra Leone. On his return to the Gold Coast, he worked as a teacher and school principal in Accra and was subsequently a newspaper editor on several local journals, starting with his uncle James Brew's *Western Echo.* Finding the law to his taste while working as a law clerk, Casely Hayford went on to study law at Cambridge, completed his professional training in London, and in 1896 returned to the Gold Coast to set up a practice. Hayford would combine a vigorous journalistic vocation with his law practice, nationalist politics, and membership, from 1916, in the Gold Coast Legislative Council. Until his death in 1930, he would remain the proprietor and editor of *The Gold Coast Leader.*

Hayford stepped into the political and cultural limelight of Gold Coast nationalism in 1896. He became its leading figure after the demise of Sarbah in 1910, and went on also to command the leadership in British West African nationalism at the end of the First World War. The Gold Coast colonial sphere, when Hayford started out professionally, was a largely restrictive one professionally and politically for the European-educated middle class, and it would remain so throughout his career. As Edsman points out, however, there were opportunities available within the colonial order for those who "knew how to work opposition and make themselves heard in

such a way as to make an impression on the [British] rulers." These were
the self-employed and independently successful lawyers, knowledgeable in
"the constitutional obscurities relating to British rule."[2] And, by virtue of
this specialized know-how, it was inevitable that these native proprietors of
a modern, politically useful knowledge would become the Gold Coast's
leading public spokesmen. The lawyers, thrust into the vanguard of middle-
class nationalism, would step forward as the defenders of a corporate native
interest, conservative espousers of the merits of native ways of life, and
leaders of political agitation against the colonial shortcomings of imperial
overrule.

Hayford, with his training in constitutional and other branches of
British law, was one of these. He was a member of a group, then, which had
an interest in maintaining and preserving the hegemony of the modern in
the particularly British institutional form—albeit not its specific colonial
political form—that it had come to the Gold Coast. We find Hayford pro-
claiming, throughout his career, an aggressive allegiance to British institutional modernity in its liberal-constitutionalist legal and political forms.
The qualification must be added, though, that this was a modernity whose
transformative power he preferred to see adapted to already existing native
institutions—a modernity institutionally nativized, as it were. Hayford's
allegiance to a British modern makes an early appearance in his 1903 *Gold
Coast Native Institutions* where he critiques Crown Colony administration
as the defect within an otherwise endorsable imperial governance.

> [T]he Aborigines of the Gold Coast triumph in the wave of imperialism
> which at present sways the public sentiment of Britain. It may overwhelm
> . . . all that is dear to them of law, custom and practice; it may reduce them
> to the condition of bondsmen and captives. . . . [B]ut, for all these things,
> they would rather have the ills they know of than to fly to others that they
> know not of.[3]

In Hayford's view, therefore, the problem is systemic rather than one of
fundamentals, for in the fundamentals, "The people of the Gold Coast . . .
see in the civilisation you offer much that is fair." If, however, they also
"cannot fail to perceive the weak spots and blemishes in the same" (*Native
Institutions,* 7), then systemic reform is what is called for, one that will
make the fundamentals premised on fair play to shine through.

Hayford's allegiance to the modern had a pragmatic dimension, too,
centered on its promise of material amelioration of Africa's comparative
backwardness in the matter of infrastructure, social amenities, scientific
agriculture, and industrial forces. It may have been true, in the diagnosis of

Hayford's mentor Blyden, that an exogenous modernity was having a ruinous impact on Africa. Nevertheless, for the pragmatic modernist in Hayford, good modernity, materially speaking, could in theory be separated from bad, hence, in his words, "There is no reason why we, as Africans, should not also harness the discoveries of Science to our everyday need and make them productive of Wealth and prosperity within our borders."[4] Hayford does not fail, therefore, to don the progressive mantle of African advocate of a developmental modernity for the Gold Coast and West Africa.

Hayford had also, like many of his generation of West African nationalists, come under the influence of Blyden, with whom he had become acquainted when he was a student in Freetown. Blyden's cultural nationalism, centered on the core thesis of an inalienable African Personality and a questioning on this basis of an assimilationist modern, had become Hayford's, too. Having taken to heart the message of "the greatest living exponent of the true spirit of African nationality and manhood" (*Ethiopia Unbound*, 164), therefore, the Hayford who steps forward as a cultural and political activist at the turn of the nineteenth century does so as a conservative nativist. *Ethiopia Unbound* is in part a nativist manifesto of Ethiopianism, according with the prescriptions of Blyden.

It is not surprising, then, that in *Ethiopia Unbound* Hayford gives his autobiographical alter ego, the lawyer Kwamankra, the attribute "Ethiopian conservative." This surrogate persona is, however, more than this: Kwamankra as the reader encounters him is "spatially" wedged between the conservative and the progressive, the native and the modern. He inhabits a temporality on which converges, at one and the same time, the claims of the past and (its) priority and the claims of a future which beckons in the form of present (or modernist) originality. Hence these orders fold into each other in a Hayfordian form of imagining and projecting the African nation as an intermediate order, a third space, over which a modern originality, to be rooted in, and made subject to, a native (or African) priority, intervenes. In ontological and performative terms, therefore, Kwamankra is what we might call a "conjunctural persona." Hayford casts his quasi-autobiographical self-construction in the overlap between (native) permanence and (modern) emergence; between the integral and the alien(ating); between metaphysical pieties to an African essence and the telling necessities of responding to the accidental order of the real-historical.

We see an autobiographical persona, therefore, which, in its double allegiance to the historical and the metaphysical, inhabits the overlap of the orders of "fact" and "figura."[5] By the former is to be understood the historical and the sociopolitical, in their empirical weightiness, that weightiness about which Yambo Ouologuem, the Malian novelist, has aphoristically remarked: "Man is in history, history is in politics, and politics is cleavage."[6] Insofar as historically, the facts of colonial politics are damning, therefore, we find Hayford's persona performatively inhabiting those facts in *Ethiopia Unbound,* marshalling them in evidentiary fashion for a prosecution and indictment of the colonial-imperial order. The third section below reviews the autobiographical persona wedded, in political, social, and cultural critique, to the empirical. It shows Kwamankra documenting in topical protest the political and social failings of Crown Colony administration as well as other systemic and humanistic shortcomings of Empire.

To turn now to the order of the figural in *Ethiopia Unbound*: we might see this aspect of Hayford's work—its "literariness" alongside its "literalness"—as conforming with what Blyden referred to as the "poetry of politics." And we may understand by Blyden's expression the creative effort to politically secure agency, mobilization, solidarity on an affective basis in representation, in mythmaking. So, then, what does Hayford's quasi autobiography yield in the overlap between the "poetical" and the "political"—that is, in being a "literal" political document which seeks an affective anchor in the "literary"?

In autobiography as a literary form we encounter the narrative unfolding of the story of the life of the *I,* the first person singular, over time. In this unfolding, the autobiographical persona is interpretively given, or finds, a complementary predicate: what the self authoring itself in retrospection does, that is, is signify onto itself forms of existential and moral predication (or attribution).

For an example of autobiographical self-predication, we might consider a political autobiography whose Pan-African motivations may be usefully compared to that of *Ethiopia Unbound.* This is Du Bois's *Dusk of Dawn* (1940), whose subtitle "An Essay toward an Autobiography of a Race Concept" speaks volumes about the attribution of the *I* of his autobiography. Into this *I* the autobiographer contrives to displace the predicate of a racial *We.* Du Bois is declaring, as it were: "I am We. For my story is not uniquely mine at all; indeed, the whole of my race is included within it." Hence in Du Bois's political mythmaking, his autobiographical persona comes vested with the *We* as its special existential responsibility. This persona—a part—takes on the moral challenge of bearing testimony to the suffering, hope, and aspiration that identify a black collectivity—the whole: Du Bois's *I* is conceived inspirationally as a spark for the struggles of the *We.* Autobiography, under the auspices of the racial nationalism of the great African American leader, is transmuted into allegory: the "race concept" takes over, and speaks its existential and sociohistorical significances through, what Du Bois intends us to see as its opposite, the "individual concept."

Like the Du Boisian one, the surrogate persona of Hayford's quasi autobiography, Kwamankra, is conceived at a juncture between autobiography and allegory and projected very much in the terms outlined above. As a student in London, "He could not help feeling that he had a call to duty, and that in the service of his race" (25). The outspoken Kwamankra is a conduit of Hayford's critical anticolonialist views as well as an exemplary embodiment of his nationalist advocacy. His Akan-Fanti name is well chosen; it is a name in whose significances Hayford seeks to confirm and legitimize the public role he takes on as *the* voice of "the people." As for these people, they are now identified by Hayford with a Gold Coast nativity mediated within an Akan-Fanti ethnoculturalism; now with a conception of Gold Coast and West African collectivity, mediated in a notion of African nationality. The people are also, above all, subsumed by the autobiographer, in a Pan-African dimension of racial advocacy, into "Ethiopia."[7] That Kwamankra embodies the people in these interlocking dimensions is reflected in his well-chosen name. Broken down etymologically into its three Akan-language parts, his name can be resolved thus: *Kwa*: bearer of, or emissary at the service of; *(o)man*: popular collectivity; *kra*: soul/*entelechial* creative life-force/transcendent (self)-consciousness.

Kwamankra is thus constructed as the allegorical character *par excellence*. Indeed, before the fifth chapter of *Ethiopia Unbound* opens, we find Kwamankra in a dream allegory being vested by the ancestors of his people to be a public witness, a popular spokesman charged to seek out and speak the truths of what ails his bonded people and race. He comes away also as the portentous medium through which the divinity of African nationality, its sacred guardianship entrusted to him, will find a this-worldly incarnation. Hayford's quasi autobiography may well be the premier narrative example of the "national allegory" in African letters. In it the "native concept" (allegorical)—displaced into the national and race concepts—inspirationally speaks through the individual concept (autobiographical).

Persona and Publics

> *Ethiopia Unbound* . . . is a product of the times, when races are feeling after harmony and co-operation. [I]t is hoped [the author's] words will be listened to as a contribution to an eirenicon.
>
> —*African World,* London (1911)

We hope that [*Ethiopia Unbound*] may help towards a Negro renaissance.

—*Morning Post,* London (September 5th, 1912)

[*Ethiopia Unbound*] Will help cause in America.

—N. Barnett Dodson in the *Freeman,* Indianapolis (*c.* 1912)

If Kwamankra the nativist must also be a modernist persona, a compelling reason for this joint predication is that Hayford, the critic of colonial rule, intuits that to lock the self in a purely inward-looking nativism is to deprive it cognitively and morally of the predicates of rationalism and humanism. It is to rob the self, that is, of the resources available for a critique and reform of a colonialist modernity. For Hayford not to take these elements of the modern into his autobiographical self-attribution would be to squander the opportunity to deprive colonial rule of a logical *raison d'être* on its own intellectual ground, the ground furnished by the Enlightenment culture of imperialism. It is an enlightened Hayford who defensively affirms: "We would not if we could, and we could not if we would, alienate our intellectual allegiance to Great Britain, for that allegiance is a guarantee of political and religious liberty and stimulus to the highest possible attainment."[8] Hence it is that, as will be outlined below, we find Kwamankra, appealing in a modernist mode to rational and progressive principles, making a logical and moral absurdity out of colonial rule in the Gold Coast. And, again, this persona is well served by Enlightenment and Christian humanism, whose tenets he directs towards a critique of the Social Darwinist, mammonist, and racist shortcomings of Empire in its political, socioeconomic, and cultural dimensions.

Ethiopia Unbound demonstrates also that for Hayford not to admit the modern into his autobiographical self-predication would be to squander the advantage of an emergent inter-imperial public sphere and an opportunity therein to prosecute his anticolonial political, and postimperial Africanist cultural, crusade. This was a "nonracial" public sphere that the Enlightenment culture of Empire, by virtue of its being shared *across* the colonial and metropolitan worlds, had opened up. And therein demands of accountability directed at, and discordant voices about, the imperial project increasingly found critical address. Kwamankra—figured as a sophisticated man in imperial cross talk with other sophisticates—is presented very much as belonging within, and drawing on, this inter-imperial critical formation. We find this formation marked by call and response across the metropolitan-colonial divide such that the works of Hayford, Sarbah, Blyden, Horton, and West African others dialogically respond to, and their probing, dissatisfied voices constitute a native and African augmentation of, the metropolitan calling of Empire to account. Examples of the metropolitan criticism of Empire are to be found in, for instance, the editorial advocacy of F. Fitzgerald in *The African Times,* the London-published journal of the African Aid Society (it ran from 1861 to 1886); in C. S. Salmon's *The Crown Colonies of Great Britain* (1886); in Ernest Eiloart's *Land of Death* (1887); in Mary Kingsley's *West African Studies* (1899); in the advocacy of the London-based Aborigines' Protection Society, and of the African Association (formed in 1901); in the reformist writings of E. D. Morel, and that of Rome Hall and others appearing, in the 1900s, in the Liverpool-published *The West African Mail.* To the list of important journals fostering the growth of inter-imperial public opinion must be added, too, the short-lived Pan-African journal *African Times and Orient Review,* edited out of London by the Arab-African Dusé Mohamed Ali in the teens of the twentieth century, and the veteran London-published weekly *West Africa,* which has survived to this day.[9]

For colonial West Africans of the turn of the nineteenth century and early twentieth, therefore, a modern, inter-imperial public sphere enablingly opens up a space to enact an exchange. The transaction involved, on the one hand, their conservative nationalism—i.e., "what is 'ours' as Africans"—and, on the other, a worldly internationalism—i.e., "what, in the name of a shared humanity, falls, or ought to fall, between 'ours' and 'theirs.'" *Ethiopia Unbound,* written self-consciously to publicize its conjunctural persona to African advantage, is located squarely within this turn-of-the-century internationalist problematic.

On the metropolitan side, in the same period, it is in the work of Mary Kingsley that we find the call for the spirit of internationalism to burgeon on both sides of the imperial divide registering very strongly. For instance, Kingsley, in her 1898 letter to Sarbah informing him about her difficult promotional work in England on behalf of Africa, tellingly uses the pronoun "we" in a nonracial sense in her last sentence. "I am writing [articles on Africa] for the general English public," she writes, "who are quite with you and me *if* we can make them understand the facts of the case."[10] In her letter to educated West Africans alluded to in previous chapters, what stands out is her exhortation to persons of "culture" like themselves to commit to building interracial bridges. Cross-racial solidarity, Kingsley was arguing in the letter, was necessary in order to reshape metropolitan public opinion through sustained social, cultural, and political critique, and thereby to exert a positive influence on public policy inter-imperially. It is particularly problematic for Kingsley that what goes into the shaping of Empire's Africa policy is the distorted perception of the English public that all Africans are "awful savages or silly children." It is to correct this error, therefore, that she enjoins educated Africans to "place before the English statesman the true African, and destroy the fancy African made by the exaggeration that he now has in his mind" (*Fanti National Constitution* [app.], 262).

Kingsley's is an important clarion call in the inter-imperial cross talk: Hayford, Sarbah, and Blyden, as we have seen, write approvingly of her conservative culturalist credentials as well as what they perceive as her internationalist-humanist commitment to Africa. In *Ethiopia Unbound*, we find Hayford responding to Kingsley's call to dispel the image of the "fancy African" and to produce in its place that of the "true African." "It is not the spoilt educated African that may be expected to help in the world's work" (197), Hayford argues. And so he labors out of a nationalist commitment to garner for the "true"—or "unspoilt"—African Personality its proper recognition within the internationalist-humanist frame afforded by the inter-imperial public sphere.

This nationalist commitment to internationalism means that Kwamankra, when he claims a place in the exchanges within this sphere, does so not only as he is autobiographically figured in his special character as an Ethiopian conservative, the bearer of the true African character. Additionally, he seeks to negotiate an exchange value for the conservative imprint on the soul of Ethiopia that he bears within himself. That is, Ethiopian nativity conserved is Ethiopia conserved not only for itself but, in the internationalist imagining, also for the world. For, as Blyden had admonished in "Race and Study," "If you . . . surrender your personality, you have nothing left to give the world. You have . . . no use, nothing which will attract and charm men" (*Origins,* 250).

It is as a symbolic bearer of an Ethiopian value of world significance, therefore, that we encounter Hayford's alter ego in the opening chapters of *Ethiopia Unbound.* Kwamankra in these chapters is presented as a student in England which appears as one of the "nations in the world who call themselves Christians." These nations, "who claim a monopoly of culture, knowledge and civilisation," are "mostly whites"; and "they think that they have a heaven-born right to survive and thrive while all others go under" (109). A skeptical Kwamankra must make destabilizing inroads into the cultural and civilizational monopoly on the Universal unjustifiably claimed by these white nations. Hence we might read England, in these opening chapters, as enabling the opening up of a critical space for dialogue, in the

Universal, as it were. Over this space, by way of the agency of Kwamankra, African nativity, otherwise devalued in imperial representation (Kingsley's "fancy Africa"), enacts a return to the Universal as humane critique and corrective of those problematic features of a colonialist European modernity, presented in Hayford's analyses as Europe's inhuman and exterminatory character.

Kwamankra's African Personality appears in the inter-imperial domain, then, as the divine and humane presentment of a resurgent nativity, a nativity which has returned to "probe" the "inner nature" of his English interlocutor, the aptly surnamed Silas *Whitely*. As for this inner nature of the latter, the returned native discovers it to be "shallow" (10). In a reversing of the counters, Nothingness—once, in the monopolistic and monologic scheme of imperial worlding, the preserve of African nativity—is projected onto Whitely: he functions as Hayford's emblem of a decadence eating at the heart of European civilization. It is because this neurotic formation has perversely distanced itself from a "divine influence" (10) that it has disastrously forgotten its obligations to a commonwealth of humanity.

By contrast, Kwamankra functions figurally as the affirmative symbol of a nativity that is rooted in a humane universal sanctioned by the divine influence itself. Hayford in this mode answers the negrophobes by asserting that "Before [the dawn of the twentieth century], it had been discovered that the black man was not necessarily the missing link between man and ape" (1). In a language that reveals the influence of Blyden's promotional racial internationalism, he goes on to proclaim:

> Moreover, [the black man] was the scion of a spiritual sphere peculiar unto himself; for when Western Nations would have exhausted their energy in the vain struggle for the things which satisfy not, it was felt that it would be to [the Africans] to whom the world would turn for inspiration, seeing that in them only would be found those elements which make for pure altruism, the leaven of all human experience. (2)

In a contest framed as a Socratic dialogue, Whitely, the emblematic European, is therefore forced to concede to Kwamankra, the African, the moral and spiritual upper hand and, with it, those empty tokens of "culture, knowledge and civilization" by which Western nations have arrogated to themselves global overlordship. In prospect, Kwamankra declares: "the nation that can show the greatest output of spiritual strength, that is the nation that shall lead the world, and as Buddha from Africa taught Asia, so may Africa again lead the way" (9).

Imperial "internationalism," wherein relations between European and non-European, white and nonwhite peoples, are defined in accordance with a racial hierarchy of Humanity, leaves to its detriment the "African race" at or near the bottom, lowly among the "inferior races," as defined by the Europeans. In reaction to the detrimental definition of the race, the African participation in the internationalism that emerges in the metropolitan-colonial crossover, as abetted by liberal-humanist and radical metropolitans, is predicated on a project of the vertical integration of Africa with Humanity. *Ethiopia Unbound* is an important literary contribution to this project of vertical integration, a project that seeks a human parity with others for the African. In this respect the nonracial public sphere that emerges in the metropolitan-colonial dialogue is an important one for opening up a worldly, or internationalist, space for nationalist self-articulation by Africans (and for a humanistic articulation of Africa by non-African Afrophiles).

That said, the metropolitan-colonial public sphere is not the only one of salience in and for the internationalism of *Ethiopia Unbound.* For Hayford's quasi autobiography reveals also that there is an emergent public sphere of the black Atlantic, an internationalism with a basis in racial solidarity, whose intellectual and political geography is comprised of the three corners of the Atlantic: Africa, Europe, and the Americas (including the West Indies). In addition to the vertical, there is a project of horizontal integration, too, that Hayford feels pressured to contribute to. "Pan-Africanism" emerges as the name of this project of horizontal integration, the making of an imagined transcontinental community that will take in black Africa and its diaspora.

Notable early figures promoting the internationalist nationalism that, after 1900, became "the Pan-African movement" include African Americans Delany (1812–85), Crummell (1822–98), and his protégé, the long-lived Du Bois (1868–1963), who became the symbol of Pan-Africanist continuity in the twentieth century. We must count among the early figures, too, the Trinidadian Sylvester Williams (1868–1911) who, in 1897, formed the African Association in London and went on, in the same city in 1900, to convene the first Pan-African Conference. And this is not to leave out the African connection, represented by such precursors as the ubiquitous Blyden and Horton.[11]

These and the later intellectuals prosecuting a Pan-African politics came to do so as a result of discovering that, in Africa and the diaspora alike, they occupied and shared the problems and possibilities of the front-line commonly resolved out of the Africa-Europe encounters. Pan-Africanism arose in the awareness by these frontline intellectuals that they might be the elevated vanguard of their race, but this was a race commonly disinherited by an imperial modernity, built on a long history of white European enslavement of their kind. Moreover, they could see, from the latter nineteenth century on, that this modernity which marginalized their race in global and colonial economy, polity, and society was being consolidated in a program of expropriation. The same white Europeans, the erstwhile enslavers, were forcibly taking over, and abrogating native rights to, the ancestral land "Africa," or interchangeably "Ethiopia," land that was— or, from a diasporic perspective, ought to be considered—a common racial patrimony. Consider, for instance, the viewpoint of Delany on Africa in 1861:

> Africa is our fatherland and we are its legitimate descendants. . . . I have determined to leave to my children the inheritance of a country, the possession of a territorial domain, the blessings of a national education and the indisputable right of self-government. . . . Our policy must be . . . Africa for the African race and black men to rule them. By black men I mean, men of African descent who claim an identity with the race. (qtd. in *Pan-African Movement*, 165)

Delany's is an early sounding of the Pan-Africanist demand for a holistic black power, a power territorially anchored: hence a state nationalism. "Africa, to become regenerated," he wrote, "must have a national character and her position among the existing nations of the earth will depend mainly upon the high standard she may gain compared with them in all her relations, morally, religiously and commercially" (165).

"Whether in the east, south, or west of the African Continent, or yet among the teeming millions of Ethiopia's sons in America," Hayford writes, "the cry of the African, in its last analysis, is for scope and freedom in the struggle for existence" (*Ethiopia Unbound*, 167). The crises befalling the race at the turn of the nineteenth century will make black power an ever more urgent demand as a global quest. There was the disillusionment of African Americans as the gains of Emancipation and Reconstruction were rolled back by Jim Crow;[12] and paralleling this was the sowing of the seeds of apartheid in South Africa. There was, too, the rise of the new-imperial culture of racism. With access to colonial administrative positions they could occupy with relative ease before now barred to them on account of their color, this meant for educated middle-class West Indians and Africans "a discrepancy between the expectations engendered by modern education and the reduced chances of applying its fruits" (*Pan-African Movement*, 174).

The atmosphere could not be more congenial, therefore, for questions to emerge in a commonality among these frontline intellectuals, diasporic and African, questions about a racial destiny, and about the mustering of a power and force, through forms of political solidarity, that would give the race charge of this destiny. The question of a solidarity politics would be seen, too, as potentially mediated by culture. Pan-Africanism needed to invent the poetry of its political mission; it needed a foundational (or norm-setting) and orientational (or destiny-directing) cultural nationalism with which it would distinctively brand its activist self.

If the question that the race on the whole was in historical crisis, a crisis born of its colonial-imperial mode of insertion into modernity, was not in doubt, the great programmatic question haunting all sociopolitical endeavor, "What is to be done?" certainly was a matter of Pan-Africanist contention and debate. And not only was the triangular black Atlantic debate involving these frontline intellectuals about substantive program; this debate emerged also as the question of the cultural-philosophical basis—the foundational question—on which a Pan-African supranationalist program was to be erected and directed. Not just "What is to be done?" (program), therefore, but also "From where?" (cultural-political philosophy), and "Towards what?" (public agenda). There arose in a Pan-Africanist public domain contentious questions about an activist program and its informing and directing philosophy, of practice and its affective basis, of a supranationalist mode of being and becoming in the world. We might see these as the issues centrally driving the three discursive chapters—16, 17, 18—similarly titled "Race Emancipation," in *Ethiopia Unbound*.

The dedication page of Hayford's quasi autobiography reads: "To the sons of Ethiopia the world wide over."[13] From the Gold Coast and West African frontline, the Hayfordian persona images a Pan-African public, "an imagined community among a specific assemblage of fellow readers,"[14] as a main co-respondent: "the thinker would through the medium of *Ethiopia Unbound* greet members of the race everywhere in the world" (167). Kwamankra also addresses a fictive Pan-African Conference held in the Gold Coast in 1905—fictive because we know no such conference took place historically. And we are informed further that Kwamankra is behind the, again, fictive newspaper *The Gold Coast Nation and Ethiopian Review* which had started by promoting "the interests of Gold Coast national conservancy; but as time went on . . . had broadened out in sympathy to embrace the needs of the entire race" (207). Through this medium Kwamankra is imagined to have emerged in 1925 as a Race Man, an influential Pan-African opinion leader.

Kwamankra, on Hayford's behalf, forcefully claims a place in a racial vanguard on a Pan-Africanist public platform. And he does so because, by his own diagnosis, "What, indeed, can be more certain than that the African in the United States, in the West Indies, and in the mother country, East, West and South, has need to unlearn a good deal?" In the matter of Pan-Africa,

> [few will doubt] that she requires emancipation from the thraldom of foreign ideas inimical to racial development. . . . But the unfortunate part of it is that the way out is at [*sic*] yet but dimly dawning even upon such as would otherwise be qualified to lead the masses. It becomes, therefore, the sacred duty of those who can see a little more clearly ahead to point the way. (183)

If these words join Hayford-Kwamankra with those "qualified" race leaders—Du Bois's "Talented Tenth" of the Negro race—he is poised as such to set before his tripartite black Atlantic co-respondents and public a nativist manifesto and its conservative public agenda. The informing genius behind manifesto and agenda is no other than his mentor, Blyden, in comparison to whom other race leaders like Booker T. Washington and Du Bois can only come off unfavorably. For:

> "[W]hile Booker T. Washington seeks to promote the material advancement of the black man in the United States, and W.E. Burghardt Du Bois his social enfranchisement amid surroundings and in an atmosphere uncongenial to racial development, Edward Wilmot Blyden has sought for more than a quarter of a century to reveal the African everywhere to himself; to fix his attention upon original ideas and conceptions as to his place in the economy of the world; to point out to him his work as a race among the races of men; lastly, and most important of all, to lead him back unto self-respect. . . .
>
> "To emphasise an important consideration, in the Afro-American school of thought the black man is seeking intellectually and materially to show himself a man along the lines of progress of the white man. In the African school of thought, represented by Dr. Blyden, the black man is engaged upon a sublimer task, namely the discovery of his true place in creation upon natural and national lines." (163–64)

If the Afro-American dreamers of an assimilationist modern for the race have missed the mark,[15] Blyden, in urging "man, know thyself," Hayford argues, is the one who has most perspicaciously dealt with the question of a relevant foundational philosophy for an activist (or political) culture for Pan-Africa. "[A] leader among leaders of African aboriginal thought" (165), it was Blyden who was uncompromisingly urging the intellectual necessity of seeking out of an African nativity an ontological a priori, a nonnegotiable "natural" first principle. On this alone, in Blyden's thought, could a modernist Pan-African agenda of racial restitution be programmatically erected and given a meaningful worldly orientation.

A conjunctural modernity, then, was what Blyden was advocating, a combination that *subjects* the originality of a Western *techne* to the priority of an African *logos*. In his Blydean self, Kwamankra, the conjunctural persona, embodies this combination. And he pontificates accordingly: "Not only must the Ethiopian acquire proficiency in the arts and sciences, in technical and industrial training, but he must pursue a course of scientific inquiry which would reveal to him the treasure house of his own nationality" (170). This goes contrary to Washington's program at the Tuskegee Institute, founded on a materialist philosophy foreign to the "true . . . racial instincts" (173), as Hayford, in strong Blydean tones, implies—and for protégé as for mentor "Nature's way" (169, 176) for racial Africanity cannot be anything but the native way. Thus Kwamankra demands, "it is not so much *Afro-Americans* that we want as *Africans* or *Ethiopians*" (173). To restore themselves to their authentic African nature, therefore, diasporic Africans, "must bring themselves in touch with some of the general traditions and institutions of their ancestors," even "though sojourning in a strange land" (165).

Kwamankra, delivering Hayford's polemic, works his nativism vitally into the question of the normative basis and the end-orientation of a Pan-African pedagogic practice. We find in this concern an anticipation in the preindependence era of what Ngugi, in the postindependence era, would term "Education for a National Culture."[16] For the earlier nationalist and his mentor Blyden—and this would be Ngugi's postindependence position, too—a worthwhile program of education for a supranational Pan-African culture was one that did not merely seek to advance black power but one that additionally would seek to make this power self-sustaining. And the culturalist justification for this was that power operating in an ontological vacuum did not make existential sense. That is, outward material power not backed by inward soul power—i.e., the state in which the race was in possession of the whole world but had forfeited its native self-possession (or soul)—could not be self-sustaining power. The great danger, then, was the acculturating Western education which produced artificial black Westerners, uncritical mimics who at the core were hollow and substanceless. "The crux of the educational question, as it affects the African," Kwamankra critically affirms, "is that . . . [h]e becomes a slave to foreign ways of life and thought." This African, in Kwamankra's nativist resolution, "will desire to be a slave no longer" (192–93).

On the matter of the pedagogical furtherance of the ends of a national culture, a culture which guarantees a harmonious combination of material power and soul power for the Ethiopian race, Kwamankra imagines himself founding "a national University for the Gold Coast and for Ashanti" (194). This institution, designed with a view to Africa's "conquer[ing] the spiritual world" (197), will be open in a spirit of Pan-African internationalism to "students from the United States, the West Indies, Sierra Leone . . . Lagos and the Gambia" (196). Here is the pedagogical agenda, in essence Blydean, that Kwamankra projects for the national University:

> "I would found in such a University a Chair for History; and the kind of history I would teach would be universal history with particular reference to the part Ethiopia has played in the affairs of the world. I would lay stress on the fact that while Rameses II was dedicating temples to "the God of gods and secondly to his own glory," the God of the Hebrews had not yet appeared unto Moses in the burning bush; that Africa was the cradle of the world's systems and philosophies, and the nursing mother of its religions. In short, that Africa has nothing to be ashamed of of its place among the nations of the earth. I would make it possible for this seat of learning to be the means of revising erroneous current ideas regarding the African; of raising him in self-respect." (194–95)

Kwamankra would also set up "professorships for the study of the Fanti, Hausa, and Yoruba languages" (195). The reasoning behind this is that, as the "examples of Ireland and Denmark" had shown, "the vehicle of a national language [is] much the safest and most natural way of national conservancy and evolution" (175). The product of the national University, therefore, must be the African who "commands the uses of his native tongue"; who "has a literature of his own, enriched by translations from standard authors of other lands." This African "respects the institutions and customs of his ancestors"; and is aware of "an intelligent past which inspires him" (170). Hayfordian pedagogy is intended, then, to refine "off the face of the African continent" the "superfine African gentleman who, at the end of every second or third year, talks of a run to Europe, lest there should be a breakdown" (193). It would promote, instead, in Sarbah's words, "the sturdy and vigorous development or growth of [a] national character racy of the soil" (*Fanti National Constitution*, 235). Apparently not open to Ethiopian women, Hayford's University will vest education consequentially in the characterological production of "*men*— no effete, mongrel, product of foreign systems" (*Ethiopia Unbound*, 197).

Afric's sons but not her daughters, and then only the "cultured"—albeit "unspoilt"—among these sons, it would seem, are the chosen ones who would function as "co-worker in the uplifting of man to nobler effort" (195). But, then, as Kwamankra shows us in *Ethiopia Unbound,* even among the chosen ones, the frontline Talented Tenth, the question of what region of, and which ideological bloc in, the black Atlantic should provide the "natural" leadership of the imagined community of Pan-Africa—the leader among the leaders—is in contention. And the location where native culture is an environing reality becomes crucial for the leadership question for the conservative ideological bloc, the school of Blyden, which Hayford's alter ego represents. Once Blyden had been of the opinion that "the solution of Africa in America, is America in Africa; and further . . . the solution of Africa in Africa, is Africa in America" (*Negro Race,* 356–57). This was Hayford's mentor in 1886 writing as an apologist of "African Colonization" by African Americans who, in his projection, had the manifest destiny of taking the leadership role in the "regeneration" of the continent. It is the self-same Blyden, however, whose *African Life and Customs* would provide ammunition for Hayford to shift the orientation of "natural" Pan-African leadership from Africa America to West Africa, and then only to its conservative school of nationalism.[17] In Blyden's contention Pan-African regeneration—"the solution of Africa in America"—was premised on the priority of African regeneration—"the solution of Africa in Africa." And the latter, to remain true to the Personality of Africa, had to proceed in accordance with the natural idiosyncracies of African societies. It was those therefore who understood these idiosyncracies, as he abstracts and synthesizes them in *African Life and Customs,* who would have equipped themselves for race leadership. And if for Gold Coast intellectuals in particular, a native culture was an environing reality to a greater degree than elsewhere in West Africa, then West Africa's leadership of the imagined Pan-African community, centered on the Gold Coast's own leadership in West Africa, was beyond question.

Culture, as a return to source, the Orphean/*sankofa* problematic, therefore, had strategic political implications in the calculus of Pan-African leadership. In *Ethiopia Unbound,* it is a calculating Hayford who urges through his autobiographical surrogate:

> Here, then, is work for cultured West Africans to start a reform which will be world-wide in its effects among Ethiopians, remembering as a basis that we, as a people, have our own statutes, the customs and institutions of our forefathers, which we cannot neglect and live. (174)

Kwamankra, quoting an authority, additionally avers, "'Our history, our customs, our characters are unintelligible to us until we know it [*sic*]'" (195). In that also is an affirmation of the Gold Coast in a Pan-African conservative vanguard, the intellectual leader in the archival work of what Soyinka, in the postindependence era, would call "race retrieval." Regarding this task, "We on the Gold Coast," Kwamankra reports, "are making a huge effort in this direction." There could not be any doubt about this, what with Hayford's and Sarbah's hugely influential seminal nativist works and the former's establishment of the Gold Coast National Research Association, which would nurture the radical nativism of Sekyi, the man who would keep the Blydean flame burning into the 1950s. About a Gold Coast nationalist archeology, the painstaking effort to recover the soul of the race, Kwamankra adds prophetically, "though European habits will die hard with some of our people . . . if we don't succeed quite with this generation, we shall succeed with the next" (174–75).

Considering a politics of the possible in the context of the early-twentieth-century colonial-imperial order, Hayford avers, "The African's way to proper recognition lies not at present so much in the exhibition of material force and power." On the contrary, following "the line of least resistance in meeting any combination of forces against him," the African's political road to recognition lay "in the gentler art of *persuasion by the logic of facts* . . . before which all reasonable men must bow" (168; emphasis added). In 1928, the same could still be heard coming out of the Gold Coast, as J.W. de Graft Johnson quotes an authority to the effect that, in metropolitan/colonial relations, "'Facts and not opinions' should be the basis of understanding."[18] The next section looks at how this principle informs the autobiographical predication, the "national character," that Hayford authors upon his alter ego, Kwamankra, as he makes him into a crusading figure of "resistance" and protest in *Ethiopia Unbound.*

Protest and Commitment: The National-Popular Persona, the "Logic of the Facts," and the Jural Addressee

> We [Gold Coasters] notice . . . that, in your (i.e., imperial Britain's) haste to fill the colonial exchequer, little regard is paid to what will work for the material advancement of the Aborigines, whose mites fill the coffers, forgetful that the greatest good of the greatest number is the keynote of healthy administration.
>
> —Casely Hayford, *Gold Coast Native Institutions*

The early stage of the acquaintanceship between the Flag and the Aborigines is in the nature of what is euphemistically called a protectorate. Now, the term "protectorate" connotes the dependence of a weaker upon a stronger. And as the Gospel of Jesus Christ, which . . . was in good faith taught the Aborigines, insists on the full brotherhood of the human race—and the Native, you must grant, whether you like it or not, is a member of that race, surely, you must mean the dependence of a weaker upon a stronger brother. But here, again, facts falsify impressions. The very missionary who preaches the gospel of universal brotherhood seems to scout the idea of the black man, cultured and uncultured, being on the same plane of life as himself. He beholds the Aborigines afar off, and believes in the Native being kept in his place. He merely intends to raise him a wee bit higher in order that he may be useful to his white brother by more intelligently hewing his wood and drawing his water, which the latter is too good to do for himself. This is the black man's burden.

—Casely Hayford, *Gold Coast Native Institutions*

We may pretend not to see these things. We may elect not to know them. But we cannot prevent people thinking and drawing conclusions. And some of the facts are decidedly ugly.

—Casely Hayford, *The Truth about the West African Land Question*

The fifth chapter of *Ethiopia Unbound* begins on a (topical) note of protest by Kwamankra against governmental dereliction in early-twentieth-century colonial Gold Coast. "In the year of grace, 1904," Kwamankra reports, "there was no such thing as a water supply in the town of Sekondi. . . . Nor was this . . . strange. The Government and the people of the Gold Coast had always depended upon Providence for such a common necessity of life as water" (65). Here we encounter the autobiographical persona wedded, in social and political critique, to the facts on the ground, as it were. This persona emerges in the guise and role of an investigative journalist, marshalling the facts in an exposé of the scandalous, that which offends logic and common sense, in colonial Gold Coast affairs. Kwamankra's role is a testamentary one, too: it involves him not simply in stating the bald and disquieting facts but also in a weighing of these facts in a crusade for justice and humanity on the Gold Coast's behalf. We encounter a persona cast in the mold both of protest and commitment.

If Hayford protests, it is because, for nigh one generation since it became a formal colony, the desire of the Gold Coast's progressive inhabitants for the country's material reconstruction had remained unfulfilled. A central reason for the country's retardation was that what passed for its politics under alien control had no genuine basis in the social life of the Gold Coast's inhabitants. For, "If the Gold Coast were a country with free institutions," that is, a country with representation and governance rooted in, and nourished by, a popular will, then

> we should soon have good wharves and harbours, gas works, water works and railway communication all over the country. Prosperous cities would grow up, and knowledge would spread among all classes of the people, producing a willing and an efficient body of workmen for the material development of the vast wealth and resources of the country. (*Native Institutions*, 130)

"*We* should soon have . . .": a popular "we" is subsumed in the Hayfordian persona, and represented, in this persona's point of view, in desire and demand for progressive development.

But by what measure is Hayford entitled to speak in the name of, and on behalf of, this popular "we"? Wherever we find anticolonial protest and demand for reform in Hayford's writings, they are directed at an addressee identified as "you," generally a reference to the colonial-imperial administration and its personnel. But there is rhetorically more to this "you"; and we may gauge this from an illustration, titled "Africa at the Bar of Justice," from another text of Gold Coast protest nationalism, Hayford protégé De Graft Johnson's *Towards Nationhood*. In Johnson's drawing, we have an advocate pleading Africa's cause before a jural and judicial assembly—whose multiracial composition gives it the appearance of an international court of appeal (although the figures of judicial authority appear to be white). It would appear that this court is assembled to hear the advocate's African plaint, and to weigh the evidence he reasonably presents of metropolitan indifference to the needs and aspirations of colonized Africa. At issue is not only the British Empire's sins of omission. The direct acts of colonial injustice visited on the native, in the interpenetrating domains of politics, society, law, and culture, must be admitted in evidence as well for proper remedial action to be taken by those who have it in their power to do so.

Black faces are missing from Johnson's picture, and we are to assume that this is so because colonial oppression has kept their worldly presence from view. The lone black figure able to make an appearance before the Bar of Justice, then, represents the rare African. This is the African privileged by virtue of his professional (legal) training; by virtue of his sharing an imperial language and culture; and by virtue of his participation in colonial-metropolitan networks and cross-racial alliances that guarantee him access to a metropolitan public and publishing. This, in short, is the modern

African who has gained the social wherewithal and cosmopolitan credentials to acquire visibility and speak in a worldly context. It is the African, too, who, inserted into these cosmopolitan networks, has gained the requisite cultural and political capital, the international stature, to emerge as a credible critic-prosecutor of Empire and its unjust colonial order.

Johnson's modernist persona is set apart from the masses by his having these privileges. But, appearing before the Bar of Justice, it is implied that he is identified, in his nativity as African, with these masses in their worldly exclusion. The *rara avis* of a lone advocate cannot but contain within himself, and give expression to, the voice of the people and the race. On a popular Africa's behalf, then, he is tasked to speak at the Bar of Justice as a translator and transmitter, giving worldly intelligibility to the desires and feelings of his otherwise inarticulate people and race.

It is in this aspect of bringing a popular nativity into the purview of a just worldliness, then, that imposes on Johnson's modernist persona to be inhabited by the (Gold Coast) people, the (African) race, collectivities whose aspirations for social advancement speak in translation through him. And in this gesture where a popular *We* is displaced into the middle-class *I,* he is anticipated by Hayford who, in what might be the expression of the elitist hauteur of a modern African, asks rhetorically in *Ethiopia Unbound,* "But for the educated native where would the unsophisticated native be?" And he goes on to pledge: "Heaven grant that the educated native may never be wanting in his duty to his less privileged brethren, or betray their trust in him" (193). And so for the "sophisticated" nationalist, Hayford, a self-made compact to identify in his person and carry the burden of those sorely put upon by the exactions of colonial-imperialism is treated as a matter that goes without saying.

We might consider in this connection Hayford's perception of his role as a newspaper editor under the colonial order:

> Above all things, I would study to make the people feel that they had in the columns of the journal a mouth-piece, and in the editor a ready friend, one who sympathized with them in all their troubles and who will give his very life's blood to ameliorate their condition. In brief, I would say with that distinguished journalist, Mr. W. T. Stead: "The people are silent. I will be the advocate of this silence. I will speak for the dumb. I will speak of the small to the great, and of the feeble to the strong. I will speak for all the despairing silent ones. I will interpret the stammering, I will interpret the grumbling, the mourning, the tumults, of crowds, the complaints ill-pronounced and these cries of beasts that through ignorance and other suffering man is forced to utter." (*Native Institutions,* 181)

"'I will be the word of the people,'" Hayford declares in conclusion, in a pious wish that, through his instrumentality, the inarticulate voice, the "raw" protest, of the "unsophisticated" people will accede to a representation adequate to the demands of the modern colonial sphere. As the nationalist assumes the popular word in and for himself—and in and for those who fall in the middle, between power and the people—he points to the making of a middle-class mimetic contract. And by mimetic contract, we might under-stand a voluntary covenant in terms of which the middle-class persona pledges fealty to "the people," therein to be the conduit of and a mirror reflecting, in Nkrumah's terms, "the dominant [popular] wish and aspiration."[19]

For Hayford, as for De Graft Johnson after him, the model of resis-tant protest is above all one in which the powerless speak the truth to power. And this is in a manner not unlike that of Richard Wright performatively taking on in his writings the role of a public defendant, and demanding, in the context of the problematic relationship of his people to a dominant white America, "White Man, Listen!" That said, however, the African de-mands as articulated by our two Gold Coast advocates hardly come across in the brusque tones of Wright's angry black man. Nor are these two, im-passioned though their advocacy is, threatening "the fire next time," as in the prognosis of black/white race relations in America made by James Baldwin (who also, in his writings, as it were, hauls white America before the Bar of Justice). The fiery rhetoric of protest would be heard stridently and pack more force in post–World War II Gold Coast nationalism after its takeover by Nkrumah, albeit we find its prefiguration in interwar anti-imperialist activity by a few like Awoonor-Renner, Wallace-Johnson, and Azikiwe. These figures, Pan-Africanists on the political left, would be as-sisted by the metropole-based International African Service Bureau, led by its tireless founder George Padmore, as they worked a tributary anticolo-nial politics on Gold Coast and West African location coherently into the mainstream of a general anti-imperialist movement of colonial peoples.[20]

Anticolonialists Hayford and Johnson may have been, insofar as the rule offered by the Crown Colony system offended legal and moral prin-ciples of equity and justice, but they were no revolutionary anti-imperial-ists. Advocating colonial reform within the framework of Empire, their nationalist politics was of the liberal-constitutionalist variety.[21] And this was also the politics generally of the organizations to which they belonged: the A.R.P.S. and its rival from 1920 to 1930, the National Congress of British West Africa. It would be the politics, too, of the United Gold Coast Convention, the first genuine political party in the Gold Coast that emerged in the 1940s.

A model of agitation confined strictly to liberal-constitutionalist principles was dominant, then, in Gold Coast anticolonial politics until the end of World War II. The original cue for this came from the way the protonationalist Fanti Confederation envisaged a modern political self-construction for the Western-educated middle class. In spite of the Confederation's being effectively destroyed by British colonialism, its last leader, the educated King Ghartey IV, had exhorted the A.R.P.S. in a letter written on his deathbed in 1897: "Be constitutional!" As Geiss points out, "These two words became the motto of West African nationalism, at least of its conservative wing" (*Pan-African Movement,* 69).

The British in colonizing the Gold Coast may have demonstrated that might *is* right, but being constitutional in anticolonial agitation, as permitted under its order, Ghartey was exhorting, would be the way for the colonized to ensure that might *does* right. The way forward politically lay, therefore, in enlightened middle-class "collaboration" with the political agencies of Empire. Collaboration, however, did not mean slavish endorsement of imperial policy by the middle class. Rather, it was an order of activity imagined in the mode of a critical contributionism; that is, of critique executed in the spirit of contributing to a reform of imperial praxis in ways that would make its order beneficial for European and native alike.[22] The subtitle of Hayford's *Native Institutions,* "Thoughts upon a Healthy Imperial Policy for the Gold Coast and Ashanti," reflects the conception of this work—and virtually his entire oeuvre—in a contributionist mode. It is a nationalist undertaking wherein Hayford, taking upon himself the "thankless task . . . of criticism," ventures "to indicate the moral duty of Great Britain to the country and the hinterland" (xiv). What contributionism meant in principle, therefore, was the political self-fashioning of the middle class in a watchdog role and the projection of this class as the defender of the interest of a native public. And it is in this role that we find the leading middle-class spokesmen, like Hayford, holding Empire morally accountable to a premise of African Reconstruction that they could see in its expansionist logic and which they endorsed.[23] Hayford had taken Ghartey's exhortation to heart, for as a critic of British rule, he appeals to the colonizer's good sense: "We know we have only to point out these [shortcomings in Crown Colony rule] and England will remedy them" (*Native Institutions,* 237).

It is as a progressive voice of the people, a marshaller of facts in justiciary protest on their anticolonial behalf, and in contributionist protest towards imperial reform, therefore, that we encounter Kwamankra in the committed modernist aspect of his persona. When in the fifth chapter of

Ethiopia Unbound he launches his topical protest about what is wrong with the Gold Coast, as inaugurally pointed out above, it is directed at a "you," an addressee onto whom Kwamankra projects his own enlightened reasonableness. Hence this is an addressee poised to be lessoned to tell political— and cultural—good faith from the chicanery that passes for the thing under the colonial order. Here, in the fifth chapter, the addressee is to be presented with a representative snapshot of the Gold Coast as Kwamankra takes his hand, as it were, and conducts him on a *tour d'horizon* of Sekondi, the western commercial hub of the colony. The end of this guided tour is to reveal the true condition of the country and its people under alien rule.

It is in the mode of truthful witnessing, then, that the addressee and interlocutor, in the company of Hayford's autobiographical persona, is afforded a "passing view of Sekondi" (70). He/she is with Kwamankra as they make a seaborne approach to a "city of great promise." Yet this statement about Sekondi's—and by extension the Gold Coast's—potential is immediately undercut by what may be intended as a metaphor of colonial blight. It is March, the start of the rainy season, and every sign of rain is evident as the approach to Sekondi is being made.

> [R]aindrops patter on the ship's deck. But even while you are wondering what a wet landing you are going to have, a blaze of light breaks on the north-east, and the Titan of the upper sphere leaps forth triumphantly over thunder and storm. As you divest yourself of your mackintosh, a cynical old coaster says to you: "That's Sekondi all over; I shouldn't be surprised if the tanks are all dry." (66)

It may be that "Progressive people in the country . . . are burning to transform the Gold Coast into a fairly decent country; but the Authorities do not seem to be in touch with the times somehow" (*Native Institutions,* 115).

With regard to the provision of public amenities and modern conveniences required to advance the well-being of the communities of the Gold Coast, then, an alien government's approach remains half-hearted. And this is because colonial power, practicing a politics of domination rather than representation, has demonstrated that it is not accountable to the populace over which it rules. The matter is put in perspective elsewhere in *Ethiopia Unbound* as Kwamankra, imparting political lessons to his son, draws an analogy to explain how the Crown Colony system works. "Now, what would you boys think of your schoolmaster in these enlightened days," Kwamankra asks, "if he should, from time to time, ask you to contribute out of your pocket money funds for the laying out of a recreation ground without allowing some of you boys to have a say as to how things were to be done?" (110–11). The analogy with colonial governance follows: "Under the [Crown Colony System] . . . the schoolmaster is the Governor, and the lads are the people of this country whose contributions are in the shape of heavy duties they pay on all imported articles." As yet, however, the people of the Gold Coast "have no voice in the spending of their contributions" (111). Gold Coast people are prevailed upon by the system they live under to unjustly suffer the burden of taxation without representation. Indeed, in the nonconsultative model of colonial politics, it is absurdly "The [colonial] Titan only [who] knows what the Titan wants, or what he means" (69).

The indictment of the Crown Colony system, for which Hayford has called out the jury (as imaged in the addressee), is that under its aegis politics in the colonial sphere is divorced from an *organic* connection with society. Politics, as a matter of policies determining the destiny of the ruled, is made at the top, the colonial apex occupied by the alien functionaries of Empire, the place of the so-called man on the spot. And if in the application policy was to be brought down to a social base occupied by the generality of the native people, it came to them in a nonnegotiable form. The shaping of policy was the prerogative of Whitehall, the Colonial Office falling under the Secretary of State for the Colonies, and Whitehall was charged with imperial oversight of Britain's far-flung colonies. But the absurdity, as Hayford will point out, was that the policy emanating from Whitehall was based on "facts" and advice coming from the man on the spot, who did not, and could afford not to, consult those who were the objects of policy. And the word of the man on the spot, because he was three thousand miles away, was, at any rate, not verifiable; what is more, such distance guaranteed that policy could not be effectively monitored. It was true, then, that the Titan—the Governor and the administrative machine he controlled—alone knew what the Titan was doing. What had transpired under the Crown Colony system of rule, for Hayford, therefore, was executive despotism, with the colonial governor wielding and exercising powers that not even the monarch in England had.[24]

On this reading, then, the Crown Colony system as operated by Whitehall was analogous to a feudal overlord parceling out fiefdoms to handpicked despots. It is true that the liberal democratic *form* of governance was in operation, with executive, legislative, and judicial branches of government in place in a colony like the Gold Coast. But the democratic form did not secrete a democratic *substance*; rather it tended towards a reinforcement of autocracy. Based on a system of gubernatorial nomination of its members, the colonial legislature was nothing more than an official rubberstamp for a despotic Governor who could access, beyond the limits of his constitutional authority, a feudal (i.e., arbitrary) power to unmake any member refusing to toe his line.

Reform may have come to these colonial legislatures, enough to have made Hayford a member of the Gold Coast Legislative Council in 1916, and enough to have given the "natural rulers" representation from 1910 on. However, critics have scoffed at the system of "advisory democracy" that these colonial legislatures remained in practice.[25] Some thirty-six years after the publication of *Ethiopia Unbound,* an expatriate observer describes the Gold Coast Legislative Council as "in . . . form not parliamentary," and in "psychology . . . paternalistic and not democratic." He concludes: "The *ultima ratio* of the government in constitutional practice has hitherto been its official majority; its *ultima ratio* in controversy is an appeal for a recognition of its beneficent wisdom."[26] The liberal principle of the separation of powers was inoperative, therefore, in colonial Gold Coast. And if this is Hayford's anticolonial contention in the early twentieth century, it is similar in content to the one to be made by the Ghanaian legal critic Fui Tsikata, reviewing the history of his country's judiciary. He notes: "[T]he colonial judiciary, which began as an extension of colonial rule, remained practically all its life an active part of the machinery of colonial government, and did not pretend to be a controlling arm against the administration."[27] And therein lay the absurdity that Hayford points out. For in spite of colonialism's vaunted claim that it was bringing the rule of law to natives it had negatively stereotyped as lawless, their rulers without exception given to despotic excess, the democratic rule of law is not what obtained under its order. What obtained instead was the iron law of rule, of despotic rule (i.e., law serving the ruler, not the people ruled). And this is a part-premise, as will come up shortly, of Hayford's prosecution of colonialism, in *Ethiopia Unbound,* as an inhumane and unethical incarnation of the principles of Social Darwinism.

Hayford dealing with issues of the moment in protest raises for imperial overrule awkward questions about its putatively superior claim to be rationalizing, modernizing, and civilizing. In the constitution of the short-lived Fanti Confederation, the educated native had shown the will to be a rational instrument of a sovereign project of African modernization. This project of Reconstruction was to have been executed in an alliance, a partnership, between a middle class and a chiefly elite. The New Imperialism had, however, intervened with force and defeated that sovereign aspiration. And yet, in Hayford's assessment, as he makes the facts unfold before the jury, as it were, what does a colonialist modernity hold out before a subject people but faux modernization and a daily reminder that might is right.

In the circumstances, Hayford might be seen to be putting before the "jural" addressee the questions that animated the Confederation in the late 1860s. Who understood not only the welfare needs of the people of the Gold Coast and did so not at a remove but in affective identification with this popular need? Why not, then, a political voice and role for a class of enlightened Gold Coasters, identified with the place, and rationally and emotionally committed to its collective interest as their own? If the New Imperialism had displaced these enlightened ones from the executive role promised by the nationalism of the Confederation, under the colonial order could they not, on behalf of the people, at least have a decisive legislative and policy-making role? Hayford had written: "the very difficulties which beset the path of the British Administrator can be correctly indicated sometimes only by the intelligent ones of the country." It followed, therefore, that "the method, if not the means, of solution must also be with [the intelligent ones]" (*Native Institutions*, 3).

The questions arise in the mode of imagining an advocacy for a class-for-power—the political modality in which we have previously identified the middle class—and they had become necessary to the extent that the Machiavellian cunning of colonial reason left a middle-class being confronting its existential absurdity. Under a new-imperial scheme, his race had become a convenient basis to exclude the educated native from the political apex of the colonial social order, and his European finish—liable to make him a trouble-maker—was cause enough for colonial authority to block his political access to a native base. It was a part of colonial stratagem, then, to representationally deprive this class of a "natural" constituency in nativity. And this is what leaves an embattled Hayford complaining: "the sagacious black man offers a point of resistance when he pleads his peculiar customs and institutions, and presto! the cry of the 'educated native peril' is raised, as if forsooth, the native ceases to be a 'native' the moment he is educated" (*Ethiopia Unbound*, 118).

Here was the politics of divide and rule in Gold Coast colonial practice, Hayford could see, politics of the same kind that had overtaken Sierra Leone, where colonial manipulation had succeeded in sundering the "cultured" black Englishmen of the Colony from the "vulgar" indigenes of the Protectorate. Thus Hayford laments in *Land Question*:

[T]oday there is a Sierra Leone Colony as distinct from the Sierra Leone Protectorate. There is no fear of the two ever coming together. . . . A gulf as insuperable as that between lost souls and the blessed in Milton's dream, is fixed. An educated Colonist dare not openly advocate the cause of a Protectorate chief. . . . Alas for education! Alas, also for the introduction of civilisation into Africa! (10)

Sierra Leone is far from being unique for "the principle of isolation is proceeding in other parts of West Africa. . . . It seems to be part of British policy to sever the educated African from the uneducated" (11).

If in political terms this artificial divide amounted to a competitive neutering of the middle class, the Orphean problematic of this class finding the people could not have been more urgent for Hayford. For the middle class, small in numbers as Hayford was writing, had little competitive force in itself. A class-for-power needed a popular constituency—a quantitative people—behind itself. But as yet it could summon this constituency only through a form of (nativist) displacement which, as we find in the writings of Hayford and his contemporaries, was a conversion of quality into quantity. That is, the claim that the middle class was invested with nativist value, the claim that it was culturally representative, was transformed into a claim for its *political* representativeness, of the multitudinous popular voice speaking through the middle (as we see in Hayford's construction of the mimetic contract). In the fourth section of this chapter, we will see how this conversion is buttressed in Hayford's Orphean version of the national allegory.

It was Blyden, defender of the "Race integrity" and "Race individuality" of the African, who had pointed out that what made these attributes he prized hard to retain in his time is a dogmatic and insurgent Western civilization. The "fringe of European civilization is violence," Blyden had concluded. Kwamankra, in the manner of the Foucauldian genealogical reconstruction that reveals in the histories of human formations "systems of subjection," and "the hazardous play of dominations,"[28] brings Blyden's thesis of modern civilization at the margin as aggravated violence to the post-encounter history of the Gold Coast. And in this emotion-charged genealogical reconstruction, Kwamankra contrives to produce this specific location as a subset of the larger history of imperial violence at the European fringe.

As Hayford's alter ego positions his addressee-companion to get a splendid "bird's eye view of Sekondi, bathed in the twilight," a scene "[s]o restful" (*Ethiopia Unbound*, 68), therefore, this romantic view of the colonial town is one that cannot be sustained. Quickly, romance is belied as the narrator moves on to retell the sordid history of European-African relations on this portion of the Gold Coast, its theme Anglo-Dutch rivalry over imperial trade and what this meant for the Sekondi of the 1860s.

> If you know the history of this town, a momentary sweep of the eye will bring back to memory signs of a former strife; for overlooking the Bay, there stands the old Fort, a symbol of the strife between the Dutch and the English in the pre-locomotive days. The struggle, in name, was between two European nations, in reality between two aboriginal factions, who, for aught one knows to the contrary, might have otherwise lived in peace. The Dutch or the English flag was the standard which drew the natives in thousands into opposing camps, and for which they shed their blood freely, only that the white man might obtain freer scope to barter spurious drinks for the precious metal which the torrential rains washed to the very doors of the aborigines. (67–68)

It is a tale of native Africans manipulated into identifying with causes that could in no way coincide with their own interests; their bodies requisitioned by aliens to prosecute conflicts which went to the benefit of the latter. In historical excursus, then, Kwamankra advances the theme of the Gold Coast's colonial absurd but compounds it with the tragic. His addressee is encouraged to understand that this more or less has been the character of the African experience in the European-African encounter. Political trends on the Gold Coast since the British bought out the Dutch (1872) and established themselves as the sole colonial power (1874) have only gone to confirm the absurdly tragic tendency of post-encounter African history:

> [I]n the present day the successors of the leaders, who bore the heat and the burden of the day in order that British commerce might gain a footing on these shores, are not remembered as they should be by the British Government. But it is true that they are protected; it is feared very much protected. To be accurate, they are remembered sometimes in the partitioning of their territories, the minimising of their authority, and, worse than all, in some cases, in the sowing of those seeds of discord, calculated to destroy the integrity of a people. (68)

To survive, to safeguard the commercial interests whose political expression it is, colonialism must purposefully orchestrate the destruction of the aboriginal integrity, as Kwamankra understands it, of the ways of life of the colonized. Kwamankra's probing perspective reveals that, as a part of this political design, a secret war is being waged on the psyche of the native— secret because he is unaware of it. Its aim is to inflict upon him an enervating schizophrenia—to leave him burdened with a conflicted double consciousness calculated to sap his will to resist alien domination. Colonial commercialism and profit-making, as supported by state policy, and colonial soul-making, as mediated by the so-called Christian missions—the one pandering to the temptations of native flesh, the other waving standards of moral excellence in the native's face—are responsible for the affective despoliation of the native. And as Kwamankra explains, this is a "work of destruction" that

> speaking generally, goes on not in the light of day, but metaphorically, in the dark hours of night. The mighty Titan does not knock down his victim and deprive him of life outright. Oh no! that would be too crude a way. With the gin bottle in one hand, and the Bible in the other, he urges moral excellence, which, in his heart of hearts, he knows to be impossible of attainment by the African under the circumstances; and when the latter fails, his benevolent protector makes such a failure a cause for dismembering his tribe, alienating his lands, appropriating his goods, and sapping the foundations of his authority and institutions. (68–69)

It is imperial policy to weaken those already vanquished. This calls for strategies of colonially infantilizing the African, producing him—and giving him back an image of himself—as one in need of adult supervision in the political sphere and as a candidate for Christian salvation, made to appear as the only worthwhile one, in the spiritual sphere. Thus the mighty Titan bolsters his claims to legitimate African overrule with the useful self-justifying myth of the white man's civilizing burden.

However, beyond the romantic myth of white responsibility to the inferior races so-called, the reality is that of Europeans carrying "in the one hand a patent from the Almighty and absolution in the other to snatch away the patrimony of others" (117–18). The enterprise of colonial imperialism is Darwinian, a matter of the strong bullying the weak into submission on the flimsiest of pretexts. Empire's exterminatory ethic of live and let die is central in the fifth chapter as Kwamankra quotes in full Guy Eden's poem "King of the Blacks," with its refrain: "Far o'er the sea came the pitiless cry: / Why should they live? Fate has writ large its doom for them, / Land for the whites! Let the black fellows die" (70). The Darwinian thesis of Empire will be taken up again in two successive chapters of *Ethiopia Unbound,* the ninth and the tenth titled "The Yellow Peril" and "The Black Peril," respectively. Both chapters stage scenes of instruction where Kwamankra patiently explains to his son the sources of the self-aggrandizing myths of the white builders of modern empire, the dangerous realpolitical consequences of these, in essence, racist myths for the "weaker races." The lesson insists on the need on the part of the African for a vigorous prosecution of the resistance that will make for his own racial and national survival.

Jumping ahead to chapters 9 and 10, then, we find Casely Hayford projecting a politics of African resistance and survival through Kwamankra's tutelary relationship with his son. Before we get to this, however, as the addressee-companion traverses Sekondi with Kwamankra, *Ethiopia Unbound* shows us how in the Gold Coast the affective basis of a resistance politics is vitiated by a will-sapping colonial presence. Political critique modulates into a cultural key, as Hayford's alter ego evaluates the changes that European cultural imperialism—"half a century of [Christian] missionary zeal and effort" (74)—has wrought on the Personality of his Fanti people. Kwamankra tells a pathetic story of self-loss: the friends with whom, as youngsters, he "joined hands together in the moonlight under the open sky and sang [traditional] *Sanko* songs," are the Christian converts he now espies worshipping in the missionary church in Sekondi. What for Kwamankra remains the "familiar *Sanko*"—symbolizing the self-affirming institutions of the past that the others seem to have rejected—was "full of meaning" (72); it was "simple . . . natural . . . spontaneous" (73). By contrast, "as he listened today to the wheezing sound of an old harmonium upon which a missionary boy was performing, he could not help thinking how much his people lost in passing from their ways to those of the white man" (72). Other signs of alienation include the schoolmaster at the head of the choir who, although he looked a veritable "'swell'" in his "elegantly cut-away black morning coat and beautifully-glazed cuffs and collar, not to speak of patent leather shoes," in the end "did look a veritable fool" (73–74).

The history and spectacle being presented to the addressee-companion is that of the native African exiled from self-consciousness on his home soil, the African denatured and thus reduced to functioning as a mere subordinate appendage, subservient to the purposes of a colonizing Other. Not only is the African robbed of his authenticity, the originality in which he creatively preserves his authentic nature is being compromised. Kwamankra's Gold Coast stands in for an increasingly demoralized Ethiopia where, as he points out in the chapter "The Black Man's Burden," in obedience to a new, alienating rationality, addiction to the white man's drink reigned supreme. And in the Gold Coast Christian sectarianism was also to be witnessed as a compelling force, dividing "children who had suckled at the same breast and had played with the same toy gods" such that, "as men [they were] feign to slay one another" (159). The soulless materialism of a colonialist modernity had produced an "unthinking crowd

. . . beside themselves in emulation of the white man's ways, and when they bowed the knee in the House of Mammon, they thought they worshipped the true God, and seemed to forget that once they were Ethiopians" (160). Corrupted by an alien and alienating temporality, the body of Ethiopia was diseased in the temporal/physical plane; and Ethiopia's soul had for the same reason lost touch with its own divinity, its spiritual godhead. If the quest for a healing reconnection of Ethiopia's body-soul with its divinity is mandated in the circumstances, it is the figural proposition that informs the national allegory in *Ethiopia Unbound,* as outlined below.

The extent of Ethiopia's alienation is underlined when, as the fifth chapter winds down, we see Kwamankra encounter a friend of his youth, now a convert to the new faith. Kwamankra, presenting himself in a mode of fidelity and constancy to the old ways—"I, at least, am not changed," he tells his friend—proposes to her to join him and other *Sanko* performers to relive the old days in an evening of song and dance. In reaction, we are told, "She raised her eyes in holy horror as much as to say: 'Get thee behind me Satan'" (74). Forced to retreat "like a beaten man," Kwamankra makes a pledge that commits him "Henceforth . . . to devote the rest of his life in bringing back his people to their primitive simplicity and faith" (75).

Kwamankra's revivalist call for a return to authentically aboriginal (or first) principles grows out of his Darwinist understanding of cultural imperialism which, as he intuits, is putting the national and racial integrity of his people, their very survival, on the line. Hence his assertion of a vigorous practice of cultural nationalism: "If my people are to be saved from national and racial death, they must be proved as if by fire—by the practice of a virile religion, not by following emasculated sentimentalities which men shamelessly and slanderously identify with . . . Christ" (75). With the native's practical relation to his own natural sphere distorted by a religion falsified in its Euro-Christian packaging, what Ethiopia needed was a patriotic religion. Culture, a matter of the affect behind and informing a people's practical relationship with the world, needed to be understood in, and worked into, a directly political function. Kwamankra gives his reader to understand in this mode that the return to the Ethiopianist/nativist first principles that he preaches, and embodies in himself, are not incompatible with precepts in the Japanese "Bushido (Shintoism)." These are patriotic precepts that exhort (manly) self-dedication to the service and defense of people and polity. Thus, among other things, Bushido demands "self-sacrifice"; it upholds "the care of the interest of the State" over "that of the individual"; it "preaches submission to authority and the sacrifice of all private interests, whether of self or family, to the common weal" (75). It demands, in short, that self-will be abolished in a collective will. Bushido, in short, is the patriotic gospel of unanimism—a doctrine premised on the submergence of one in all, the individual part in the group whole[29]—very much in the mythological mode in which Hayford, by way of Kwamankra, presents his political persona. It is this persona that is entrusted with the salvific role—rescuing "my people . . . from national and racial death"—as, in *Ethiopia Unbound*, a private poetics of privation in Hayford's quasi autobiography is resolved, in a unanimist mode, into the public performance of the national allegory.

Hayford's first wife, Beatrice Madeline Pinnock, had died from complications during her second childbirth, and the baby, a girl, did not survive her mother either. This is recorded and explored by Hayford as an experience of deep personal privation in *Ethiopia Unbound* by way of Kwamankra, portrayed—in the chapter "Love and Death"—in quasi-fictional parallel as a man who has lost his wife and baby daughter.

> He had been a father once before—the happy husband of a happy wife in a home where love dwelt; and when death first took the wife and then the new born babe, he left darkness behind where first was light. It all looked so strange. He only half realised it in the first flush of his sorrow. But as the days wore on, and the old familiar chair by the hearth remained vacant, the darkness in his heart seemed to deepen. (42)

The intensely personal quality of the experience notwithstanding, Kwamankra's private loss as a paterfamilias—much in the manner we find Du Bois doing in the chapter of *Souls,* "Of the Death of a Son"—is one we see transformed into a public gesture. Gendered as masculine loss of a complementary principle of femininity, the death of Mansa, Kwamankra's wife, is able to function as such as a synonym of national loss. This gendered complementarity is outlined in the previous chapter, "Love and Life," which treats the subject of Kwamankra's courtship of Mansa, both of similar educational attainment. When Kwamankra proposes to Mansa, it is to cast her in a conjugal role as the biblical "little child [who] shall lead them." Furthermore, he objects in a conventionally Victorian masculine manner to Mansa's plan to take up an appointment as a headmistress—won in her own right as a highly educated woman—asking her to abandon any plans for a career and marry him instead. "I was hoping," Kwamankra pleads with her, "that yours would be the task to teach me the way of duty, and that when found you would help me tread it." The conversation repays extensive quotation:

Mansa: But how do I know what your duty is? Who can tell you better than yourself? Moreover the gods of our fathers can teach you it, if you need guidance. Don't you know that?

Kwamankra: Yes, I know that. But this also I do know, that the gods are wont to make use of human instruments in approaching men. The Infinite finds expression in the finite, and the ideal is realised in the actual. And it has often occurred to me that the child-like hand that shall guide me through life's labyrinthine ways is the self-same one that I now hold tenderly in my own. (34)

The reader is informed next that "She began to understand. She made an effort as if she would withdraw her hand. She hesitated and the next moment she surrendered the other also." Kwamankra asks, "half-persuasively, half-triumphantly," "You will be my teacher, then?" to which Mansa responds, "simply," "Yes," and pledges, "So may the gods of our race help me!" (35).

In Kwamankra's suit, therefore, the person-to-person commitment of man and woman is understood and negotiated through a public structure of being and meaning. Conjugal love is projected beyond the private towards the patriotic duty and civic obligation the partners *must* owe the Fatherland, native and racial. Furthermore, duty and obligation to nativity and racial Africanity specially command an instrumental and sacrificial role, with the godly and patriarchal sanction of the Ethiopian racial pantheon, for the feminine as masculine helpmeet.

As in "Love and Life" for Mansa, so in "Love and Death": her demise is a "fortunate" one, for it carries her instrumentality to a nationalist masculine to another level of expression—a political poetry of the Sublime. That is, in the sublation wherein private loss is nationalized, this loss becomes figurally personal gain for Kwamankra. For the reader is given to understand that "Sorrow was the path that led him to the innermost shrine where he met God, the *Nyiakropon* of his race, and understood. . . . Yes, he had touched . . . the depths of human sorrow, and had come to know that the way to God led from the one to the other" (43). With this Hayford readies the reader for a figural performance of Kwamankra's return for inspiration in the Ethiopian soul-Source, rendered in Fanti as *Nanamu-Krome,* the sublime "city of the ancient dead of his race" (44). There, in a dream allegory, Kwamankra will re-encounter Mansa, who will play the otherworldly role of feminine guide and interlocutrix clarifying for him his this-worldly nationalist mission.

Back to the Future: Heroic Self-Nomination, Middleness, and the (Patriarchal) Allegory of the African Nation

> Not so very long ago in the age of the world, the Nations were gathered in council upon Mount Atlas . . . and there were no people that were not represented, save the Ethiopians. . . . [T]here was one thing concerning which these mighty men were in earnest, and that was the capture of the soul of Ethiopia. . . . "Now, before our hosts lieth the whole stretch of Ethiopia from sea to sea. Come let us partition it among ourselves. . . ." One Nation said, "How shall we do this thing, seeing we are Christians?" Another said . . . "This thing is easily done. We shall go to the Ethiopians, and shall teach them our religion, and that will make them ours, body and soul—lands, goods, and all, for all time."
>
> —*Ethiopia Unbound*, 157–58

> The Child is the father of the Man;
> And I could wish my days to be bound each to each by natural Piety.
> —William Wordsworth, "Ode: Intimations of Immortality"

The first epigraph above is taken from the chapter "Through a Glass Darkly" in *Ethiopia Unbound*. There, Kwamankra, in a narrative redolent of the Chronicles of the Old Testament, renders the Africa-Europe encounters in a telescopic sweep of history. We glimpse through a biblical form of quasi allegory the histories of Europe's "discovery" of Africa and the Euro-Christian missionizing of African peoples—that is, the European imperialism of the soul—that followed in its wake. Europe's spiritual imperialism in Africa has been the source of a debilitating infection of the composite body-soul of the African Personality. It is an Ethiopian body deprived of its soul which had become an easy prey of Europe's Scramble for Africa. At the ratification of the Scramble during the Berlin Conference of 1884–85, therefore, what the "gathering of [European] Nations" had partitioned among themselves was a continent already robbed of its bodily will and soul force. The real essence of Africa's colonial bondage, Kwamankra-Hayford leads his addressee to conclude, was not the physical thralldom that came with the territorial partitioning of the continent—this was merely accidental. Rather, it was the intangible "capture of the soul of Ethiopia."

On the strength of this reading, then, anticolonial and nationalist wisdom began in the intangible, in a retrieving and renovation of Africa's imperially denuded spirituality. The premise of "Ethiopia Unbound" for

Hayford was spiritual prior to being anything else. The nationalist slogan of Kwame Nkrumah, who dominated post–World War II Gold Coast nationalism was, "Seek ye first the political kingdom and the rest shall be added unto you." In Hayford's case, the nationalist demand had to be, as it were, "Seek ye first the kingdom of the soul and the rest shall be added unto you." It is a Hayford disposed to think along these lines who shows Kwamankra in *Ethiopia Unbound* congratulating a Lafcadio Hearn for his "remarkable work, *Kokoro,* which 'treats of the inner rather than of the outer life of Japan.'" Clearly Kwamankra-Hayford sees a reflection of himself and his vocation in Hearn; they both "belonged to that band of men who force their fellowmen to think. They are not always popular; but whether or not, they are the saviours of the race" (211).

In its sweep, Kwamankra's history in *Ethiopia Unbound* is (secular) history interpreted towards the formulation of an Ethiopianist eschatology. "Eschatology" in Judeo-Christian religion is the "doctrine of final things" dealing with the afterlife destiny of the individual soul. But, in one of its prominent Old Testament meanings, as the *Catholic Encyclopedia* explains, eschatology takes up the question of the destiny of the soul of the corporate individual, this corporate individual being the Hebrew "nation." This aspect of Old Testament eschatology turns on "the tendency to sink the individual in the nation and treat the latter as the religious unit."[30] And this was

> one of the most marked characteristics of the Hebrew faith. . . . Deferred and disappointed personal hopes could be solaced by the thought of their present or future realization in the nation. . . . It is true of the O[ld] T[estament] as a whole that the eschatology of the people overshadows that of the individual, though it is true at the same time that, in and through the former, the latter advances to a clear and definite assurance of a personal resurrection from the dead.

The *Encyclopedia* concludes: "[T]he several phases of this national eschatology . . . centres in the hope of the establishment of a theocratic and messianic kingdom on earth."[31]

Three elements stand out here; and they are all of moment for a reading of the symbolic rendering of Kwamankra's nationalist itinerary as figura in Hayford's quasi autobiography. These are, first, the sinking of the individual in the people—the unanimist problematic, as we have seen Kwamankra advocating, with reference to the Japanese Bushido. In Kwamankra's nationalist eschatology, the Ethiopian people, read through the Akan-Fanti, "So familiar [as they are] with the essence of Godhead"—

a godhead infused in "the innermost consciousness of the people" (214)—are positioned in the a priori status of a divinity.

Secondly, there is the projection of personal hopes—or the hopes of a small corporate group, such as the politically negligible (West) African middle class—which are unfulfilled in the present, into a mode of future realization. The fulfillment of the part, then, comes to be imagined by this part through, and as owing its ultimate derivation from, the fulfillment of the whole: the conception of a future Jubilee. It is the middle-class dilemma of being a colonially excluded middle that compels Hayford to project the destiny of this class onto a future time. This is a future when Ethiopia is unbound, a time of the free nation when personal and class fulfillment are assured in the sovereign warranty of national salvation.

The third point follows from this: the nation's soul is saved—Ethiopia is unbound, that is—when it has overcome its (colonially) enforced division from, and restored its centeredness in, its own divinity, its natal soul-Source. To save Ethiopia is for Kwamankra-Hayford, then, to recall her to her native divinity; it is to restore Ethiopia's soul wholesomely to, and rejoin it thus with, her profane body. The nativist merger (again) of the African Personality in soul and body becomes the sole guarantor for Hayford that this divinely given African Personality will weather the adverse and corrupting storms of the colonial temporality which has overtaken it.

Hayford's figural self-production emerges thus in terms of Kwamankra's resolute commitment to a messianic role. In this role he will unbind the corporate individuality of the Ethiopian national soul from colonial thralldom, the success of which will leave a beloved Ethiopia to chart its own destiny, in a secular eschatology. And, to pick up once more a theme introduced already, Kwamankra's commitment is cast in the mode of the mimetic contract between middle and a national-popular base below it. "I will be the word of the people": we have heard Hayford make of this a secular pledge as he fashions the mimetic contract. This pledge takes on a quasi-religious character, too, given the figurations, in the Judeo-Christian mode, of allegory and quasi mysticism in *Ethiopia Unbound*. These are figurations wherein Kwamankra, as the word of the people, seeks to be accredited and ratified at and by the (divine) Source of a popular nativity, conceived in a manner not unlike what we find at the opening of the Gospel of John in the New Testament. "In the beginning was the Word," John testifies, "and the Word was with God, and the Word was God. . . . And the Word became flesh." In its Infinitude the Word, the Judeo-Christian *logos*, is permanently anchored in a metaphysical priority; however, still in touch with its priority in the Infinite, the Word descends from its immaculate and sacred (a)temporality to enter the profane, time-bound world, the or-der of historical finitude. The Word, embodied in Christ the Messiah, be-comes the incarnation of originality in historical time: Christ, the God made flesh, originates the messianic kingdom in an earthly temporality. Kwamankra could be glossing John's gospel, and therein putting his Ethiopianism in a messianic frame, when, in relation to his own worldly vocation, he reminds Mansa: "The Infinite finds expression in the finite, and the ideal is realised in the actual." It is on this idealist basis that the national allegory emerges in performance in *Ethiopia Unbound.*

The heroic poetry of Kwamankra's allegorical return to, and immer-sion in, the Ethiopian soul-Source in the fourth chapter of *Ethiopia Un-bound* records, then, Hayford's reaching in a native *logos* for an inspira-tional Sublime. "Bending the full force of his will to the task," Kwamankra embarks on a journey to seek his "beloved" (47) in *Nanamu-Krome* where he finds the "the scene around him, though weird, was by no means unfa-miliar." For Kwamankra "had the feeling of one who, travelling to a far distant country, and for the nonce forgetting the physical aspects of his native land, upon returning, in a moment, recalls the old place again" (44). It is colonial alienation that is to blame for the hero's forgetting, for Kwamankra was there with the *logos* in the beginning, consecrated in *Nanamu-Krome* as man-god and hierophant:

> Even as the home-sick traveller, returning to his native shore, suddenly re-calls distant echoes of the past, so did Kwamankra. . . . It seemed to him as if in some bygone age from this self-same abode of the ancient dead, the gods had sent him on an errand to mortals. Even as he thought, the impression deepened in his mind that one day the gods had said to him: "Kwamankra, this day we send thee forth into the nether sphere to be for us a witness unto the truth. . . . Go, as a thinker among the thoughtless, convince them of their error, proclaim unto them the sovereignty of truth and the eternal maj-esty of *Nyiakrapon,* the god of truth." It seemed to him that in obedience to this call, he had gone forth, full of courage, full of zeal, resolved to obey the command of the gods; and lo! before his work was half done, here he was, as it were in a dream, back to *Nanamu-Krome.* (52–53)

Kwamankra's symbolic journey of return rejoins him with a natal prin-ciple—the soul-Source—of nativity and race, a principle we see displaced (in part) onto his beloved Mansa. Mansa in her feminine interchangeabil-ity with a racial nativity, then, might be seen as the allegorical emblem of a prized and complementary progenitive value from which the male quester has long been distanced. This bereavement has left Kwamankra, the heroic quester, "[o]ver and over again . . . wondering whether his beloved was truly dead, or dead only to his physical senses." The acknowledgement of the reality of *physical* privation, however, cannot overcome in Kwamankra an affirmation of (nationalist) faith in a *metaphysical* order of Ethiopianist permanence. Thus his "confidence renewed, evermore building upon adamantine foundations," Kwamankra "wafted a vow to heaven that his one quest would be to learn the way to her" (50).

We might see Kwamankra's desire and his vow to "build upon adamantine foundations" as arising out of the elements he protests: the "bad methods of the missionary" (186), the pedagogical methods which "separate those . . . educated from their own race" (196), and the philanthropic practice that "denationalises" the African (192–93). If these leave the body-soul of the Ethiopian bereft of its native divinity, it is this misfortune of death-in-life wrought on Ethiopia that calls for his resolute foundationalism. The anxious themes of *finding his way* to a prior metaphysical principle and of *founding himself* are not separable concerns. Kwamankra's recovery in Mansa and the Sublime of *Nanamu-Krome* of the natal principle guarantees that, in a matrix of being and knowing, he is figurally "born again" as the (metaphysical) child who will father forth—that is, whose being will be the foundational becoming of—the Ethiopian nation.

"The child is the father of the man," as the English Romantic Wordsworth opines in the lines reproduced in the third epigraph above. This is a statement affirming a constant principle conserved amid change; an affirmation of the visionary power of the poetic eye to discern continuity within, and hence able to overcome a distracting, historical contingency. Wordsworth, that is, hands us a conservative entelechy,[32] a poetry of the abiding soul, on whose basis he wishes his days to be bound each to each in natural piety. That is to say, the poet invests in self and its memory a morality that keeps an unwavering faith in, and unyieldingly holds on to, an enduring soul-principle. And the poet does so with the awareness of the blandishments of a corrupting temporality, blandishments that ever threaten to overwhelm and rob of its integrity the remembering self.

"Child" and "man" are Wordsworth's images of past and future; and the continuum whose preservation the poet imagines in the fidelity of memory makes the future a time and a state shot through with, and therefore undivided from, the past. The poet transits confidently through the present into the future because in doing so the visionary eye faces backwards and inwards, fixed, in remembrance of a time past, on an Origin, and seeing, in a time now and to come, an enduring Being. And visionary cognition is to be seen as creatively enabling the poet to mold the future in the image of the past. On account of the self that keeps faith with itself, then, the future emerges reassuringly prefigured in the past; the child of soul endures as an abiding principle in the man of the world. Visionary cognition performs a conservative dialectic which secures Permanence in emergence, Immanence in change, Sameness in difference, Whole in part, Nature in art(ifice), Foundation in transition, Being in becoming, Conservatism in progress, and so on.

Allegorical representation in *Ethiopia Unbound* mirrors this model of Romantic conservative idealism. Hayford's visionary-cognitive act of finding the Source ("*learning* the way to her")—the metaphysical *arche* and *logos* of nativity—is the guarantee of a normative ("adamantine") act of founding, of a historic rebirth premised on a re-membering of a dismembered Ethiopia. Hayford's foundationalism posits a *telos,* too, since it is future (self)-realization, and the nationalist ownership thereof, that are to be given a principled foundation in the nativist return to Source.

Additionally, the Orphean recouping of beginnings in *Ethiopia Unbound* is to be vested in the making of a consequential (national) character. Hayfordian national allegory signals a theme of aspiration in whose terms Ethiopia's reemergence is presented as a historic bodying forth of a preexisting characterological essence. When the emissary of the gods is shown "rising up a new structure of considerable beauty and strength" in *Nanamu-Krome,* Mansa is quick to point out structural imperfections in this architectural representation of the national character: "Behold . . . the symmetry of this building. It is such as displeases not the gods. Yet, if thou perceivest clearly, thou wilt see a seam here, a fissure there, unevenness in places where there should be uniformity. Much as I love you . . . I cannot be unmindful of thy imperfections" (60–61). Insofar as these blemishes remain in Kwamankra, the bearer of the essential national character, the "guardian angel" continues, "Reunion may not take place." The rejoining of the divine soul of Ethiopia with its historic body, that is, remains suspended "till thou has laid the apex to a character, fit for a god to dwell in" (61). Mansa explains to the uncomprehending Kwamankra:

> In the beginning evil and good were created, and to man was given the command to rule and subdue the evil, and to foster and cause the good to prevail. That is the final reason of human existence, and man becomes a god when he has won the victory. It consists in the building of character. . . . When mortality fails, the immortal in man prevails and finds its home here where . . . it becomes a god dwelling in the temple which character hath fashioned. The temple hath truth for foundation, love for superstructure, and child-like trust for apex. (61)

Mansa, in exhortation to Kwamankra, elaborates Hayford's Ethiopianist eschatology in which the individual (middle-class) soul fulfills itself in immortality only in self-commitment and dedication, in truth, love, and trust, to the greater (national) soul, the collective of which it is but a part.

Mansa affirms to Kwamankra further that, "[Thou art] a god," adding, "only thy warfare is not yet accomplished." After his supplication to *Nanamu,* the gods of the race, Kwamankra has been given permission on this account to "visit this sacred abode, that thou mightest carry hence a knowledge which will aid thee in thy work" (58). The inspirational message for the one who both seeks after and embodies the godhead of Ethiopia is that before attaining a "translation" to the eternal, "our beings must be rounded off, and every phase of development completed." And for this purpose we are "given opportunity after opportunity" (60). The message of the inspirer acknowledges that Kwamankra's earthly (i.e., anticolonial) warfare is not over. It could be read in this regard as a reminder to the Ethiopian nationalist that, as constrained as he is by having to operate within the sociohistorical and political limits set by the colonial dispensation, this dispensation is still to be thought of as a conjunctural one. If, as such, it leaves possible spaces of negotiation and maneuver, these are the windows of "opportunity" through which nationalist avocation must will its self-translation, as it were, into the worldly self-affirmation of Ethiopia. Hence Kwamankra-Hayford's charge to the middle class to practice a strategic opportunism. "African manhood," observes Hayford, "demands that the Ethiopian should seek not his opportunity, or ask for elbow room from the white man, but that he should create the one or other for himself" (182). It is in this opportunistic mode that in *Ethiopia Unbound* we are asked to witness the nationalist seizing himself as a pro-creative agency. His historical task is that of promoting the maturation and advancement of a native Ethiopian character from the minority forced upon it by a colonialist modernity towards the majority of national "manhood," the majority of African modernity.

Through the figurations of a nativist characterology for the middle class, then, Hayford seeks to define the institutional basis, and hence to procure the authority and legitimation, to make a class-for-power into the people's representative. Additionally, if an Ethiopianist characterology is posited by Hayford in a framework linking Infinite and finite, between the two he salutarily interposes the middle-class character as the transitional image of opportunity and time to come. Here, in the third space of a transitional middle, he imagines the representative form-content of the nation which will be the consummate embodiment of the soul of a popular nativity. The middle-class character is projected onto nationalist praxis—i.e., the domain which creatively seizes and transforms opportunity—as the end-foreshadowed beginning of the Ethiopian people's motion towards (re-newed) self-realization in the world. With beginning and end conjoined in his figure, Kwamankra, the representative middle-class character, must appear in the joint aspect of a future-past: his *sankofa* return to Source, "the abode of the ancient dead" (53), is also a return to the future. The city of the gods itself has a dual aspect: if it is "majestic" and "ethereal" in an otherworldly way, its appearance is also "earthly," compatible with a this-worldliness, to the observing Kwamankra. With the sight of the city leaving him "feeling . . . that he had seen the like before in some forgotten age" (54), Hayford's alter ego is vouchsafed, in the image of this "native" city of *Nanamu,* a blueprint for the future modern Ethiopia. And this is what becomes his privilege, as the middle-class character, to materialize. The proviso is that the future, and the middle class which makes it, must remember and keep faith with the past perfect if it is to guarantee that a dismembered Ethiopia is re-membered in the image of the past, the perfect past.

We have heard Blyden exhorting the West African middle class: "If you are not yourself, if you surrender your personality, you have nothing left to give the world" (*Origins,* 250). It is in response to this challenge that the ideologeme[33] of character in Hayford's idealist national allegory emerges. And this ideologeme projects the middle-class persona as a figural pathway through which a reconstructive energy might be generated and channeled for the purposes of relating the Ethiopian or African Personality, in a humanly validating way, to itself and to the world. This renewed humanist selving and worlding of Africa is what we find in passionate preparation in the initial expenditure by Hayford—and other frontline intellectuals of his middle-class kind—of what the American feminist poet Adrienne Rich has termed "energy of relation."[34] If the expenditure of this energy involved the frontline intellectual in a (modernist) return to a popular source, he was tasked therein with taking on the burden of being a middleman. As such his was to knowledgeably project a racialized and nationalized "Africa"/"Ethiopia" in a culturally affirmative and politically useful nativist *gnosis* (order of knowing) and ontology (order of being).

Ultimately, *Ethiopia Unbound* is a work self-consciously written to show the self straddling the frontline in a difficult negotiation of a double legacy, with all the paradoxes that this entails. Hayford's struggles with and in a difficult temporality, necessary if he was to win for his Ethiopian nationality the terms of its own being in the world, rewards us nearly a hundred years on with insights into the African post-encounter condition, captured at once in the predicament of being modern and the challenge within this being modern of having to be(come) African.

In 1935, five years after Hayford had passed on, an ardent Gold Coast youth passing through the imperial center on his way to America registered his nationalist commitment to Africa in this protest:

> But just as I was feeling particularly depressed about the future . . . on [a] placard I read: "*MUSSOLINI INVADES ETHIOPIA*. . . ." At that moment it was almost as if the whole of London had suddenly declared war on me personally. For the next few minutes I could do nothing but glare at each impassive face wondering if those people could possibly realize the wickedness of colonialism, and praying that the day might come when I could play my part in bringing about the downfall of such a system. My nationalism surged to the fore; I was ready and willing to go through hell itself, if need be to achieve my object. (*Ghana*, 27)

Nkrumah's passion is a tribute to those, Hayford prominent among them, who, in the political and cultural formation of African nationalism, pioneered a redirection of the energy of a middle class towards the task of unbinding Ethiopia-at-large from colonial captivity.

In 1942, when Nkrumah graduated from the Lincoln Theological Seminary in Pennsylvania, the subject of his graduation oration was "Ethiopia shall stretch forth her hands unto God." At the time "Ghana," like the Ethiopia to come, was still an "empty" name, an ideal form whose patent in the Gold Coast was wielded, as we have seen, by J. B. Danquah. For the longest while, it was the fate of Danquah's "Ghana," to employ a Hayfordian allegorical conceit, to remain a semblance (i.e., an ideal form), as such awaiting its infusion with characterological content (i.e., a national-popular substance). This was the "Ghana" that would be wrested from Danquah by Nkrumah after 1947. Framing "Ghana" in a tantalizing politics of the possible as the foreshortened name of (Pan)-Africa, Nkrumahist idealism would project it as a temporary if pragmatically necessary incarnation of Pan-Africanism's symbolic Ethiopia, an Ethiopia towards which "Ghana" therefore was and would always be enjoined to strive. "The Independence of Ghana," as would be spelled out with Pan-Africanist conviction by Nkrumah, "is meaningless unless it is linked with the total liberation of the African continent." As it turned out, Ghana's nationalist part-fulfillment of Ethiopia's eschatological promise of liberation did not happen until 1957, and then only after a political "characterology" reinvented by Nkrumah had intervened in the Gold Coast. It is this nationalist figure, on the ascendent after 1947, who came to augment the relational Orphean energy of an earlier phase of African nationalism with a dynamic Promethean energy of creation. *Ghana: The Autobiography of Kwame Nkrumah,* to which we turn next, is a cultural and political record of this extraordinary historic event.

7

PROMETHEUS UNBOUND

NKRUMAH'S GHANA: THE AUTOBIOGRAPHY OF KWAME NKRUMAH

The times are changing and we must change with them. In doing so we must combine the best in Western culture with the best in African culture. The magic story of human achievement gives irrefutable proof that as soon as an awakened intelligentsia emerges among a so-called subject people, it becomes the vanguard of the struggle against alien rule. It provides the nucleus of the dominant wish and aspiration, the desire to be free to breathe the air of freedom.

—Kwame Nkrumah, *Ghana*

Here is a man of great magnetic force, evoking love and sympathy wherever he goes. But he is a mere man. The corresponding force which he attracts and calls into play here and there becomes created entities, begging for life and claiming the right to live. Tell me, what is the duty of the giver of this life? . . . Must he allow free scope to the play of sympathy, or must he ruthlessly set to work to destroy the hope of light which he bids spring up in a human soul?

—Casely Hayford, *Ethiopia Unbound*

Even his most severe critics have not thought this claim to be excessive: "To the black man in all parts of the world Nkrumah gave a new pride." His admirers have thought it certain: "He was above all . . . the strategist of genius in the struggle against colonialism."

—Basil Davidson, *Black Star*

248

Writing the Self-Nation

> Those . . . who are deluded by the false promises of "preparing" colonial peoples for "self-government," who feel that their imperialist oppressors are "rational" and "moral" and will relinquish their "possessions" if only confronted with the truth of the injustice of colonialism are tragically mistaken.
>
> —Kwame Nkrumah, *Towards Colonial Freedom*

Nearly five decades elapse between the appearance of Hayford's *Ethiopia Unbound* and Nkrumah's *Ghana*. In *Ghana* the story is retold of another seminal nationalist figure. Emerging from the ranks of the middle class, Nkrumah is able to pose challenging questions of its modernist situation—as in the epigraph at the head of the section—and therewith to articulate its historical tasks and possibilities in a style that radically departs from that of his predecessors. The title of Nkrumah's work alone—and we should keep in mind that its appearance was timed to coincide with Ghana's independence—points to an autobiography imagined in the classic mode of communal narrativity earlier identified as a recurrent feature of the nationalist writing of African modernity.[1]

Like *Ethiopia Unbound* before it, *Ghana* is another example of a frontline middle-class narrative in which the story of the self-as-part, or the design of autobiography, seeks its subsumption within the story of the self-as-whole, or the design of national allegory. Of the two works, however, it is the latter that urges itself on us as a successful reconciliation of part and whole. The reasons are historical. As we saw in the previous chapter, Hayford's earlier effort in *Ethiopia Unbound* was calculated to produce a form of nationalist address that was visionary and boldly prospective. However, emanating as it did from the leader's politically and existentially uncertain situation in the heyday of colonial power, what we get in this work also is a hesitant and groping narrative: the self-as-whole proves elusive.[2] Nkrumah's *Ghana,* on the contrary, is historically fated to appear under the sign of nationalism's imminent victory over the forces of colonialism. Hence its mode of being is more resolutive, admitting of the closure of story in the round. Nine or so years of consummate politicking by the latter nationalist leader—falling between 1948 and 1957—assures him the benefit of historical hindsight, and hence a full-bodied story, the very element of fulfillment denied his predecessor. Ending on the eve of Ghana's independence from colonial rule, the first in black Africa, Nkrumah's autobiography could and does assume its epochal significance.

For this reason, autobiography functions in *Ghana* in a mode that retrospectively justifies the life: it is designed to yield a full-bodied (hi)story wherein the nationalist leader's life over time is narrativized into a meaningful, allegorical congruence with the birth of the nation-state Ghana. And, beyond this, the conditions that make for a holistic fit between the individual life and the pattern of nationalist meaning must also at once appear in, and disappear into, an expansive logic. Nkrumah writes: "I have never regarded the struggle for the Independence of the Gold Coast as an isolated objective but always as part of a world historical pattern" (290). Thus if the life (the subjective "I") is presented as being strictly subordinated to a national will (the collective subject of "Our struggle"), the self-nation (or the "I-We"), whose narrative the autobiography constitutes, also appears as an allegorical subformation falling within, and subject to, another, larger holistic narrative logic. In Nkrumah's dialectic, the particular self-nation of Ghana is projected as an entity which seeks out and finds its necessity or rationality in a world-historical (or universal) national-allegorical pattern.

Nkrumah's autobiographical performance—the writing or narrative constitution of the self-nation—is thus posited within a world-historical logic which, if it is "given," is certainly not appropriated without struggle. On the contrary, the singular self-nation appears as a possibility which, in and out of a colonial time, is to be wrested, recuperated, in heroic, Promethean terms. Such an observation falls into place in Nkrumah's avowed preparedness to "go through hell itself" in order—to quote James Joyce's Stephen Dedalus—"to forge in the smithy of my soul the uncreated conscience of my race."[3]

In *Ghana,* the self-presentation of the leader is proposed in just such terms. The autobiographical gesture nominates him as a mediating self, a catalyst, in a struggle aimed at creatively reconciling a formal universal, nation, with a local initiative and meaning. Hence Nkrumah, the native son, having successfully discharged this medial role in and for his time, permits himself to project in and through his self-presentation the emergent figure of his nation. This is a nation that has managed, or will soon manage, to pour a unique formal content, its own, into a world-historical mold. The perception fostered by the autobiographical gesture, therefore, is that Nkrumah "is" and completes Ghana, a Ghana meaningful because it is now possessed of a worldly formal content.

We need to also add that, much in the same manner in which we saw Hayford envisioning the middle-class dialectic, Nkrumah's Ghana *had to be,* had to have a worldly meaning, in order that his (class) identity might find its completion. Nkrumah brings a radical interpretation to this desire by an African middle class to take the full measure of its nationalist identity in the world. This is evident in his disagreement with his mentor, the renowned early-twentieth-century African internationalist, the Gold Coast's Kwegyir Aggrey. In Aggrey's understanding, the achievement of middle-class worldliness called for unconditional cooperation between the black and white races. Hence, contrary to the call for "Africa for the Africans," a position especially identified in the 1920s with Marcus Garvey, he had observed in a famous dictum: "You can play a tune of sorts on the white keys, and you can play a tune of sorts on the black keys, but for harmony you must use both the black and the white" (qtd. in *Ghana,* 14). To this Nkrumah, the self-confessed Garveyite,[4] responds: "[O]nly a free and independent people—a people with a government of their own—can claim equality, racial or otherwise, with another people" (14). Looked at in its worldly aspect, then, Nkrumah's dream of independence, as exemplified by his comments here and elsewhere in the autobiography, is shaped within a powerful desire to make an African middle class, a colonial class-for-power, attain to its worldly identification in *competitive equivalence.*

Going by Nkrumah's argument, we might grasp competitive equivalence in terms of the principle that only in a more or less perfectly competitive—i.e., equal—world is cooperation of the kind desired by Aggrey enjoined between nations, thus making for a truly international world. This, we must suppose, is the sense contained in Fanon's argument to the effect that "[i]t is at the heart of national consciousness that international consciousness lives and grows."[5] For Fanon, as for Nkrumah, an Nkrumah who claims Mazzini as one of his inspirers, the international dimension—a morality of global cooperation—begins from and terminates in national self-consciousness. True national consciousness, then, is that which has adapted itself to the worldly demand of competitive equivalence. If so, being one of the ruling "ideologemes" of the middle class allegory of nation, competitive equivalence compels us to pursue a further implication carried by Nkrumah's autobiography. In *Ghana,* the autobiographical composite of self and nation is posited as standing at the end of one pattern of history, the unequal time of the colonial, and at the beginning of another, the projected equal time of the nation. The middle-class self-nation, having wrested its own necessity from the "hell" of colonial times, is thus one that is poised to divert the latter into the promise of a "new Jerusalem." Thus the self-nation in *Ghana* is imagined in a time when it will have freely reshaped in its singular image, according to its own *competitive* design, the mold of the world historical. And, as we shall see, for Nkrumah the rationality of the world historical is embodied in the modern state, that very institution which had given itself in Africa first in the negative guise of the colonial.

That image of nation as a new Jerusalem appears in Nkrumah's last sermon in America, a sermon whose prophetic theme, as the autobiography recalls, was "I saw a new Heaven and a new Earth" (166). The future leader, it is obvious, was not averse to speaking figuratively. Hence we may follow suit and suggest—as, for instance, Padmore does in his "hagiography" of Nkrumah, *The Gold Coast Revolution*[6]—that, in *Ghana,* Nkrumah's self-presentation is that of the middle-class *logos,* Hayford's "Ethiopia," epochally made flesh. The credit for the popularization of "Ghana" may belong to Nkrumah's nationalist contemporary Danquah, but the latter's gesture, fixated on pastness, was in many respects that of an empty epic formalism. Nkrumah's "Ghana," on the other hand, shown in its actualization on the ground, reveals its meaning in the epic content of its own present, the future-oriented present of struggle. Nkrumah will declare in the Gold Coast Legislative Assembly Debates of 18th May 1956: "[W]e take pride in the name ['Ghana'], not out of romanticism but as an inspiration for the future."[7]

In writing the nation, Nkrumah presents himself in the aspect of the fulfilling middle-class complement. This gesture nominates and confirms him as the one representative of the many. He is the leader who, bridging different orders of time and space, the local and the universal, transforms the otherwise "empty" colonial duration of the Gold Coast into the meaningful advent of a Ghanaian and African secular modernity. Making intelligible this way the motions of time and figure in the leader's life-over-time allows us to see why his autobiography insists on bearing the exemplary title it does.

Ghana offers an account of Nkrumah's life from 1909 (or 1913), when he was born, to 1957, when we have a final image of him at the threshold of Independence preparing to assume the stewardship of a new nation-state of Ghana. The autobiography of the leader begins by recounting in selective detail the events of his early life as a boy growing up in his native Nzima, on the extreme southwestern flank of the Gold Coast colony. We may locate here, in Nkrumah's brief but lovingly executed detail of a "simple" Nzima-land (as he himself refers to it), the formative elements that will lead to the emergence of the future "man of the people." Receiving an honorary degree in 1953 from Lincoln University,[8] his American alma mater, at a time when he had become the first native and black "Leader of Government Business" in an African colony, Nkrumah will display a self-consciousness about his humble origins. He will declare, "Truly . . . it is not the heights to which a man climbs that matter, but the depths from whence he came" (163).

That comes as an emphatic reminder to his reader that *Ghana* is the story of a man who, unlike Sarbah, Hayford, Sekyi, Danquah, and others, was not a scion of the merchant class and/or traditional chiefly "aristocracy" of the Gold Coast. To this group belonged an elite group of men, mostly lawyers, for whom nationalist leadership had been an exclusive preserve for the longest period. On the contrary, rising, so to speak, out of the metaphoric "depths"—Nkrumah's father was an unlettered rural goldsmith and his mother had no formal schooling either—the autobiography bespeaks the extraordinary story of a self-described "very ordinary looking African" (122).

If, however, the "handicap" of ordinariness accompanies Nkrumah's first appearance on the flank of what he saw as an undynamic Gold Coast nationalism, in the end he comes out as the heroic figure who puts his "handicap" to positive advantage. For he utilizes it to overcome the more or less retrograde elitism of the nationalism of the few. This he does by objectifying and renewing in his person Gold Coast nationalism's promissory narrative of collective emancipation. As his story unfolds we encounter the nationalist of the many, the charismatic awakener of the masses, the man of the people who takes over a flagging nationalist praxis and kindles it into assuming a historic shape equal to its vaunted ideological content.

This is the substance of the heroic story whose retelling begins with the sights, scenes, and experiences of Nkrumah's early life. The details of the opening pages quickly shade off into Nkrumah's experiences as a youthful student at Achimota School, the elite government institution of the Colony. We learn of Nkrumah's encounter at Achimota with the influential and widely admired Aggrey. Acting as an early role model for Nkrumah, Aggrey, a returnee from an American sojourn, fired in the future leader of Ghana a determination to study in America. Nkrumah will set the realization of that wish in motion soon after he graduated as a teacher from Achimota in 1930. Five years after his graduation, wish becomes reality when, after ceaseless exertions on his own behalf, Nkrumah is accepted to study at the Theological Seminary of Lincoln University in Pennsylvania.

An account of Nkrumah's ten-year sojourn as a student in America follows. These are years in which he suffers material hardship. He will, however, justify them retrospectively in Promethean terms:

> Just as in the days of the Egyptians, so to-day God had ordained that certain among the African race should journey westwards to equip themselves with

> knowledge . . . for the day when they will be called upon to return to their motherland and to use the learning they had acquired to help improve the lot of their brethren. (166)

America marks the high point of the tutelary phase of Nkrumah's life. As Kofi Awoonor points out, those ten years stamp him decisively as a product of post-Depression American liberal intellectualism. The names that feature prominently in his intellectual formation, however, will have to include not only Jefferson, Paine, and Lincoln but also Marx, Engels, and Lenin. Ultimately, it will be with "tools from creeds as diverse as Marxism, Jeffersonian democracy and Gandhian non-violence [that Nkrumah will begin] an incredible stripdown of Britain's African empire."[9]

After America, Nkrumah spends two politically active years in England. There he becomes a protégé of George Padmore—after independence one of the Ghanaian leader's closest and trusted advisers in Accra—who imparts to Nkrumah his considerable experience in political activism and publicity organizing.[10] England, then, marks the intensification of the activist-political phase of Nkrumah's life, a phase where we see the future leader striving to engage thought with practice. The practical successes he chalks up in this short period include his initiating a Coloured Workers' Association of Great Britain, and, with the active cooperation of a dedicated cadre of students and activists, the formation of a nationalist organization, the West African National Secretariat. The Secretariat, conceived in part as a vanguard liberation movement, will serve at this time as a political clearing house where affairs of vital concern to (West) African nationalism come up for debate.[11] Nkrumah also mentions his association at the time "with all [the British] parties ranging from the extreme right to the extreme left" (79). The purpose was to learn about techniques of organization that would "help me in organizing my own nationalist party on the best possible lines when I eventually returned to my country" (80).[12]

Thus the Nkrumah who returns to the Gold Coast from England in 1947 leaves with valuable knowledge about modes and techniques of sociopolitical organization and representation. The experience gained will make the difference when the time comes for Nkrumah to wrest the mantle of nationalist leadership from an organizationally defective and politically ineffective United Gold Coast Convention, the then elite vanguard of Gold Coast nationalism. This organization, which invited Nkrumah to become its general secretary in the first place, did so, we are told, because it was "faced with the problem of how to reconcile the leadership of the intelligentsia with the broad masses of the people" (*Ghana*, 61). "It was in an effort to make [the U.G.C.C.] appear a popular movement," Nkrumah informs us further, "that I was invited to become its general secretary" (69). Yet the U.G.C.C. was led by men whose political philosophy Nkrumah saw as "contrary to the political aspirations of the people of the Gold Coast" (62). Hence, the inevitable differences between his radical populist style and the more sedate, laid-back politics of the other leaders of the organization provoked a split that led to the formation of Nkrumah's own Convention People's Party (C.P.P.).[13]

What the autobiography furnishes subsequently are the quotidian details of political engagement—constitutional wrangles, strike actions, mass boycotts, Party rallies, and so on—those details of the decolonizing struggle that have passed into the stuff of history and legend. The Nkrumah of this stage is the nationalist leader remembered for his ability to effectively mobilize the masses of the people; the man whose agitprop—disseminated through the newspaper and fiery public speaking—popularizes such catchwords as "Freedom!" "Positive Action," "Tactical Action," and other such slogans of popular mobilization. With these grand propagandist themes the leader will conduct the great task of reorganizing a Gold Coast social narrativity. He will impart therein a teleological solidity to a dream of collective emancipation otherwise confined to a dead end within the moribund exclusivism, in Nkrumah's perception, of elite nationalism.

Consider, then, the moment when Nkrumah breaks away from the U.G.C.C., over the latter's footdragging on the independence question, to form the C.P.P. as the reformed vanguard platform for the campaign for "self-government now!" The autobiographical recall of the occasion and events of Sunday, 12 June, 1949, at the Arena, Accra, presents the paradigmatic moment of the leader's linkage[14] with "the people," the "sixty thousand" who had gathered to hear him speak:

> "May I," I asked them, "in the present stage of our political struggle, pack my things and leave this dear Ghana of ours?"
> "No! No! Certainly not!" yelled the crowd indignantly.
> "Or may I remain here and keep my mouth shut?"
> "No! No! Speak! Stay and open your mouth!" they cried.
> "Then may I break away from any leadership which is faltering and quailing before imperialism and colonialism and throw in my lot with the . . . people of this country for full self-government *NOW?*" The unanimous shout of approval . . . was all that I needed to give me my final spur. I was confident that whatever happened, I had the full support of the people. . . . We had decided to take our future into our own hands and I am sure that in those few minutes everyone became suddenly conscious of the burden we had

undertaken. But in the faces before me I could see no regret or doubt, only resolution. (*Ghana*, 104–5)

Thus "a people" capable of, and committed to, *making* history, their own, appear at the instigation of a leader who exhorts them: "The time has arrived . . . when a definite line of action must be taken if we are going to save our country from continued imperialist exploitation and oppression" (103).

The autobiographical Nkrumah emerges as one of the people's own. He has become so to the extent that he has succeeded in taking the ideology of nationalism out of the elite ranks of a middle class and has given it renewed articulation within the felt but as yet "formless" desires—the "uncreated conscience"—of a broad-based popular-social narrativity. Nkrumah is the autobiographical hero who invests this social domain of narrative with a teleological solidity. He is embodied as such in his dramatic ability, as we have seen, to represent his person as the only rationally desirable symbol of this narrative's authority. Nkrumah emerges as an authoring and authorizing symbol that is able to represent to communities and groups, differentiated horizontally and vertically but nevertheless sharing a common fate of colonial degradation, their collective, heroic characterization in what appears to be the only narrative rationally possible for their time.

This is the timely essence contained in the leader's rallying "Freedom!" and "Self-government *NOW!*"—the latter being the slogan he opposes to his elite opponents' disembodied and feeble "Self-government as soon as possible." These opponents, we are given to see, are of the same order as those nationalist literati denounced by Nkrumah during his London days as "idealists contenting themselves with writing theses but quite unable or unwilling to take any active part in dealing with the African problem" (53). Drawing on the autobiography's mode of existing as a full-bodied sign of successful political and social adventure, we might say that its movements signal the consummation of the mimetic contract of the middle-class allegory of nation beyond this contract's mere idealization. Here, Nkrumah seems to say in *Ghana*, is a presentation of the mimetic contract, as captured in Hayford's "I will be the voice of the people," that finally escapes the confines of the merely symbolic, the domain of its previous enactments. With the advent of Nkrumah's "Ghana," this contract enters a properly social domain of performance.

Hence, as autobiography gives us a privileged inside view of the tireless and astute political organizer embarked on a renewed performance of the mimetic contract, we are encountering also, compared with Hayford and others, a figure who is *more* than a "thinker." *Ghana* presents a social "doer" in whom secular advent is given symbolic inscription. In the name of Nkrumah, the communally diffuse and colonially repressed elements of emancipatory desire in the social narrativity of the Gold Coast are concentrated and refashioned into the content of a *palpable* manifest destiny.[15] This, as we see in the second epigraph at the head of the chapter, was the creative élan that Hayford sought charismatically to embody. We must acknowledge, though, that it is Nkrumah who gives this creative force one of its most vigorous expressions in the annals of African nationalism. For Nkrumah the Promethean understood what his Orphean predecessors had not quite come to understand: that "a middle class elite without the battering ram of the illiterate masses, can never hope to smash the forces of colonialism" (*Ghana*, 215).[16]

Take Danquah, for instance, for whom it was a datum of faith that the nationalist intellectual unproblematically stood in for the people. "It is only in the study of the lives of our great men," Danquah was convinced, "that we can approach a general or universal history of the Gold Coast."[17] Hence Danquah's intellectual, unlike Nkrumah's, did not stand *alongside,* and make history *with,* the people; he made history *for* the people. Richard Wright's interview of Danquah is revealing in this respect:

> Wright: Why don't you try to win the masses to your side?
> Danquah: Masses? . . . I don't like this thing of masses. There are only individuals for me. . . .
> Wright: But masses form the basis of political power in the modern world today. . . .
> Danquah: You believe that? . . . I know you fellows dote on this thing of masses. . . . I've read that you claim that this mass unrest comes from the industrialization of the Western world.
> Wright: Where else could it come from? . . . Look, how did Nkrumah learn his techniques of organization? In New York, in Chicago, in Detroit, and in London he saw men organizing and he studied their methods. Then he came to Africa and applied them. . . . You're facing the twentieth century, Dr. Danquah. . . . Why is it that you cannot appeal to the masses on the basis of their daily needs? You're a lawyer; you are used to *representing*. . . . Well, *represent* them. As we say in America: Be a mouthpiece for them.
> Danquah: I can't do things like that. . . . It's emotion. (*Black Power,* 220)

Wright is forced to conclude: "It was no use. He was of the old school. One did not speak for the masses; one told them what to do." And what is more, "the destiny of the disinherited will never be his" (221).

Nkrumah having acquired the "battering ram" of the "masses," he brings more than a supposition, then, of his being the bearer of the manifest destiny merely of a middle class to his address before the Gold Coast Legislative Assembly in 1953. This is the occasion when he moves his historic "Motion of Destiny." "My independence motion," as he refers to it, is therefore made on behalf a "united people."

Yet, if the "Motion of Destiny" speech is couched in the idiom of popular demand, this demand, taking place in the Legislative Assembly, is still framed by the institution of the colonial state. Nkrumahist nationalism was in effect beholden to the imperative of etatism or *state ideology.* What this means is that if the teleological solidity conferred on a Gold Coast social narrativity by the leader had made the destiny of a middle class manifest as a popular destiny and vice versa, this destiny was also manifest as one inevitably approaching its consummation in etatism.

It is to Chatterjee's elaboration of etatism in a discussion of Nehru in the context of Indian nationalism that we will now turn to shed some light on Nkrumah's situation in the Gold Coast. Like Nkrumah's, Nehru's reconstruction of Indian nationalist ideology was one whose "specific form was to situate nationalism within the domain of state ideology." In either case this was because the historical constraints imposed by the colonial social formation on an emergent middle class were such that

> its intellectual-moral leadership could never be firmly established in the domain of civil society. Of historical necessity, its revolution had to be passive. The specific ideological form of the passive revolution . . . was an *étatisme,* explicitly recognizing a central, autonomous and directing role of the state and legitimizing it by a specifically nationalist marriage between the ideas of progress and social justice.[18]

Chatterjee's insights into the colonial problem of social representation—the question of intellectual-moral leadership broaches the question of hegemony—supply lessons for understanding what a modernist class-for-power had to confront in a preindependence Gold Coast. As in other African colonies, the discontinuities within the Gold Coast—discontinuities primarily of ethnicity—for strategic reasons, had been confirmed and reinforced by the contrivances of colonial power. The impact of indirect rule had over colonial time hardened what had precolonially been the flexible social spaces of the Gold Coast into quite differentiated "tribal" formations. For the natives of the colony, of course, these were spaces hardly integrated one in another—whether politically, or economically, or culturally—in any salutary fashion. Given the circumstance of this enforced and uneven plurality—uneven even in the sameness of colonial duration—by the time Nkrumah appeared on the stage of Gold Coast nationalism, the real nativity that we saw Hayford pursuing in *Ethiopia Unbound* was one whose Akan-Fanti parochialism could seem to have exhausted itself. The Orphean propositions of an earlier phase of nationalism, it was apparent, were no longer able to provide the terms that would *adequately* represent the diverse geographical, ethnocultural, class, gender, generational, and occupational panorama of a Gold Coast comprised of the Colony, Ashanti, the Northern Territories, and Trans-Volta Togoland.

It is for this reason that in the sections following, this reading of *Ghana* will attempt to account for an Nkrumah who is compelled to leave a pure *ethnos*—Hayford's ideal order of a real nativity—(partially) behind. This chapter reads an Nkrumah therefore who, reaching for Ghana in etatist terms, is able to invest the ideology of state in a different ethos of nativity. As the symbol authorizing etatism, I see Nkrumah, among other things, as standing at the inception of a *virtual* nativity. Far from the theogony of Hayford, the Nkrumahist state is dreamed in terms of a secular cosmogony whose rationale is the invention of a people who are spatially, rather than lineally, one. That, and only that, is the basis of the brave new world rhetoric of the leader: "Seek ye first the political kingdom and all things shall be added unto you" (*Ghana,* 164). These are words spoken by one hopeful of mending into a lateral continuity a popular socioscape that has been fractured by colonial power. This theme will be taken up in the third section of the chapter.

Autobiography as a Fulfilling Reflex of a Gold Coast Social Narrativity: Inventing a Pre-text for <u>Ghana</u>

> There is such a thing as the poetry of politics.
> —Blyden, *Christianity, Islam and the Negro Race*

Nkrumah has been written about extensively as a political figure and ideologue of African unity towering above the Ghanaian and African landscape, and as an anti-imperialist theoretician and statesman looming large in the politics of Pan-African, Third World, and socialist internationalism. Not much has been written, however, about the poetry of Nkrumah's politics, an aspect of the man's endeavors which invites a mode of reading that weds culture—in the aspect of (social) dramaturgy, narrativity, and symbolism—to political understanding; and politics, for that matter, to cultural understanding.

What is offered in this chapter is a contribution to a reading of the poetry of Nkrumah's politics.[19] What follows gives a probabilistic account of Nkrumah's autobiography as contributing to a critique of, and project-ing beyond, the theocratic essentialism of the discourse of Orphean nativism. This is what is given a classic embodiment, as we saw in the previous chap-ter, in Casely Hayford's *Ethiopia Unbound*. It is, therefore, a reading of the moment of *Ghana* as a revisionist one, a moment where the national alle-gory is negotiated away from a spiritual towards a secular coding. I will give myself here the large freedom of reading Nkrumah's first chapter back into an inchoate social narrativity, giving a sense of how its tropes and figures of desire are given shape within, and in terms of, a native setting in the grip of a colonialist modernity. I will, in other words, be inventing the first chap-ter as a narrative pre-text from which *Ghana* detaches itself as the condi-tion of its own possibility. This will be a pre-text whose claims on the autobiography *Ghana negotiates* and *advances*; a pre-text to which the auto-biography finally circles back as a *fulfillment* of its own precondition. It should be apparent by now that in saying this I am also instituting this pre-text as a subtext, a kind of "unconscious," that accompanies Nkrumah's autobiographical narrative over the range of its performances. I hope to show, in retrieving this "unconscious," how the theme and structure of a virtual nativity are already implicitly contained in the inaugural movements of narrative in *Ghana*.

To begin from the beginning, with the account Nkrumah gives of his birth and early childhood in the setting of Nzima-land. About Nzima, where he was born at an uncertain date (either 1909 or 1913), he informs us: "[T]ime did not count in those peaceful communities." Strictly speak-ing this is not accurate. We may infer, rather, that what he means is that timekeeping in the Western sense went unremarked for the reason that the space of a domestic nativity was already accounted for in an order of tem-porality that was all its own. Nevertheless, even here a Western time scheme was on the ascendent. The inception of this time scheme, as Nkrumah recounts it, went back to when Nzima had been "discovered" by Europeans and christened "Appollonia because it was on the feast day of St Apollo that the white man first set foot in Nzima Land" (1). Having been inserted into Christendom, Nzima locality had more and more become subject to the influential chronometry of Anno Domini. And if anything, a colonial power in the land was hastening this process.

From the manner in which Nkrumah recalls the Nzima of his birth, then, we may deduce that the unequal meeting of two temporalities—one forceful, the other "peaceful"—had ensured that the economic imperatives of an invasive West and its discursive and political supports had come to lie heavily athwart his homeland. This process had fractured Nzima and inserted it into a framework of multiple, unevenly overlapping spaces. For instance, as Nkrumah recounts—perhaps with understated heat—his native land had, of necessity, to confront a colonial reality daily in the fact that, not only was it yoked with other Gold Coast ethnic groups by colonial diktat, but it was also forcibly divided. One part of it belonged to the British Gold Coast and the other to the French Ivory Coast. Nzima had also sustained a sundering within, between a sector of traditional observances and a modern sector to which, complexly, belonged another tradition, that of the "priest who . . . baptised me into the Roman Catholic Church [and] recorded my birth date as 21st September, 1909" (1).

Local knowledges were still operative in Nzima at the time of the future leader's birth. Nevertheless, even for Nkrumah's unlettered mother, who had been weaned on these knowledges, the shape of her son's life seemed to lie beyond a pure locality, and more in a location in between, a location angled in the direction of the exogenous modern school. We are told: "Although my mother had never had the benefit of a formal education herself, she was determined that I should be sent to school at the earliest opportunity" (10).

We may produce the "common sense" at the basis of a mother's decision as the intuitive grasp by an Nzima nativity of its existence in a virtual alignment of plural worlds. There was its own world which, falling under the dispensation of a colonialist modernity, was articulated with that of worlds other than its own. And if the tag of Gold Coasters borne by the natives of Nzima meant anything at all, it meant that an impinging power had compelled the natives of both Nzima and beyond to partially concede a recognition of Self within the powerful presence, real and symbolic, of the Anglo-British Other. Uneven though a colonial structure made this alignment of worlds appear, the transverse relationships the colonial encounter had created could yield a dream—as is obscurely manifest in the wish of an unlettered mother—of a potential link that will "thread" or "suture" into ideal proportion these different times and spaces.

It is in just such a manner that Nkrumah, in his intellectual and political formation, appears in *Ghana*. Hence we might grasp his career as a confirmation of the modernist covenant of a native mother. Madam Nyaniba, Nkrumah's mother—the autobiography is dedicated to her—and others like her had to have been staking their faith on their native sons and daughters being able to find in and through the modern school a rigorous formulation with which to materialize that sense of African worldliness which, for their untutored generation, could only have remained on the level of intuitive common sense.

A folk anecdote that Nkrumah recounts as he sketches his early years "justifies" a mother's commonsensical yearnings on behalf of her son and opens a preliminary window for us onto the issues that will animate the life over time represented in *Ghana.* In August of 1913, we are told, a cargo ship, the *Bakana,* had run aground off the Nzima coast and its captain had perished. Those are the facts. The English vessel's accident, however, is transformed by the Nzima folk imaginary into a consequential story of heroic appropriation. In the fantastic version circulating among the Nzima, it is the god of a local river who, wishing to visit his goddess in a neighboring river, had engineered the shipwreck so that he would have a boat at his command for his middle passage. That a domestic god-figure would feel the need to seize, on his own behalf and for his own purposes, a *man*-made object, an instrument, moreover, that was the metonym, the technological emblem *par excellence,* of the global power of early-twentieth-century Europe, must surely speak volumes.

Reading the "political unconscious" of this folk anecdote puts us in a position to see a locality already groping towards a model of empowering reconciliation with a universality which at this time, willy nilly, bore the powerful imprint of Europe. And it would seem that this reconciliation had to want to find its way through the vessel of a global European modernity, a symbol whose local manifestation was not only the disproportionately powerful colonial state but also, as presented in a mother's wish for her native son, the techniques conferred by the seductive new school.

And yet, if this is the case, we are also required, complementarily, to see the ongoing negotiation captured in a folk anecdote not simply as an act of African domesticity paying homage to the puissant universality of Europe. Hardly. Rather, the parable of the local god who commandeers the European ship requires us to envision, in a theme of secular emergence, an African nativity's Promethean abrogation of the vessel of a Eurocentric universality for its local self-expression.

It is here, then, in a virtuality to be aspired towards, that the heroics of the autobiographical gesture in *Ghana* must be sought. The requirement imposed on the hero, ultimately, is to refigure the domestic space of the Gold Coast and to chart its *singular* insertion into the motions of a universal history. From a land outside time—as Hegel once remarked of Africa and which Nkrumah curiously seems to confirm ("time did not count" in pristine Nzima, he tells us)—a representative native figure is enjoined to descend into a temporal dialectic in order to remake himself into the agent of historical eventuation. It is only thus that he stood to be able, so to speak, to shape the demise of the colonial captain and, seizing the vessel of colonialist design, foresee a reconstituted and self-actuating nativity. Insofar as it appears in Nkrumah's political poetry of national allegory, what could the conceit of a god whose trysts with his goddess have to be mediated by the profane artefact of a European modernity mean but this?

That implication is the one carried in the first epigraph of this chapter: an Nkrumahist nativity which, virtually renewing itself in *and* beyond Europe's terms, would produce a self-nation in a universal modernity that still kept faith with its own nature. In the circumstances, the universal will have been given a new meaning much rather as, in the process of extending itself into this universality, a new nativity will have been born. It is such a virtual coding, therefore, that we must give the tale of an African godhead— sign of the pure originality and the perfect self-identity of a pristine nativity, outside time, as we saw in *Ethiopia Unbound*—that has felt the need to descend from a lofty position of absolute figurality in order to enter the motions of secular allegory.

The point of reading the conceit contained in the folk anecdote the way I have done is because the insights it offers are transposable into a reading of Nkrumah's autobiographical performance. In the light of these insights, we might bring more than a literal consideration, then, to this detail the leader gives about his birth: "I am told," he writes, "that . . . I apparently took so long to show any signs of life that my mother had lost all interest in me as she believed me to be dead" (*Ghana,* 3). This is more Nkrumahist mythmaking. Could there not be the merest hint of an invitation to the reader to rescue from this detail the additional conceit of a nativity hesitating to keep a tryst in "impure" time with the feminine mother-figure? Perhaps not. Still, if we bear in mind the tale of a god who has perforce to descend to earth to negotiate a middle passage in order to reach his goddess, may we not discern here the conceit of a nativity seeking to reencounter its originality—symbolized by the principle of the mother— in altered circumstances? Could Nkrumah's primordially lifeless body then be the sign of a native sphere that remains bodily mute because it is consigned to a powerless ideality? That is, until he—like the god-figure who, in changed circumstances, must renew his trysts and keep faith with his goddess—is forced into the motions of secular allegory? Nkrumah continues: "my female relatives . . . were determined to put life into me [and after much effort] they finally succeeded in arousing my interest and . . . handed me back to my mother" (4). It would seem that in the humanized and relative time of secular allegory, the native *logos,* the pure but inert vocable, seeking to reencounter itself in renewal, is enjoined to condescend to suffer the profanity of being made flesh.

We will find such a sense of renewal-in-relativity (and vice versa) accompanying the attempt by Nkrumah to fix a beginning precisely for himself in addition to and beyond the Nzima calendric system which, as he informs us, his mother falls back on to calculate his age. Beginning—originality—here appears through the mediation of the shipwrecked English vessel and the tombstone of its dead captain, two landmarks of Western timekeeping which provide the means for Nkrumah to mark with relative precision his own date of birth in his opening chapter.

As it turns out, ship and captain will return once more as the autobiographer's concluding images. Anticipating this conclusion, we may observe inaugurally here that the leader's signifying of autobiographical beginning and end upon these images is not fortuitous: between and through the modernist resonances of the images of ship and captain, Nkrumah will have shown us an ideopraxis based self-consciously on renewal-in-relativity. Hence, as the conclusion will show us, what underwrites Nkrumah's self-nomination as autobiographical hero is a certain modality of recuperating the modern for Africa: in *Ghana,* in other words, we encounter an Nkrumahist stylization, essentially Promethean, of African modernity. In the end what we have is a portrait of a man who has been able to seize and put to work on his behalf those conjunctural opportunities given by a colonialist-modernist dispensation, the very ones that Hayford before him had intuited but could only ineffectually gesture at.

"The essence of politics is the realization of what is possible" (193), observes Nkrumah, and we can assume that these words are spoken as a corrective to an earlier nationalist praxis. This characterization of the realpolitical as a working with(in) and towards the virtual—i. e., "possible"—marks the distance between Nkrumah's style of self-fashioning and that of Hayford and his acolytes, Sekyi and the De Graft Johnson brothers among them. These are the ones who, under the aegis of the Gold Coast National Research Association, would completely expunge "the white man's standpoint from the black man's outlook," and go on to reconstruct the native state in its pre-contact purity "before the disintegrating foreign element . . . insinuated itself into it" (qtd. in *Political History,* 525). If on the one hand, we have a Hayfordian nationalism that hampers and constrains itself in the pursuit of a conservative nativism; on the other, the populist Nkrumah presents a radical, postnativist style of politics. Nkrumah's kind pragmatically wills its self-constitution in what is given; it is a politics that makes do with what is available. The difference between the two leaders is that be-

tween the hierophant, Hayford, ineffective for being walled up in an idealized native past, and the present-minded communicant, Nkrumah, (partially) successful for being able to invest the middle-class *logos* in a consensual national community. This theme is dwelt on at some length in the
section following.

Going through the Logic of Colonial Fracture

> I wish I had the power to bring back Osagyefo Dr. Kwame Nkrumah
> from the grave. For in Nkrumah, there was one Ghana! The Ewes,
> Gas, Dagombas, Ashantis, Krobos, etc., all lived together as one great
> people.
> —Letter to the editor, *Ghanaian Chronicle,* Aug. 7, 2000

Writing in an earlier Orphean phase of nationalism, Hayford, as we have
seen, projects the successful institution of a normative bond between himself and a popular nativity in terms of the middle-class intellectual's active
recherche du temps perdu. Hence we discover, in *Ethiopia Unbound,* his autobiographical alter ego, Kwamankra, standing in Kumasi (the capital of
Asante), far from a coast ravaged by European intrusion, and imagining an
inland preserve that answers his quest for an Ethiopian norm which he
might come to embody. From an alienated gaze trained upon the town's
inhabitants, he muses: "the men and women [of Asante] are not changed. . . .
It is easy to see that the men and women who walked the banks of the Nile
in the days of yore are not far different from . . . the sons of Efua Kobi (i.e.,
royal matriarch of Asante [1857–84])." Hayford concludes therefore: "Thus
you arrive at the heart of these people, and you are inwardly persuaded that
all symbols of European authority, responsibility are more impermanent
than the frail houses you see about you."[20]

While Hayfordian nationalism may cast itself ideally as speaking from
within a popular nativity, its style of articulation nevertheless presents impressive problems. For monologic commentary like the kind we see above
contrives only to leave a normative people in a silent, timeless order, preserved as the ahistorical signifier of an unblemished "Ethiopian" interiority. The citation concludes: "How to reach the heart of such a people would
not be an uninteresting study" (*Ethiopia Unbound,* 185–86). And this is
followed by the Blydean projection that "If you succeed, you have arrived
at the heart of the principle which may be applied to healthy race development wheresoever necessary" (186). In the projection, however, we encounter

something of the philosophical incoherence of the nativist intellectual. For how did one "develop"—i.e., articulate in an order of *relativity*—that which was confined in an absolute zone of mute ideality? And the ultimate question must surely be why it would be necessary to "develop," that is to say, alienate from itself, a state of purity presumed to be sufficient unto itself.

Hayford here—and the same goes for his intellectual heir Kobina Sekyi—articulates a characteristically conservative style of responding to that great question which has haunted all political activism down the ages: "What is to be done?" Hayford's and Sekyi's manner of locking the solution of the problem into a radically conservative mode, though, is of the kind that Nkrumah's diagnosis in *Ghana* identifies with an elite nationalism hampered by its excessive Orphean/*sankofa* idealism. Hence Nkrumah's exasperation with those he accuses of being "idealists," men out of touch with the "African problem."[21] The question, as Nkrumah mounts the nationalist platform, then, is a reformulation of what is to be done. The African problem needed a resolution, above all, in and as the pragmatic question of how a middle class could present an image of itself as a vanguard bearing the "dominant wish and aspiration" of "the people." The problem was how a class-for-power might construct a broad-based social force positioned solidly behind it in its contests with colonial authority.

Pursuing these questions, what follows presents in a comparative framework the ways in which the African problem shapes the self-presentations given by the two nationalist leaders, Hayford and Nkrumah, in their respective autobiographies. Both proceed on the assumption that "the people" are the sole basis upon which a middle class "Africanizes" itself (i.e., casts its class self as legitimately representing the "African"/"native"/"national" people). Both understand, additionally, that "the people" are to be factored into every attempt by a middle-class political vanguard to surmount "the African problem"—as an immediately *colonial* problem. If so, the comparison of the two leaders offered here will be a way of assessing two competing middle-class nationalist modes and styles, Orphean and Promethean, of articulating "the people" within the colonial conception of "the African problem."

In Nkrumah's postnativist posture we see him bringing an understanding that shifts the constitution of the people away from the nonnegotiable primordial basis Hayford gives it. What emerges is the difference between Hayford's community of a real nativity, or (African) people by *descent*, and Nkrumah's community of a virtual nativity, or (African) people by *consent*.

Historically, if Hayford's monologue, as exemplified above, remains an unfulfilled homage to a pristine past, in *Ghana* Nkrumah gives us an alternative that begins with a homage to the future. We see this in an out-standing image of the future leader as he takes his leave of America gazing up at the celebrated Statue of Liberty, "with her arm raised as if in personal farewell to me." With his eyes misted over, Nkrumah declares to the Statue: "You have opened my eyes to the true meaning of liberty. . . . I shall never rest until I have carried your message to Africa" (48). In that compact is captured the pragmatic idealism that Nkrumah will later inject into the anticolonial struggle. For, unlike Hayford the unanimist, it is not the case for Nkrumah that *all* the symbols of European authority should be rejected out of hand. Rather, for an Africa looking towards a self-renewing posture in modernity, these were symbols awaiting Promethean appropriation for the refashioning of the norms of a viable postcolonial political and cultural order.

To demonstrate the efficacy of Nkrumah's pragmatic idealism, *Ghana* gives us the testimony of an old man—an emblem of the past, if any-thing—who is moved by the leader's proclamation of a new order of postcolonial freedom—the compact of the future, if anything—at a C.P.P. rally. This rally, as it happens, takes place in Kumasi, the self-same Kumasi which Hayford preferred to be immured in an immemorial tradition. We are told that the old man asks Nkrumah in amazement: "Do you mean that *I* can stand up in Kumasi and speak of the things you have just told us? All this in *Ashanti?*" To which the leader responds in a tremendous display of reassurance: "Why not? You are the same as the rest of us. If you believe in freedom then you say so!" And the old man's final word is: "If the C.P.P. can do this for me—then *FREEDOM!*" (222).

"You are the same as the rest of us": here monologue gives way to dialogue. In this connection, George Hagan's assessment of "Nkrumah's Leadership Style" reveals a politician who had "correctly discerned that political propaganda in a culture in which communication was mainly face-to-face, had to be face-to-face." What this meant was that Nkrumah

> had to communicate his ideas through direct contact. He had to see and touch the people, and the people had to see and touch him. His body and his voice became a medium of communication—and that medium became identified with the call to arms and with *independence*. He and the people drew fresh energy from their mutual encounters. ("Leadership Style," 182; emphasis in original)

In Nkrumah's politicking, two-way exchanges take place, then, in which he is able to give a common sense projection to an oppressed "underclass," created by and in colonial inequality, of a time of the nation where each will be equally deserving of liberty. As Wright analyzes it, Nkrumah had tapped into, and become the expressive vehicle of, what had become "more than a word" for Africans, the desire for "freedom." "Freedom" was more than a word, according to Wright, because "these people knew that it meant the right to shape their own destiny as they wished. . . . [N]o threats could intimidate them about it; they might be cowed by guns and planes, but they'd not change their minds about the concrete nature of the freedom that they wanted and were willing to die for" (*Black Power,* 54).

It is meaningful exchanges of the kind we find between Nkrumah and the old man that enlist a new content, "the people," into Hayford's historically ineffective call for "reciprocity." Reciprocity, we will recall from earlier chapters, was meant to resound in the context of the struggle of the educated middle class against the white colonial structure. We may not overlook the fact that it contains the important premise that, but for the New Imperialism and its official culture of racism, the native intellectual and the white colonial functionary might share the same cultural identity and class interest after all. Hence Hayford shows us that the anticolonial struggle begins in large measure as a confrontation between two colonial factions, both positioned in a structure of privilege, however asymmetrical this positioning. One faction, white, actually wielded power. The other was black, with a European education, and privileged as such. Nevertheless its position in the colonial structure was such that the actuality of power continued to elude it.

If, in the circumstances, Gold Coast nationalism is produced under the sign of a class-for-power, the inability to see the power struggle through until the intervention of Nkrumah must be accounted for by the failure of a native elite to rally the masses to its side. A first phase of nationalism, therefore, founders in large part because a middle class is unable to represent its interests to the people as the people's own interest. All claims to the contrary, a nativity of "the people" could only remain an elitist abstraction in a contestatory nationalist discourse that nevertheless shrilly insisted that the only political reality was this people's priority. Until the moment of Nkrumah a middle-class politics confronts its failure to make good the compact of popular representation it had posited in the mimetic contract. Having excessively idealized nativity into a nonnegotiable norm, Orphean nationalism, as it turned out, had compromised on a relativist definition of the political in a colonial setting.

If the real nativity of Orphean/*sankofa* nativism posited a norm that seemed to lie beyond politics, this claim was belied by an invasive colonial authority which kept ensuring that no space was sacrosanct and nothing remained immune to politics. For colonial realpolitik dictated a capture of nativity itself. Hence, the nativist knowledge produced by the native intellectual quite simply played into the hands of the colonial state. In the policies of Indirect Rule and Native Administration, colonial authority came to use this knowledge to expediently refashion the "customary" in accordance with its authoritarian model of power and command. In Mamdani's characterization,

> customary law consolidated the noncustomary power of the chiefs in the colonial administration. . . . For the first time the reach of the Native Authority and the customary law it dispensed came to be all-embracing. Previously autonomous social domains . . . now fell within the scope of chiefly power. At the same time . . . any challenge to chiefly power would now have to reckon with a wider systemic response. The Native Authority was backed up by the armed might of the modern state at the center.[22]

The colonial establishment, engaged in the "invention and dignification of Tradition,"[23] had enormously empowered an elite of traditional rulers. These were then available to be used as a bulwark against the perceived threat to the white power structure represented by the middle class.[24] Divide and rule as a tactic for reproducing the colonial state was nothing new to colonial power.

The invention of tradition in the Gold Coast had produced colonial subjects, therefore, who were caught between two mutually reinforcing spheres of oppressive exaction: the modern state and its subservient, administratively tribalized "customary" counterpart. Thus the logic of fracture by which colonial power reproduced its authority; and it is here, within an order submitted to colonial necessity, that Nkrumah's logic of freedom would seek the modalities of its expression. For if the contrivances of colonial power had divided the social spaces of the Gold Coast it had also virtually made them the "same" since they were subjected "equally" to the burden of its exactions. When Nkrumah tells the old man "You are the same as the rest of us," therefore, he is using a language that seductively "threads" its way through the oppressive logic of colonial fracture,[25] to emerge on its utopian other side, into the time of a national modernity, a time foreshadowed as such by the uniformity imposed by the colonial state itself. That future utopia draws its authority from, and insinuates itself into, a dream of a common language—a language of freedom, popular accountability, and social justice—to which all will come as equal communicants irrespective of lineal and ethnocultural descent. Only in the originality of this conception could the worlds beyond Nkrumah's native Nzima merge into each other and into the dream of Ghana, an African nation in a world of equal nations.

A landmark shipwreck and a tombstone: when Nkrumah informs his reader in his opening chapter that these are his aids in ascertaining the date of his birth, we are given a sense of a beginning which he can grasp only relatively. We might extend this reading into a metaphor of an autobiographical performance in which his own originality appears as the timely and virtual appropriation, phoenix-like, of a self-nation from a perspective fixed in the demise of the English captain and the chronometry that marks his death as a meaningful event. In this acknowledgement of a trace of otherness on Nkrumah's beginnings, the autobiography of the self-nation signals the location of its own productivity.

It is not altogether implausible, then, to retrieve from *Ghana* the suggestion that, without this seizure of the Other, Nkrumah's own beginning and that of his nation would not have entered the order of "real" time and knowledge: that order of history which permits the life over time to find its justification in a communally transforming ideopraxis. For the Nkrumahist moment leads us to suppose that, to have immured oneself in a temporality where, so to speak, "time did not count"—in an Africa invaded by the historical imperatives of modernity—is to have rendered "unthinkable" the beginnings that make historical eventuation meaningful. This, we must suppose, is the insight that accompanies the autobiographical celebration of Nkrumah's ability to salutarily recover an expansive modernity and reconcile it with an African domesticity once merely confined to a supplementary status by European colonialist modernity.

Ghana announces an African modernity, therefore, that nation-statehood is understood to both signify and virtually guarantee. And, as we have seen, reaching for this expression of national expansiveness, Nkrumah is enjoined to abandon a theocratic guarantee of a primordial, irreducible difference—the position held by Hayford and others of his Orphean/*sankofa* kind—and enter a secular imaginary of *difference in the same*. However, even as the Promethean Nkrumah makes bold to enter the same order of the colonial ship's inscription, his future guarantee is placed in the self-nation's being able to shape the demise of the ship's colonialist captain. The self-nation is to be reborn in a guise different from its colonial phylogeny. The projection of *Ghana*, therefore, is of an African Difference not consumed by, but consummated in modernity, or the symbolic order of the Same.

The thrust of the chapter has been to draw on this relative coding of originality to demonstrate that the energy of creation Nkrumah brings to the anticolonial struggle rests on a Promethean dream of a middle-class state becoming the modernist foundation of a virtual African nativity. It is a dream which, in time, Nkrumah brings to a realization in Ghanaian nation-statehood. This is the sense of achievement borne by the concluding lines of the autobiography: as the story of *Ghana* winds down it circles back to its beginning to revise its earlier image of a sunken ship. Here, in the revised mode, Nkrumah paints a memorable portrait of himself as the African "captain" of the buoyant "ship" of a Ghanaian state which, "freshly launched," faces the "hazards of the high seas alone" (290). The modernist image captures an African nation poised for a promising navigation of the middle passage of a challenging modernity. And the new captain, standing "on the bridge of that lone vessel as she confidently sets sail," is buoyed by the hope that the time of the Ghanaian nation will prove exemplary, projecting a nation that will have become a radiant beacon to all of Africa and the black world.

The sentiment resounds grandly in Nkrumah's speech on Independence day, March 6, 1957. "[F]rom now on," he declared, "there is a new African in the world and that new African is ready to fight his own battle and show that after all the black man is capable of managing his own affairs." The new Africans "are going to demonstrate to the world, to the other nations, young as we are, that we are prepared to lay our own foundation."[26] Moreover, as he writes in *Ghana,* the country's example has "awakened" the "African in every territory on this vast continent . . . and the struggle for freedom will go on." Hence, African nationalism was not and could not be "confined to the Gold Coast—the new Ghana." Indeed, in obedience to the modernist logic of Nkrumahist virtual nativity, the modality and strategy of anticolonial struggle "from now on . . . must be Pan-African nationalism, and the ideology of African political consciousness and African political emancipation must spread throughout the whole continent." For "our task is not done and our safety is not assured until the last vestiges of colonialism have been swept from Africa" (*Ghana,* 290).

Nkrumah, the Logic of Etatism, and After

> The people have not mastered their independence until it has been given a national and social content and purpose that will generate their well-being and uplift.
>
> —Nkrumah, *Consciencism*

Nkrumah and Ghana bring us to the beginning of the end of an epoch, the colonial one, to a moment of arrival that foresees the ushering in of a brand new epoch, a decolonized time of African national modernity. In this con-nection, many will concur that the culmination of the narrative of "Ghana" reads indeed as the autobiography of Nkrumah. And as many, if not more, will agree also that the narrative of early independent Africa, heralded by Nkrumah's Ghana, reads, so to speak, as the "biography" of this dominant nationalist figure. Yet if the autobiography is a model of closure, the "biog-raphy" has hardly proved to be so. The story of black Africa, since the independence of Ghana ushered in the moment of nationalist arrival, does not permit conclusiveness of the sort imagined by the Promethean pro-tagonists of the final stages of the anticolonial struggle. Hence, as we reread the promise of "Ghana," and the premise of decolonization, some four-and-a-half decades into Independence, one question appears *de rigueur*: what to make of the legacy of Nkrumah and others in what now appears to be at worst a failed, at best an ailing, African revolution?

For all that he was "the strategist of genius in the struggle against classic colonialism,"[27] Nkrumah's words regarding the capture of the politi-cal kingdom resonate in our time not in terms of a fulfilment of their confident promise but in their compromise. Events in an unruly postindependence era have conspired to deny the vision Nkrumah and others sought to realize. In the assertion itself, Nkrumah borrows a Chris-tian formulation ("seek ye first the *kingdom of God* and the rest shall be added unto you") and transfers its *metaphysical* meaning—the kingdom of God as the be-all and end-all—to the political state. If, therefore, in secur-ing the political kingdom, Nkrumah and others of his kind envision the African struggle for an independent national-social order reaching a mo-ment of culmination—a final moment of coherence, that is—this moment coheres as such in, and is firmly underwritten by, a more or less etatist absolutism. And this absolute places the meaning of culmination by and large within its own logic, or sense, of an *ending* (i.e., as the be-all and end-all).[28] In that sense, a more or less absolute state—a state which, in Chatterjee's assessment, has a central, autonomous and directing function—remains an article of faith with Nkrumah. The advent of a national people is unimaginable without this postulate.

What does this envision in theory, if not in fact, for the daily practice of culture in the postindependence nation? It means that culture, the proper domain of nation-formation, is subordinated to politics.[29] Appearing from above, it is the *force* of the State, it would seem, that "legitimates" the nation; and not the force of the nation, from a popular below, that confers on the state its true legitimacy. To the extent that the former holds true, the native people, it would seem, become a mere object of politics, as such to be emptied or abstracted into the nationalistic pretensions and requirements of the political kingdom.

The thesis of etatist absolutism advanced here as part of the legacy of middle-class nationalism in Africa generally is not the creation of a subjective whim. On the contrary, it bears repeating that its cultural-political logic is imposed by objective circumstances. The anticolonial struggle, given the ethnocultural plurality of the colonial countries, and to the extent that its purposes had to terminate in what Gramsci refers to as "passive" or "reform-revolution,"[30] had no choice but to begin by positing an antithesis, the exogenous state, which middle-class nationalism positioned as prior to a thesis it had then to seek out. As for this thesis, middle-class African nationalists imagined it as an endogenous principle of modern popular selfhood whose definition, beyond the merely ethnic and ethnocentric, would be national. In the progressive nationalist imaginary, the modernity of the nation points hopefully in the direction of a dialectical entry into a "higher" synthesis of antithesis and thesis, of exogenous and endogenous components.

Inasmuch as this etatist vision of culmination is driven by the dialectical priority of the political kingdom, in retrospect its Promethean positivism seems, perhaps, too brash. And one speaks here bearing in mind the convulsions, upheavals, and setbacks that have beset (and continue to beset) many nation-states on the African continent since Independence. What has transpired is a political kingdom which, stamped on the continent by colonial imposition, continues to define an imperative alien to the deepest aspiration of the peoples of Africa.[31] This historical and cultural antithesis has proven durable and too strong, becoming a structure that insinuates itself into and pre-empts the normative constitution of endogenous national selfhood.[32] This, more or less, sums up the argument of Abiola Irele in an exercise in direct political critique that brings an impassioned judgment to bear on "The Crisis of Legitimacy in Africa."[33] Irele's article marks once more the consistency with which, as failed practice, the political has featured as a major *cultural* theme in the creative projects and critiques of African modernity in the last forty years.

Yet, in all the critiques of a failed African nationalist practice that have emerged, one value-constant, perhaps, remains implicitly or explicitly upheld. This, as most centrally projected by Nkrumahist nationalism, is the ideal of a virtual or consensual nativity as the foundation and goal of African cultural and political modernity. Perhaps, then, it is in the unflinching drive to realize a consensual nativity that we need to locate the enduring legacy of this species of African nationalism. And yet, if this vision bears, as we have seen in Nkrumah's representative example, its own impressive baggage of etatist liability, then we need to register other possibilities beyond its moment. And, perhaps, more than any figure in the front ranks of African nationalism, it is Amilcar Cabral who, in his difficult reflections on the relations between the political and the cultural in nationalist practice, suggests the modalities of this going beyond.

It is Cabral, then, who attempts to bring the metaphysics tainting Nkrumah's political kingdom to earth by arguing in outstanding fashion the priority of the cultural in the political, the latter as represented by the antithesis of the colonial state against which the struggle for national liberation contends. In an oft-quoted piece, "National Liberation and Culture," Cabral argues that to the extent that "imperialist domination has the vital need to practice cultural oppression, national liberation is necessarily an act of *culture*" (*Unity and Struggle*, 13). The point is that the political act of liberation begins and ends in culture. Cabral thus redefines liberation or independence as a culmination whose logic is—which must be posited in a sense of—a *beginning*. And in this beginning the cultural and the political, people and power, are seen as elements that must negotiate their way, without the grand political preconception, towards their mutual reconciliation in practice.

This proposition shifts from the etatist positivism that sees the people as a singular political *object*—an abstraction emptying into the political kingdom—to the people, in their variety, as cultural *subjects*. As such, from below, their variety is radically formative of, rather than waiting to be singularly reformed from above by, the politics of national liberation. For Cabral, the foundation and goal of African cultural and political modernity, a virtual/consensual nativity, reads as a datum of gradualism. It is reached at a "*confluence of the levels* of culture of different social groups" (*Return to Source*, 53, emphasis in original). But the reality is that such convergence is never "reached," in the sense of arriving at an ideal equilibrium. On the contrary, it is a vanishing point which, for this reason, enjoins a nationalist practice able, with the beacon of democracy before it, to renew its goals in, and adapt its means to, the ever changing demands of cultural, political, and economic life.

These brief reflections on Cabral must remain at this stage a simplified interpretation of the by no means simple thought of the late Guinéan (Bissau) leader. His necessarily difficult insights into the cultural-political logic of the African nation are in themselves a critical reflection on the fragility, the hollowness even, of the grand constructs of nationalist legitimation of the middle-class founders—the world-historically mediated State, representing the ulterior Reason towards which the grand narratives of the nation must strive—when tested against the ground realities of everyday practice in the postindependence African nation.[34]

And yet the assertion that "the way out is the way through"—attributed to Kenneth Burke—is one that Cabral would appreciate. If so, what he leaves us Africans is the insight that we must be prepared to revisit constantly what it is we are going through (and cannot help but go through), treating it not as a process once understood but responding to it as one responds to a protean challenge. In that sense, then, what is required in the imaginary and practice of the African nation is not the "metaphysical" sense of an ending. What is required, rather, is a radical sense of beginning that, regarding ends as vanishing points, places the emphasis on continually renewed nationalist effort, in theory as in practice.

POSTSCRIPT

ETHICAL TRANSNATIONALISM, POSTCOLONIALISM, THE BLACK ATLANTIC

WRITING GHANA, IMAGINING AFRICA VIS-A-VIS THE CONTEMPORARY REVISIONISMS

> A true respect for the past—a consciousness of a real national history—has not only a binding force but a stimulating effect, and furnishes a guarantee of future endurance and growth. That which has been achieved in the past is a prophecy of what may be done in the future. You may call this poetry if you like, but it is the kind of thing on which nations thrive.
>
> —Blyden, *Christianity, Islam and the Negro Race*

"Intellectuals everywhere," Appiah reports from the trenches of the so-called culture wars of the late twentieth century, "are now caught up . . . in a struggle for the articulation of their respective nations." And variously waging this struggle are "volunteers, draftees, and resisters."[1] This book, *Writing Ghana, Imagining Africa,* poised in nationalist defense of "Africa"—as read frequently through its subsidiary "Ghana"—will presumably have to count in Appiah's reckoning as a "volunteer draftee."

It is Appiah also who, disposing of the fiction of disinterested knowledge in his essay "Tolerable Falsehoods," has alerted us to the interest-relativity of all knowledge. Having this awareness makes it pertinent, as this book winds down, for its author to ask what *interest* exactly informs his articulation of the African nation in an intellectual-cum-activist history.

276

"History," as we have heard Mudimbe declare, "is a legend, an invention of our present. It is both a memory and reflection of our present."[2] If so the interest that informs this book's historical retrospection has been to recuperate for the present a knowledge of African and Pan-African figures, engaged in a drawn-out struggle to articulate African nationality, as *model* agent-protagonists in and of the modern. It has been a matter in what has gone before in this book's pages, then, of seeing these agents seizing themselves, not without difficulty and perplexity, contradiction and paradox, flaws and shortcomings, as *subjects* of modernity, a would-be *African* modernity. It is that, this book has endeavored to show, rather than their consenting to remain merely fixed in *object* status by and in the modern, in the manner purposed for them by the forces of colonial-imperialism. Hence this study has recovered, and evaluated as positive, *to a greater or lesser degree,* African intellectual agency navigating and negotiating the categorical and conceptual givens of the culture of imperialism in an effort to clear a space for an "authentic" knowledge and practice of the African nation to emerge. It is this effort that is consummated, in however compromised and problematic a fashion, in African Independence.

But how to answer the philosophically engaged critique by Appiah, worked out in a transnationalist repudiation of the "isms" of nation, race, and nativity, that has put in question the navigations and negotiations of these modernist givens in African activist intellection?

"Africa" and/in Ethical Necessity

Looking at the dominant terms of collective self-representation furnished by the modern, Appiah finds no way of producing an intellectual history of the post-encounter world except as a narrative here, there, and everywhere of monumental moral error. For contained in the modernist categories of "nation," "race," "native," and the ideological "isms" that ratify and legitimize them, are now globalized ways of knowing which starkly divide and reduce that which ought to be indivisible and irreducible: humanity transcendent. Pioneering nineteenth-century black intellectuals—Blyden, his Pan-Negroist collaborator Crummell, Crummell's protégé Du Bois, etc.— and their Pan-African heirs who took these categories over and maneuvered them into an invention of a useable "Africa" were only perpetuating dangerously antihuman illusions and falsehoods. It may have been that those dispossessed by those who imposed these categories in power took the selfsame categories up in a quest to re-empower themselves. But special pleading of this kind makes no difference to Appiah, whose transnationally articulated appeal is to a Kantian "ethical universal," one that enjoins us to "universalize our moral judgments" (*In My Father's House,* 152, 18, 19). In the name of this ethical universal the powerful and the dispossessed, the West and the Rest, are indifferently and equally culpable of the antihumanist and unreasonable errors of racism, nationalism, and nativism. With one broad Kantian stroke, therefore, Appiah the "resister" consigns virtually all of Pan-African nationalist and racialist thought to ethical worthlessness: all sound and fury, racialist, nationalist, and nativist Africanism signifies nothing.

It does seem to Appiah that modern (Pan)-African intellectual history has no inspirational human story to tell. Apparently, true humanistic consciousness dawns in African philosophico-cultural thought some time in the late 1980s and early 1990s, when *In My Father's House* was being worked on by its author. As facetious as this may sound, this is precisely the effect that Appiah's critique produces. However, the ethical imperative that Appiah takes from a Western philosopher to judge a thought and practice whose concrete situation is (Pan)-African should not be allowed to have the last word. The story of African modernity, as retold in this book, is one which shows nationalist intellectuals under a compulsion to affirm a common humanity through a *prior* affirmation of (their) African humanity. And in retrospection this African priority ought to read as an ethical necessity insofar as continental peoples and their counterparts in the black diaspora had, as their special modern existential legacy, been denied a share by Westerners in a common fund of humanity and a meaningful place in the human family. The evidence reviewed in this book therefore makes the case for an ethics that is positioned not in humanistic abstraction, as Appiah's transnationalist posture will have it, but in *context,* rooted in the interconnected particulars of an African and diasporic experience. "Africa" as a self-sufficient ethical postulate is to be seen in the light of the necessities pressing down on nationalist intellectuals as they faced a formidable Western, and unethically enslaving, imperializing, and colonizing adversary at the frontline.

Appiah has argued elsewhere, as noted above, for the validity of "tolerable falsehoods," these being myths, ideologies, and theories—such as nationalism, racialism, nativism, Negritude—that are tolerable because they structure the world for the agents who invent and manipulate them in humanly livable ways. *Writing Ghana, Imagining Africa* views the thesis of tolerable falsehoods as a better ethical proposition with which to assess the African activist intellection produced at the frontline. Looking at these frontline African intellectuals is to see them engaged in the slippery task of transforming the unethical and error-prone modernist terms and categories of their appropriation into a situated ethics. What is given them imperially in error becomes, in a postimperial rethinking and working out of African modernity, negotiable—a matter for the frontline intellectuals of making ethical virtue out of unethical necessity. It is in this light that, for instance, we must see Blyden's original inspirational appropriation of "Africa" in the "unethical" falsehoods of race, nativity, and nation. Setting out the Africa so appropriated in a comprehensive philosophizing, as we have seen, Blyden sets the tone and agenda for much that would follow in Pan-Africanist and African nationalist thought.

What does it mean for the present, then, to recover and reinterpret as more or less tolerable falsehoods, as this book has done, the Pan-Negro and Africa-centered thought of Blyden and those who in adaptation, modification, revision, and extension of this thought on African soil continued on the trail he had blazed? The question is an urgent one for how "Africa" is to be viewed and positioned in contemporary debate in the light of new conceptualizations of political and cultural modernity that are based on notions of contingency and discontinuity, of heterogeneity and overdetermination. For these are conceptualizations that endanger the contemporary validity of "Africa" as a boundary marker of collective aspiration, "Africa" as a more or less nonnegotiable limit-term for a particular way of being, knowing, and acting in the world. This, one might add, is "Africa" as it has been resolved in the solidarity ideopraxis of transcontinental Pan-Africanism—a Pan-Africanist praxis mediated in significant ways by the "crossover" Blyden and also other New World blacks such as Delany, Crummell, and Du Bois.

"Postcolonial" and "black Atlantic" are two of the new conceptualizations referred to; within the terms of their formulation by two influential critics of the African diaspora, Stuart Hall and Paul Gilroy, "Africa" can never have more than the problematic status of an intolerable cognitive and political falsehood. I turn to Hall's formulation of the "postcolonial" below.

Black Folk, Then and Now: Postcolonialism and the Question of "Africa"

What is a proper knowledge here, there, and everywhere of encounter's aftermath? And how, construing the "field" of a post-encounter modernity properly, might we arrive at a tolerable grounding in it of a politics of "postcoloniality"? Pondering these themes in the question "When Was 'the Post-Colonial'?" Stuart Hall provides the following answer:

> But isn't the ubiquitous, soul-searing lesson of our times the fact that politi-cal binaries do not (do not any longer? did they ever?) either stabilise the field of political antagonism in any permanent way or render it transparently intelligible? *"Frontier effects" are not "given" but constructed*; consequently political positionalities are not fixed and do not repeat themselves from one historical situation to the next or from one theatre of antagonism to another, ever "in place," in an endless iteration.[3]

The essential character of a postcolonial politics lies in its being given *only* in the contingency of its making. For we find ourselves—indeed, we have in the colonial past as in the nominally decolonized present always found ourselves—as the influential cultural theorist avers, "in a necessarily open and contingent political field" ("When Was the Post-Colonial'?" 244). And this can only dictate a politics that is situational, and a matter of choosing, rather than "eternal," and a matter of being chosen. There are, as Hall insists, no pre-given—and permanently fixed—"frontier effects"; these ap-pear only as they are "constructed." In short, Hall, arguing a positional politics "which has no absolute guarantee in an unproblematic, transcen-dental 'law of origin,'"[4] brings what we might term a flexible "construc-tionist" view of the political to the contemporary postcolonial debates.

The evidence of African activist intellection presented by *Writing Ghana, Imagining Africa* challenges this constructionist postcolonial para-digm. For this intellection proffers a knowledge of a post-encounter mod-ern in which "Africa" is inescapably *given* as a "frontier-effect"—or "front-line," as the book has rendered it—a given which is also there, available politically, *for the taking.* The perspectives on Africa reviewed in this book are consistent with the existential "postcolonialism" of Fanon as he looks at the colonial situation and finds that in it "not only must the black man be black; he must be black in relation to the white man."[5] In effect, the pow-erless black man in the colonial relation is not simply black in and for himself. His blackness is given as an imposition on him by his powerful opposite, a given that functions productively as that frontier-effect which demarcates the post-encounter colonial field knowledgeably into the place of superior self and the place of the inferior other, of white fulfillment and black lack. Blackness as a given and lived knowledge on the part of Fanon's black person of white-imposed human incompleteness is a powerful constraint on his choices—it is Hall's "transcendental 'law of origin,'" more or less—with regard to what a "postcolonizing" politics entails.

Are we to consign Fanon's self-conscious reading of blackness as a frontier-effect to the past tense because it is given to him in the special circumstances of a colonial relation? Is the political knowledge Fanon works out of blackness in colonial contingency superseded therefore with the passing of formal colonialism?

The answer has to be a "no" if Chinua Achebe's contemporary postindependence African sense of the way "the world is moving" is anything to go by. Here is Achebe explaining the worldly positionality given him to occupy by the currents of a post-encounter history, and the kind of "postcolonial" politics that this must necessarily entail for him as a *black* creative writer:

> I'm . . . black first, then a writer. . . . I must see what it is to be black—and this means being sufficiently intelligent to know how the world is moving and how the black people fare in the world. This is what it means to be black. *Or an African—the same*: what does Africa mean to the world? When you see an African what does it mean to a white man? . . . [I]f somebody meets me, say, in a shop in Cambridge [England], he says "Are you from Africa?" Which means that Africa means something to some people. Each of these tags has a meaning, and a penalty and a responsibility. All these tags unfortunately for the black man are tags of disability. (qtd. in *In My Father's House*, 73; emphasis added)

Achebe concludes: "I think it is part of the writer's role to encourage the creation of an African identity" (74).

What we get from the thought of Fanon and Achebe—thought continuous with that of the activist intellectuals reviewed in this book—therefore, is not Hall's sense of the postcolonial political field. For Hall's field, then as now, is unconditionally open, its frontier-effects never given in advance, and thus it allows us to conclude that on it politics is only (given in) construction. Rather, the proposition the first two ask us to entertain, a proposition which the evidence of this book should render axiomatic, is that the interchangeable givens of "black" and "Africa," given in advance as "tags of disability," set an all-embracing existential limit on black, hence an inclusively *Pan-African,* politics. They ask therefore that we enlist these tags of negativity which their bearers have in no way shaken off, in a Pan-Africanist understanding of a politics of the "postcolonial" whose validation is not in the *contingency* of constructionism but in the *continuity* of *re*constructionism. We are to see in "Africa," therefore, a post-encounter frontier-effect, a limit of endeavor and aspiration, which requisitions a continuous existential engagement by intellectuals, then and now, here in Africa *and* there in the diaspora, of a Pan-African politics of Reconstruction.

But if then and now, and here and there, are continuous in a Pan-African model of the "postcolonial," this historically and existentially validated formulation is exactly what threatens to disappear from the "black Atlantic." I refer to the conceptual geography of black intellectual and cultural endeavor advanced influentially by Paul Gilroy. As with Appiah's and Hall's revisionism, Gilroy's claims require the searchlight of Pan-African "postcolonialism," as presented here, to be thrown on them.

Black Folk, Here and There: The Black Atlantic and the Question of "Africa"

In what can only amount to a ratification of the politics of contingency recommended by Hall, Gilroy, looking to locate "the dialectics of diasporic identification," has proclaimed, "It ain't where you're from, it's where you're at."[6] On this basis we find Gilroy's black Atlantic referenced in a new topography of cultural reconstruction for which "Africa," reduced to a retrograde term of ambivalent and atavistic identification in diasporic blacks, ceases to function existentially as a valid frontier-effect. "I am seeking," Gilroy announces in *The Black Atlantic,* "to contribute to some *re*constructive intellectual labour" (45). And his intellectual labor, conducted from a perspective on "the internality of blacks to the West" (5), takes as its "starting point" the "*distinctive* historical experiences of [the black Atlantic] diaspora's populations [which] have created a unique body of reflections on modernity and its discontents" (45; emphasis added). In keeping, therefore, with his intellectual interlocutor Jürgen Habermas's concern that as yet (Western) "modernity [is] an incomplete project,"[7] it is the modernity of the West that Gilroy, questioning its Enlightenment philosophic and cultural formulation, sets out to "complete." And this completion is to be carried out within the alternative terms furnished by the new black Atlantic. Gilroy demands a transcendence of

> the unproductive debate between a Eurocentric rationalism which banishes the slave experience from its accounts while arguing that the crises of modernity can be resolved from within, and an equally occidental anti-humanism which locates the origins of modernity's current crises in the shortcomings of the Enlightenment project. (*Black Atlantic,* 54)

"The time has come," he announces in the mode of this transcendence, "for the primal history of modernity to be constructed from the slaves' point of view" (55).

In a gesture that in a Gilroyan perspective will seem far-fetched, George Padmore, among the greatest Pan-Africanists of the twentieth century, writing about *The Gold Coast Revolution,* subtitled his work "The Struggle of an African People from Slavery to Freedom." What this titular gesture discloses is a New World imaginary (Padmore was Trinidadian-born) "Africanizing" the slave experience, mapping the enslaved blackness of the New World onto the colonized blackness of the Old World. The experience of the one is rendered readable through that of the other, the black New World and Old World then united in the figure of a degradation they share in common in the modernity which oppressively absorbs them into the imperializing West. Padmore's interest is in creating—just as Achebe recommends the black writer's "postcolonial" role must be—a Pan-African moral community, a transcontinental community of solidarity, engaged in an agenda of common racial uplift. Africa and the diasporic black Atlantic thus comprise a continuous terrain of reconstructive "postcolonial" endeavor in Padmore's evocation.

Not so for Gilroy, who invokes the black Atlantic distinctively in a complexly configured diasporic transnationalist "nationalism." The black Atlantic "is a non-traditional tradition, an irreducibly modern, ex-centric, unstable, and asymmetrical cultural ensemble that cannot be apprehended through the manichean logic of binary coding" (*Black Atlantic,* 198). Yet, for all that, Gilroy's black Atlantic world comes coded in a binary, bordered clearly in being what Africa is *not,* and in that, perhaps, what Africa must be barred access to. "Diaspora time is not, it would seem, African time" (196), Gilroy waveringly affirms. And even if "Africa is retained as one special measure of . . . authenticity" by diasporic blacks, this "enthusiasm for [Africa as authentic] tradition . . . expresses not so much the ambivalence of blacks towards modernity, but the fallout from modernity's protracted ambivalence towards the blacks who haunt its dreams of ordered civilisation" (191). In this reading "Africa" is no self-assumed galvanizing symbol for a blackness disinherited everywhere by (Western) modernity, as politically figured in Achebe's, Fanon's, and Padmore's—and before them Blyden's, Horton's, etc.—Pan-African reconstructionism. In Gilroy's reading, "Africa" as it circulates in the diasporic black Atlantic has no "reason" behind it. Its appearance and persistence must be marked as an irrational symptom, an *unreasoned* compensatory reflex—mere "fallout," as he terms it—(spontaneously?) engendered by the oppressive conditions endured by modern blacks inside the West. "Africa" in the black Atlantic, therefore, is a bad faith symptom of black self-denial, not a sign of self-affirmation—for diasporic blacks *are* irreducibly Western. As with Appiah so with Gilroy as he assesses the "back to Africa" racialist, nationalist, and traditionalist mythmaking of "Africentrism" and the system building of "Africalogical thought" (127). All these intellectual and quasi-intellectual attempts to produce a "reason" for the Africanist reflex of modern black oppression must quickly be flung back into what Gilroy figures as the abyss of unreason from which they emerge. The black Atlantic must be freed from the atavistic weight of "Africa" in order that it might reconcile with "one of [its] adoptive parental cultures" (2), the West, and be in filial step with this parent in completing, as Habermas recommends, the project of (Western) modernity.

The brothers J. C. and J. W. de Graft Johnson, Gold Coast and Pan-African nationalists, noted in the 1920s that "it is a far greater pleasure helping build a tradition than being obliged to live on the memory of one."[8] In a general way this proposition is what informs the reconstructive labor of intellectual history in both *The Black Atlantic* and *Writing Ghana, Imagining Africa.* Both works are helping to build a tradition by evoking a certain vision of past black self-construction as valuable for the present and the future. But Gilroy's project builds on past black Atlantic endeavor that he has only read selectively, on a past he has willfully distorted therefore. We find Gilroy, for instance, pushing Blyden to the margin of black Atlantic thought, making him interesting only insofar as his links with Jews and Jewish thought ratify the ex-centrism and transnationalism of cultural formation that the critic will claim for his "authentic" version of the black Atlantic (see *Black Atlantic,* 208–12). To have put Blyden's Pan-Negro and Africa-centered thought where it deserves to be—squarely at the center of black Atlantic intellectual history—would have been for Gilroy to acknowledge with the former what he cannot: that as a black person where you are from is not *existentially* separable from where you are at. Blyden in effect had reasoned that diaspora time in its blackness overlaps with African time— a time shared by both in their common displacement into, and racial disinheritance by, a Western imperial modernity. It is on this basis that Blyden, his Pan-Negroist contemporaries of the mid- to late nineteenth century— Delany, Crummell, the young Du Bois, among them—and the prominent Pan-Africanists who came after them in the twentieth century, worked to establish continuities between diasporic and African endeavor, to rearticulate the modern in a time of African Reconstruction.

A conceptualization of the black Atlantic in an authentic cultural geography, then, is one that must acknowledge Old World and New World in fraternal step with each other, delimiting in "Africa" the agenda of a black modernity. This modernist black/African agenda is by no means uncomplicated, contrary to what Gilroy's caricature of an essentialist "Africentrism" purports it to be. For, as this study has shown, insofar as the politics of African Reconstruction is obliged to appropriate its categories of self-representation— "nation," "race," "nativity," indeed "Africa" itself—from the very imperial modernity into which blackness has been negatively displaced, "Africa" emerges in a complicated negotiation of modernist dessert in a "hybrid" language of political and cultural demand. Double disposition in consciousness and cognition, that fracture in black ontology produced by Western imperialism, is not the exclusive property of the diasporic branch of the black Atlantic: it is to be seen both here, in the Old World, and there, in the New.

Recuperating the joint implication of "black" and "Africa," "diaspora" and "home," in each other—the joint implication whose willed occlusion we find in Gilroy's *The Black Atlantic*—therefore, is a part of what this study is about. This is why it has been the interest of this study to produce the preindependence Ghanaian and West African nationalist intellectuals it reviews in a knowledge of their sharing "Africa" as a post-encounter frontier-effect with others elsewhere, in a Pan-African beyond. As we have seen, they share with these others also the problems and possibilities, the imaginings and constraints thereon, that arise from being so placed as African. Understanding this shared basis of being and imagining—also a shared basis of problematizing this being and imagining—preindependence middle-class nationalism in West Africa could draw on generally Pan-African currents of thought and practice, and, in fraternal confirmation, revision, and critique, feed into the same.

What to make then, finally, of this double reconstruction—then and now, here and there—of the intellectual and activist genealogy of the African nation? In conclusion, let me circle back to the question of the interest-relativity that structures the historical knowledge produced in *Writing Ghana, Imagining Africa* by repeating the assessment I gave in chapter 5 of what genealogical reconstruction entails:

> [G]enealogical reconstruction traces a dual movement: it preserves in one continuum the movement of past in present and present in past. In such reconstruction, that is, the past is brought forward and preserved as present memory, and present memory itself reaches back towards and into the past for an investment of its own future possibility. Past and present are thus inscribed in each other, and the genealogical exercise reads as an attempt to capture both in a continuum whose points it defines always as the *creative* or *original* moments of a future anterior.

What is at stake in reclaiming past and present for each other this way is best summed up in what Walter Benjamin offers, in his "Theses on the Philosophy of History," as both caveat and encouragement. Benjamin writes, "Only that historian will have the gift of fanning the spark of hope in the past who is firmly convinced that even the dead will not be safe from the enemy if he wins." And if in Benjamin's estimation, "the enemy has not ceased to be victorious,"[9] it is enough for us to recall in this that (Pan)-African intellectual and activist endeavor is fated to take place at, and is recurrently called into being by, a troublingly ambiguous, but ever-present, frontline.

ABBREVIATED TITLES

Many titles are abbreviated in the notes. The following is a list of the abbreviated titles; full bibliographic information is to be found in the bibliography.

Affairs	Sampson, Magnus. *Gold Coast Men of Affairs (Past and Present).*
"African Past"	Jenkins, Ray. "In Pursuit of the African Past: John Mensah Sarbah (1864–1903 [*sic*]) Historian of Ghana."
Akan Peoples	Balmer, Rev. W. T. *A History of the Akan Peoples of the Gold Coast.*
Black Spokesman	Lynch, Hollis. *Black Spokesman: Selected Published Writings of E. W. Blyden.*
"Brutes"	Lindqvist, Sven. *"Exterminate All the Brutes."*
Celebrities	Attoh Ahuma, S. R. B. *Memoirs of West African Celebrities.*
Colonial Intelligentsia	La Guerre, John Gaffar. *The Social and Political Thought of the Colonial Intelligentsia.*
Colonial Subjects	Zachernuk, Philip. *Colonial Subjects: An African Intelligentsia and Atlantic Ideas.*
Crown Colonies	Salmon, C. S. *The Crown Colonies of Great Britain.*
Gold Coast	Attoh Ahuma, Rev. S. R. B. *The Gold Coast Nation and National Consciousness.*
"Gold Coasters"	Jenkins, Ray. "Gold Coasters Overseas, 1880–1919."
Heroes	Okonkwo, Rina. *Heroes of West African Nationalism.*
History	Reindorf, C. C. *The History of the Gold Coast and Asante.*
Ideologies	Langley, J. A. *Ideologies of Liberation in Black Africa, 1856–1970: Documents on Modern African Thought from Colonial Times to the Present.*

Land Question	Casely Hayford, J. E. *The Truth about the West African Land Question.*
Lawyers	Edsman, Bjorn. *Lawyers in Gold Coast Politics, c. 1900–1945: From Mensah Sarbah to J. B. Danquah.*
"Leadership Style"	Hagan, George P. "Nkrumah's Leadership Style—An Assessment from a Cultural Perspective."
"Manichean Allegory"	JanMohamed, Abdul. "The Economy of Manichean Allegory: The Function of Racial Difference in Colonialist Literature."
"Myth"	Goody, Jack. "The Myth of a State."
Nationalist Thought	Chatterjee, Partha. *Nationalist Thought and the Colonial World: A Derivative Discourse.*
Native Institutions	Casely Hayford, J. E. *Gold Coast Native Institutions.*
Negro Race	Blyden, E. W. *Christianity, Islam and the Negro Race.*
Origins	Wilson, Henry S. *Origins of West African Nationalism.*
Pan-Africanism	Langley, J. A. *Pan-Africanism and Nationalism in West Africa, 1900–1945: A Study in Ideology and Social Classes.*
Pan-Negro Patriot	Lynch, Hollis. *Edward Wilmot Blyden: Pan-Negro Patriot.*
Papers	Arhin, Kwame. *The Papers of George Ekem Ferguson: A Fanti Official of the Government of the Gold Coast, 1890–1897.*
Political History	Kimble, David. *A Political History of Ghana: The Rise of Gold Coast Nationalism, 1850–1928.*
Protestant Ethic	Weber, Max. *The Protestant Ethic and the Spirit of Capitalism.*
Return	Cabral, Amilcar. *Return to the Source.*
Souls	Du Bois, W. E. B. *The Souls of Black Folk.*
Towards Nationhood	De Graft Johnson, J. W. *Towards Nationhood in West Africa.*
Wretched	Fanon, Frantz. *The Wretched of the Earth.*
Writings	Mazzini, Joseph. *Life and Writings of Joseph Mazzini.*

NOTES

Introduction

1. Anderson, *Imagined Communities.*

2. Balakrishnan, "The National Imagination," in *Mapping the Nation,* ed. G. Balakrishnan, 212.

3. Chatterjee, *Nationalist Thought and the Colonial World* (cited hereafter as *Nationalist Thought*).

4. Greenfeld, *Nationalism: Five Roads to Modernity,* 14.

5. Gellner, *Nations and Nationalism,* 124.

6. Ibid., 124. Emphasis in original.

7. See, among others, Appadurai, *Modernity at Large*; Gaonkar, ed., *Alternative Modernities*; S. Newell, *Ghanaian Popular Fiction.*

8. With regard to the Gold Coast/Ghana, the designation "preindependence" should cover strictly the period between 1874 (when the British began formal colonial rule of the territory) and 1957(when the Gold Coast became independent and was renamed Ghana). The historical record, however, discloses that Britain informally exercised dominance, going back to roughly the 1830s, over parts, mostly on or near the littoral, of what by 1901 had become consolidated as the colony of the Gold Coast, comprising the Colony, Ashanti, and the Northern Territories. "Preindependence" in this book thus covers the forty- to fifty-year period before 1874 as well. The turning over to the British of their coastal settlements by the Danes, in 1850, and by the Dutch, in 1872, aided the colonial consolidation of Britain's power. So too did the conquest, in 1874, and, again, decisively in 1897, by British colonial forces of the imperial kingdom of Ashanti (or properly Asante), located in the Gold Coast hinterland. For much of the nineteenth century, the Asante war machine remained a credible threat to British imperial and commercial interests on the coast—interests allied with the Fanti, ethnic Akan and cousins of the Asante—with the Asantes dealing the British a number of serious military setbacks. In 1918, with the defeat of the Germans in World War I and the consequent loss of their African colonies, the one half of German Togoland contiguous with the eastern flank of the Gold Coast was turned over to Britain. Trans-Volta Togoland, as this territory became known, would thus fall under the administrative oversight of the Gold Coast as a trust territory, later to be amalgamated with the three aforementioned Gold Coast territories into independent Ghana.

9. The argument for accounting for the different (anglophone) West African territories as one sociohistorical and cultural unit has been made in a number of works. This is on account of the experiences shared intercolonially by these territories, and of the similar cultural trends that took shape in them under the (British) colonial order. Rina Okonkwo, in *Heroes of West African Nationalism,* notes that:

British West Africa . . . was something of a unit in [the colonial] period. There was an intellectual community . . . among the educated elite. They shared a common educational experience from the missionaries . . . [and] often felt a greater kinship with members of their class in neighbouring colonies than with the uneducated indigenes of their own colony. . . . The African-owned newspapers also contributed to building the West African community. They reprinted news from other colonies and created a dialogue and forum for the exchange of ideas. (viii–ix)

Imanuel Geiss, in *The Pan-African Movement*, notes the differences in the historical origins and cultural formation of the elite of the various West African colonial territories alluded to by Okonkwo. The Sierra Leone Creole elite in the nineteenth century, made up of descendants of migrants—resettled Africans, emancipated New World Africans, and the repatriated Black Poor of England—was different from the Gold Coast one. Unlike the latter, which had ties of kinship with the peoples of the Gold Coast, the non-native Creoles were not affiliated with any of the indigenous societies of the Sierra Leone colony. Likewise, the prominent educated elite in Southern Nigeria at first consisted largely of so-called "native foreigners." These were returnees from Sierra Leone (Saro) and Brazil (Amaro) who, at best, could hope to renew the indigenous connections that the enslavement of their forebears had snapped. Nevertheless elite identification emerged in a coherent cross-territorial form because "The steamship line increased the horizontal mobility of the modern elite on the West African coast," and this "facilitated the tendency of the West African elites to coalesce into a homogeneous urban class along the coast from Gambia as far as Cameroon." This process of amalgamation was "aided by their common experiences at school at Freetown [in Sierra Leone], later on the Cape Coast [*sic*] and at Lagos [in Nigeria], and by intermarriage." Eventually, it would lead to "a feeling that the whole West Africa shared a common destiny" (54).

10. Said, *The World, the Text, and the Critic,* 169.

11. Jonathan Rée, quoted by Malkki in "Citizens of Humanity: Internationalism and the Imagined Community of Nations," 42. The "imagined international community," Malkki notes, "is not a supranational or cosmopolitan world but precisely an international one, a world where *globality is understood to be constituted by interrelations among discrete 'nations'* (41; emphasis in original).

12. Adrian Hastings has contested Anderson's "'modernist' view" of the nation—a view he identifies also in the work of J. Breuilly, Hobsbawm, and Gellner. For Hastings the origin of the nation-form goes back to European antiquity, with England supplying the prototype as early as the end of the tenth century A.D. See the first chapter in his *The Construction of Nationhood.*

13. See, for instance, Paolini, "The Place of Africa in Discourses about the Postcolonial, the Global and the Modern."

14. For critical inventories of, and commentary on, the invention of Africa as incurably unmodern, see, among others, Hammond and Jablow, *The Africa That Never Was*; Miller, *Blank Darkness: Africanist Discourse in French.*

15. James, *Nkrumah and the Ghana Revolution,* 36.

16. The designation "modernist" employed here might provoke some confusion since the term is conventionally associated with a Euro-American literary movement and its aesthetic, as well as with a particular periodization of literary expression. I attach the suffix "ist" to a number of substantives in this study—modern, native, colonial, for instance—to point to a state or condition having to do with, derived from the being or meaning of, or from the objectivity captured in, the relevant substantive.

17. Spivak, "Who Claims Alterity?" in *Remaking History,* ed. B. Kruger and P. Mariani, 269–70.

18. Davidson, *The Black Man's Burden: Africa and the Curse of the Nation-State.*

19. Concerning the African middle class, its mode of being such is defined in its straddling everywhere on the continent the divide between African and European in the colonial encounters. It is a "native" fraction placed, in colonial racial and social prescription, between dominant "Europeans" above and the general group of dominated "Natives" below. I give the thesis of an African middle class a fuller historical and sociocultural review in the following chapter.

20. Blyden, "Study and Race," in Wilson, *Origins of West African Nationalism,* 252 (emphasis added).

21. Nandy, *The Intimate Enemy.*

22. Appiah, *In My Father's House,* 149.

23. The essence of the Faustian allegory is the alienation of (a) man's sovereign, if limited, creativity (his soul) to a greater (Mephistopheles, the devil) in whose comprehensive power—it covers the whole world—he hopes thereby to participate. After acquiescing to the blandishments of the devil (the overreaching, ultimately self-destructive principle), Faust is thenceforth held captive by the former; and, in the long term, he must suffer the everlasting agony that, we must suppose, comes with the knowledge of having lost sovereign control over his human destiny.

24. Varadharajan, *Exotic Parodies,* xiii. (I owe to Varadharajan the characterization I make above of African middle-class consciousness constituted in an interplay of "friend and foe." See *Exotic Parodies,* xxv, xxvi.)

25. Zeleza, "The 'Posts,' History, and African Studies," in *Rethinking Africa's Globalization,* 1:248–49. Cf. also A. Vanaik in his *The Furies of Indian Communalism,* in which he offers this defense of the nation-form:

> The exceptional character of nationalism . . . lies in its unique combination of politics and culture, of civic power (e.g. the importance of citizenship) and identity. The nation-state for the first time invests ordinary people (through the principle of equal citizenship rights) with an authority and importance that is historically unique. To date the zenith of popular individual empowerment is political citizenship, whose frame of operation is the nation-state or multinational state. (42)

26. Chatterjee apparently finds his "No Exit" reading of Third World nationalist agency in *Nationalist Thought* defeatist and does an affirmative reappraisal on that question in *The Nation and Its Fragments.* In this later work, he credits "Asian and African" anticolonial nationalism with an agency located in nation grasped as an "inner domain," therefore "spiritual," and "bearing the 'essential' marks of cultural identity." This inner, inviolate domain claimed as "sovereign territory," then, is opposed to the "domain of the 'outside,'" a "domain where the West had proved its superiority and the East had succumbed." The paradox, however, is that even though the "colonial state . . . is kept out of the 'inner' domain of national culture . . . it is not as though this so-called spiritual domain is left unchanged." For "here nationalism launches its most powerful, creative, and historically significant project: to fashion a 'modern' national culture that is nevertheless not Western" (6).

The interpretation of the "African" evidence I offer in this book is generally in sympathy with Chatterjee's revised "Asian" reading. However, I must question the Indian critic's purely defensive interpretation of the inner domain of the nation. For him this domain is walled off, a metaphysical cocoon, and thus he affirms the "nation" too easily in an indigenist sovereignty and autonomy. In contrast, the African evidence suggests that, because colonial discourse fixed Africa's "inner domain" in a debilitating, dehumanizing image of otherness, this "interiority" has been required to "extravert" itself in African nationalism's creative reconstruction of it. The interior "purity" of the African nation, as I show recurrently in the forthcoming chapters, has had to be made answerable to a compelling "universalizing" demand on it to be articulated in a humanistic parity with Africa's detractors. The projects of Asian and African nationalist modernity are perhaps, then, not as easily conflated as Chatterjee's indigenist reading would want them to be.

For a critique of how conceptually and politically problematic Chatterjee's proposition is that the "authentic" nation in Asia and Africa falls "outside" and "beyond" the reach and claims of universal history (i.e., the history of Western global-capitalist dominion), see Neil Lazarus, *Nationalism and Cultural Practice in the Postcolonial World,* 128–33.

27. I owe the portmanteau term "ideopraxis"—which captures concisely the sense both of ideology as a practice and of practice as ideology-informed—to the Ghanaian writer Ayi Kwei Armah. Armah uses the term in "Masks and Marx."

28. Delany is quoted by George Shepperson in his introduction to Horton's *West African Countries and Peoples,* xiv.

29. Cited by Robert July in *The Origins of Modern African Thought,* 119.

30. The Gold Coast/Ghana version of the historically, geographically, and experientially variegated phenomenon historians have dubbed "colonial encounter"—the unequally negotiated contact between European and non-European peoples—goes back in time to the late fifteenth century. The Portuguese, who made landfall at Elmina in 1482 and built a castle there, are believed to be the first European presence on that portion of the West African littoral that became known by the trademark name of "the Gold Coast." The British, who would come, over the course of the nineteenth century, to dominate the Gold Coast colonially, were late arrivals, making their appearance in the seventeenth century, as did other Europeans, for the purposes of trade.

31. Frantz Fanon offers an uncomplicated evolutionary schema wherein he sees the consciousness of "native writers" under colonialism passing through three stages of maturation. In the first, the native intellectual is a figure of "unqualified assimilation," giving "proof that he has assimilated the culture of the occupying power." In the next phase, "we find the native is disturbed; he decides to remember who he is," and so immerses himself in the native culture. The third and final phase sees the writer emerging as a producer of a revolutionary literature of engagement. He is the "awakener of the people"; from the barrel of his pen comes "a fighting literature . . . a national literature." We see in Fanon's typology a rewriting of the history of nationalist consciousness to privilege as superior his historical and ideological kind: those intellectuals in the intense heat of the decolonizing struggle of the 1950s. See his *The Wretched of the Earth,* 222, 223 (cited hereafter as *Wretched*).

32. Philip Zachernuk, *Colonial Subjects: An African Intelligentsia and Atlantic Ideas.* Zachernuk acknowledges as "invaluable"—and rightly so—the pioneer work of modern African intellectual history, July's *The Origins of Modern African Thought,* which stands out because it focuses on the earliest native intellectuals to emerge out of *both* the French and the British colonies of West Africa (and independent Liberia, as well). However, Zachernuk (justly) critiques July for employing a "biographical structure" in his presentation of modern African intellection with the result that this intellection emerges in a form that is "episodic rather than systematic" (*Colonial Subjects,* 11).

33. Joyce, *A Portrait of the Artist as a Young Man,* 189.

34. J. A. Langley, introduction to Sekyi, *The Blinkards,* 2.

35. F. K. Drah, introduction to J. W. de Graft Johnson, *Towards Nationhood in West Africa,* xxiii (cited hereafter as *Towards Nationhood*).

Chapter 1

1. Spivak, "Theory in the Margin," in *Consequences of Theory,* ed. J. Arac and B. Johnson, 172.

2. Blyden, *Christianity, Islam, and the Negro Race,* 79 (cited hereafter as *Negro Race*).

3. Casely Hayford, *Gold Coast Native Institutions,* 8.

4. Horton, *Letters on the Political Condition of the Gold Coast,* iii.

5. De Graft Johnson, *Towards Nationhood in West Africa,* vi (cited hereafter as *Towards Nationhood*).

6. "Ethiopia" is the long-lived symbolic name of Africa in the religious, mythological, and intellectual usages of a transatlantic Pan-Negroism and Pan-Africanism. The name both draws on and exceeds the bounds of the historic East African country of Ethiopia. Ethiopianism was invented by the displaced Africans of the New World but gained currency in the Old from the mid-nineteenth century on. Blyden was the African popularizer of the designation "Ethiopia" in nationalist intellectual circles. Around 1872 Blyden founded a newspaper, with a circulation among the educated West African elite, called the *Ethiopian.* Proudly referring to himself as an "Ethiopian," Casely Hayford, Blyden's Gold Coast nationalist protégé, titled his 1911 quasi autobiography *Ethiopia Unbound.* The racialist, religious, and humanistic attributions Ethiopianism gave the continent were drawn from ancient Greek sources, the Bible, and traditions of European mysticism. The historic Ethiopia had held out against the forces of both Islam and European colonialism. For this reason, Ethiopianism could resolve out of the intact sovereignty of the East African country a free and independent Pan-African image to bolster a resistant anticolonial nationalism, as it does in Casely Hayford's *Ethiopia Unbound.* On Ethiopianism and its varied Pan-African manifestations, see, among others, Drake, *The Redemption of Africa and Black Religion*; Howe, *Afrocentrism: Mythical Pasts and Imagined Homes*; Shepperson, "Ethiopianism and African Nationalism"; Moses, *The Golden Age of Black Nationalism, 1850–1925.*

7. Soyinka, *Myth, Literature, and the African World,* 115.

8. Cf. Rev. Samuel Johnson, of Yoruba ethnicity (like Soyinka), who a century or so before Soyinka grappled with producing, in a Yoruba cultural identity, a difference that is nevertheless compatible with—hence lying in the same cultural continuum as—Christianity and the characterological tenets of Anglo-European civilization. Johnson's 1897 *The History of the Yorubas* (not published until 1921), invokes a tradition of Yoruba origin from the Near East to deal with the contradiction of a convergent divergence. According to Johnson, the Yorubas practiced primitive Christianity at their point of origin. Having migrated to their present location, there has been, over time, a falling off from the original— and this accounts for the divergence. Johnson believed that the fortuitous presence and influence of Christian missionaries among his contemporary Yorubas would restore to them the pure identity rooted in their Christian prehistory. Divergence (difference) negotiating a convergence (similarity) would not be lost to itself; the premise and promise of the modern in Johnson's history is self-restoration, not alienation. On the contradictory necessity of this

form of frontline cultural-nationalist thought, see Law, "Constructing 'A Real National History . . .'" in *Self-Assertion and Brokerage,* ed. P. F. de Moraes Farias and K. Barber.

9. Casely Hayford, *The Truth about the West African Land Question,* 101 (cited hereafter as *Land Question*).

10. Curtin, *The Image of Africa,* 413, 414.

11. Buxton, *The African Slave Trade and Its Remedy,* 457.

12. Cf. this letter dated 12 April 1844 from George Nicol, a "colony-born Sierra Leonean clergyman," to J. Warburton: "I am deeply convinced . . . that if Africa could be raised from her present degraded state of barbarism, superstition and vice, to any equal with the civilized world, recourse must be had to native agencies," in Wilson, *Origins of West African Nationalism,* 129 (cited hereafter as *Origins*).

13. Macaulay, "Minute on Indian Education," in *The Post-Colonial Studies Reader,* ed. Bill Ashcroft et al.

14. This is Sarbah, in his 1906 *Fanti National Constitution,* 250.

15. See Wilson, "T. J. Bowen on the Need to Develop a West African Middle Class," in his *Origins,* 129–30. Wilson takes the extract from Bowen's *Adventures and Missionary Labours in Several Countries in the Interior of Africa.*

16. The validity of the concept-category of class to an understanding of African social relations remains an ongoing debate in African(ist) sociologies of politics, history, anthropology, and literature. The debates are conducted from perspectives coming out of the radical traditions of Marxism, Fanonism, and dependency theory, on the one hand, and the relatively "conservative" traditions of Weberian and American sociology, on the other. A sampling of the debates (in English) can be found in the following works: For a political sociology, see, among others, Gutkind and Waterman, eds., *African Social Studies: A Radical Reader*; Hodgkin, *Nationalism in Colonial Africa.* The "Weberian" perspective in a political sociology is represented in the essays gathered in Lloyd, ed., *The New Elites of Tropical Africa*; a Weberian manifestation in a historical sociology is perhaps found in Kilson, "Nationalism and Social Classes in British West Africa." A critical review of the state of the debate on class from various political-sociological perspectives, including that of dependency theory, is provided in Katz, *Marxism, Africa and Social Class: A Critique of the Relevant Theories.* For the Fanonian perspective, there is of course Fanon's two-in-one political and cultural critique of class in Africa in *The Wretched of the Earth.* For a Fanonian perspective in a literary sociology, see Lazarus, *Resistance in Postcolonial African Fiction*; Ngugi, *Decolonising the Mind.* The debate on class in an African literary sociology is represented, either explicitly or implicitly, in Amuta, *The Theory of African Literature*; Gugelberger, ed., *Marxism and African Literature*; Irele, *The African Experience in Literature and Ideology*; Obiechina, *An African Popular Literature.* For a critical review of the debates in a historical sociology, see Zeleza, "The Rise and Mutation of African Historiographies"; Temu and Swai, *Historians and Africanist History: A Critique.*

17. On the *asikafo* of Asante, see Wilks, *Asante in the Nineteenth Century,* 692–705. Wilks characterizes the *asikafo* as "a well defined class" (693), possessed of an identifiable "middle class interest" (699), and whose "level of consciousness [by the 1880s] . . . was such that they should probably be regarded as constituting a small but growing bourgeois middle class" (705).

18. R. Jenkins, "Gold Coasters Overseas, 1880–1919," 7 (cited hereafter as "Gold Coasters"). In nineteenth-century Gold Coast, Jenkins finds three distinctive "Euro-African" constellations. Created within the spheres of control and influence of different Euro-

peans—Danish, Dutch, German-Swiss, and British—they each have different histories and degrees of European acculturation.

19. Hall, "New Ethnicities," in *The Post-Colonial Studies Reader*, ed. Bill Ashcroft et al.

20. From the 1850s on, conversion and Western education of Africans generated, as Zachernuk notes, middle-class "products of the colonial system, created to provide the clerical and other skills required by the colonial government, missions and commercial firms." Zachernuk, whose focus is on colonial southern Nigeria, implies further that special circumstances under the new dispensation made for the socioeconomic differentiation of this middle class as such. The members of the emergent middle class "were well placed to adapt to the new opportunities of the colonial era"; and "Because the colonial order required their skills, the educated community was able to reach new standards of wealth and prestige." Privileged, relative to others, to be a significant shareholder in and beneficiary of a colonial economic, social, and cultural dividend, this group emerges in vertical differentiation from these others, characterized by Zachernuk as "peasant producers and laborers." "They were an elite in the sense that they possessed advantages not available to the unlettered." Geiss, surveying the Gold Coast scene, confirms that an emergent group, "termed by the British 'educated natives' or 'middle class,'" whose members "gained their living as merchants and lawyers and also in the infant colonial administration," formed "a kind of aristocracy vis-à-vis the African population during the latter half of the nineteenth century."

This group was a privileged intermediary, too, since, according to Zachernuk, its members "could communicate directly with the British" and were recognized by others among the colonized not similarly privileged as "valuable allies in dealing with colonial authorities." In this function the African middle class, especially its articulate intelligentsia, bridged the otherwise wide communicative, social, and cultural gap between the alien rulers and the generality of the ruled. In the Gold Coast, as Bjorn Edsman has established, it was a minuscule intelligentsia of lawyers, especially, who occupied the vanguard of the intermediary role of the middle class, combining in that role what Farias and Barber have called "self-assertion and brokerage."

Above this middle class, in the vertically differentiated colonial society, Kilson finds an "imported oligarchy" functioning as an "upper or ruling class" and comprised of the "small but economically dominant group of European entrepreneurs, business administrators, senior colonial officials, district officers, and the array of lesser civil servants."

Farias and Barber further point out the origins of the West African middle class in a social geography of coastal and near-coastal; hence its "middleness" is also a matter of its being sociogeographically "poised between the African hinterland and the tiny but powerful class of white administrators, missionaries and traders." The West African middle class "mediated in politics, trade, and in cultural activities, representing the Africans to the Europeans and the Europeans to the Africans."

See, variously, Zachernuk, *Colonial Subjects*, 13–14, and also 19–46; Geiss, *Pan-African Movement*, 19; Edsman, *Lawyers in Gold Coast Politics* (cited hereafter as *Lawyers*); Farias and Barber, *Self-Assertion and Brokerage*, 1–10; Kilson, "Nationalism and Social Classes in British West Africa," 374–75.

"Middle class" in the singular is a useful analytic category since over time and space this sociocultural stratum bears an invariant intermediary character. "Middleness" is not just given; it is a position *self-consciously* occupied by those to whom it is given. In *The Nation and Its Fragments*, Chatterjee, describing a colonial Indian middle class placed similarly as the colonial African middle class, assesses the positionality in between as comprised of "social agents who are conscious [of themselves and their possibilities] as a 'middle term' in a social relationship" (35). And this (self)-consciousness about being such is persistent over time and space. Nevertheless, Zachernuk, with an eye to restoring "heterogeneity to representations of colonial subjects" (*Colonial Subjects,* 9), importantly shows us how substantively this sociocultural formation is also a heterogeneous assemblage. Zachernuk details, in the southern Nigerian setting: the historical formation; the alterations in ethnocultural, demographic, and geo-spatial composition; and the changing historical, ideational, and ideological contexts of the ideas and action of the middle-class colonial intelligentsia over the span of roughly a century. As with southern Nigeria, so with the Gold Coast/Ghana and elsewhere. Middle-classness is to be understood in the African setting in the variety of its incarnations, across genders, generations, and fractious ethnicities; in the relative distributions of privilege and "unprivilege" within and across it; and in its varied locations in geography, culture, and power. (Hence Zachernuk settles on "medial classes" rather than "middle class" as his working proposition.)

Somewhat comparable to Zachernuk's analysis of southern Nigeria, Bhekizizwe Peterson provides in his *Missionaries, Monarchs and African Intellectuals* an analysis of an intermediate "kholwa" group produced by missionary education in para-colonial Natal and the Rand in South Africa. In the Nigerian and South African instances, as in the Ghanaian, we see a middle-class intelligentsia negotiating a problem they share in common at the post-encounter frontline: figuring out a modernity that would also be "African."

21. In Davidson's memorable characterization in *Black Man's Burden,* those entering the colonial schools encountered a sign that read: "ABANDON AFRICA, ALL YE WHO ENTER HERE" (42).

22. Okonkwo, *Heroes of West African Nationalism,* 1 (cited hereafter as *Heroes*).

23. *The Lagos Standard,* 11 March 1896, quoted in Zachernuk, *Colonial Subjects,* 57.

24. Appiah, *In My Father's House,* 149.

25. "Extract of a letter . . . dated Aug. 12, 1910, from Blyden to Casely Hayford," appendix B in Casely Hayford, *William Waddy Harris, the West African Reformer,* lix.

26. Mudimbe, *The Invention of Africa,* 185.

27. Blyden, *Liberia's Offering,* v.

28. This is Attoh Ahuma's lead essay in his similarly titled collection, *The Gold Coast Nation and National Consciousness* (cited hereafter as *Gold Coast*).

29. Kimble, *A Political History of Ghana,* 91 (cited hereafter as *Political History*).

30. See, among others, Bolt, *Victorian Attitudes to Race*; Stepan, *The Idea of Race in Science.*

31. On Creole Pan-African identification in Sierra Leone and how it grew out of, and contributed to, problematic relations between the Creoles and indigenous Sierra Leoneans, see K. Kanneh, *African Identities,* 48–62.

32. Sartre, "Black Orpheus," in his *"What is Literature?" and Other Essays,* 296.

33. Marx writes: "Men make their own history, but they do not make it just as they please; they do not make it under circumstances chosen by themselves, but under circumstances directly encountered, given and transmitted from the past." Marx, *The Eighteenth Brumaire of Louis Bonaparte,* 15.

34. West, "Marxist Theory and the Specificity of Afro-American Oppression," in *Marxism and the Interpretation of Culture,* ed. C. Nelson and L. Grossberg, 24.

35. Fanon, *Black Skin, White Masks,* 134.

36. Bakhtin, *The Dialogic Imagination,* 293–94.

37. The phrase "emotive intentionality" is JanMohamed's. See *Manichean Aesthetics,* 6.

38. Nkrumah, *Ghana,* 185.

39. I derive "Blank Darkness" from Christopher Miller's *Blank Darkness: Africanist Discourse in French.*

Chapter 2

1. Casely Hayford, *The Truth about the West African Land Question,* 99. (Cited hereafter as *Land Question.*)

2. Appiah, *In My Father's House,* 80.

3. Mudimbe, *The Invention of Africa,* 17.

4. Spivak, *A Critique of Postcolonial Reason,* 211, 212.

5. Brantlinger, *Rule of Darkness,* 196.

6. Mudimbe, *The Invention of Africa,* 199–200.

7. Appiah, *In My Father's House,* 54.

8. Foucault, "What Is an Author?" in *Textual Strategies,* ed. J. Harari, 160.

9. Bhabha, *The Location of Culture,* 45. Emphasis in original.

10. On the ordering of natural and social worlds as knowledge that bolsters—and is bolstered by—the wielders of social power, see, among Foucault's many works on the subject, *The Order of Things*; *Power/Knowledge.*

11. For Weber's elaboration of "rationalization," see such works as his *The Protestant Ethic and the Spirit of Capitalism* (cited hereafter as *Protestant Ethic*); and his *The Theory of Social and Economic Organization.*

12. Marcuse, *One Dimensional Man.*

13. On modernity as inaugurating a global society, see A. Giddens's *The Consequences of Modernity.* See also the contributions by S. Hall and A. McGrew, chapters 6 ("The West and the Rest: Discourse and Power") and 14 ("A Global Society?"), respectively, in S. Hall et al., *Modernity.*

14. Among others, see P. Gilroy's critique in *The Black Atlantic* of Habermas, preeminent theorist of the modern, for being blinkered by ethnocentrism.

15. Spivak, "Can the Subaltern Speak?" in *Marxism and the Interpretation of Culture,* ed. C. Nelson and L. Grossberg, 291.

16. Elsewhere Weber appears to recognize the error of his ways in proposing the West as the be-all and end-all. He writes, in an acknowledgement of the relativity of truth and plurality of worldviews:

> The fate of an epoch that has eaten of the tree of knowledge is that it must . . . recognize that general views of life and the universe can never be the products of increasing empirical knowledge, and that the highest ideals, which move us most forcefully, are always formed only in the struggle with other ideals which are just as sacred to others as ours are to us.

Quoted by D. Harvey in his *The Condition of Postmodernity,* vii.

17. Bhabha suggests that we see "the image of post-Enlightenment man tethered to . . . his dark reflection, the shadow of colonized man" (*Location of Culture,* 44).

18. Chow, "Where Have All the Natives Gone?" in *Contemporary Postcolonial Theory: A Reader*, ed. P. Mongia, 124.

19. On imperial calculation and strategy, see A. JanMohamed, "The Economy of Manichean Allegory," in *"Race,"Writing, and Difference*, ed. H. L. Gates, Jr., 78–106. (Cited hereafter as "Manichean Allegory.")

20. Coetzee, *Foe*, 121–22.

21. Beckett, *Three Novels*, 31.

22. See, among others, Bhabha, "The Other Question," in *Location of Culture*, 66–84; Said, *Orientalism*; S. Slemon, "Monuments of Empire"; and Spurr, *The Rhetoric of Empire*. On the production of "Africa" in imperial allegory, specifically, see, among others, McClintock, *Imperial Leather*; and Miller, *Blank Darkness*.

23. Toynbee is quoted by Abraham in *Africa in Search of Ideology*, 60.

24. Quoted by Lindqvist in *"Exterminate All the Brutes"*, 8. (Cited hereafter as *"Brutes"*.)

25. Spivak, "Theory in the Margin," in *Consequences of Theory*, ed. J. Arac and B. Johnson, 172.

26. Fanon, *The Wretched of the Earth*, 212.

27. Awoonor-Renner, *This Africa*, 27.

28. The theme of African regeneration is a staple of preindependence nationalist writings across the continent. There is, for instance, "The Regeneration of Africa" (1905–1906), by the South African Pixley I. Seme, a cofounder and one-time president of the African National Congress. See *Ideologies of Liberation in Black Africa, 1856–1970*, ed. J. A. Langley, 261–65. (Cited hereafter as *Ideologies*.) A chapter of the same title is to be found in the Nigerian B. Omoniyi's *A Defence of the Ethiopian Movement*. The theme resounds in the 1937 work *Renascent Africa* by Omoniyi's compatriot N. Azikiwe.

29. Gikandi gives the designation a central analytical value in his examination of the postindependence works of Achebe. See his *Reading Chinua Achebe*. Gikandi deploys "national allegory" also in "The Politics and Poetics of the National Formation," in *From Commonwealth to Post-Colonial*, ed. A. Rutherford. Gikandi reads Achebe, in the domain of African modernist aesthetics, as being in some profound sense the origin. Part of the argument of this book, however, is that the middle-class making of the national allegory has not only a relevance to understanding the preindependence writers, but is an activity in fact inherited from these precursors by their postindependence successors.

30. See Ahmad, "Jameson's Rhetoric of Otherness and the 'National Allegory,'" 3–25.

31. Jameson, "Third World Literature in the Era of Multinational Capital," 15.

32. *Transition* was the name given to the major African intellectual journal produced on African soil in the early postindependence era, founded by the Ugandan (and Asian-African) Rajat Neogy. Captured in the name is the African nationalist imaginary of the still-to-come. Soyinka's appropriation of Yoruba mythology and metaphysics to mediate his—and an African—literary-nationalist role in his *Myth, Literature and the African World* speaks to the same point. In a reading of the god-figure Ogun, from the Yoruba pantheon, Soyinka explains that, in Yoruba existential metaphysics, this god-figure "correlates . . . with the fourth area of existence . . . labelled the abyss of transition." As in African middle-class nationalist self-invention, Ogun emerges in a myth-allegory as the exemplary embodiment of pioneer activism: his "unique essentiality" in Yoruba metaphysics is as "*the embodiment of the social, communal will invested in a part of its choice.*" This, as we have seen, is the

postimperial allegorical proposition at the nationalist frontline of whole displaced into, hence represented in, part. Soyinka proposes further:

> Ogun is the embodiment of challenge, the Promethean instinct in man, constantly at the service of society for its full self-realization. Hence his *role of explorer through primordial chaos,* which he conquered, then bridged, with the aid of the artifacts of his science. . . . Ogun experienced the process of being literally torn asunder in cosmic winds, of rescuing himself from the precarious edge of total dissolution by harnessing the untouched part of himself, the will.

Soyinka's retrieval of Ogun as Muse of (a tragic) metaphysics of Will thus makes the god-figure into a relevant metaphor for the challenge, at the frontline, of African modernity—as yet giving itself as "chaos" to be navigated, of middle-class self-rescue from exogenously imposed alienation ("dissolution"). The frontline is of course what is given a poetic cast by the writer as "the abyss of transition." See pp. 26 and 30. Emphases added.

33. Sarbah, *Fanti National Constitution,* 250.

34. See Appiah's "Tolerable Falsehoods: Agency and the Interests of Theory," in *Consequences of Theory,* ed. Arac and Johnson, 63–90. Myths (or representations that are "falsehoods") come out in Appiah's argument as pragmatically invested with an interest in structuring the world for their makers in tolerably livable—and for the critic always necessarily incomplete—ways.

35. Danquah, "Self-Help and Expansion," in *The Political Awakening of Africa,* ed. R. Emerson and M. Kilson, 53.

36. Hall, "Cultural Identity and Diaspora," in *Identity: Community, Culture, Difference,* ed. J. Rutherford, 222.

37. Nkosi, *Tasks and Masks,* 1.

38. Nkrumah, *Ghana,* 215.

39. Varadharajan, *Exotic Parodies,* xiv.

40. Casely Hayford, *Gold Coast Native Institutions,* 81. (Cited hereafter as *Native Institutions.*)

41. See, for instance, the revisionist reading in *Location of Culture* by Bhabha of Fanon's political self-representations. The expression "politics of narcissism" (63) is Bhabha's.

42. Zachernuk, *Colonial Subjects,* 45.

43. Horton, *West African Countries and Peoples,* 175.

44. See Lynch, ed. *Black Spokesman: Selected Published Writings of E. W. Blyden.* (Cited hereafter as *Black Spokesman.*) Lynch authors, additionally, *Edward Wilmot Blyden: Pan-Negro Patriot.* (Cited hereafter as *Pan-Negro Patriot.*)

45. Brantlinger notes this contradiction: "Paradoxically, abolitionism contained the seeds of empire. . . . [A]bolition was not purely altruistic but . . . economically conditioned. . . . Applied to Africa . . . humanitarianism did point insistently to imperialism" (*Rule of Darkness,* 174).

46. Buxton proclaims in his book that Africa, "bound in the chains of the grossest ignorance, is prey to the most savage superstition" (10–11). Africa is ruled over by "a rabble of petty chiefs . . . most ignorant . . . and the greatest vagabonds on earth" (289); the "African population [is] in a state of callous barbarity, which can only be effectually counteracted by Christian civilization" (244).

47. On the justifications of extermination, see Knox, *The Races of Man*; and W. W. Reade, *Savage Africa.* Lindqvist paraphrases the latter thus:

W. Winwoode Reade . . . ends his book *Savage Africa* . . . with a [Darwinist] predic-
tion on the future of the black race.

Africa will be shared between England and France. . . . Under European rule, the
Africans will dig the ditches and water the deserts. It will be hard work, and the
Africans themselves will probably become extinct. "We must learn to look at this
result with composure. It illustrates the beneficent law of nature, that the weak must
be devoured by the strong."

A grateful posterity will honor the memory of the blacks. One day, young ladies
will sit tearfully beneath the palm trees and read *The Last Negro*. And the Niger will
be as romantic a river as the Rhine. (*"Brutes"*, 130–31)

48. Blyden, "Study and Race," in *Origins of West African Nationalism*, by H. Wilson,
252. (Cited hereafter as *Origins*.)

49. Blyden, *Christianity, Islam and the Negro Race*, 277. (Cited hereafter as *Negro
Race*.)

50. See such essays as "The Origin and Purpose of African Colonization" (94–112);
"Echoes from Africa" (130–52); and "African Colonization" (337–73), in *Negro Race*.

51. Irele, *The African Experience in Literature and Ideology*, 97.

52. Mazzini, "Principles of Cosmopolitanism," in *Life and Writings of Joseph Mazzini*,
vol. 3, 15. (Cited hereafter as *Writings*.)

53. See, for a classic example, Du Bois's 1897 "The Conservation of Races," in *The
Seventh Son: The Thought and Writings of W.E.B. Du Bois*, vol. 1, ed. J. Lester. Du Bois's
piece shows the influence of the thought of his mentor, Alexander Crummell, who spent
twenty years in Liberia (1853–73) and collaborated with Blyden in working out the po-
litico-intellectual agenda of Pan-Negroism.

54. Malkki, "Citizens of Humanity," 42.

55. Crummell quotes Mill's doctrine as set out below in his 1870 piece "Our National Mistakes and the Remedy for Them." See *Origins*, 105–17.

56. Comparing the German and the Liberian, Lynch notes that

Herder did not believe in the inherent superiority of one nation over another, just as
Blyden did not believe that one race was inherently superior to another. They both
believed that the ultimate goal of a nation or race was to serve humanity at large, and
that the individual could fulfill himself best through unselfish, dedicated service to
nation or race. (*Pan-Negro Patriot*, 61)

57. Hegel, *Phenomenology of Spirit*, 47. Emphases added.

58. Fanon could be characterizing Blyden's endeavors when he writes in *The Wretched
of the Earth*:

The concept of negritude . . . was the emotional if not the logical antithesis of that
insult which the white man flung at humanity. This rush of negritude against the
white man's contempt showed itself in certain spheres to be the one idea capable of
lifting interdictions and anathemas. . . . The unconditional affirmation of African
culture has succeeded the unconditional affirmation of European culture. (212–
13)

59. Blyden privileges educated West Africans in his project of African modernity
apparently because "By the early 1870s," as Lynch notes, "it had become clear to Blyden
that the modern trans-tribal West African nation which he envisaged would not come
about through any large scale New World black emigration to West Africa" (*Black Spokesman*, xix).

60. Kingsley and Blyden met in London in 1898. Lynch notes that "Miss Kingsley became a powerful ally of Blyden in the task of getting Europeans to understand and appreciate the African social system" (*Pan-Negro Patriot,* 206).

61. Langley, *Pan-Africanism and Nationalism in West Africa,* 112.

62. See also Sarbah, *Fanti National Constitution,* xi-xii, xiii-xiv, 127, 248, for other approving references to Kingsley.

Blyden eulogizes this public-spirited woman—she had died en route to South Africa on a humanitarian mission in 1900—as "a spirit sent to serve Africa and the African race in a way which it was not given to others to serve them." Kingsley was to be commended for "introducing the African to Europe, and pleading for more patient and accurate study of his character . . . his customs, and his institutions." In Blyden's reading—naïve, no doubt— Kingsley was a redeemer of the imperial idea in showing that British imperialism, in spite of its militarism, was reconcilable with a humanitarian and egalitarian internationalism. See Blyden, *West Africa before Europe,* 2–5.

63. About the "public sphere in the political realm," a public sphere of "civil society," Habermas, looking at its modern European emergence, has noted that "through the vehicle of public opinion it put the state in touch with the needs of society." Nancy Fraser has recently clarified the public sphere further as

> designat[ing] a theatre in modern societies in which political participation is enacted through the medium of talk. It is the space in which citizens deliberate about their common affairs, and hence an institutionalized arena of discursive interaction. This arena is conceptually distinct from the state; it is the site for the production and circulation of discourses that can in principle be critical of the state.

See Habermas, *The Structural Transformation of the Public Sphere,* 30–31; and Fraser, "Rethinking the Public Sphere," in *The Cultural Studies Reader,* ed. S. During, 519.

The Gold Coast Aborigines' Rights Protection Society, founded in 1897, gives the Gold Coast public sphere its most practical and vigorous political expression in the late-nineteenth and early-twentieth century. But the A.R.P.S. does not invent this public sphere. We must credit that to the original "public intellectuals" of the Gold Coast, Charles Bannerman (1828–1872) of Accra, in the eastern Gold Coast, and James Hutton Brew (1844–1915) of Cape Coast, in the west. These two are the indigenous pioneers of public-interest journalism in the country, Bannerman by founding the *Accra Herald* in 1857 (later the *West African Herald*), and Brew the *Gold Coast Times* in 1874, followed by the *Western Echo/Gold Coast Echo* in 1885. The two, then, stand out as originals in the creation, in a Gold Coast fourth estate, of a critical institutional space under the colonial order, a public sphere, where "opinion could present itself as that of society." Casely Hayford acknowledges the inspirational contribution of Bannerman and Brew (Hayford's uncle, and the man under whom he served as subeditor of the *Times*) in his honor roll of nineteenth-century Gold Coast journalism in his chapter "Landmarks," in *Native Institutions* (see pp. 171–81). See also Jones-Quartey's updating of the contributions of the two pioneers in his *History, Politics and Early Press in Ghana.*

The discussion in the following chapter of the thought and writing of figures who self-consciously project themselves as public intellectuals should be seen in the light of critical challenges confronting these intellectuals of forging a viable Gold Coast (nationalist) public sphere under the colonial order.

64. Loomba, "Overworlding the 'Third World,'" in *Colonial Discourse and Post-Colonial Theory: A Reader,* ed. P. Williams and L. Chrisman, 305–23.

Chapter 3

1. Reindorf, *The History of the Gold Coast and Asante.* (Cited hereafter as *History.*)

2. On the various "genres" of Gold Coast historiography, see R. Jenkins, "Intellectuals, Publication Outlets and 'Past-Relationships,'" in *Self-Assertion and Brokerage,* ed. de Moraes Farias and K. Barber, 69–70, 73.

3. "Accra" and "Akra" were more or less interchangeable, in the nineteenth century, with "Ga." The Gas are a sub-division of a larger collectivity of cognate groups, the Ga-Adangme. These groups share a myth of a common eastern origin—southwestern Nigeria—and common migration to the east-central seaboard of Gold Coast/Ghana and the interior districts behind it.

4. See "British Letters of Patent, Constituting the Office of Governor and Commander-in-Chief of the Gold Coast Colony, and Providing for the Government Thereof. Westminster January 13th, 1886," app. X of Sarbah's *Fanti Customary Laws,* 302.

5. Casely Hayford quotes the British paper, the *Times,* protesting the intentions of the British to invade Asante in 1864: "What good can come out of that? If we capture Kumasi [capital of Asante] . . . [and] we destroy it, we destroy at once the commercial value of Cape Coast." *Gold Coast Native Institutions,* 264. (Cited hereafter as *Native Institutions.*)

6. See Priestley's "The Emergence of an Elite," in *The New Elites of Tropical Africa,* ed. P. C. Lloyd; and her *West African Trade and Coast Society.*

7. See the section "Native Institutions: the Commercial System," in Casely Hayford's *Native Institutions,* 95–100.

8. Reindorf provides a history of missionary activity in Chapter XIX of the *History.* For more on mission history in the Gold Coast/Ghana, see Bartels, *The Roots of Ghana Methodism;* Debrunner, *A History of Christianity in Ghana;* Graham, *The History of Education in Ghana;* Odamtten, *The Missionary Factor in Ghana's Development up to the 1880s;* Smith, *The Presbyterian Church of Ghana, 1835–1960;* Wiltgen, *Gold Coast Mission History, 1471–1880.*

9. R. Jenkins, "In Pursuit of the African Past," in *Under the Imperial Carpet,* ed. R. Lotz and I. Pegg, 113. (Cited hereafter as "African Past.")

10. Kimble, *A Political History of Ghana,* 521. (Cited hereafter as *Political History.*) Kimble compares Reindorf's *History* and Ellis's 1893 *A History of the Gold Coast of West Africa,* and points out that, in contrast to Reindorf's self-conscious "nativism," Ellis's is a Eurocentric account. For where the former shows us Gold Coast natives as initiators of, and actors in, their own history, the focus of the latter is on European discovery of this portion of Africa and on what European actors did in, over, and to it.

11. Consider, for instance, Claridge's monumental 1915 two-volume *A History of the Gold Coast and Ashanti* (London: Frank Cass, 1966). Kimble notes that Claridge's imaginary is an imperial one, showing in the way he "displayed a marked bias in favour of the Ashantis," whom he presented as "'the most powerful and in fact the only really important kingdom and empire that the Gold Coast has ever seen'" (*Political History,* 526).

12. "Tshi" is a nineteenth-century spelling of what is now exclusively spelled "Twi."

13. Kimble sees the *History* as "lacking in general perspective," "overloaded with unimportant detail" (*Political History,* 521), a point which the interpretation offered above is in total variance with. The failure to work out a general perspective is Kimble's, not Reindorf's.

14. Kimble, citing "Petition of 9 Apr. 1895, to Secretary of State (of the British Colonies) from King, Chiefs, natives and other inhabitants . . . of Cape Coast" (*Political History,* 337).

15. The words of Mary Kingsley in her letter of July 1898 to Sarbah (see app., *Fanti National Constitution,* 260).

16. Sarbah, "Petition of 5 June 1889, to the Secretary of State [for the Colonies]." Quoted by Crabbe in *John Mensah Sarbah,* 102 n. 5.

17. See Sarbah, *Fanti Customary Laws,* 3–6. The subject of the Akan as an ethnocultural federation is also treated in Danquah's *The Gold Coast Akan;* and in his earlier *Gold Coast: Akan Laws and Customs and the Akim Abuakwa Constitution.*

18. Attoh Ahuma, *The Gold Coast Nation and National Consciousness,* 1. (Cited hereafter as *Gold Coast.*)

19. See *Political History,* 331.

20. Salmon, *The Crown Colonies of Great Britain,* 75. (Cited hereafter as *Crown Colonies.*)

21. Casely Hayford is bitter in *Native Institutions* about the way "British . . . aggrandisement" has "shattered" the "trade based on good-will and mutual confidence between merchants on the Gold Coast and their friends . . . in Ashanti" (95). Sarbah traces a history in which initiatives in African economic enterprise in the Gold Coast in the nineteenth century had quickly been overwhelmed by unfair European competition in *Fanti National Constitution* (xv-xvi). See also S. Rohdie's "Gold Coast Aborigines Abroad."

22. See app. B of Casely Hayford's *The Truth about the West African Land Question,* 162. (Cited hereafter as *Land Question.*)

23. Sarbah is adamant that there is a "similarity of the constitution of town and village communities and of the principles regulating national public administration and government among the aboriginal tribes of Africa," a matter "now admitted by students of jurisprudence and others" (*Fanti National Constitution,* 232).

24. Langley, *Pan-Africanism and Nationalism in West Africa,*133. See also chap. 6 n 22 of this study.

25. Chambers, *Room for Maneuver,* 1–2.

26. Chambers makes a distinction between "oppositional behavior" and "resistance," the former more or less unselfconscious, the latter more or less self-conscious, while conceding also that this distinction is a fragile one. He notes:

> That there is a very large gray area straddling the categories of resistance and opposition is demonstrated, for example, by guerilla warfare . . . —a mode of resistance that relies on oppositional tactics—but also by the way oppositional behavior shades towards resistance as it becomes more self-conscious and/or in 'tight' contexts where . . . it is *regarded* as a form of resistance. (12)

The anticolonial politics prosecuted by the A.R.P.S., and the N.C.B.W.A. after it, may be seen as straddling these unstable poles, now weakly (if always self-consciously) oppositional, now strongly resistant. The "oppositional mode" would then be the politics of sending deputations to the metropopole to plead the Gold Coast/West African case; of submitting petitions, memoranda, etc., questioning colonial policy to either the Colonial Office in London or the colonial Governor; of producing books such as Hayford's *Land Question.* The "guerilla" mode of resistance will be the insurgent battles waged in colonial courtrooms in the 1920s and 1930s for which the A.R.P.S. legal luminary, Sekyi, and his sidekick, Kojo Thompson, have earned themselves permanent fame in the annals of Ghanaian nationalism (and notoriety in the eyes of the British colonial apologists and their historian-sympathizers). On the activities of Sekyi and Thompson in this regard, see Edsman, *Lawyers in Gold Coast Politics, c. 1900–1945,* esp. chapters 5 and 7. (Cited hereafter as *Lawyers.*)

27. Wilson, *Origins of West African Nationalism,* 38, 37. (Cited hereafter as *Origins.*)

28. Fanon, *The Wretched of the Earth,* 210.

29. Scott, "Colonial Governmentality," 191. Scott acknowledges his indebtedness to Talal Asad's essay "Conscripts of Western Civilization." For Asad, the modern, as it transpires in the encounter between the West and the Rest, is a scene of creative destruction where "new possibilities are constructed and old ones destroyed," and modernist origination brings into being "conditions in which only new (i.e., modern) choices can be made. The reason for this is that the changes involve the re-formation of subjectivities and the re-organization of social spaces in which subjects act and are acted upon." In Asad's view, "The modern state—imperial, colonial, post-colonial—has been crucial to these processes of construction/destruction." The notion of the modern as a predicament which furnishes "a way out" only in accordance with its preset terms and no other is what sounds in Asad's formulation; and it is that which this study argues confronts the frontline African nationalist intellectuals. Asad is quoted by Scott (p. 191). See also Gailey, ed., *Dialectical Anthropology,* 1:337.

30. Hegel, *The Philosophy of History,* 93.

31. Lynch, new introduction to the 3rd edition of *Fanti Customary Laws,* xii, xiii.

32. "The Meaning of the Expression Thinking 'in English'" is the title of a series of lectures delivered by Kobina Sekyi in 1943. In the summary of the Ghanaian historian Kofi Baku, these lectures "highlighted Sekyi's profound realization that language was no more than thought in words. Every language, therefore incorporated prejudices peculiar to it, and by implication, the adoption of a foreign language meant the adoption of a foreign viewpoint." See Baku, *Kobina Sekyi of Ghana: An Annotated Bibliography,* 9.

33. For the story of Mfantsipim and its preeminent place in the middle-class imagining and making of Ghana, see Boahen, *Mfantsipim and the Making of Ghana.* Current UN Secretary General Kofi Annan is a product of Mfantsipim.

34. See "Reviews: 'Fanti Customary Laws,'" app. in Attoh Ahuma, *Memoirs of West African Celebrities,* 249, 251. (Cited hereafter as *Celebrities.*)

35. See chap. 3, "Indirect Rule Elaborated," in *Lawyers.* Edsman quotes the 28th Aug. 1944 edition of the Accra-based newspaper *African Morning Post* complaining against the recently passed Gold Coast Native Authority Bill for endeavoring "to keep native customary laws in a static condition" (207). What had materialized under a manipulative colonial order was the fear Sarbah had expressed some fifty years before in *Fanti Customary Laws.* He wrote then:

> I am quite alive to the danger of reducing Customary Law to a condition of fixity in a semi-developed state of society, the effect of which may hinder the gradually operating innate generation of law by a process of natural development . . . which best accords with the varying needs and spirit of a people so circumstanced as the inhabitants of the Gold Coast. (xi)

36. The expression is Mahmood Mamdani's, and it recurs in his characterization of the nature of indirect rule in Africa in *Citizen and Subject.*

37. Blyden, "The Aims and Methods of a Liberal Education for Africans," in *Black Spokesman,* ed. H. Lynch, 231–45.

38. Cited by K. K. Prah in his *Essays on African Society and History,* 18.

39. Achebe, *Hopes and Impediments,* 160.

40. Sekyi, "Education with Particular Reference to a West African University," 1920, Acc. 325/64, Ghana National Archives, Cape Coast.

41. Langley, introduction to Sekyi, *The Blinkards,* 3.

42. "Been-to" is an anglophone West African designation for one who has returned home after visiting or living in the imperial metropole.

43. Du Bois, *The Souls of Black Folk,* 45.

44. Serialized in the journal *West Africa* from May to September 1918, excerpts from *The Anglo-Fanti* also appeared in Nancy Cunard's 1934 anthology *Negro,* 774–79. The full text has been published recently in *The Blinkards: A Comedy and the Anglo-Fanti* (1997).

45. Armah, *Fragments.*

46. Blyden's "Christianity and the Negro" appeared as an essay in 1876 and was included in his 1887 *Christianity, Islam and the Negro Race.* (Cited hereafter as *Negro Race.*)

47. Fanon, *Black Skin, White Masks,* 14.

48. Blyden, "Study and Race," in *Origins,* 249–50.

Chapter 4

1. The first deputation scheme, mooted in the period between 1885 and 1887, united eastern and western Gold Coast in a common demand for representative institutions in the colony. King Tackie's letter, which provides the epigraph to the chapter, is cited by F. Agbodeka in *African Politics and British Policy in the Gold Coast,* 126.

2. Cust, "Reflections on West African Affairs . . . Addressed to the Colonial Office," as quoted in Bhabha, *The Location of Culture,* 85.

3. Ibid., 85.

4. See app. D, "Bond, 6th March, 1844," in Casely Hayford's *Gold Coast Native Institutions,* 367–68.

5. Kimble, *A Political History of Ghana,* 550.

6. Horton proposes in *West African Countries and Peoples* a republican eastern Gold Coast and a western counterpart, the Fanti Confederation, with a constitutional monarchy.

7. See "Resolutions of the Select Committee of the House of Commons, 26 June 1865," in H. Wilson's *Origins of West African Nationalism,* 151–52.

8. This would be the agitation of the Fanti Confederation and its imitator in the eastern Gold Coast, the Accra Native Confederation. Horton's influence would be writ large over the constitution drawn up by the former.

9. Attoh Ahuma, "Colony or Protectorate? Thoughts on the Present Discontent," app. B in Casely Hayford's *Native Institutions,* 316.

10. Atto Ahuma, *The Gold Coast Nation and National Consciousness,* 1. (Cited hereafter as *Gold Coast.*)

11. The duration of sixty years begins, of course, with the signing of the Bond of 1844.

12. Rodger in *The African Mail* of 9 July 1909, qtd. in *Political History,* 93.

13. Bakhtin, *The Dialogic Imagination,* 362.

14. Mudimbe, *The Invention of Africa,* 195.

15. As argued by Appiah in "Tolerable Falsehoods," cognitive idealizations, whether of the natural or human world, proceed from an interest in influencing that world. Idealization

then is the containing mold by which interested men and women *will* the reduction of the real world to a predictable, hence controllable, shape. See *Consequences of Theory*, ed. J. Arac and B. Johnson, 63–90.

16. Rev. J. B. Anaman's *Gold Coast Guide* (1895) is perhaps the first native statement in print of the Gold Coast–ancient Ghana connection. Imperial Ghana, which covered parts of what more or less makes up present-day Mali, is said to have lasted for more than a thousand years. Danquah first mentions the link in *The Akim Abuakwa Handbook* in 1928.

17. Goody, "The Myth of a State," 473. (Cited hereafter as "Myth.")

18. Quoted in "A Great Ghanaian: Dr. J. B. Danquah, 'Doyen of Gold Coast Politics,'" by *The West African Review* (March 1957). Reproduced by H. K. Akyeampong, compiler of Danquah memorabilia in *Liberty: A Page from the Life of J. B.*, 6.

19. Edsman, *Lawyers in Gold Coast Politics*, 217.

20. Danquah, *Liberty of the Subject*.

21. K. G. Konuah, cited by Kwa O. Hagan in "The Literary and Social Clubs of the Past: Their Role in National Awakening in Ghana," 85. Membership of the Youth Conference was by way of these Literary and Social Clubs, widely distributed in and open to the youth of the Colony. Danquah's canalization of the activities of the Clubs into a would-be central directorate, the Conference, can be seen, as in Konuah's terms, as one of the effective ways in which a middle class vanguard had begun to assert an enabling pedagogical, if not political, counterweight against colonial hegemony. Consider, for instance, Danquah's versifying charge to the Youth of the Gold Coast (1938), reproduced by Hagan on the same page cited: "Buck up, O Youth and kill the bogey! / The bogey that your race is infant! / Know ye not that God is busy, / And helps only the few who are constant?" (For a recent update of scholarship on the Clubs see S. Newell, *Ghanaian Popular Fiction*, 53–59.)

22. Wright, *Black Power*, 65.

23. Balmer, *A History of the Akan Peoples of the Gold Coast*, 14. (Cited hereafter as *Akan Peoples*.)

24. Tempels, *Bantu Philosophy*, 16, 18.

25. Lord Cromer is quoted by Said in *Orientalism*, 37.

26. Rhodes, as quoted by Oldstone-Moore, "European Empires," <*http://www.wright.edu/~christopher.oldstone-moore/empires.htm*>.

27. Horsman, "Origins of Racial Anglo-Saxonism in Great Britain Before 1850," 410. Anglo-Saxonist doctrines and ideologies of racial supremacy are discussed in, among others: Brantlinger, *Rule of Darkness*; Curtin, *The Image of Africa*; Curtis, *Anglo-Saxons and Celts*.

28. Balmer's influence on Gold Coast nationalist hagiographer Magnus Sampson is obvious. Sampson devotes his 1937 *Gold Coast Men of Affairs* to the "memory of my old Principal and devoted Guardian, the late Rev. W. T. Balmer . . . a true lover of the African." In a work honoring the achievements of Gold Coast nationalism, it is Balmer's portrait which takes pride of place by appearing on the frontispiece. The rather lengthy introduction to the work (some thirty pages), incidentally, is furnished by J. B. Danquah, who writes:

> The Gold Coast people are everlastingly in [Sampson's] debt for rendering them this service of inestimable value, for, from these cameo pictures of the life stories of our great men and leaders, the youth of Mr. Sampson's age and those coming after would draw their inspiration, emulate the work of their forebears, and wherever possible, attempt to excel in the greatness of their contribution to our common inheritance. . . .

I have yet to meet a historical study of the kind more faithful to our articulate national ideal. (38)

29. Kwa Hagan quotes the revered Gold Coast internationalist, Dr. Aggrey ("Aggrey of Africa"), urging the youth of the Clubs in 1924 "to equip themselves intellectually and morally in order to be able in the near future to shoulder responsibilities as citizens and leaders of an emerging country" ("Literary and Social Clubs," 85). On Aggrey's influence on the young Nkrumah, see the latter's *Ghana,* 14–15.

30. The ideological inevitability of Akanization is revealed, for instance, in the nationalist imaginings of J. W. de Graft Johnson. In *Towards Nationhood in West Africa,* the Akan-Fanti Johnson wishfully foresees "the auspicious moment" when "Ashantees, Akims, Akwapims, Fantees [all Akan], Gas [non-Akan], Ewes [non-Akan], Ahantas [Akan], *and all,* would be drawn together *in one great Akan organization,* such as would have *naturally* evolved if Britain had not intervened too early in the history of the Gold Coast and Ashanti" (127, emphases added).

31. Cf. Peter Carstens's insight that "the retention or revival of tenuous [ethnic] loyalties are resources available to persons to establish prestige or esteem. . . . [T]he surest way to achieve recognition, prestige and esteem in the eyes of the ruling class as well as from the local(s) . . . is to participate in the externally imposed educational and religious institutions." [Here we might add "externally imposed *discursive* institutions," as also appropriate to our discussion]. He concludes: "it is only by manipulation of . . . internal [ethnic] status systems that [such persons] are able to gain access to other status sytems which are located in a higher class. The strategy of status manipulation is best seen then as a means of crossing class [or colonial race-caste, in our case] boundaries." Carstens is cited by I. Wallerstein in "Class and Status in Contemporary Africa," in *African Social Studies: A Reader,* ed. P. Gutkind and P. Waterman, 279.

32. Danquah's thesis is that "Ghana" is an Arab corruption of an original "Akane" or "Akana," "said to mean 'foremost, genuine.'" These names, he further suggests, should be seen as coinciding with the "old Babylonian race known as Akkad, Agade or Akana." See the entries on "Akan" and "Ananse," app. II, "Notes and Glossary of Akan Words," in his *The Akan Doctrine of God,* 198–99, 199–200.

33. Mauny's essay appears in *Africa* (July 1954): 200–213; Danquah's in *West African Review* (Nov. 1955): 968–70 and (Dec. 1955): 1107–11. Meyerowitz's "The Akan and Ghana" appears in *Man* 57 (June 1957): 83–88.

34. Meyerowitz, *The Akan of Ghana,* 21. Emphasis added.

In her article, "The Akan and Ghana," Meyerowitz concludes from the available "evidence" that "over a thousand years the Ghana people and the Akan (Saharan Libyan Berbers) by intermarrying with negro aboriginals in the western Sudan, underwent considerable racial modifications and admixtures" (87).

35. Meyerowitz, *The Akan of Ghana,* 15. Emphases added.

36. Meyerowitz, *Akan Traditions of Origin,* 124. Emphasis added.

37. Goody, "The Ethnohistory of the Akan in Ghana," 79.

38. Wallace-Johnson, the labor activist and left Pan-Africanist, was the leader of the militant West African Youth League. He and Azikiwe were deported from the Gold Coast in 1936 by the colonial authorities for fomenting "sedition." Johnson went on to found with Nkrumah, Bankole Awoonor-Renner, and others in 1945 the radical West African National Secretariat in London, with the manifesto that "Imperialism and colonial liberation are two irreconcilable opposites; a compromise between them is impossible. The death

of the one is the life of the other" (Adi, *West Africans in Britain, 1900–1960,* 129). Azikiwe became the first President of independent Nigeria in 1960.

39. As a long term objective "Ghana" has proved elusive, as witnessed by the titles of Armah's negative *The Beautyful Ones Are Not Yet Born* (1968) and Kojo Laing's "groping" novel *Search, Sweet Country* (1986). On the question of elusive Ghanaian nationhood, see the rather pretentious essay by P. Skalnik, "Why Ghana Is Not a Nation-State."

40. *Selected Poems of Edith Sitwell,* 67. Consider what might be an apologetic response to "Gold Coast Customs" in the following lines by Ghanaian poet Dorothy Kurankyi-Taylor, aptly titled "The Sensible Attitude":

> No, no, we do not believe in these things,
> these relics of the pre-imperial days.
> They have their place beside the buccaneers,
> the slave-marts, and Arabian merchandize,
> and warring tribesmen, and blood fueds [*sic*] and things;
> and they have left their tears about the hours
> and in the very laughter of the years,
> and cursed the places and the names with tales.
> Yes, they are things far better left to die. . . .
> But there is pathos in these foolish faiths,
> these last strongholds of a defeated race
> whose gods have played them false . . .
> these dark beliefs of a forgotten time,
> these whispers from the dead. How mystery-laden
> are their parent sepulchres, how vacant.

See *Reflected Thoughts,* 31.

Chapter 5

1. Symptomatic readings, we will recall, are based on the principle that texts, whether social or literary, cannot mean what they say (i.e., manifestly or overtly) and cannot say what they mean (i.e., latently or covertly). Textual and social meanings, then, are not fully present to themselves but are derived in the domain of the Other (rendered as Ideology and/ or the Unconscious). It is the task of elaborating the content of this Other, "buried" or "ghostly" scene of meaning—and how, in a "live" manner, it distortingly interferes with and insinuates itself into a manifest content—that falls on the critic who reads symptomatically. For Ngugi, of course, it is the structure of the colonial relationship, one that produces a serviceable African ancillary for its ends, that produces this Other scene, the Unconscious that alienates an African middle class from a sovereign meaning ("message") of its own.

2. Achebe's "Girls at War"—this short story appears with others in a collection whose title goes by the same name—is set during the civil war that killed a million Nigerians in the late 1960s. It is by situating himself in the events behind this story that Ngugi finds in Achebe's novelistic oeuvre an occasion to read not so much a culmination as a falling apart. The African nation, in this reading, is not a positive coming to coherence but a compromised structure, whose threatened falling apart must reveal the blemished truth of a contemporary African middle class to itself: its "hidden" messenger status. For Ngugi this status

makes this *pseudo*nationalist class, as he sees it, a bearer of, and a secret sharer in, a message historically not of its own fashioning. This is a message, moreover, which this class is condemned to secrete neocolonially even at a distance from, and in the absence of, the Source.

3. On the essence of the Faustian allegory, see note 23 of the introduction.

4. Casely Hayford, *The Truth about the West African Land Question,* 101. (Cited hereafter as *Land Question.*)

5. Ibid., 100. What Hayford refers to as "death"(-in-life), we might translate as the Unconscious.

6. In its original version, Hayford's piece was delivered on his behalf before students of a colonial institution in Lagos, Nigeria, going by the suggestive name New High Class School.

7. Cf. the second epigraph to the chapter. Attoh Ahuma, for all his rhetoric of self-consciousness and the nationalist exhortation to go back to the way of the fathers, experiences the imposed burden of the Nothingness of the past quite keenly. He is subject to this burden in a way that does not permit him to fully escape the language that makes savages out of the precolonial fathers and demonizes their culture. Yet these are the very fathers he idealizes elsewhere in *The Gold Coast Nation and National Consciousness.* What we see in the circumstances is the voice of a desirous middle class which, as it seeks, in the Orphean mode, the original terms with which to world Africa anew, is compelled to speak—and this is the dilemma of doubling Hayford addresses in his lament—with a forked tongue.

8. Kane, *Ambiguous Adventure,* 50.

9. Arhin, preface to *The Papers of George Ekem Ferguson,* vii. (Cited hereafter as *Papers.*)

10. In *Gold Coast Men of Affairs,* M. Sampson writes: "There is enough evidence for saying that the Colonial Office to-day owes more to no African of the Colonial Civil Service whose name stands on its roll of fame, than to . . . Ferguson." Sampson's Ferguson is a "dutiful" man whose "daring and brilliant achievements commanded the attention not only of Colonial administrators and authorities at the Colonial Office, but also the British and Foreign War Offices" (129). Ferguson's expeditions derived their urgency in the West African context of the Scramble for Africa, the intense struggle to acquire territory waged between the rival New Imperialisms of Britain, Germany, and France.

11. Such imaginings are reflected in Ferguson's speculations on the possible pre-ethnic linguistic unity of the Gold Coast and Hinterland. He writes:

> When we reflect that a thousand years ago resemblances amounting to mutual intelligibility existed among the languages of Anglo-Saxon England, of Upper and Lower Germany and of Holland but that now, whatever radical affinity scientific dissection may reveal among English, German or Dutch, it is well known that a person speaking only one of these needs an interpreter for the other two, it is not difficult to conceive that all the aborigines of the Colony and its Hinterland are of one stock. (*Papers,* 126)

If a greater Gold Coast is envisaged by Ferguson's work on the ground, these imaginings, in the mode of linguistic and ethnographic "science," amount to this groundwork's (ideological) justification. As we shall see in the next chapter, the "scientific" imaginary—articulated by Ferguson here—in which the middle class sees a role for itself of bridging past perfect (one people before) and future perfect (one people to come) has a parallel with the culturalist principles and practice defined in a middle-class nativist nationalism.

12. Cf. Sarbah's advocacy of "scientific colonization" in *Fanti National Constitution* (xx). And Hayford affirms: "There is no reason why . . . Africans should not also harness the discoveries of Science to our everyday need." See Sampson, ed., *West African Leadership,* 79.

13. Before Ferguson's analyses of the political economy of the Gold Coast (and its) Hinterland, Horton had written his pioneer *Political Economy of British Western Africa* (1865), revised and expanded into his *West African Countries and Peoples.* In this work, we read an agile mind utilizing the idea of *political economy* to rope the discontinuities between the so-called West African countries into a standard of uniform understanding. If Horton's effort translates these countries into measurable units in a relation of statistics, economic history and politics, the idea-concept that sustains their understanding as such, political economy, is itself part of the interlocking discourses of post-Enlightenment Europe investigating— and legitimating the transformations of—the foundations of society. These are discourses whose "scientific" self-emplacement in relation to their object, society, name them not only as modern but promote also a prestigious ideology of the modern. Before Ferguson, then, Horton's thoughtful action thus already desires the infusion, if not the imposition, of the modern and its ideology across a native sphere.

14. Take the case, for instance, of middle-class father, Samuel Ajayi Crowther, the southern Nigerian (Yoruba) who, in the era before the new-imperial rise of official racism, rose to occupy the high position of Anglican Bishop of West Africa. Crowther, the most prominent native linkman to modern Euro-Christian civilization in nineteenth-century West Africa argued in 1865:

> Africa has neither knowledge nor skill to devise plans to bring out her vast resources for her own improvement; and for want of Christian enlightenment, cruelty and barbarity overspread the land to an incredible degree. Therefor [*sic*] to claim Africa for the Africans alone, is to claim for her the right of a continued ignorance to practice cruelty and acts of barbarity as her perpetual inheritance. For it is certain, unless help come from without, a nation can never rise much above its present state.

See Wilson, *Origins of West African Nationalism,* 150.

15. Anderson, *Imagined Communities,* 18–19.

16. Conrad, *Heart of Darkness,* 52.

17. See, among others, Brantlinger's *Rule of Darkness,* 173–97.

18. *OED Online,* s.v. "distantiation": "The action or process of distantiating; putting or keeping at a distance."

19. Thus, for instance, Ocansey recounts—and chooses to be taught to forget—a moment on the streets of London when he is taunted by some English boys reminding him of his racial affiliation: "Halloa! blacky, can't you wash your face . . . and make it white?" To this racist insult he defers a response to his English companion who "kindly said, 'You must not take any notice of them, because they do not know any better'" (*African Trading,* 42). Compared to Fanon's reaction, in a similar moment where a white child points at him and says "Mama, a Negro!" Ocansey's silence is deafening. See Fanon, *Black Skin, White Masks,* 111 ff.

20. Before Ocansey, what we might call a syndrome of resignation to fatality—as it appears in the native son's "The past no longer is in my power," etc.—registers, for instance, in the careers of two eighteenth-century middle-class prototypes from the Gold Coast, Jacobus Capitein and Philip Quaque. On Capitein, see Abraham, *The Mind of Africa,* 124–25; and Prah, *Jacobus Eliza Johannes Capitein, 1717–1747*; and on Quaque, see Bartels, "Philip Quaque, 1741–1816."

21. Casely Hayford, *Ethiopia Unbound,* 183.

Chapter 6

1. The accolade is M. Sampson's. See his *Gold Coast Men of Affairs,* 163. (Cited hereafter as *Affairs.*) F. N. Ugonna repeats it in his introduction to the second edition of *Ethiopia Unbound* (p. vii). Between 1920 and 1930, Hayford dominated British West African nationalism as the founder and leader of the interterritorial National Congress of British West Africa.

2. Edsman, *Lawyers in Gold Coast Politics,* 249–50. (Cited hereafter as *Lawyers.*)

3. Casely Hayford, *Gold Coast Native Institutions,* 6. (Cited hereafter as *Native Institutions.*)

4. Sampson, *West African Leadership,* 79.

5. *OED Online,* s.v. "figura": "a person who represents some higher or supervening reality." See also Kermode, *The Genesis of Secrecy,* 104.

6. Ouologuem, *Bound to Violence,* 175.

7. On the history and significances of the designation "Ethiopia" see chap. 1, n. 6.

8. Quoted by La Guerre in *The Social and Political Thought of the Colonial Intelligentsia,* 15. (Cited hereafter as *Colonial Intelligentsia.*)

9. Geiss places the beginnings of the formation of the inter-imperial public sphere in "the philanthropic and humanitarian element in England, which from the late eighteenth century onwards time and time again stood up for the rights of Africans and Afro-Americans." He adds: "[I]n the beginning of the twentieth century elements of the British left . . . as well as Quakers and other groups, provided practical and political assistance to the nascent Pan-African and African nationalist movements . . . by their impact on Parliament and on public opinion" (*Pan-African Movement,* 13).

Hayford's criticisms of E. D. Morel's advocacy for Africa as being dangerously misguided lends a piquancy to the debates within the inter-imperial public sphere described. It was not a matter of metropolitans proposing and Africans meekly following, Hayford shows. See the opening chapters of his *The Truth about the West African Land Question.* (Cited hereafter as *Land Question.*)

10. See app., *Fanti National Constitution,* 260. Emphasis in the original.

11. Geiss notes of the twentieth-century career of Pan-Africanism that "It was the West Indies . . . that produced men of great significance in [its] development . . . such as . . . Sylvester Williams, Marcus Garvey, George Padmore and Claude McKay." If these were all English-speaking, "A role of similar importance was played by West Indians from the French possessions in the development of nationalism in francophone Africa and the 'Négritude' movement after World War I: René Maran, Gaston Monnerville, Aimé Césaire . . . Frantz Fanon . . . Jean Price-Mars." Du Bois, organizer of four Pan-African Congresses between 1919 and 1927, became the twentieth century's "Grand Ol' Man" of Pan-Africanism, with "most of [his] followers . . . in France after 1919 [being] politicians and intellectuals from the French Antilles" (*Pan-African Movement,* 11). After the 1945 Congress in Manchester, the dominant voices in Pan-Africanism became the Africans—centrally Kwame Nkrumah of the Gold Coast/Ghana.

12. For an emotion-filled history of these developments, see Du Bois's *The Souls of Black Folk.* (Cited hereafter as *Souls.*)

13. A dedication to Ethiopia's "sons" not her "daughters": the masculinist unconscious of Pan-Africanism in general and African nationalism in particular is on display here. The mission to save the race and to restore the nation in a decolonizing agenda remains the

prerogative of an elite of "men of light and leading," imagined by Hayford much in the same terms as Du Bois's African-American "Talented Tenth."

For critiques of masculinism in the black and Pan-Africanist agenda, see Carby, *Race Men*; also, the Jamaican Brodber's short story "Sleeping's Beauty and Her Prince Charming"; and Amadiume, *Re-Inventing Africa*. A broad-based feminist critique of masculinist nationalism, both of the imperial and anti-colonial variety, is McClintock's *Imperial Leather: Race, Gender, Sexuality in the Colonial Contest*.

14. Anderson, *Imagined Communities,* 62.

15. Hayford's assessment of Washington and Du Bois as two sides of the same assimilationist coin does not hold much water. Washington, yes, but not Du Bois. The foundational racial conservatism that Hayford credits Blyden with exclusively is present in Du Bois's 1897 "The Conservation of Races"; and "Africanity," as I have argued elsewhere, is the nonnegotiable organizing principle of *Souls* (the text on which Hayford's critique is based). See Korang, "As I Face America: Race and Africanity in Du Bois's *The Souls of Black Folk*," in *W.E.B. Du Bois and Race,* ed. Fontenot and Morgan, 166–86.

16. Ngugi, *Barrel of a Pen,* 77–86.

17. Cf. Sekyi *circa* 1925: "The salvation of the Africans in the world cannot but be most materially assisted by the Africans in America but must be controlled and directed from African Africa and thoroughly African Africans. . . . We claim that we should be the architects." Cited in Langley, *Pan-Africanism and Nationalism in West Africa,* 99, 100. (Cited hereafter as *Pan-Africanism.*) Casely Hayford reiterates Sekyi's point: "we must be in advance of the current racial thought of the day . . . the right inspiration must come from the mother continent." See Sampson, *West African Leadership,* 78–79.

18. De Graft Johnson, *Towards Nationhood in West Africa,* 49. (Cited hereafter as *Towards Nationhood.*)

19. Nkrumah, *Ghana,* 91.

20. On these figures and others on the Pan-Africanist left, see Langley, *Pan-Africanism.* An insider's account is Makonnen's *Pan-Africanism from Within.*

21. On the political thought and action of these nationalists under the aegis of a liberal constitutionalism, see La Guerre, *Colonial Intelligentsia*; and Langley, *Pan-Africanism.*

22. In the assessment of Langley, the liberal-constitutionalist nationalists of West Africa before World War II were "essentially co-operationists . . . a sub-elite whose interests generally coincided with, and were in fact protected by, the foreign rulers they were agitating against." Despite their claims to the contrary, "the interests of the nationalist petty bourgeoisie were not identical with those of the people" (*Pan-Africanism,* 133).

Basil Davidson endorses this "co-operationist" reading in *Black Man's Burden* (28), and it is a central thesis also in Edsman's *Lawyers,* where the latter calls into question the notion that what transpired in the way of anticolonial agitation before World War II could adequately be grasped by the term "nationalism."

For Martin Kilson, in "Nationalism and Social Classes in British West Africa," West African nationalism was merely the ideological reflex of the *ressentiment* of the well-educated members of the middle class. This was a group frustrated by white expatriate personnel blocking their access to the higher and well-remunerated positions in the colonial establishment.

A dissenting voice, however, is F. K. Drah's. In his introduction to the 1971 reissue of De Graft Johnson's *Towards Nationhood,* Drah castigates the reductive "realism"—as he puts it—of these readings. The viewpoint made fashionable by Kilson and others, he points out, "only blunts the sharp edges of the kind of interpretation the colonialists themselves put on the motives of the educated Africans." Drah concedes the Hobbesian point that "altruism is not only intermittent but also limited in range." Nevertheless, "if men are not angels, neither are they predominantly selfish." For Drah, therefore, the matter is the complex one that "the educated Africans were naturally concerned with their own comparative social status and advantage vis-à-vis the colonial oligarchy"—and more beside and beyond that (*Towards Nationhood*, x-xi).

23. Cf. the following: "We in West Africa are ardent imperialists. But our imperialism is tempered with common sense" (*Land Question*, 83). See also chapter 7, "Signs of Empire: Loyal Hearts" in *Ethiopia Unbound*.

24. "What system is this," Hayford remonstrates,

which places in the hands of the Governor . . . a power beyond that exercised by the . . . Emperor-King of the British Dominions? A curious arrangement this, surely, by which the Governor is not responsible to the taxpayers, who keep the machine going, and who do know what is really good for them, but to an over-tasked official, some 3,000 miles away . . . who gleans his information as to the local conditions from his obedient servant, the Governor! (*Native Institutions*, 125)

How well-informed the man on the spot was can be gleaned from Hayford's pointing out "the fault of a system [of governance] that . . . has seen nothing, and known nothing, save through the eyes of the local man." And if Hayford means by "local man" the governor, the "farcical" fact for him was that "Our Governors . . . have not governed. They have not been in touch with the people. They have been occasional travelling inspectors of a magnificent order" (*Land Question*, 93).

25. Hayford notes that the unofficial members of the colonial legislature were, contrary to good sense, "supposed to support the Government." "They never initiate legislation"; and suffered to keep "their seats during the pleasure of the Government," their "province is not so much to criticise as to advise." And when "they do advise, they must do it in such a way as to fall in with the view of the moment entertained by the Government" (*Native Institutions*, 124).

26. Wight, *The Gold Coast Legislative Council*, 82.

27. Tsikata, "Towards an Agenda of Constitutional Issues under the Kwame Nkrumah Regime," in *The Life and Work of Kwame Nkrumah*, ed. K. Arhin, 210.

28. Foucault, *Language, Counter-Memory, Practice*, 148.

29. "Unanimism" in strict usage describes the forms peculiar to "a French poetic movement . . . which emphasized the submersion of the poet in the group consciousness." See *OED Online*, s.v. "unanimism."

30. *Catholic Encyclopedia* <http://www.newadvent.org/cathen/05528b.htm>, s.v. "Eschatology," 15 pages: quotations from p. 9.

31. Ibid.

32. *OED Online*, s.v. "entelechy": "The soul itself as opposed to the body": "that which gives perfection to anything: the informing spirit."

33. An "ideologeme" is a "minimal unit"—in the form of "a conceptual or belief system, an abstract value, an opinion or idea"—around which class discourses are organized. Its "essential . . . characteristic may be described as its possibility to manifest itself as . . . a protonarrative, a kind of ultimate class fantasy about . . . 'collective characters.'" See Jameson, *The Political Unconscious*, 87.

34. Rich, "When We Dead Awaken," in *Adrienne Rich's Poetry and Prose*, ed. Gelpi and Gelpi, 174. From the same piece comes Rich's expression "energy of creation," which I utilize below.

Chapter 7

1. As in Appiah's observation, Nkrumah as an African is existentially predisposed to ask not "who am I?" but "who are we?" Displacing the imagined community into the writing self, and the writing into a mode of communal ownership, is what the title and substance of Nkrumah's autobiography are all about.

2. Cf. Henry Wilson's correct assessment in *Origins of West African Nationalism* that "Hayford had sensed the problem of fusing his two roles, of middle-class politician and theorist of West African populism" (41). In Wilson's reading, this dilemma is symbolically resolved in Hayford's 1915 study in charisma and (Christian) faith, *William Waddy Harris, the West African Reformer*. "The people" were as yet an elusive political quantity in Hayford's time. If therefore a nationalist mass politics lay for the nationalist in a distant and unreachable future, that "promised land" which was not yet for Hayford could nevertheless wishfully be read into "the explosive symbiosis of charisma and the crowd" that he saw in Harris's religious mass revivalism.

3. Joyce, *A Portrait of the Artist as a Young Man*, 253.

4. Nkrumah writes: "I read Hegel, Karl Marx and Lenin and Mazzini. . . . But I think . . . the book that did more than any other to fire my enthusiasm was *Philosophy and Opinions of Marcus Garvey* . . . with his philosophy of 'Africa for the African' and his 'Back to Africa' movement." (*Ghana*, 45).

5. Fanon, *The Wretched of the Earth*, 247–48.

6. Padmore concludes that "[i]n many respects Mr. Casely Hayford was a sort of John the Baptist, preparing the way for . . . Nkrumah." Padmore obviously means Nkrumah to be "Christ" to Hayford's "John the Baptist." See *The Gold Coast Revolution*, 52.

7. Cited in Kimble, *A Political History of Ghana*, xviii. See also *Ghana*, 198.

8. Nkrumah actually graduated from the Theological Seminary of Lincoln University; he uses the two names—the seminary and the university—interchangeably.

9. Awoonor, "Africa's Literature beyond Politics," 23.

10. D. Birmingham, *Kwame Nkrumah*, 7. In Birmingham's assessment, "Padmore's death [in Accra] in 1959 coincided, perhaps not altogether fortuitously, with the apogee of Nkrumah's career."

11. For more historical details, see "Africanisation and Radicalisation: Cold War Responses 1945–49," in Adi, *West Africans in Britain, 1900–1960*, 120–50.

12. For a recent and well-researched book that complements Nkrumah's account of his years abroad, see Sherwood, *Kwame Nkrumah*.

13. Danquah's version of what provokes the split lays the blame on Nkrumah's treachery and overweening ambition. "Nkrumah is selfish," he reported to Richard Wright during Wright's visit to the Gold Coast in the early 1950s. "With wiles and tricks he stole power . . . while pretending to work for us [i.e., U.G.C.C.]. . . . Ruthlessly, he split the national front." See Wright, *Black Power*, 219–20. See also Ofosu-Appiah's Introduction to the collection of Danquah's writings, *The Ghanaian Establishment*, xix-xx. In Ofosu-Appiah's assessment, "Nkrumah's popularity was partly based on his shrewd assessment of [the] base qualities [of lust for power arising from greed and ambition] in his countrymen. . . . [H]e managed to put worthless men in his debt and find agents for his evil deeds" (xxv). There appear to be not a few dissenters on the question of the epochal significance of Nkrumah. But cf. the letter to the editor of the *Ghanaian Chronicle* which provides the epigraph to the third section of the chapter.

14. I take "moment of linkage" from Frank Lentricchia's work—itself an extended footnote of Kenneth Burke's writings—on ideology and hegemony in the domain of social representation. According to Lentricchia/Burke, "form" (read Nkrumah), in the moment of hegemonic "linkage," "would seize and direct ideological substance, transform it into power over the subject audience. . . . The . . . moment of linkage, then, is the manipulative moment at which the subject-audience is submitted ('subjected') to the productive force of ideology." See Lentricchia, *Criticism and Social Change,* 104. Other Nkrumahist moments of linkage in the Gold Coast are recorded as eyewitness accounts by Wright—he confesses that he is "thunderstruck" (60) by them—in his *Black Power,* 53–61, 75–79, 86–92.

15. Armah puts his finger on this charismatic quality of Nkrumah by making a character in his first novel worshipfully say of the leader and awakener: "How can a man born of woman tell me my thoughts even before I know them? I ask you how can he?" See his *The Beautyful Ones Are Not Yet Born,* 87. (The Nkrumah so described, however, is only the nationalist of the era of decolonization. The postindependence Nkrumah is a disappointment for Armah as he is for C. L. R. James. In the latter's words, in *Nkrumah and the Ghana Revolution,* Nkrumah "failed to create a new society" ([7]).

The secular apotheosis of the leader is also very much in evidence in Party loyalist Krobo Edusei's admiration for the man. After Nkrumah fails to honor a mass rally of the C.P.P. in Kumasi, Edusei is reported to have said: "Tell me, Kwame—what sort of man *are* you? . . . There was something sadly lacking. When you are there it makes so much difference both to the crowds and to us" (*Ghana,* 271). The element of hero worship also appears in a little vignette in *Ghana* about a woman who renames herself Ama Nkrumah (Ama is the feminine form of Kwame). At a rally, this woman slashes her face with a blade, "smearing the blood all over her body"; she challenges the men present "to do likewise in order to show that no sacrifice was too great in their united struggle for freedom and independence" (109).

If Nkrumahist ideopraxis is driven in part by the dictum that "the degree of a country's revolutionary awareness may be measured by the revolutionary awareness of its women," as noted by Takyiwah Manuh, her assessment of C.P.P. rule shows the revolutionary gains of Ghanaian women under it as modest but significant. See "Women and Their Organizations during the Convention Peoples' Party Period," in *The Life and Work of Kwame Nkrumah,* ed. K. Arhin, 101–27. See also Wright, *Black Power,* 102–3.

16. Hence this assessment of Hayford and Nkrumah given by Padmore: "[U]nlike men of the type of Gandhi and Nehru and Kwame Nkrumah, [Hayford] failed to realize that without the active support of the plebeian masses . . . who form the bulk of the population, the middle class intellectuals were ineffective." See his *The Gold Coast Revolution,* 52. Padmore's pro-Nkrumah assessment perhaps weighs too harshly against Hayford. For the historical record discloses that the objective conditions under which nationalism could court the support of the "plebeian masses" had not materialized in Hayford's time as they had in Nkrumah's (see note 2 above). In the late 1940s, social change in the Gold Coast had advanced to a point where, unlike Hayford, Nkrumah could count on "a broad social group of elementary-school-leavers [as] leaders of the radical wing of the nationalist movement." This "commoner class," disdained by the chiefly functionaries of indirect rule as "malcontents" and "agitators," may have been "locally rooted in the village." Yet they were "beneficiaries also of an educational system which . . . endowed them with a common language—English—and an awareness of common interest which cut across tribal boundaries. In 1948 they burst suddenly upon the political scene, attributing their grievances to colonial rule and sweeping aside the U.G.C.C." See Austin, *Politics in Ghana,* 17.

17. Danquah, introduction to Sampson, *Gold Coast Men of Affairs,* 10.

18. Chatterjee, *Nationalist Thought and the Colonial World,* 132.

19. D. Apter's *The Gold Coast in Transition* is one of the two(?) earliest books that bring a cultural-anthropological reading to Nkrumah's successful politicking (the other has to be Wright's *Black Power* and its ungainly attempts to delve into the psychocultural dynamics of the C.P.P. revolution). Apter earns the ire of C. L. R. James, in *Nkrumah and the Ghana Revolution,* for locating Nkrumah's success in a "tribal" cultural logic. Apter's "greatest discovery," a disapproving James writes, "is that in Nkrumah the people of the Gold Coast found the authority of an individual as a substitute for the lost authority of the chiefs" (61). In short, Nkrumah appears to Gold Coasters in the image of a hero in a past- not future-referenced mode: Apter's Gold Coast improbably marks time in a past tense. James offers his own mythology of Nkrumah as Promethean, placing his politics in a modernist cultural logic. Through Nkrumah's forward-looking instrumentality, the people of the Gold Coast successfully steal the thunder from colonialism. Nkrumah, therefore, "is the exact opposite, antithesis, negation of the tribal chief. In actuality and symbolically he fulfills and completes the strivings of the Ghanaian people to become a free and independent part of a new world" (62).

But James goes completely overboard in suggesting that Nkrumah "could lead the people because his genealogical tree is to be found not among African flora but because he is the fine flower of another garden altogether, the political experiences and theoretical strivings of Western civilization" (62). The evidence provided by George Hagan in "Nkrumah's Leadership Style" gives the lie to James's reading. Without a knowledge of traditional (or "African") symbolism, body language, forms of oratory, and propaganda, all elements which Nkrumah cobbled together to produce his political style, the man, Hagan suggests, would have been as ineffective as the elite opponents against whom he was competing for the prize of Gold Coast/Ghanaian nationalism. See Hagan, "Nkrumah's Leadership Style," in *The Life and Work of Kwame Nkrumah,* ed. K. Arhin, 177–206. (Cited hereafter as "Leadership Style.")

When it comes to Nkrumah's understanding of where he stands himself, he is Blydean in positing African modernity (or "African renaissance" (63), as he terms it) and African Personality in his *Consciencism* in terms of reconciling a triple heritage: African tradition, (Eastern) Islam, and (Western) Christianity. "*[P]hilosophical consciencism,*" Nkrumah proposes, "will give the theoretical basis for an ideology whose aim shall be to contain the African experience of Islamic and Euro-Christian presence as well as the experience of the traditional African society, and, by gestation, employ them for the harmonious growth and development of . . . society" (70).

Nkrumah's notion of African modernity in a triple heritage may be compared to Wright's alternative conception of the same, as spelled out at the end of the latter's *Black Power.* In Wright's understanding, the African renaissance demands nothing short of a stringent "militarization of African life." Hence his counsel to Nkrumah is that he must ensure "a military form of African society [which] will atomize the fetish-ridden past, abolish the mystical and nonsensical family relations that freeze the African in his static degradation. . . . [I]t is the one and only stroke that can project the African immediately into the twentieth century!" (348–49).

20. Casely Hayford, *Ethiopia Unbound,* 185.

21. Langley confirms Nkrumah's assessment in his reading of Sekyi as an armchair political theorist who "'failed' to lead. . . . Right up to the eve of independence, he still clung

to his somewhat elitist and patrician view that the natural rulers and intelligentsia should rule within a federal Ghana. . . . He was trapped in Cape Coast by [an A.R.P.S.] ideology and organization . . . that had long outlived its usefulness." See Langley, introduction to Sekyi, *The Blinkards,* 10–11.

22. Mamdani, *Citizen and Subject,* 110.

23. The phrase is A. F. Robertson's. See his "Anthropology and Government in Ghana," 54.

24. Hayford's own bitter quarrel in the 1920s with Nana Sir Ofori Atta over who was naturally qualified to represent the people of the Gold Coast, the middle class or the chiefly elite, is a case in point. The cunning of the colonial administration had ensured that the conduct of the argument involved not colonized natives and their white colonizers but two colonized native factions.

25. We can understand the logic thus, in the voice of a hypothetical colonial apologist: "By and through our actions we know you are (potentially) One people. But we have to divide you internally into the Many so that you can serve the purposes of the imperium whose interests we conduct through and manifestly embody in the localized colonial state."

26. Nkrumah, *I Speak of Freedom,* 107.

27. Cabral, *Unity and Struggle,* 115.

28. The phenomenon of one-party states that in quick succession became the norm in post-independence Africa generally supports this interpretation. In Ghana, the slogan was: "The C.P.P. is Ghana and Ghana is the C.P.P."—making Nkrumah's ruling Party indistinguishable from the nation whose totality it had come erroneously to imagine itself as synonymous with.

29. In this regard, the fates of the late Keita Fodéba, cultural worker and Minister of State, executed in 1969 by Guinea-Conakry's Sékou Touré, and writer-activist Ken Saro-Wiwa, murdered in 1995 by the Abacha regime in Nigeria, are emblematic. The Fodéba story is retold in C. Miller, *Theories of Africans,* 31–60. For a sustained reflection on the state/people, power/culture contradiction in Africa, see the later works of Ngugi.

30. "Passive revolution" as proposed by Gramsci, Chatterjee explains, arises "in situations where an emergent bourgeoisie lacks the social conditions for establishing complete hegemony over the new nation." Hence it attempts a

> "molecular transformation" of old dominant classes into partners in a new historical
> bloc and only a partial appropriation of the popular masses, in order first to create
> the state as the necessary precondition for the establishment of capitalism as the
> dominant mode of production.

Gramsci's ideas, though, "provide only a general, and somewhat obscurely stated, formulation of this problem." Hence Chatterjee recommends that "To sharpen it, one must examine several historical cases of 'passive revolutions' in their economic, political and ideological aspects." See *Nationalist Thought,* 30.

31. A lot has been written on the issue. See, among others, Davidson, *Black Man's Burden*; Achebe, *The Trouble with Nigeria*; and Soyinka, *The Open Sore of a Continent.*

32. Armah's "An African Fable" offers a powerful illustration of this point.

33. Irele, "The Crisis of Legitimacy in Africa," 296–302.

34. See Achille Mbembe's vigorous but flawed exposé of the realities of daily practice in the African "postcolony" in "The Banality of Power and the Aesthetics of Vulgarity in the Postcolony." Mbembe's flaws are taken up in T. Olaniyan's response, "Narrativizing Postcoloniality: Responsibilities."

Postscript

1. Appiah, *In My Father's House*, 53.

2. Mudimbe, *The Invention of Africa*, 195.

3. Hall, "When Was 'the Post-Colonial'?" in *The Post-Colonial Question*, ed. I. Chambers and L. Curti, 244. Emphasis added.

4. Hall, "Cultural Identity and Diaspora," in *Identity, Community, Culture, Difference*, ed. J. Rutherford, 226.

5. Fanon, *Black Skin, White Masks*, 110.

6. Gilroy, "It Ain't Where You're From, It's Where You're At."

7. See Habermas, "Modernity—An Incomplete Project," in *The Anti-Aesthetic: Essays on Postmodern Culture*, ed. H. Foster.

8. Quoted by D. Kimble, *A Political History of Ghana*, 528.

9. Benjamin, "Theses on the Philosophy of History," in his *Illuminations: Essays and Reflections*, 255.

BIBLIOGRAPHY

Abraham, Jerome. *Africa in Search of Ideology.* Vol. 1 of *National Agrarianism.* Kampala, Nairobi, and Dar es Salaam: East African Literature Bureau, 1973.

Abraham, W. E. *The Mind of Africa.* London: Weidenfeld and Nicholson, 1962.

Achebe, Chinua. *The African Trilogy.* London: Picador, 1988.

———. *Girls at War and Other Stories.* New York: Anchor-Doubleday, 1972.

———. *Hopes and Impediments: Selected Essays.* New York: Anchor-Doubleday, 1989.

———. *Morning Yet on Creation Day.* London: Heinemann, 1975.

———. *The Trouble with Nigeria.* London: Heinemann, 1984.

Addo-Fening, R., et al. *Akyem Abuakwa and the Politics of the Inter-war Period in Ghana.* Basel: Basler Afrika Bibliographen and the Historical Society of Ghana, 1975.

Adi, Hakim. *West Africans in Britain, 1900–1960: Nationalism, Pan-Africanism and Communism.* London: Lawrence and Wishart, 1998.

Africa and the American Negro: Addresses and Proceedings of the Congress on Africa. Atlanta, 1896.

Agbebi, Mojola. *Inaugural Sermon Delivered at the Celebration of the First Anniversary of the "African Church," Lagos, West Africa, December 21, 1902.* New York: Edgar Howorth, 1903.

Agbodeka, Francis. *African Politics and British Policy in the Gold Coast, 1868–1900: A Study in the Forms and Force of Protest.* Evanston, Ill.: Northwestern University Press, 1971.

Ahmad, Aijaz. "Jameson's Rhetoric of Otherness and the 'National Allegory.'" *Social Text* 17 (Fall 1987): 3–25.

Akyeampong, H. K, comp. *Liberty: A Page from the Life of J. B. [Danquah].* Accra: H. K. Akyeampong, 1960?

Amadiume, Ifi. *Re-Inventing Africa: Matriarchy, Religion, and Culture.* London and New York: Zed, 1997.

Amuta, Chidi. *The Theory of African Literature: Implications for a Practical Criticism.* London: Zed, 1989.

Anaman, Rev. J. B. *Gold Coast Guide.* London, 1895.

Anderson, Benedict. *Imagined Communities: Reflections on the Origin and Spread of Nationalism.* London: Verso, 1983.

Appadurai, A. *Modernity at Large.* Minneapolis: University of Minnesota Press, 1996.

Appiah, Joseph. *Joe Appiah: The Autobiography of an African Patriot.* New York: Praeger, 1990.

Appiah, Kwame Anthony. *In My Father's House: Africa in the Philosophy of Culture.* New York: Oxford University Press, 1992.

———. "Tolerable Falsehoods: Agency and the Interests of Theory." In *Consequences of Theory,* edited by Jonathan Arac and Barbara Johnson, 63–90. Baltimore, Md.: The Johns Hopkins University Press, 1991.

Apter, David. *Ghana in Transition.* 2nd rev. ed. Princeton, N.J.: Princeton University Press, 1972.

Arac, Jonathan, and Barbara Johnson, eds. *Consequences of Theory.* Baltimore, Md.: Johns Hopkins University Press, 1991.

Arhin, Kwame, ed. *The Life and Work of Kwame Nkrumah.* Trenton, N.J.: Africa World Press, 1993.

———, ed. *The Papers of George Ekem Ferguson: A Fanti Official of the Government of the Gold Coast, 1890–1897.* Cambridge and Leiden: African Studies Centre, 1974.

Armah, Ayi Kwei. "An African Fable." *Présence Africaine* 68 (1968): 193–96.

———. *The Beautyful Ones Are Not Yet Born.* London: Heinemann, 1969.

———. "Masks and Marx: The Marxist Ethos vis-à-vis African Revolutionary Theory and Praxis." *Présence Africaine* 131 (1984): 35–65.

Asad, Talal. "Conscripts of Western Civilization." In *Civilization in Crisis.* Vol. 1 of *Dialectical Anthropology: Essays in Honor of Stanley Diamond,* edited by C. Gailey, 333–51. Gainesville: University Press of Florida, 1992.

Asante, Molefi K. *The Afrocentric Idea.* Philadelphia: Temple University Press, 1987.

Ashcroft, W. D., Gareth Griffiths, and Helen Tiffin. *The Empire Writes Back: The Theory and Practice of Post-Colonial Literature.* London: Routledge, 1989.

Asika, Ukpabi. "A Social Definition of the African Intellectual." In *The African Reader: Independent Africa,* edited by Wilfred Cartey and Martin Kilson, 143–52. New York: Vintage-Random, 1970.

Attoh Ahuma, Rev. S[amuel] R[ichard] B[rew]. "Colony or Protectorate? Thoughts on the Present Discontent." Addressed to the Gold Coast Aborigines' Rights Protection Society, Cape Coast Castle. *The Gold Coast Methodist Times* April 30, 1897. Appendix B in *Gold Coast Native Institutions,* by J. E. Casely Hayford.

———. *The Gold Coast Nation and National Consciousness.* 1911. 2d ed. London: Frank Cass, 1971.

———. *Memoirs of West African Celebrities.* Liverpool: Marples, 1905.

Austin, Dennis. *Politics in Ghana, 1946–1960.* London: Oxford University Press, 1964.

Awoonor, Kofi. "Africa's Literature beyond Politics." *Worldview* (March 1972): 21–25.

———. "Kwame Nkrumah: Symbol of Emergent Africa." *Africa Report* (June 1972): 22–25.

———. "Nationalism: Masks and Consciousness." *Books Abroad* 45, no. 2 (1971): 207–11.

Awoonor-Renner, Bankole. *This Africa.* 1928. London: Central Books, 1943.

Ayandele, E. A. *The Missionary Impact on Modern Nigeria, 1842–1914: A Social and Political Analysis.* London: Longmans, 1966.

Azikiwe, Nnamdi. *My Odyssey: An Autobiography.* New York: Praeger, 1970.

———. *Renascent Africa.* 1937. London: Frank Cass, 1968.

Bakhtin, Mikhail M. *The Dialogic Imagination: Four Essays.* Translated by Caryl Emerson and Michael Holquist. Austin: University of Texas Press, 1981.

Baku, Kofi. *Kobina Sekyi of Ghana: An Annotated Bibliography of His Writings.* Boston: Boston University, African Studies Center, 1991.

Balakrishnan, Gopal. "The National Imagination." In *Mapping the Nation,* ed. G. Balakrishnan. London and New York: Verso/New Left Review, 1976.

———, ed. *Mapping the Nation.* With an introduction by Benedict Anderson. London: Verso, 1996.

Baldwin, James. *Collected Essays.* New York: Library of America, 1998.

Balmer, Rev. W[illiam] T[urnbull]. *A History of the Akan Peoples of the Gold Coast.* 1925. New York: Negro Universities Press, 1969.

Bartels, F. L. "Jacobus Eliza Capitein, 1717–1747." *Transactions of the Historical Society of Ghana* 4, no. 1 (19—): 3–13.

———. "Philip Quaque, 1741–1816." *Transactions of the Gold Coast and Togoland Historical Society* 1, no. 4 (1955): 153–77.

———. *The Roots of Ghana Methodism.* Cambridge: Cambridge University Press, 1965.

Beckett, Samuel. *Three Novels: Molloy, Malone Dies, The Unnameable.* New York: Grove Press, 1955, 1956, 1958.

Benjamin, Walter. *Illuminations: Essays and Reflections.* Edited and introduced by Hannah Arendt. Translated by Harry Zohn. New York: Schocken Books, 1969.

Berman, Marshall. *All That Is Solid Melts into Air: The Experience of Modernity.* New York: Simon and Schuster, 1982.

Bhabha, Homi K. *The Location of Culture.* London and New York: Routledge, 1994.

———, ed. *Nation and Narration.* London and New York: Routledge, 1990.

Birmingham, David. *Kwame Nkrumah: The Father of African Nationalism.* Rev. ed. Athens: Ohio University Press, 1998.

Blake, William. *Songs of Innocence and Experience.* New York: Orion Press, 1967.

Blyden, E. W. *African Life and Customs.* London: C. M. Phillips, 1908.

———. *Christianity, Islam and the Negro Race.* 1887. Edinburgh: Edinburgh University Press, 1967.

———. *Liberia's Offering.* New York, 1862.

———. "Study and Race." 1893. Reprinted in Henry S. Wilson. *Origins of West African Nationalism,* 249–53. London: Macmillan, 1969.

———. *West Africa before Europe.* London: C. M. Phillips, 1905.

Blyden, Nemata A. *West Indians in West Africa, 1808–1880: The African Diaspora in Reverse.* Rochester, N.Y.: University of Rochester Press, 2000.

Boahen, A. Adu. *Mfantsipim and the Making of Ghana: A Centenary History, 1876–1976.* Accra: Sankofa, 1996.

Bolt, Christine. *Victorian Attitudes to Race.* London: Routledge and Kegan Paul, 1971.

Bowen, T. J. *Adventures and Missionary Labours in Several Countries in the Interior of Africa.* New York, 1857.

Brantlinger, Patrick. *Rule of Darkness: British Literature and Imperialism, 1830–1914.* Ithaca and London: Cornell University Press, 1988.

Breuilly, John. *Nationalism and State.* 2nd ed. Manchester: Manchester University Press, 1993.

Brodber, Erna. "Sleeping's Beauty and Her Prince Charming." *Kunapipi* 11, no. 3 (1987): 1–4.

Buxton, Thomas Fowell. *The African Slave Trade and Its Remedy.* 1839, 1840. London: Dawsons, 1968.

Cabral, Amilcar. *Return to the Source: Selected Speeches of Amilcar Cabral.* New York: Monthly Review Press, 1973.

———. *Unity and Struggle: Speeches and Writings.* Translated by Michael Wolfers. New York: Monthly Review Press, 1979.

Carby, Hazel V. *Race Men: The W. E. B. Du Bois Lectures.* Cambridge, Mass. and London: Harvard University Press, 1998.

Cartey, William, and Martin Kilson, eds. *The Africa Reader: Independent Africa.* New York: Vintage-Random, 1970.

Casely Hayford, Joseph Ephraim. *Ethiopia Unbound: Studies in Race Emancipation.* 1911. 2nd ed. London: Frank Cass, 1969.

———. *Gold Coast Native Institutions.* 1903. London: Frank Cass, 1970.

———. *The Truth about the West African Land Question.* 1914. 2nd ed. London: Frank Cass, 1971.

———. *William Waddy Harris, the West African Reformer: The Man and His Message.* N.p., 1915.

Catholic Encyclopedia. <http://www.newadvent.org/cathen/ 05528b.htm>.

Césaire, Aimé. *Discourse on Colonialism.* New York: Monthly Review Press, 1972.

Chabal, Patrick. *Amilcar Cabral: Revolutionary Leadership and People's War.* Cambridge: Cambridge University Press, 1983.

Chambers, Ross. *Room for Maneuver: Reading (the) Oppositional (in) Narrative.* Chicago: University of Chicago Press, 1991.

Chatterjee, Partha. *The Nation and Its Fragments: Colonial and Postcolonial Histories.* Princeton, N.J.: Princeton University Press, 1993.

———. *Nationalist Thought and the Colonial World: A Derivative Discourse.* Minneapolis: University of Minnesota Press, 1986.

Chow, Rey. "Where Have All the Natives Gone?" In *Contemporary Postcolonial Theory: A Reader,* edited by Padmini Mongia, 122–46. New York: Arnold, 1996.

Claridge, W. W. *A History of the Gold Coast and Ashanti from the Earliest Times to the Commencement of the Twentieth Century.* 2 vols. 1915. London: Frank Cass, 1966.

Coetzee, J. M. *Foe: A Novel.* New York: Penguin, 1987.

Cohen, Robin. "Class in Africa: Analytical Problems and Perspectives." In *The Socialist Register 1972,* edited by D. Miliband and J. Savile, 231–55. New York: Monthly Review Press, 1972.

Conrad, Joseph. *Heart of Darkness.* Harmondsworth: Penguin, 1973.

Crabbe, John Azu. *John Mensah Sarbah, 1864–1910.* Accra: Ghana Universities Press, 1971.

Cromwell, Adelaide. *An African Victorian Feminist: The Life and Times of Adelaide Smith Casely-Hayford, 1868–1960.* London and Totowa, N.J.: Frank Cass, 1986.

Cunard, Nancy. *Negro: Anthology, 1931–1933.* New York: Negro Universities Press, 1969.

Curtin, Philip D. *The Image of Africa: British Ideas and Action, 1780–1850.* Madison: University of Wisconsin Press, 1964.

———, ed. *Africa and the West: Intellectual Responses to European Culture.* Madison: University of Wisconsin Press, 1972.

Curtis, L. P. *Anglo-Saxons and Celts: A Study of Anti-Irish Prejudice in Victorian England.* Bridgeport, Conn.: 1968.

Cust, Edward. "Reflections on West African Affairs . . . Addressed to the Colonial Office," Hatchard, London, 1839. Quoted in Homi K. Bhabja, *The Location of Culture.* London and New York: Routledge, 1994, 85.

Danquah, J[oseph] B[oakye]. "The Akan Claim to Origin from Ghana." *West African Review* (November 1955): 968–70 and (December 1955): 1107–11.

———. *The Akan Doctrine of God: A Fragment of Gold Coast Ethics and Religion.* 1944. 2nd ed. Edited by K. A. Dickson. London: Frank Cass, 1968.

———. *Akim Abuakwa Handbook.* London: Forster Groom, 1928.

———. "The Culture of the Akan." *Africa* 22 (October 1952): 360–66.

———. *An Epistle to the Educated Young Man in Akim Abuakwa.* Accra: Palladium Press, [192–].

———. *Friendship and Empire.* London: Fabian Publications and Victor Gollancz, 1949.

———. *The Ghanaian Establishment: Its Constitution, Its Detentions, Its Traditions, Its Justice and Statecraft, and Its Heritage of Ghanaism.* Edited by A. Adu Boahen. With an introduction by L. H. Ofosu-Appiah. Accra: Ghana Universities Press, 1997.

———. *Gold Coast: Akan Laws and Customs and the Akim Abuakwa Constitution.* London: George Routledge and Sons, 1928.

———. *The Gold Coast Akan.* London and Redhill: United Society for Christian Literature, 1945.

———. *Liberty of the Subject.* Accra: George Boakie, n.d.

———. *Self-Help and Expansion: A Review of the Work and Aims of the Youth Conference, with a Statement of Its Policy for 1943, and the Action Consequent upon That Policy.* Accra: Gold Coast Youth Conference, 1943.

Davidson, Basil. *The Black Man's Burden: Africa and the Curse of the Nation-State.* New York: Times Books, 1992.

———. *Black Star of Africa: The Life and Times of Kwame Nkrumah.* London: Allen Lane, 1973.

———. "On Revolutionary Nationalism: The Legacy of Cabral." *Race and Class* 27, no. 3 (1986): 21–45.

Debrunner, Hans W. *A History of Christianity in Ghana.* Accra: Waterville, 1967.

De Graft Johnson, J. W. *Towards Nationhood in West Africa: Thoughts of Young Africa Addressed to Young Britain.* 2nd ed. With an introduction by F. K. Drah. London: Frank Cass, 1971.

Delany, Martin R. *The Condition, Elevation, Emigration and Destiny of the Colored People of the United States, Politically Considered.* Philadelphia, 1852.

Diop, Cheik A. *Black Africa: The Economic and Cultural Basis for a Federated State.* 1960. Westport: Lawrence Hill, 1978.

Drake, St. Clair. *Black Folk Here and There: An Essay in History and Anthropology.* Vol. 1. Los Angeles: UCLA, Center for Afro-American Studies, 1987.

———. *The Redemption of Africa and Black Religion.* Chicago: Third World, 1970.

Du Bois, W. E. B. *Black Folk, Then and Now: An Essay in the History and Sociology of the Negro Race.* New York: H. Holt, 1939.

———. "The Conservation of Races." 1897. In *The Seventh Son: The Thought and Writings of W. E. B. Du Bois.* Vol. 1. Edited by Julius Lester. New York: Random House, 1971.

———. *Dusk of Dawn: An Essay toward an Autobiography of the Race Concept.* 1940. New York: Schocken Books, 1968.

———. *The Souls of Black Folk.* 1903. New York: Signet Classic, 1969.

———. *The World and Africa.* 1947. New enlarged edition. New York: International Publishers, 1965.

Duffield, Ian. "Dusé Mohamed Ali, Afro-Asian Solidarity, and Pan-Africanism in Early Twentieth-Century London." In *Essays on the History of Blacks in Britain,* edited by J. S. Gundara and I. Duffield. Aldershot: Avebury, 1992.

Echeruo, Michael. *Victorian Lagos: Aspects of Nineteenth Century Lagos Life.* New York: Africana; London: Macmillan, 1978.

Edsman, Bjorn. *Lawyers in Gold Coast Politics, c. 1900–1945: From Mensah Sarbah to J. B. Danquah.* Uppsala: University of Uppsala, 1979.

Ellis, A. B. *A History of the Gold Coast of West Africa.* 1893. New York: Negro Universities Press, 1969.

———. *The Tshi-Speaking Peoples of the Gold Coast.* London, 1887.

Emerson, Rupert, and Martin Kilson, eds. *The Political Awakening of Africa.* Englewood Cliffs, N.J.: Prentice-Hall, 1965.

Esedebe, Olisawunche P. *Pan-Africanism: The Idea and Movement, 1776–1991.* Washington, D.C.: Howard University Press, 1994.

Falola, Toyin. *Nationalism and African Intellectuals.* Rochester, N.Y.: University of Rochester Press, 2001.

Fanon, Frantz. *Black Skin, White Masks.* Translated by Charles Lam Markmann. New York: Grove Weidenfeld, 1967.

———. *Toward the African Revolution: Political Essays.* Translated by Haakon Chevalier. New York: Monthly Review Press, 1967.

———. *The Wretched of the Earth.* Translated by Constance Farrington. New York: Grove Weidenfeld, 1969.

Farias, P. F. de Moraes, and Karin Barber, eds. *Self-Assertion and Brokerage: Early Cultural Nationalism in West Africa.* Birmingham: University of Birmingham, Centre for West African Studies, 1990.

Foucault, Michel. *Language, Counter-Memory, Practice: Selected Essays and Interviews.* Translated by D. Bouchard and S. Simon. Edited by D. Bouchard. Ithaca, N.Y.: Cornell University Press, 1977.

———. *The Order of Things: An Archaeology of the Human Sciences.* New York: Vintage-Random, 1973.

———. *Power/Knowledge: Selected Interviews and Other Writings, 1972–1977.*

Translated by C. Gordon, L. Marshall, J. Mepham, K. Soper. Edited by Colin Gordon. New York: Pantheon Books, 1980.

———. "What is an Author?" In *Textual Strategies: Perspectives in Post-Structuralist Criticism,* edited by J. Harari, 141–60. Ithaca, N.Y.: Cornell University Press, 1979.

Frank, Catherine. *A Voyager Out: A Life of Mary Kingsley.* Boston: Houghton Mifflin, 1986.

Fraser, Nancy. "Rethinking the Public Sphere: A Contribution to the Critique of Actually Existing Democracy." In *The Cultural Studies Reader,* edited by Simon During, 518–36. 2nd ed. London and New York: Routledge, 1999.

Fyfe, Christopher. *Africanus Horton: West African Scientist and Patriot.* New York: Oxford University Press, 1972.

Gaonkar, Dilip Parameshwar, ed. *Alternative Modernities.* Durham, N.C.: Duke University Press, 2000.

Garvey, Marcus. *Philosophy and Opinions of Marcus Garvey.* 2 vols. 1923, 1925. Edited by Amy J. Garvey. New York: Arno, 1968–69.

Gates, H. L. Jr., ed. *"Race," Writing, and Difference.* Chicago and London: University of Chicago Press, 1986.

Geiss, Imanuel. *The Pan-African Movement: A History of Pan-Africanism in America, Europe and Africa.* Translated by A. Keep. New York: Africana Publishing, 1974.

Gellner, Ernest. *Nations and Nationalism.* Oxford: Basil Blackwell, 1983.

Gerth, H. H. and C. W. Mills, eds. *From Max Weber: Essays in Sociology.* London: Kegan Paul, 1948.

Giddens, Anthony. *The Consequences of Modernity.* Cambridge: Polity Press, 1990.

Gikandi, Simon. "The Politics and Poetics of the National Formation: Recent African Writing." In *From Commonwealth to Post-Colonial,* edited by Anna Rutherford, 377–89. Sydney: Dangaroo, 1992.

———. *Reading Chinua Achebe: Language and Ideology in Fiction.* London: James Currey, 1991.

Gilroy, Paul. *The Black Atlantic: Modernity and Double Consciousness.* Cambridge, Mass.: Harvard University Press, 1993.

———. "It Ain't Where You're From, It's Where You're At: The Dialectics of Diasporic Identification." *Third Text* 13 (Winter 1990/1991): 3–16.

Gocking, Roger S. *Facing Two Ways: Ghana's Coastal Communities under Colonial Rule.* Lanham, Md., New York, and Oxford: University Press of America, 1999.

Goody, Jack. "The Ethnohistory of the Akan in Ghana." *Africa* 29, no. 1 (1959): 67–80.

———. "The Myth of a State." *Journal of Modern African Studies* 6, no. 4 (1968): 461–73.

Graham, C. K. *The History of Education in Ghana.* Tema: Ghana Publishing, 1976.

Gramsci, Antonio. *Selections from the Prison Notebooks.* Translated and edited by Q. Hoare and G. N. Smith. New York: International Publishers, 1971.

Greenfeld, Liah. *Nationalism: Five Roads to Modernity.* Cambridge, Mass.: Harvard University Press, 1992.

Gugelberger, Georg M., ed. *Marxism and African Literature*. Trenton, N.J.: Africa World Press, 1985.

Gutkind, Peter C. W. and Peter Waterman, eds. *African Social Studies: A Radical Reader*. London: Heinemann, 1977.

Habermas, Jürgen. "Modernity—An Incomplete Project." Translated by S. Benhabib. In *The Anti-Aesthetic: Essays on Postmodern Culture*, edited by Hal Foster, 3–15. Port Townsend: Bay Press, 1983.

———. *The Structural Transformation of the Public Sphere: An Inquiry into a Category of Bourgeois Society*. Translated by T. Burger. Cambridge, Mass.: MIT Press, 1989.

Hagan, George P. "Nkrumah's Leadership Style—An Assessment from a Cultural Perspective." In *The Life and Work of Kwame Nkrumah*, edited by K. Arhin, 177–206. Trenton, N.J.: Africa World Press, 1993.

Hagan, Kwa O. "The Literary and Social Clubs of the Past: Their Role in National Awakening in Ghana." *Okyeame* 4, no. 2 (1969): 81–86.

Hall, Stuart. "Cultural Identity and Diaspora." In *Identity, Community, Culture, Difference*, edited by Jonathan Rutherford, 223–37. London: Lawrence and Wishart, c. 1990.

———. "New Ethnicities." In *The Post-Colonial Studies Reader*, edited by Bill Ashcroft et al., 223–27. London and New York: Routledge, 1995.

———. "The West and the Rest: Discourse and Power." In Stuart Hall et al., *Modernity: An Introduction to Modern Societies*, 185–227. Cambridge, Mass., and Oxford: Blackwell, 1996.

———. "When Was 'the Post-Colonial': Thinking at the Limit." In *The Post-Colonial Question: Common Skies, Divided Horizons*, edited by I. Chambers and L. Curti, 242–60. London and New York: Routledge, 1996.

Hall, Stuart, David Held, Don Hubert, and Kenneth Thompson. *Modernity: An Introduction to Modern Societies*. Cambridge, Mass., and Oxford: Blackwell, 1996.

Hammond, Dorothy, and Alta Jablow. *The Africa That Never Was: Four Centuries of British Writing about Africa*. 1970. Prospect Heights, Ill.: Waveland, 1992.

Harvey, David. *The Condition of Postmodernity: An Enquiry into the Origins of Cultural Change*. Cambridge, Mass., and Oxford: Blackwell, 1989.

Hastings, Adrian. *The Construction of Nationhood: Ethnicity, Religion and Nationalism*. Cambridge: Cambridge University Press, 1997.

Hegel, G. W. F. *The Phenomenology of Spirit*. Translated by A. V. Miller. Oxford: Oxford University Press, 1977.

———. *The Philosophy of History*. Translated by J. Sibree. Buffalo, N.Y.: Prometheus Books, 1991.

Hobsbawm, Eric J. *Nations and Nationalism since 1870: Programme, Myth, Reality*. Cambridge: Canto, 1991.

Hodgkin, Thomas L. *Nationalism in Colonial Africa*. New York: New York University Press, 1957.

Horsman, Reginald. "Origins of Racial Anglo-Saxonism in Great Britain Before 1850." *Journal of the History of Ideas* 37, no. 3 (1976): 387–410.

Horton, James Africanus Beale. *Letters on the Political Condition of the Gold*

Coast. 1870. 2nd ed. With an introduction by E. A. Ayandele. London: Frank Cass, 1970.

———. *West African Countries and Peoples British and Native . . . and a Vindication of the African Race.* 1868. Reprinted with an introduction by George Shepperson. Edinburgh: Edinburgh University Press, 1969.

Howard, Rhoda. *Colonialism and Underdevelopment in Ghana.* London: Croom Helm, 1978.

Howe, Stephen. *Afrocentrism: Mythical Pasts and Imagined Homes.* London and New York: Verso, 1998.

Hutchinson, John, and Anthony D. Smith, eds. *Nationalism.* Oxford and New York: Oxford University Press, 1994.

Irele, Abiola. *The African Experience in Literature and Ideology.* Bloomington and Indianapolis: Indiana University Press, 1981.

———. "The Crisis of Legitimacy in Africa." *Dissent* 39 (Summer 1992): 296–302.

———. "In Praise of Alienation." In *Surreptitious Speech: Présence Africaine and the Politics of Otherness, 1947–1987,* edited by V. Y. Mudimbe, 201–24. Chicago and London: The University of Chicago Press, 1992.

Ita, Eyo. *Reconstructing towards Wider Integration: A Theory of Social Symbiosis.* Calabar: West African People's Institute Press, [1946?].

Jahn, Janheinz. *Muntu: An Outline of the New African Culture.* New York: Praeger, 1967.

James, C. L. R. *The Black Jacobins: Toussaint L'Ouverture and the Santo Domingo Revolution.* 1938. New York: Vintage-Random, 1989.

———. *Nkrumah and the Ghana Revolution.* London: Allison and Busby, 1977.

Jameson, Fredric. *The Political Unconscious: Narrative as a Socially Symbolic Act.* Ithaca, N.Y.: Cornell University Press, 1981.

———. "Third World Literature in the Era of Multinational Capital." *Social Text* 15 (Fall 1986): 65–88.

JanMohamed, Abdul R. "The Economy of Manichean Allegory: The Function of Racial Difference in Colonialist Literature." In *"Race," Writing and Difference,* edited by Henry Louis Gates, Jr., 78–106. Chicago and London: University of Chicago Press, 1986.

———. *Manichean Aesthetics: The Politics of Literature in Colonial Africa.* Amherst: University of Massachusetts Press, 1983.

Jenkins, Paul, ed. *The Recovery of the West African Past—African Pastors and African History in the Nineteenth Century, C. C. Reindorf and Samuel Johnson.* Basel: Basler Afrika Bibliographien, 1998.

Jenkins, Ray. "C. C. Reindorf's 'Traditions and Historical Facts': From *Geschichte des Volkes der Goldkuste* to a Provisional National History of the Gold Coast: 1889–1895." In *The Recovery of the West African Past,* edited by P. Jenkins, 165–94. Basel: Basler Afrika Bibliographien, 1998.

———. "Gold Coasters Overseas, 1880–1919." *Immigrants and Minorities* 4, no. 3 (1985): 5–52.

———. "In Pursuit of the African Past: John Mensah Sarbah (1864–1903 [*sic*]) Historian of Ghana." In *Under the Imperial Carpet: Essays in Black History, 1780–1950,* edited by R. Lotz and I. Pegg, 109–29. Crawley, England: Rabbit Press, 1986.

———. "Intellectuals, Publication Outlets and 'Past-Relationships': Some Observations on the Emergence of Early Gold Coast-Ghanaian Historiography in the Cape Coast, Accra and Akropong 'Triangle.'" In *Self-Assertion and Brokerage*, edited by de Moraes Farias and K. Barber, 68–77. Birmingham: University of Birmingham, Centre for West African Studies, 1990.

Johnson, Rev. Samuel. *The History of the Yorubas.* 1921. Edited by O. Johnson. Lagos: C.M.S. Bookshop, 1966.

Jones-Quartey, K. A. B. *History, Politics and Early Press in Ghana: The Fictions and the Facts.* Accra: Afram Publications, 1975.

———. "Sierra Leone and Ghana: Nineteenth Century Pioneers in West African Journalism." *Sierra Leone Studies* 12 (December 1959): 230–44.

———. "Sierra Leone's Role in the Development of Ghana." *Sierra Leone Studies* 10 (June 1958): 73–84.

Joyce, James. *A Portrait of the Artist as a Young Man.* Harmondsworth: Penguin, 1960.

July, Robert W. *The Origins of Modern African Thought.* New York: Praeger, 1967.

Kane, Cheik Hamidou. *Ambiguous Adventure.* Translated by Katherine Woods. London: Heinemann, 1972.

Kanneh, Kadiatu. *African Identities: Race, Nation and Culture in Ethnography, Pan-Africanism and Black Literatures.* London and New York: Routledge, 1998.

Katz, Stephen. *Marxism, Africa and Social Class: A Critique of Relevant Theories.* Montreal: McGill University Centre for Developing Area Studies, n.d.

Kaunda, Kenneth. *Zambia Shall Be Free: An Autobiography.* New York: Praeger, 1962.

Kenyatta, Jomo. *Facing Mount Kenya: The Traditional Life of Gikuyu.* 1938. London: Heinemann, 1979.

Kermode, Frank. *The Genesis of Secrecy.* Cambridge, Mass.: Harvard University Press, 1979.

Kilson, Martin. "Nationalism and Social Classes in British West Africa." *The Journal of Politics* 20 (1958): 368–87.

Kimble, David. *A Political History of Ghana: The Rise of Gold Coast Nationalism, 1850–1928.* Oxford: Clarendon Press, 1963.

Kingsley, Mary H. *Travels in West Africa.* 1897. London: Everyman, 1993.

———. *West African Studies.* 1899. London: Frank Cass, 1964.

Knox, Robert. *The Races of Man: A Philosophical Enquiry of the Influence of Race over the Destinies of Nations.* London, 1850, 1862.

Korang, Kwaku Larbi. "As I Face America: Race and Africanity in W. E. B. Du Bois's *The Souls of Black Folk.*" In *W. E. B. Du Bois and Race: Essays Celebrating the Centennial Publication of "The Souls of Black Folk"*, edited by C. J. Fontenot and Mary A. Morgan, 166–86. Macon, Ga.: Mercer University Press, 2001.

———. "Crisis and Accounting: Towards a Spatial History of the African Nation." In *Sacred Spaces and Public Quarrels: African Cultural and Economic Landscapes*, edited by E. Kalipeni and P. T. Zeleza, 251–69. Trenton, N.J. and Asmara: Africa World Press, 1999.

Krafona, Kwesi. *The Pan-African Movement: Ghana's Contribution.* London: Afroworld, 1986.

Kurankyi-Taylor, Dorothy. *Reflected Thoughts.* Ilfracombe: Stockwell, 1959.

La Guerre, John G. *The Social and Political Thought of the Colonial Intelligentsia.* Mona, Jamaica: Institute of Social and Economic Research, University of the West Indies, 1982.

Laing, Kojo. *Search, Sweet Country.* London: Heinemann, 1986.

Langley, J. A. *Ideologies of Liberation in Black Africa: Documents on Modern African Thought from Colonial Times to the Present.* London: Rex Collings, 1979.

———. "Modernization and Its Malcontents: Kobina Sekyi (1892–1956) of Ghana and the Re-Statement of African Political Theory." *Research Review* (University of Ghana) 6 (1971): 1–61.

———. *Pan-Africanism and Nationalism in West Africa, 1900–1945: A Study in Ideology and Social Classes.* Oxford: Clarendon Press, 1973.

Law, Robin. "Constructing 'a Real National History': A Comparison of Edward Blyden and Samuel Johnson." In *Self Assertion and Brokerage,* edited by Farias and Barber, 78–100. Birmingham: University of Birmingham, Centre for West African Studies, 1990.

Lawrence, A. W. *Trade Castles and Forts in West Africa.* Stanford, Calif.: Stanford University Press, 1964.

Lazarus, Neil. *Nationalism and Cultural Practice in the Postcolonial World.* Cambridge: Cambridge University Press, 1999.

———. *Resistance in Postcolonial African Fiction.* New Haven, Conn.: Yale University Press, 1990.

Lentricchia, Frank. *Criticism and Social Change.* Chicago and London: University of Chicago Press, 1983.

Lindqvist, Sven. *"Exterminate All the Brutes."* Translated by J. Tate. London: Granta Books, 1998.

Lloyd, P. C., ed. *The New Elites of Tropical Africa.* London: International African Institute and Oxford University Press, 1966.

Loomba, Ania. "Overworlding the Third World." In *Colonial Discourse and Postcolonial Theory: A Reader,* edited by Patrick Williams and Laura Chrisman, 305–23. New York: Columbia University Press, 1994.

Lorimer, Douglas. *Colour, Class and the Victorians.* New York: Holmes and Meyer, 1978.

Lynch, Hollis R. *Edward Wilmot Blyden: Pan-Negro Patriot, 1832–1912.* London: Oxford University Press, 1967.

———, ed. *Black Spokesman: Selected Published Writings of Edward Wilmot Blyden.* New York: Humanities Press, 1971.

———, ed. *Selected Letters of Edward Wilmot Blyden.* New York: KTO Press, 1978.

Lyons, Charles. *To Wash an Aethiop White: British Ideas about Black African Educability 1530–1960.* New York: Teachers College Press, 1975

Macaulay, Thomas Babington. "Minute on Indian Education." In *The Post-Colonial Studies Reader,* edited by Bill Ashcroft et al., 428–30. London: Routledge, 1989.

Makonnen, Ras. *Pan-Africanism from Within*. As recorded and edited by Kenneth King. London: Oxford University Press, 1973.

Malkki, Liisa. "Citizens of Humanity: Internationalism and the Imagined Community of Nations." *Diaspora* 3, no. 1 (1994): 41–68.

Mamdani, Mahmood. *Citizen and Subject: Contemporary Africa and the Legacy of Late Colonialism*. Princeton, N.J.: Princeton University Press, 1996.

Manuh, Takyiwah. "Women and Their Organizations during the Convention Peoples' Party Period." In *The Life and Work of Kwame Nkrumah*, edited by K. Arhin, 101–27. Trenton, N.J.: Africa World Press, 1993.

Marable, Manning. *African and Caribbean Politics: From Kwame Nkrumah to the Grenada Revolution*. London: Verso, 1987.

Marcuse, Herbert. *One Dimensional Man: Studies in the Ideology of Advanced Society*. Boston: Beacon Press, 1964.

Marlowe, Christopher. *Doctor Faustus*. London: Methuen, 1989.

Marx, Karl. *The German Ideology*. New York: International Publishers, 1970.

———. *The Eighteenth Brumaire of Louis Bonaparte*. 1852. New York: International Publishers, 1963.

Mauny, Raymond. "The Question of Ghana." *Africa* 24 (July 1954): 200–213.

Mazrui, Ali A. "Kwame Nkrumah: Leninist Czar." In his *On Heroes and Uhuru Worship: Essays on African Independence*. London: Longmans, 1967.

———. *Towards Pax Africana*. London: Weidenfeld and Nicholson, 1967.

Mazzini. *Life and Writings of Joseph Mazzini*. Vol. 3. London: Smith and Elder, 1905.

———. *Life and Writings of Joseph Mazzini*. Vol. 5. London: Smith and Elder, 1908.

Mbembe, Achille. "The Banality of Power and the Aesthetics of Vulgarity in the Postcolony." *Public Culture* 4, no. 2 (1992): 1–30.

Mbonjo, Pierre Moukoko. *The Political Thought of Kwame Nkrumah: A Comprehensive Presentation*. Lagos: University of Lagos Press, 1998.

McCarthy, Mary. *Social Change and the Growth of British Power in the Gold Coast: The Fante States, 1807–1874*. Lanham, Md.: University Press of America, 1983.

McClintock, Ann. *Imperial Leather: Race, Gender, Sexuality in the Colonial Contest*. New York and London: Routledge, 1995.

McGrew, A. "A Global Society?" In *Modernity*, ed. S. Hall et al. Cambridge, Mass. and Oxford: Blackwell, 1996.

Meer, Fatima. *Higher Than Hope: A Biography of Nelson Mandela*. Harmondsworth: Penguin, 1990.

Meyerowitz, Eva L. R. "The Akan and Ghana." *Man* 57 (June 1957): 83–88.

———. *The Akan of Ghana: Their Ancient Beliefs*. London: Faber, 1960.

———. *Akan Traditions of Origin*. London: Faber, 1952.

———. *The Divine Kingship in Ghana and Ancient Egypt*. London: Faber, 1960.

———. *The Early History of the Akan States of Ghana*. London: Red Candle Press, 1974.

———. "A Note on the Origins of Ghana." *African Affairs* 51 (1952): 319–22.

———. *The Sacred State of the Akan*. London: Faber, 1960.

Miller, Christopher. *Blank Darkness: Africanist Discourse in French*. Chicago: University of Chicago Press, 1985.

———. *Theories of Africans: Francophone Literature and Anthropology*. Chicago: University of Chicago Press, 1990.

Mongia, Padmini, ed. *Contemporary Postcolonial Theory: A Reader*. New York: Arnold, 1996.

Moses, Wilson J. *The Golden Age of Black Nationalism, 1850–1925*. New York: Oxford University Press, 1988.

Mudimbe, V. Y. *The Invention of Africa: Gnosis, Philosophy, and the Order of Knowledge*. Bloomington and Indianapolis: Indiana University Press, 1988.

Myers, Robert A., comp. *Ghana*. World Bibliographic Series. Oxford: Clio Press, 1991.

Nairn, Tom. *The Break-up of Britain: Crisis and Neo-Nationalism*. London: NLB, 1977.

Nandy, Ashis. *The Intimate Enemy: Loss and Recovery of Self under Colonialism*. Delhi: Oxford University Press, 1983.

Nelson, Cary, and Lawrence Grossberg, eds. *Marxism and the Interpretation of Culture*. Urbana: University of Illinois Press, 1988.

Newell, Stephanie. *Ghanaian Popular Fiction: 'Thrilling Discoveries in Conjugal Life' & Other Tales*. Oxford: James Currey, 2000.

Ngugi wa Thiong'o. *Barrel of a Pen: Resistance to Repression in Neo-Colonial Kenya*. Trenton, N.J.: Africa World Press, 1983.

———. *Decolonizing the Mind: The Politics of Language in African Literature*. London: James Currey, 1986.

———. *Detained: A Writer's Prison Diary*. London: Heinemann, 1981.

Nkosi, Lewis. *Tasks and Masks: Themes and Styles of African Literature*. Harlow: Longman, 1981.

Nkrumah, Kwame. *Africa Must Unite*. 1963. New York: International Publishers, 1970.

———. *Consciencism*. London: Heinemann, 1964.

———. *Ghana: The Autobiography of Kwame Nkrumah*. 1957. New York: International Publishers, 1971.

———. *I Speak of Freedom: A Statement of African Ideology*. 1961. Westport, Conn.: Greenwood Press, 1976.

———. *Neo-Colonialism: The Last Stage of Imperialism*. New York: International Publishers, 1966.

———. *Revolutionary Path*. New York: International Publishers, 1973.

———. *Towards Colonial Freedom: Africa in the Struggle against World Imperialism*. London: Heinemann, 1962.

Nyerere, Julius. *Freedom and Unity*. Dar es Salaam: Oxford University Press, 1966.

Obiechina, Emmanuel. *An African Popular Literature: A Study of Onitsha Market Literature*. Cambridge: Cambridge University Press, 1973.

Ocansey, John E. *African Trading; or The Trials of William Narh Ocansey of Addah, West Coast of Africa, River Volta*. Liverpool, 1881.

Odamtten, S. K. *The Missionary Factor in Ghana's Development up to the 1880s*. Accra: Waterville, 1978.

Ofosu-Appiah, L. H. *Joseph Ephraim Casely Hayford: The Man of Vision and Faith.* Accra: Academy of Arts and Sciences, 1975.

Ojike, Mbonu. *My Africa.* New York: John Day, 1946.

Okonkwo, Rina. *Heroes of West African Nationalism.* Enugu: Delta, 1985.

Okoth, P. G. "The Creation of a Dependent Culture: The Imperial School Curriculum in Uganda." In *The Imperial Curriculum,* edited by J. Mangan. London: Routledge, 1993.

Olaniyan, Tejumola. "Narrativizing Postcoloniality: Responsibilities." *Public Culture 5,* no. 1 (1992): 47–55.

Oldstone-Moore, Christopher. "European Empires," *http://www.wright.edu/~christopher.oldstone-moore/empires.htm*

Omari, Peter. *Kwame Nkrumah: The Anatomy of an African Dictatorship.* New York: Africana, 1970.

Omoniyi, Bandele. *A Defence of the Ethiopian Movement.* London: St. James Press, 1908.

Omu, Fred I. A. "'The Anglo-African,' 1863–1865." *Nigeria Magazine* 90 (Sept. 1966): 206–12.

———. *Press and Politics in Nigeria, 1880–1937.* London: Longman, 1978.

Osadebay, Dennis C. *Building a Nation (An Autobiography).* Yaba: Macmillan, 1978.

Osei-Nyame, Kwadwo. "Pan-Africanist Ideology and the African Historical Novel of Discovery: The Examples of Kobina Sekyi and J. E. Casely Hayford." *Journal of African Cultural Studies* 12, no. 2 (1999): 137–53.

Ouologuem, Yambo. *Bound to Violence.* Translated by R. Manheim. Oxford: Heinemann, 1971.

Owusu-Ansah, David, and Daniel McFarland. *Historical Dictionary of Ghana.* 2nd ed. Metuchen, N.J.: Scarecrow Press, 1995.

Padmore, George. *The Gold Coast Revolution: The Struggle of an African People from Slavery to Freedom.* London: Dennis Dobson, 1953.

———. *Pan-Africanism or Communism? The Coming Struggle for Africa.* London: Dennis Dobson, 1956.

Paolini, Albert. "The Place of Africa in Discourses about the Postcolonial, the Global and the Modern." *New Formations* 31 (1996): 83–118.

Pathak, Avijit. *Indian Modernity: Contradictions, Paradoxes and Possibilities.* New Delhi: Gyan Publishing House, 1998.

Patton, Adell. *Physicians, Colonial Racism, and Diaspora in West Africa.* Gainesville: University Press of Florida, 1996.

Peterson, Bhekizizwe. *Missionaries, Monarchs and African Intellectuals: African Theater and the Unmaking of Colonial Marginality.* Trenton, N.J., and Asmara: Africa World Press, 2000.

Plaatje, Sol. *Native Life in South Africa before and since the European War and the Boer Rebellion.* 1916. Athens: Ohio University Press, 1991.

Porter, Bernard. *Critics of Empire: British Radical Attitudes to Colonialism in Africa, 1895–1915.* London: Macmillan, 1968.

Powell, Erica. *Private Secretary (Female)/Gold Coast.* New York: St. Martin's Press, 1984.

Prah, K. K. *Essays on African Society and History.* Accra: Ghana Universities Press, 1976.

————. *Jacobus Eliza Johannes Capitein 1717–1747: A Critical Study of an Eigh-teenth Century African.* Braamfontein: Skotaville, 1989.

Priestley, Margaret. "The Emergence of an Elite: A Case Study of a West Coast Family." In *The New Elites of Tropical Africa,* edited by P. C. Lloyd, 87–103. London: International African Institute and Oxford University Press, 1966.

————. *West African Trade and Coast Society: A Family Study.* London: Oxford University Press, 1969.

Reade, W. Winwood. *Savage Africa.* London, 1864.

Rée, Jonathan. "Internationality." *Radical Philosophy* 60 (1992): 3–11.

Reindorf, C[arl] C[hristian]. *The History of the Gold Coast and Asante.* 1895. 2nd ed. Accra: Ghana Universities Press, 1966.

Rich, Adrienne. "When We Dead Awaken." In *Adrienne Rich's Poetry and Prose,* edited by B. Gelpi and A. Gelpi. New York and London: Norton, 1993.

Robertson, A. F. "Anthropology and Government in Ghana." *African Affairs* 74, no. 294 (1975): 51–59.

Rohdie, Samuel. "Gold Coast Aborigines Abroad." *Journal of African History* 6, no. 3 (1965): 389–411.

Said, Edward. *After the Last Sky.* London: Faber, 1986.

————. *Culture and Imperialism.* New York: Knopf, 1993.

————. *Orientalism.* New York: Vintage-Random House, 1978.

————. *The World, the Text, and the Critic.* Cambridge, Mass.: Harvard University Press, 1983.

Salmon, Charles Spencer. *The Crown Colonies of Great Britain.* London, 1886.

Sampson, Magnus. *Gold Coast Men of Affairs (Past and Present).* With an introduction by J. B. Danquah. 1937. London: Dawsons, 1969.

————, ed. *West African Leadership: Public Speeches Delivered by the Hon. J. E. Casely Hayford.* 1951. London: Frank Cass, 1969.

Sarbah, John Mensah. *Fanti Customary Laws.* 1897. 3rd ed. With an introduction by Hollis Lynch. London: Frank Cass, 1968.

————. *Fanti National Constitution.* 1906. 2nd ed. With an introduction by Hollis Lynch. London: Frank Cass, 1968.

Sartre, Jean-Paul. "Black Orpheus." In his *"What is Literature" and Other Essays.* Cambridge, Mass.: Harvard University Press, 1988.

Scott, David. "Colonial Governmentality." *Social Text* 43 (1995): 191–220.

Sekyi, Kobina. *The Blinkards.* With an introduction by J. A. Langley. London: Heinemann, 1974.

————. *The Blinkards: A Comedy and the Anglo-Fanti—A Short Story.* Accra: Readwide; Oxford: Heinemann, 1997.

————. "Conflict of Loyalties." *Gold Coast Times,* September 15 1925.

————. "Education." *The Gold Coast Leader,* 13 and 27 November, 4 December 1920.

————. "Education with Particular Reference to a West African University." 1920. Acc. 325/64. Ghana National Archives, Cape Coast.

————. "The Essentials of Race Manhood." *The African Telegraph and Gold Coast Mirror,* December 1914.

————. "The Future of Subject Peoples." 1917. In *Ideologies of Liberation in Black Africa,* edited by J. A. Langley, 242–51. London: Rex Collings, 1979.

———. "The Meaning of the Expression 'Thinking in English,'" 1940. Acc. 531/64. Ghana National Archives, Cape Coast.

———. "The Parting of Ways." 1924. Acc. 464/64. Ghana National Archives, Cape Coast.

Senghor, Léopold Sédar. "Edward Wilmot Blyden, Precursor of Negritude." Translated by D. L. Schalk. Foreword to *Selected Letters of Edward Wilmot Blyden,* edited by Hollis Lynch, xix-xxii. New York: KTO Press, 1978.

———. "Negritude: A Humanism of the Twentieth Century." In *The Africa Reader: Independent Africa,* edited by William Cartey and Martin Kilson, 179–92. New York: Vintage-Random, 1970.

Shaw, Flora. *A Tropical Dependency: An Outline of the Ancient History of the Western Soudan.* London: J. Nisbet, 1905.

Shepperson, George. "Abolitionism and African Political Thought." *Transition* 3, no. 12 (1964): 22–26.

———. "Ethiopianism and African Nationalism." *Phylon* 14, no. 1 (1953): 9–18.

———. "'Pan-Africanism' and 'pan-Africanism': Some Historical Notes." *Phylon* 23, no. 4 (1962): 346–58.

Sherwood, Marika. *Kwame Nkrumah: The Years Abroad, 1935–1947.* Legon: Freedom Publications, 1996.

Shils, Edward. "The African Intellectuals." In *Christianity and African Education,* edited by R. P. Beaver. Grand Rapids, Mich.: W. B. Erdmans, 1966.

Sitwell, Edith. *Selected Poems of Edith Sitwell.* London: Macmillan, 1965.

Skalnik, Peter. "Why Ghana Is Not a Nation-State." *Africa Insight* 22, no. 1 (1992): 66–72.

Slemon, Stephen. "Cultural Alterity and Colonial Discourse." *Southern Review* (1987): 102–7.

———. "Monuments of Empire: Allegory/Counter-Discourse/Post-Colonial Writing." *Kunapipi* 9, no. 3 (1987): 1–16.

Smith, Edwin. *Aggrey of Africa: A Study in Black and White.* New York: Richard R. Smith, 1930.

Smith, J. N. *The Presbyterian Church of Ghana, 1835–1960.* Accra: Ghana Universities Press, 1966.

Solanke, Ladipo. *United West Africa (or Africa) at the Bar of the Family of Nations.* 1927. London: African Publication Society, 1969.

Soyinka, Wole. *Myth, Literature and the African World.* Cambridge: Cambridge University Press, 1976.

———. *The Open Sore of a Continent: A Personal Narrative of the Nigerian Crisis.* New York: Oxford University Press, 1996.

Spitzer, Leo. *The Creoles of Sierra Leone: Responses to Colonialism, 1870–1945.* Madison: The University of Wisconsin Press, 1974.

———, and LaRay Denzer. "I. T. A. Wallace-Johnson and the West African Youth League." *International Journal of African Historical Studies* 6, no. 3–4 (1973): 413–52, 565–601.

Spivak, Gayatri. "Can the Subaltern Speak?" In *Marxism and the Interpretation of Culture,* edited by Cary Nelson and Lawrence Grossberg, 271–313. Urbana: University of Illinois Press, 1988.

———. *A Critique of Postcolonial Reason: Toward a History of the Vanishing Present.* Cambridge, Mass., and London: Harvard University Press, 1999.

———. "Theory in the Margin: Coetzee's *Foe* Reading Defoe's *Crusoe/Roxana.*" In *Consequences of Theory,* edited by Jonathan Arac and Barbara Johnson, 154–80. Baltimore, Md.: The Johns Hopkins University Press, 1991.

———. "Who Claims Alterity?" In *Remaking History,* edited by B. Kruger and P. Mariani, 269–92. Seattle: Bay Press, 1989.

Spurr, David. *The Rhetoric of Empire: Colonial Discourse in Journalism, Travel Writing, and Imperial Administration.* Durham, N.C., and London: Duke University Press, 1993.

Stepan, Nancy. *The Idea of Race in Science, Great Britain, 1800–1960.* London: Macmillan, 1982.

Tempels, Placide. *Bantu Philosophy.* Translated by Colin King. Paris: Présence Africaine, 1959.

Temu, A., and B. Swai. *Historians and Africanist History: A Critique.* London: Zed Press, 1981.

Toll, William. *The Resurgence of Race: Black Social Theory from Reconstruction to the Pan-African Conferences.* Philadelphia: Temple University Press, 1979.

Tsikata, Fui S. "Towards an Agenda of Constitutional Issues under the Nkrumah Regime." In *The Life and Work of Kwame Nkrumah,* edited by K. Arhin, 207–14. Trenton, N.J.: Africa World Press, 1993.

Ugonna, Nnabuenyi. "Casely Hayford: The Fictive Dimension of African Personality." *Ufahamu* 7, no. 2 (1977): 159–71.

UNESCO. "Symposium on African Elites." *International Social Science Bulletin* 8 (1956): 413–98.

Vanaik, Achin. *The Furies of Indian Communalism: Religion, Modernity and Secularization.* London and New York: Verso, 1997.

Varadharajan, Asha. *Exotic Parodies: Subjectivity in Adorno, Said and Spivak.* Minneapolis and London: University of Minnesota Press, 1995.

Wallace-Johnson, I. T. A. "British Oppression in West Africa." *The Negro Worker* (Dec. 1931).

———. "The West African Youth League: Its Origins, Aims and Objects." *The Negro Worker* (May 1937).

Wallerstein, Immanuel. "Class and Status in Contemporary Africa." In *African Social Studies: A Radical Reader,* edited by P. C. Gutkind and P. Waterman, 277–83. London: Heinemann, 1977.

———. "Elites in French-Speaking West Africa: The Social Basis of Ideas." *Journal of Modern African Studies* 3, no. 1 (1965): 1–23.

Weber, Max. *The Protestant Ethic and the Spirit of Capitalism.* Translated by Talcott Parsons. London: Unwin, 1968.

———. *The Theory of Social and Economic Organization.* New York: Oxford University Press, 1947.

West, Cornel. "Marxist Theory and the Specificity of Afro-American Oppression." In *Marxism and the Interpretation of Culture,* edited by C. Nelson and L. Grossberg, 17–33. Urbana: University of Illinois Press, 1988.

West African Review. "A Great Ghanaian: Dr. J. B. Danquah, 'Doyen of Gold Coast Politics.'" (March 1957).

Wight, Martin. *The Gold Coast Legislative Council.* London: Faber and Faber, 1947.

Wilks, I. *Asante in the Nineteenth Century.* London: Cambridge University Press, 1975.

Williams, Patrick, and Laura Chrisman, eds. *Colonial Discourse and Post-Colonial Theory: A Reader.* New York: Columbia University Press, 1994.

Wilson, Henry S. *Origins of West African Nationalism.* London: Macmillan, 1969.

Wiltgen, Ralph. *Gold Coast Mission History, 1471–1880.* Techny, Ill.: Divine Word, 1956.

Wordsworth, William. "Ode: Intimations of Immortality from Recollections of Early Childhood." In *The Poetical Works of William Wordsworth,* edited by E. de Selincourt and H. Darbishire. Oxford: The Clarendon Press, 1947.

Wright, Richard. *Black Power: A Record of Reactions in a Land of Pathos.* New York: Harper and Brothers, 1954.

———. *White Man, Listen!* 1957. Westport, Conn.: Greenwood, 1978.

Young, Robert A. *The Ethiopian Manifesto, Issued in Defense of the Black Man's Rights in the Scale of Universal Freedom.* New York, 1829.

Zachernuk, Philip. *Colonial Subjects: An African Intelligentsia and Atlantic Ideas.* Charlottesville: University Press of Virginia, 2000.

Zeleza, Paul Tiyambe. "The 'Posts,' History and African Studies." In his *The Intellectual Challenges.* Vol. 1 of *Rethinking Africa's Globalization.* Trenton, N.J., and Asmara, Eritrea: Africa World Press, 2003.

———. "The Rise and Mutation of African Historiographies." In his *Manufacturing African Studies and Crises.* Dakar: Codesria, 1997.

INDEX